The Horror Comics

ALSO BY WILLIAM SCHOELL

Creature Features: Nature Turned Nasty in the Movies (McFarland, 2008, paperback 2014)

The Opera of the Twentieth Century: A Passionate Art in Transition (McFarland, 2006)

The Horror Comics

Fiends, Freaks and Fantastic Creatures, 1940s–1980s

WILLIAM SCHOELL

McFarland & Company, Inc., Publishers
Jefferson, North Carolina

Illustrations are from the author's collection.

LIBRARY OF CONGRESS CATALOGUING-IN-PUBLICATION DATA

Schoell, William.
The horror comics : fiends, freaks and fantastic creatures, 1940s–1980s / William Schoell.
    p.   cm.
Includes bibliographical references and index.

ISBN 978-0-7864-7027-3 (softcover : acid free paper) ∞
ISBN 978-1-4766-1835-7 (ebook)

1. Horror comic books, strips, etc.—History and criticism.
2. Comic books, strips—United States—History and criticism.
I. Title.
PN6725.S376 2014   741.5'973—dc23   2014019889

BRITISH LIBRARY CATALOGUING DATA ARE AVAILABLE

© 2014 William Schoell. All rights reserved

No part of this book may be reproduced or transmitted in any form or by any means, electronic or mechanical, including photocopying or recording, or by any information storage and retrieval system, without permission in writing from the publisher.

On the cover: Octopus and background landscape © 2014 iStock/Thinkstock

Printed in the United States of America

*McFarland & Company, Inc., Publishers
Box 611, Jefferson, North Carolina 28640
www.mcfarlandpub.com*

To the memory of my grandfather,
Jacob Schoell,
whom I take after in many ways

Table of Contents

Preface ... 1

Part I: The Golden Age, Pre–1956 ... 3

One: American Comics Group (ACG) ... 5
Two: EC Comics ... 19
Three: Prize Comics ... 42
Four: Atlas, Timely and Marvel ... 52
Five: DC, Fawcett, Charlton and Harvey ... 67
Six: Ace and Ajax-Farrell ... 92
Seven: Avon, Better/Nedor, Comic Media and More ... 105
Eight: Key, St. John's, Story, Quality, Smaller and Canadian Publishers ... 119

Part II: The Silver Age, 1956–1969 ... 137

Nine: Marvel, DC and Charlton ... 139
Ten: Dell and Gold Key ... 158

Part III: The Bronze Age, 1970–1983 ... 173

Eleven: Dracula, Frankenstein and Werewolf by Night ... 175
Twelve: Man-Thing, Morbius and More ... 193
Thirteen: DC's Horror Anthologies ... 209
Fourteen: More Sinister Houses ... 223
Fifteen: Phantom Strangers and Swamp Things ... 237
Sixteen: Charlton, Gold Key and Atlas ... 248

Bibliography ... 271
Index ... 273

Preface

When most people think of horror comic books the first thing that comes to mind is the often grisly and controversial *Tales from the Crypt* and similar series from EC Comics. These comics are justifiably famous and certainly deserve their chapter in this book, but they are neither the beginning nor the end of the story. Horror stories appeared in comic books in the golden age of the 1940s, the same decade in which the first full-fledged horror anthology comic, *Adventures into the Unknown*, made its debut. Although horror comics were all but obliterated by the comics code—most metamorphosing into science fiction and fantasy comics—they began reappearing in the silver age of the '60s, when there were long-running comic adaptations of such shows as *The Twilight Zone* and when Dell Comics came out with *Ghost Stories*, the first issue of which contained one of the most nightmare-inducing classics ever published. In the '70s—the bronze age—a general horror boom in films and fiction, along with a relaxation of the comics code, brought about a virtual avalanche of horror material from all publishers, with Marvel boasting its *Tomb of Dracula* and *Werewolf by Night*, DC and Charlton mass-producing such anthologies as *The Witching Hour* and *Scary Tales*, and such publishers as Dell, Gold Key and the short-lived Atlas releasing much horrific and supernatural material.

Said material—be it in the golden age or much later—came from a variety of sources. On occasion it ushered forth from the fertile imaginations of writers, but there was also quite a bit of borrowing, with plots influenced by or simply lifted from literature (Poe, Mary Shelley), radio shows (such as *Lights Out!*), movies, and even folklore. There were times, however, when it was just the opposite, and you'll find in this volume certain stories that were clear influences on some famous horror films made years later; screenwriters and producers were not above reading comic books. Certain plots or themes were used over and over: the spirits of murdered men rise to haunt their murderers; a person makes a deal with the devil but discovers that Satan is rarely outwitted; a hen-pecked or harassed man or woman finally snaps and takes an ax to his or her spouse; a protagonist kills, steals and betrays every person and principle he knows to achieve life everlasting only to spend eternity paralyzed, in endless agony, or in jail for a "life" sentence. And so on.

The discussion of these comics follows a roughly chronological order in that the three parts of the book correspond to the golden, silver, and bronze age of comics. Within these parts chapters are presented according to the comics' importance and influence. American Comics Group presented the first long-running horror comics series so it gets the first chapter, and EC Comics gets Chapter Two because it influenced countless comic books from many publishers, some of whom changed their style of storytelling just so they could seem more like EC. In general major publishers are covered first, and then the smaller ones. Due to the huge amount of material, black and white larger-format horror *magazines* such as *Eerie* and *Creepy* are not included, although some of Marvel's black and white periodicals are mentioned for purposes of continuity, as some of their fearsome characters appeared in both comics and magazines. Horror comics of the golden age have been examined in other tomes with varying degrees of success—most books on the subject simply reproduce covers or stories without critical assessment—but horror comics of the '60s and '70s have never come in for serious study before now.

This volume covers thousands of comic books from an historical and critical perspective. Most of the research for this book has consisted, simply, of reading or re-reading all of these comics, which was a dream come true for an author who loves both comic books and the horror field. While many horror comic stories are derivative, schlocky, poorly done, or fail to properly develop some interesting premises, there are also a lot of honest-to-goodness gems hidden among the gristle.

Part I

The Golden Age, Pre–1956

One

American Comics Group (ACG)

American Comics Group (ACG) came out with what was to become the first of the long-running horror comics when they began publishing *Adventures into the Unknown* in 1948. The cover of the premiere issue shows a young couple about to enter a haunted house. Inside there is a host of stories: a creepy tale about a werewolf on the rampage, stalking a woman who suspects his true identity; Malevo, the Devil's second-in-command (but even more evil), walks the earth as "The Living Ghost"; the spirit of a murdered man whose body was dumped into the sea supposedly haunts a newly opened resort hotel; and a woman is told she will inherit a fortune if she spends the night in a house which is said to be haunted by a dead man's restless spirit. The last two stories have a similar formula in that the "ghosts" turn out to be living people enacting nefarious schemes, although the presence of a true ghost is also revealed at the end. The comic also includes an adaptation of Horace Walpole's classic 1768 Gothic story "The Castle of Otranto." An editorial on the inside cover assured the reader that "superstition is ignorance ... *There are no such things as ghosts*—there never were, there never will be" but explained that *stories* of the supernatural would live forever.

Adventures into the Unknown was an immediate hit with readers. The Living Ghost returned for more malevolence in the second issue and was to appear in the third, but the idea for turning it into a continuing feature was dropped even though many readers wrote in asking for more stories about Malevo. Instead in the fifth issue there appeared the first installment of "The Spirit of Frankenstein." In this an aging, dying scientist named Pardway is jealous of his younger associate, Dan Warren. When the two build a hulking robot together, Pardway importunes Warren to put his brain in the robot after his death, which he does. Realizing that Pardway's bitter spirit is controlling the robot and may cause it to do serious harm, Warren exorcises the spirit in a most unusual manner. As he explains it: "A ghost is dependent on the atomic structure of the body it has left. By subjecting [the body] to nuclear fission—will destroy his ghost!"

Still in the following issue Warren is not certain that Pardway's brain can't still cause problems, so he has his girlfriend Marcia pay a call on a spiritualist named Daggert. Daggert has exorcised several haunted houses and collected the spirits, several of which he instructs to take over the mind of the "Frankenstein" robot in a play for power. The robot runs amok in the city. Warren is able to free it from the spirits' devilish control but in *AITU* 8 searches

The first continuing horror anthology comic: *Adventures into the Unknown*, by American Comics Group.

for a way of keeping it forever free of outside evil influences. He hopes that a device called a "microvolt resistor" will do the job, but Pardway, in a last ditch effort before dissipating into the ether, awakens the creature's intelligence—it's still his brain inside its metal head—and the robot is able to seize control of the device. Fortunately Warren is able to prevent the robot from causing a major disaster at an atomic lab. In the next issue the robot plays good guy when a hypnotist inadvertently creates a phantom consisting of the evil impulses of hundreds of convicts. When the phantom, given physical form by Warren as he seeks to discover its true nature, tries to break those same convicts out of prison, "Frankenstein" prevents him at the scientist's urging. The robot battled the spirit of an ancient Egyptian sorcerer in *AITU* 10 as well as other strange monsters in subsequent issues but disappeared for good after about a dozen installments.

Adventures also ran whimsical fantasy tales on occasion, along with science fiction with a horrific slant. "The Beast from Beyond" (*AITU* 17) had a plot so similar to John W. Campbell's "Who Goes There?" (made into the film *The Thing from Another World* the same year) that it's unlikely the author wasn't influenced by it. Scientists discover a strange alien creature frozen in the ice and thaw it, only to discover that it can change its shape and mimic any animal or human. After a while paranoia breaks out in the camp. The story was well done, but original it wasn't. "The Magic Formula" in *AITU* 22 employed the popular theme of gigantism: a scientist enlarges animals to giant size so that they can supposedly feed the world and provide more milk, meat and wool, but the question is never raised as to how much more these big animals themselves would eat, although the problem of containing them—the usual problem in movies and stories about out-sized animals—does come up when the creatures break loose. In late 1952 when both horror and sci fi comics were proliferating, the editors asked the readers of *Adventures* to let them know if they wanted at least one weird science-fiction story per issue; the answer was a resounding no—for a time.

Occasionally there would be some novelty in one of the vampire/werewolf/zombie stories. In "Fangs of Horror" (*AITU* 22) werewolves do not attack people in general, but subsist on corpses in cemeteries. Young Enid's father has hit on a way of wiping out the werewolves, but he and his wife are killed by them—but not before he takes the precaution of hiding his secret on a piece of paper inside Enid's teddy bear. Enid is raised by the werewolf leader—who never thinks to look inside the teddy bear—and grows up almost thinking that he and his lupine friends are normal, until a cop on their trail sets her wise. They discover the secret paper and learn that the werewolves can be stopped with cyanide. The story had giant holes in it but at least it added some unique elements to the formula.

"Shadow of the Wolf" (*AITU* 23) presented a werewolf as a sociopathic young man, Kurt, who covets the ranch owned by his uncle and which will be inherited by his two cousins. He decides to get the ranch for himself by killing the two men in his werewolf form. The suspenseful story—you know who's doing what to whom but not how it will all come out—works well as a lycanthropic murder mystery. In "Werewolf Valley" (*AITU* 30) a lumber company moves in on the title location in the Blue Ridge Mountains, even though they're warned that it's home to a nest of vampires who only want to be let alone to live in their private space in peace. A beautiful woman attaches herself to the lumberjacks, and at first seems to be quite helpful, but in reality she's slowly working her way through the men, using her seductive charms to turn them into werewolves like herself. At the end the foreman confronts her but discovers to his regret that all of his men have become snarling werewolves as they attack him. "When Werewolves Howl" (33) was a moving tale in which a boy is given a were-wolf cub by a dying old were-woman (one of her family attacked and killed the boy's dog), discovers the cub can turn into a boy, and treats his pet—who only changes into human form when no one else is around—as if he were his brother as well as best friend. The young werewolf sacrifices his life to save his friend and the boy's father from an attacking pack of wolves.

"Assault from the Unknown" (*AITU* 25) was an in-joke that also worked as an effective thriller, with a writer for the comic discovering that a Legion of Evil comprised of ghosts, werewolves, vampires and the like has decided to wipe out the staff of *Adventures into the Unknown* because the comic was giving away trade secrets. (A similar story appeared in Ace's *Hand of Fate*.) The writer gives his life to save a female staffer and leaves a note saying he'll continue to send in stories from the world of the supernatural. "Maybe *Adventures into the Unknown* will start to print stories that are *really* out of this world," says the editor.

A popular theme in horror comics—and *Adventures into the Unknown* was no exception—was men who are spurned by women getting even with them until their own eventual comeuppance overtakes them. Sometimes the women were unspeakably cruel in their rejection, and almost seem to deserve their fate. Other times their only crime is not being attracted to the man in question. In "The Hideous Head" (*AITU* 28) homely Professor Griffith, who relishes statues of beautiful women who are repulsed by him in real life, discovers the snake-tressed head of Medusa in some ruins. He first kills a woman on the dig who recently rejected him by turning her to stone with the head, then advertises for models so he can turn them all into lovely dead statues, his revenge upon the world of women. A lady detective answers his ad and Griffith winds up becoming a victim of the gorgon's gaze himself. Twenty-one issues later a sculptress named Mady George—whose statues of men and women in terrified poses are amazingly lifelike and resemble people who'd vanished—is unmasked as Medusa in "Talent for Terror."

Another popular theme was the man with the shrewish, unloving or greedy wife (sometimes the wife had an evil husband) who made his life miserable with her profligate spending, leading the nominal hero to take drastic action of some kind. In "The Blind Man" in *AITU* 48 Sam wants Hilda to marry him but she wants to make sure he'll be a success. Kindly Sam gives money to an old blind beggar and thereafter has dreams that warn him of deadly future events and how to avoid them. Saving the life of men on a construction site nets him a job; saving his boss from a diabetic coma gets him a raise; and so on. Hilda marries him but nearly drives him into bankruptcy. He dreams that she's in unspecified danger and decides to take her out of the country by plane wherein the pilot turns out to be the old blind guy. The story now drops all pretense of reasonableness and brings in some beaked alien creatures who take Hilda away with them and presumably kill her. "It's better this way," says the old man. "Otherwise she would have led you both to doom. You will find happiness yet—with another girl." Thus Sam is not only spared the cost of an expensive divorce but has no need to resort to murder, either! On the other end of the spectrum were numerous stories in which the love between spouses helped save one or both of them from demonic forces.

Many stories dealt with devilish aspects of the hereafter. In "The Man Who Died Too Soon" (*AITU* 43) the pilot Stan Griffith is the only survivor of a plane crash (the story doesn't explain why he managed to fly his plane into a mountain!). But his spirit is mistakenly taken into the hereafter, then released, unfortunately, after he already signed the register.

Afraid of punishment, the spirits responsible for this mistake decide that he has to die in an another accident. Then, like something out of the *Final Destination* movies, Griffith finds himself narrowly avoiding death during one grotesque accident after another. Finally the argument is made before a supreme council that his life has already been recorded as not ending for many decades, and he is allowed to live out his full lifespan.

The Devil himself, depicted in the stereotypical fashion of red skin, horns and trident, appeared frequently. "The Devil's Disciple" (6) had a young woman named Judy reading an old diary that once belonged to Hester Prince, a woman of an earlier century. Hester was betrayed by her fiance and best friend, and sold her soul to the Devil to get revenge. As Judy reads these words in the diary, the Devil appears, and is furious that Judy has no desire to sell her soul to him. He tries to tempt her, and when that fails tries to kill her in multiple accidents. Judy falls in love with Wayne Morse, who saves her from one of those accidents, but after they're engaged, discovers him, like Hester before her, in the arms of another woman, Hester Prentiss. Judy decides that she, too, wants revenge, and winds up signing her name in the Devil's Book of Souls. But even as she drives off to kill Wayne, she realizes that Hester Prince and Hester Prentiss are one and the same, and it's all a trick the Devil's. She manages to save Wayne from Hester's demonic clutches, and the story suggests that the two of them will live happily ever after. Apparently the writer forgot that Judy signed the Devil's book....

Adventures didn't go in for giant monsters very much, but it did run a few stories in the genre: Scientists find living dinosaurs in modern-day Everglades (*AITU* 21); Merlin the magician unleashes dragons on the modern world wherein they are shot down by the Air Force (26); a tentacled sea monster devours everyone on the *Marie Celeste* and other ships whose passengers have mysteriously disappeared (41); and a scientist injects himself with a serum that turns him into a man-sized, blood-drinking spider (50), seen crawling into a terrified woman's bedroom window on the cover.

Adventures into the Unknown was rarely terribly gruesome, but it had its moments. In *AITU* 38 a witch doctor tries to use a voodoo doll to get rid of a nasty white man who threatens his son. Knowing that only a really memorable death may show the man's associates that he means business, he bites the head off of the doll—and the real man's head simply falls off (although this is not shown). In *AITU* 53 Baron Kroger, the "head man" in collecting, decides to sell off his valuable prizes because he's started a secret new collection. When a curious Herr Schwill, who assumes the collection has great monetary value, insists upon seeing it at gunpoint, Kroger directs him to a safe. Schwill sees nothing in the safe, so sticks his head inside for a better look—only to have a sharp blade come swishing down so the Baron can add his head to his collection. Generally it was only evil people who came to bad ends, but there were exceptions, such as a story in *AITU* 40 in which the wicked side of a man's nature develops a body of its own. His girlfriend kills the evil twin, only to learn that she actually murdered her boyfriend when his double walks in and proceeds to strangle her.

By 1953, with a reduced page count, *Adventures into the Unknown* was still extremely popular—ACG had come out with sister publications such as *Forbidden Worlds*, *Out of the Dark* and *Skeleton Hand*—but the series had a lot of competition. 3D comics that had fuzzy images which became clear when you wore special glasses were coinciding with the 3D rage in movies. Beginning with the fifty-first issue *AITU* published stories in what it called "Truevision," what it considered a type of 3D without the eyestrain and without glasses. The stories were printed on a black background, with objects and people stretching out of the borders,

Witches and monsters in *Adventures into the Unknown* 47.

to create an extremely simplistic 3D effect. *AITU* tested the waters with a story or two, then ran almost every story in the "process" for about a year. This actually stripped the series of much of its visual interest, with every story looking the same. It didn't help that the chief artist, Harry Lazarus, who had quite a few pages to draw every month, often turned in rushed work. (Other artists for the series were Bob Fangione, Kenneth Landau, and Edmond Good.)

The "Truevision" period didn't last long but the comic published one of its most macabre and memorable stories in that process, "The Man Who Died Laughing" (*AITU* 58). Titus Graeme takes care of his simple cousin Herman by living off the $100 a week Herman gets from a trust fund. Titus gives Herman the bare necessities while living it up on most of the money. When Herman gets sick Titus doesn't bother with a doctor, and the poor fellow dies. Titus is only upset because he's afraid of losing the weekly stipend. Using his occult knowledge, Titus manages to turn Herman into one of the living dead; since he was already dull-witted he fools the lawyer who delivers the checks into thinking he's still alive. Titus decides to live a frugal life for the next twenty years—Herman no longer needs food—and puts each weekly payment into a suitcase, hoping to have a fortune to spend while he's still reasonably young. Two decades go by during which a lonely Herman has become friends with numerous mice, whom Titus hates. When Titus opens the suitcase to count what he expects will be $100,000, he discovers that the filthy mice have *eaten* the money. Confronted with this reality, he becomes hysterical, suffers a seizure and dies. The police find two bodies in the house, but are utterly baffled by the fact that one of them has been dead for twenty years.

Readers were divided as to the effectiveness of Truevision, which was no longer touted on the cover as of *AITU* 59 although a few such stories remained, and the editors asked if they wanted "shock-suspense" stories (undoubtedly of the EC variety) intermingled with the supernatural tales. When it became clear that the days of EC Comics and others like it were numbered (see Chapter Two), ACG turned to science fiction and lighter fantasy tales instead. For instance, the lead story in *AITU* 60, "Hospitality," was a darkly amusing tale in which space explorers land on a mysterious world from which no one has ever returned. Entering a gigantic structure, they wind up caught in an alien mousetrap planted by the grotesque giants who see them only as disgusting vermin. Despite the absurd, almost comical premise, the story was nevertheless disturbing, especially the panel of the three dead astronauts, hopeful and alive only moments before, dangling from the deadly contraption as it's thrown away as debris. Future issues would frequently have sci fi stories featured on the cover. In the same issue *AITU* ran an editorial regarding the protests against horror and crime comics (so much for running shock stories). They argued that their comics always strived to remain in the boundaries of good taste, and their imitators, lacking their taste and talent, became too shocking and lurid in response. "Such protest is constructive we feel—save where it attempts to condemn the entire realm of comics because of the sins of the few."

However, the comic had already commissioned some non-supernatural suspense stories, such as the intense and excellent "The End of the Line" in *AIUW* 61. The protagonist of the story scuttles his boat for the insurance money and lets his two inebriated crew men drown, actually laughing as they desperately grab hold of a line that is attached to the sinking ship and instead of saving them only drags them down into the deep. These two men have the last laugh, however, as they neglected to put food and gas in the one life boat as ordered, so the killer finds himself alone in the middle of the ocean and starving. He manages to grab one dead fish, but it turns out to be bait for tuna, and its hook gets caught on his clothing. He winds up pulled up out of the boat and dragged under the water to his death. Harry Lazarus' art for the story was very good at depicting not only the man's desperate circumstances, but his growing hysteria and madness. In the very disturbing "Big Roar" in the following issue, a young man hoping for fame and fortune goes over Niagara Falls in a barrel, but the barrel hits a rock and breaks apart, and everyone assumes he dies when his body goes over the waterfall. Actually he was able to grab onto a jutting rock and pull himself to safety on an outcropping behind the raging falls. He makes his way into a cave but there is no exit and nobody knows he is there or even alive. Subsisting on frogs, he goes quietly mad as the falls freezes over, then thaws, over and over again until forty years have passed and he is still a prisoner of the falls. This story, although a touch far-fetched, was definitely in the category of really-awful-things-happening-to-perfectly-nice-people.

In the next issue it was announced that *Adventures into the Unknown* would conform to the new comics code, and from henceforth there would be no more stories about "zombies, vampires, and werewolves," which had been the comic's stock-in-trade from the first. In addition to sci fi tales, there would be "gripping tales of suspense," fantasy stories and even outright comedies, such as "Coward in Outer Space," in which the title character goes on a space mission to get away from his shrewish, domineering wife, lands on another planet, and winds up winning a kind-hearted princess who is her duplicate, even as he sends his own duplicate—a nasty warrior—back to earth (and his wife) in his stead. However, just because the horror stories were gone from the magazine didn't mean that horrible things couldn't happen to likable folk such as George Harris in "Your Number's Up," who develops a run of atrocious luck on his twenty-seventh birthday (all having to do with the number 27), losing his job, his fiancee, and all of his money, and then throws away a telegram that arrives because he's convinced it must be bad news—and in doing so throws away a small fortune that he would have won had he known to claim his winnings in a lottery.

Adventures into the Unknown continued well into the silver age but the final golden age issue, 69, ended on a high note—if not exactly a horrific one—with the story of a mean man who cages a variety of birds from Africa, including a very exotic creature called a starbird that can talk and develops quite a vocabulary. The starbird wants freedom for himself and the other birds, but his keeper won't relent. So the bird, calling himself "Mr. Feathers," puts in a call to the IRS and tells them where the man keeps records of his hidden assets. As the birds escape their cages and make their way back to Africa, the keeper finds *himself* in a cage—prison. The story was a far cry from the material that made the comic famous, but it *was* hilarious.

Other memorable stories during the comic's golden age period included: "Marriage of Death"—a woman marries a man who turns out to be Death and never grows any older (*AITU* 11); "Map of Magic"—a mapmaker uses special ink to make an imaginary map and he and his fiancee find themselves in the world he just created (11); "The Look of Death"—a man uses a mystical Indian spy glass to kill people but is careless where he places it (11). "Haunted Morgue," in which murderers mentioned in newspaper articles come back as ghosts (14); "Double Doom"—a machine creates evil duplicates of human beings (14); "Portrait Without a Soul"—an artist paints such a realistic picture of a fictional murderer that he literally steps out of the painting (21); "The Howling Hunters"—a dead criminal is brought back to life as a werewolf but sacrifices himself to save the life of woman who is kind to him

(24); "Dolls of Doom"—a man tries to wipe out his family for their inheritance with voodoo dolls (27); and "Demon of the Devil"—a woman tries desperately to keep her boyfriend from being manipulated and killed by a satanic imp that materializes on his shoulder and won't let go (28).

Other notable stories: "Ship of Death"—a captain mans his crew with unliving, compliant zombies (29); "Mask of Mumbo," a harrowing tale wherein a woman who sports a magic mask in her nightclub act comes afoul of a persistent demon that wants to kill her for her temerity in wearing it (31); "The Creeper"—an amorphous black mass seeps out of the walls of an old house seeking flesh (44); "Death of the Mountain God"—horrible events on a mountain top that resembles a skull (45); "The Eternal Fires"—a baby-faced mobster with three months to live tries to outwit Satan and fails (49); and "Jewels of the Deep"—a giant clam sucks in victims and turns their skulls into giant pearls (56).

The most memorable golden age cover was arguably for *Adventures into the Unknown* 9, which depicts a frigid landscape in which blocks of snow have formed a sinister face and hands.

Forbidden Worlds

Due to the success of *Adventures into the Unknown*, ACG came out with a sister title, *Forbidden Worlds*, in 1951. In the debut issue there were the usual vampires and werewolves: a man hatched an elaborate scheme to keep a woman he loved from the clutches of a werewolf; a vampire count destroyed a young couple on their honeymoon who were then reunited in death. The main story, "Demon of Destruction," had a skeptical man unleashing an ancient and monstrous demon from a locked tomb who first murders individuals and then grows big enough to tear apart bridges and knock over the Empire State Building. The best story was "The Monster Doll," in which a scientist investigates rumors than in the last century a man managed to turn an executed woman's corpse into a robot by melding mechanical parts to flesh, then discovers that this deadly living doll is his own wife.

Forbidden Worlds proved so popular that it became monthly with the seventh issue. The first ten issues of the comic had a wide variety of memorable or mediocre stories involving the usual ghosts, demons, vampires and werewolves, as well as weird, almost campy science fiction such as the silly "Realm of the Moonsters [*sic*]" in *FW* 7. As for vampires, in "Lair of the Vampire" a couple wage a desperate, action-packed struggle against a persistent bloodsucker who is determined to feast on both of them (*FW* 3). "The Unknown Vampire" in *FW* 10 concerns passengers and crew members whose plane crashes on a remote island and who try to figure out whom among them is a vampire preying upon the others (with surprising results). "The Flapping Head"—an actual head with bat's wings behind its ears—was a vampire who flew about a castle searching for the rest of its body, a bunch of entombed bones. (There was also a "Flying Head" of a Hindu Shaman in *FW* 9.)

There were plenty of ghost stories in these issues as well. "The Vengeful Spirit" was a female resistance fighter, murdered by her own collaborationist brother, who emerges from bottles of wine seeking men to help her get vengeance on the fellow who killed her (3). In "The Ghoul's Return" (7) an executioner of the French revolution who lopped off 999 heads comes back to kill the descendants of the man who was supposed to be victim number 1000 but managed to turn the tables on the headsman. Satan made several appearances as well, such as in "The Devil and the Gambler," in which a young man sells his soul to become the richest man in the world, only to discover his mind has been placed inside the corpulent body of an Indian maharajah—the world's wealthiest man—who promptly dies of a heart attack as he realizes the price he's paid to have money (7). In "The Strange Circus of Dr. Namirha" the devil puts on a show with animal-human hybrids—beasts with human heads—claiming they are illusions when they are actually real. While the audience is mesmerized by these apparitions, Satan sneaks into convalescent homes where there are heart patients, kills them, and steals their souls to merge them with animals and create more hybrids (8).

Some stories had an air of whimsy or were more out of the ordinary than usual. "The Zombie's Doom" was a bizarre, even sick romance in which a woman falls for a man who is secretly a dread zombie with a grotesque appearance, but still loves him even when she learns the truth and sees his true face (8). "Doom of the Gnomes" in *FW* 9 was a charming tale of a little boy who tries to save a group of leprechaun-like creatures who live in caverns from being destroyed by explosives planted by a construction team that is unaware of their existence (the gnomes can only be seen by people as small as they are). In "Strange Machine" a mad scientist turns many young women into old "hags" in his attempts to recalibrate a machine that is supposed to make people young again. He does manage to turn one woman into a child and her boyfriend into an elderly man, but together they're able to outwit him (10).

As the series continued evil women made their mark in several stories. In "Lure of the Snake Goddess" (*FW* 16) a beautiful Indian woman who can turn into a hideous snake comes to the United States to find fame and fortune and literally crushes anyone who gets in her way, including rival actresses who get the stage roles she covets. A man who knows her secret but can't prove it arranges for her to really be burned at the stake during her performance as Joan of Arc so that she's forced to switch to snake form to wiggle out of her ropes and get away from the fire. After he shoots her, she changes back to her human form. When a cop tries to arrest her killer, the latter points out to the audience, where hundreds of witnesses can testify that the star of the play was indeed a snake monster! In "My Fanged and Fiendish Darling" (*FW* 34) a lonely wife whose husband is in the service overseas willingly becomes a werewolf when one of them knocks on her door; she then contrives to keep her secret when her husband, who is now blind, returns home. An interesting aspect of the story is that while the housewife grows fangs, the werewolf that inhabits her takes on a separate lupine form and stalks the night while she rests at home, experiencing her other self's savage attacks on humans from the safety of her living room.

There were occasional stories with larger or especially bizarre creatures, such as "The Million-Year Monster" in which an atomic blast irradiates a dinosaur egg causing it to hatch a grotesque ten-foot abomination that can talk and has hypnotic control over humans (14). "The Winged Terror" is a race of man-eating horrors that emerge from cocoons and also put their human victims in cocoons to be fed upon later (15). "The Ant-Master" is an out-sized soldier ant with an evil, wizened face who can command humans bitten by normal soldier ants to kill people once they transform into hideous man-ant hybrids (21). In another story a mad scientist breeds creatures that are combinations of insects and animals, such as a cat-moth, and injects his two conniving servants, who are after his hidden fortune, with the formula and wonders at the end what they might become (23).

And the monsters continued: "Charah's Prey" concerns an Egyptian deity with a huge alligator-like head who goes on rampages unless he is given female sacrifices to devour in a few grisly gulps (24). "The Tree of Terror" is a man-eating tree that drags victims down to a cave beneath its roots and feeds upon them as they lay dying (26). In "The Beast in the Berg" ugly large and red insectoid creatures inside ice bergs thaw out and emit killing rays that doom the entire world. In "The Thing on the Beach" (30) a murderer marooned on a lonely atoll finds only ants to eat, with the result that he turns into a man-sized mutated ant monster that devours his former shipmates when they come for him. A creepy scene has him watching as ants carry off pieces of his flesh that have baked in the sun and fallen off. In "Terror Under the Big Top" a girl's head is squashed under an elephant's foot as a rogue spirit goes on the rampage causing deaths and horrible accidents (27).

At first the covers of *Forbidden Worlds* often had nothing to do with its contents. The cover of *FW* 5 depicts a gigantic sea serpent-centipede attacking a ferry, but the inside pages instead presented a tale of a giant man-eating merman who wants revenge for the destruction of his underworld city and people. The cover of *FW* 6 has a giant ape making like King Kong and climbing a skyscraper tower, but there was no sign of this creature within the book. Later on the comic would generally highlight its lead story on the cover, depicting all manner of were-creatures, vampires, terror trees, and unearthly creatures and spirits—along with plenty of good-looking women. Artists for the series included Art Gates, Harry Lazarus, Al McWilliams, Edmond Good and Kenneth Landau.

After the creation of the comics code and the ban on horror, *Forbidden Worlds*, like *Adventures into the Unknown*, eschewed horror stories for lighter suspense and sci fi tales. Instead of vampires and werewolves, there were stories about identical twins who could communicate psychically during times of stress, or about a pilot who crash lands into a lost civilization in the Himalayas and returns to find that 150 years have gone by in the real world. There was a mix of non-horror supernatural stories with speculative fiction and zany, light-hearted sci fi. The artwork also became less grisly and more eye-appealing.

Some other memorable golden age stories in *Forbidden Worlds* included: "The Eyes of Death"—the spirit of a man driven to suicide by a rival who took over his home extracts a terrible price for vengeance (8); "Mummy's Treasure"—a dead mummy pursues a little boy who accidentally freed him from his sarcophagus (11); "Clutching Curse"—a harrowing tale of a couple trying to stay alive in a house with an evil and murderous presence (11); "Chest of Death"—an ancient genie emerges from a box to kill in order to gain strength and size (12); "Were-Spider's Doom"—the Widow Black can turn into a giant black widow spider with a human head, but she meets up with a were-wasp and dies (12); "Werewolves of the Rockies"—the passengers of a train stalled in a snow storm have to deal with a village of werewolves who see easy prey (17).

Also: "The Recorded Monster"—a demonic god is "recorded" on audio tape and reemerges when the tape is played to wreak bloody havoc (17); "Hallahan's Head"—a human head pursues the man who ordered him murdered across the ocean and bites him to death (25); "The Talking Machine"—a parrot with artificially enhanced intelligence commits robberies for a larcenous couple and then ultimately outwits them (30); "Invasion of the Deadlings"—aliens come to earth and inhabit corpses—both of the already dead and of humans they kill—so they can walk around in earth's atmosphere until the couple who learns of their existence destroy them by making the ultimate sacrifice (32); "Bride of the Swamp"—a woman turns into an alligator and tears apart her horrified beloved (33); "The Dreamer"—

a woman's prophetic dreams initially lead to wealth and happiness but ultimately end in tragedy (35).

Forbidden Worlds continued to be published well into the silver age but it was no longer a horror comic.

Out of the Night

ACG came out with two more horror series in the fifties: *Out of the Night* and *Skeleton Hand,* neither of which lasted as long as *Adventures into the Unknown* or *Forbidden Worlds. Out of the Night* debuted in 1951, lasting 17 issues. It featured the same kind of stories as the other two series, but while many of these had interesting premises they were often poorly executed, with both scripts and art on a mediocre level.

There were some notable exceptions, however. "The Curse of the Witch" turns a pretty young woman into a hideous hag who is compelled to murder someone she loves. She prevents herself from murdering her fiance by killing her beloved pet dog, but finds it harder and harder to resist her compulsion to kill ... if she doesn't kill someone in three days time she will permanently became a slave of Satan. Fortunately, her husband is able to get her out of her predicament by destroying the witch who cursed her (*OOTN* 7). "Domain of the Were-Beast" is a variation of "The Most Dangerous Game" wherein the hunter of humans who mounts their heads on his wall is a werewolf accompanied by weird demonic creatures (9). "When the Spirit Walked" is a very unusual private eye story in which Satan hires an, at first, unbelieving gumshoe to recover a vengeful soul who managed to escape from Hades. The latter's corpse had been kept alive by the presence of microscopic creatures called diatoms, that were in salt water that seeped into his grave from the ocean nearby (10).

While most of the characters in *Out of the Night* met terrible fates, occasionally they were spared such anguish. "Destination: Unknown" (*OOTN* 14) presented the bizarre predicament of newlyweds Ted and Mary Judson, who are on a honeymoon cruise to Europe. When the ship goes down, Ted, an Olympic swimmer, tells Mary to hold on tightly to his hand and never let go. Unfortunately, the drowning Mary drags Ted to the sea bottom. When they awake, they are on a boat of dead souls being taken for final judgment. Ted realizes that he feels hunger and pain, his heart still beats—he is not really dead. He hates the idea of being separated from his beloved so hides the fact that he is still alive. When the truth is discovered, he begs to die and go with Mary, but his long life has already been ordained, as has his wife's death. However, when he wakes up again in the sick bay of the rescue ship, his dead wife is successfully revived; fate has been kind to them.

Not so Laura and Don, another couple in "Ship of Death" (10) who accidentally cause an accident and several deaths while embracing in their automobile as they rush to the dock for a honeymoon cruise. They lie about their involvement in the crash but discover that the ship is full of the spirits of the victims and that *they* are also dead. When it turns out that both are actually still alive, they are sent back to the real world but die in the operating room since their injuries are so severe. They then learn that their fate is to spend the rest of eternity being operated on—without anesthetic. As their injuries would actually have prevented them from lying to the police or indeed saying anything, this seems like an incredibly harsh punishment.

Some stories are interesting not because of their quality but because of the bizarre developments they encompass. In "The Fountain of Age" (*OOTN* 9) water-starved geologist Dan Newton shoots his native guides when they try to prevent him from drinking the waters of a mystical fountain in the sun-baked Kalahari. The water makes him see himself at different ages, then turns him into an elderly man facing death. Even though he's a murderer his girlfriend Rita sacrifices herself for him because he's a "great scientist" and at the end becomes another statue holding up the fountain. "The Weird Wager" (9) is a bet between Satan and Death, who choose a young couple as sample humans and show them what's in store for them at the end of their lives if they choose death—oblivion—or eternal damnation. Satan shows them images of Hell, such as people burning in fire pits or endlessly rolling heavy boulders up a hill but never reaching the top. Strangely the couple choose the Devil over Death. "As long as we're together we can stand any pain—so we prefer eternal torture to eternal nothingness," explains the man. It's a question if he would still feel that way after, say, a century of rolling boulders or boiling in oil.

There were occasional monster stories in *Out of the Night*. "Out of the Screen" in *OOTN* 14 featured a prehistoric monster in a 3-D movie, featured on the very effective cover, who emerges from the screen to create havoc; despite the amusing premise, the story itself was too nonsensical to be effective. "Nightmare from the Past" (16), in which Professor Callen discovers the survivor of a race of giants frozen in the ice, was better. The block of ice which contains the huge man falls during transportation, separating into two parts, one containing the head and the other the body. The head is kept alive mechanically and given a blood supply and when it revives and begins to speak, Milo, Callen's assistant, tortures him to learn details of the giants' hidden treasure. But the giant fools Milo into reuniting its head with its body with predictable results. The story, unfortunately, ended a little too abruptly to make the most of its premise.

The best story that ever appeared in the comic was "The Tunnel," expertly drawn for maximum impact by Kenneth Landau, in *Out of the Night* 16. Slim Warren works in a railroad switch house and is resentful that Bailey, the younger man he trained, has been given a promotion Slim coveted. As Bailey walks home through the nearby tunnel, Slim impulsively decides not to switch the track for the approaching express, which not only hits and kills Bailey, but derails after the initial impact, killing several passengers. Slim arranges for the late Bailey to get the blame, but needs to find his watch in the tunnel to back up his story. Slim is plagued by guilt, as well as the ghost of Bailey and images of a phantom train carrying the spirits of those who died. As a real train bares down on him, Slim lays low in the tracks and finally spots the watch. After the train—carrying the corpses from the wreck—passes over him safely, Slim reaches out for the watch in triumph, touches the third rail, and is electrocuted.

Skeleton Hand and *The Clutching Hand*

Skeleton Hand (the full title was *Skeleton Hand in Secrets of the Supernatural*) debuted in 1952 and only lasted six issues. Many of its stories seemed like rejects from ACG's other three horror titles, especially art-wise, but at least some had interesting premises. For instance, in one story there was a mirror out of which souls of the dead could emerge and come back to life (*SK* 4). "The Bat and the Brain" (*SK* 2) presents a scientist who invents a mechanical bat whose movements he can control with his brain waves, but he hasn't reckoned with the possibility that a vampire might want to control the bat for his own purposes. "The Were-Fiends of Finland" are werewolves who strike back when a doctor has come upon a possible means of wiping out their curse—and them—once and for all (5). In "The Hidden Horror" a 300-year-old wizard imprisons victims behind stone walls in his basement before a young couple manage to end his reign of terror (5).

The Clutching Hand was yet another horror comic from ACG that came out in 1954. When the comics code came into effect, bringing a new editorial slant to the macabre magazines, *Clutching Hand* became a one-shot deal, understandably, as the comic offered a couple of stories more in the lines of gruesome EC Comics. "The Real McCoy" concerned a man named Oliver, who's amassed huge gambling debts and is threatened with death if he doesn't pay up. His wealthy parents refuse to give him the money, so to keep his vicious creditor at bay he decides to pretend he's been kidnapped. The parents see through this scheme—the ransom is the exact amount he asked for, for one thing—so he steps up the game by sending a note specifying that they'll receive a different piece of him each day until they pay up. A finger arrives, horrifying Oliver's parents, until a spark hits it and it burns up like cellophane —a fake. A hand that arrives the next day also proves to be a phony. When Oliver's folks receive the next parcel, the father throws it into the fireplace with disgust. But when they smell a horrible odor they realize this wasn't fake—it is Oliver's actual severed head; seems his creditor was getting impatient.

In "The Tiny Heads" a man murders several natives simply so he can have some shrunken heads to sell, but the heads come to life and begin biting him, holding him in place while his own head is severed and he winds up in the same bag with the other "trophies." "Death of a Doll" is a grotesque concoction wherein a wealthy midget gets even with the women who shunned him by murdering them, and when chased by police winds up hiding in the cage of an ape who turns him into a twisted bloody toy. In another story a bitter old man discovers a potion that raises the dead, whom he forces to do his bidding until he makes the mistake of directing them to sacred ground. A story of a female vampire rounded out the issue.

Two

EC Comics

EC (Entertaining Comics) comics such as *Tales from the Crypt*, *Vault of Horror* and *Shock SuspenStories* have become as famous for the controversy surrounding them and the changes it engendered in the whole comics industry, as for their often admirable content. While the publisher churned out much material that was little better than the stuff presented in imitative comics from other firms, the more effective stories were often clever, deliciously macabre, well-illustrated, and quite memorable. Reading some EC stories today a modern reader may well be surprised if not startled by what these comics got away with (for a time, at least) in the 1950s, as the material in its graphic nature generally was much grosser than what teens and younger children were seeing at the drive-in, and gorier than all but the most recent horror comics. EC didn't help itself by marketing its product to kids, even printing missives from youngsters on their letters pages; even today most reasonable people would agree that most of EC's material was not for children. Some of the less sensitive youngsters responded to the black comedy aspects of the comics' cackling hideous hosts—borrowed from radio—and the tone of many of the stories, but even a mature adult mind would find many of the tales quite disturbing. (It could be argued that EC took advantage of immature minds' lack of empathy and compassion for others.) A psychologist named Fredric Wertham penned a tome entitled *Seduction of the Innocent* which criticized comics put out by EC and their many imitators, although he didn't play fair, taking panels out of context and overstating everything as if horror comics were responsible for every single evil act perpetrated on the planet. Nevertheless, many horror comics that were not in the EC mold started dropping stories of blood-suckers and ax-wielding maniacs in favor of less grisly content, a comics code authority was eventually formed by the industry that banned certain depictions of horror and gore, and EC began publishing different types of stories and eventually went out of business. Fortunately, most of the stories from the publisher have been reprinted, so they can be enjoyed—if that's the word—by the modern reader.

Tales from the Crypt

EC Comics changed the title of one of its comics to *Crypt of Terror* for its seventeenth issue in 1950 and presented all horror and suspense stories, what they called "SuspenStories"

with a cadaverous "Crypt Keeper" as host. The first new issue had tales about a man who stays young for decades by stealing glands from youthful corpses and having them transferred to his own body; an executioner who decides to take the law into his hands and kill people he thinks have gotten away with murder; a private eye who finds an unidentified corpse in a hotel room and deduces who it is; and a man who's convinced he's turned into a flesh-tearing werewolf. Only the first story was somewhat memorable, although weakened by a flat finale. "The Living Corpse" in the next issue is a clever tale in which a frightened morgue attendant keeps encountering the same lively "dead" body. "Mute Witness to Murder" is basically a rip-off of the 1946 Vincent Price movie *Shock*, in which a woman who sees a doctor murder his wife is committed by him to an institution. "The Hungry Grave" in *COT* 19 is a darkly amusing story about a woman and her lover who keep trying to kill off her husband with ironic and deadly results. Artists included Al Feldstein, Johnny Craig, Harvey Kurtzman and Wally Wood.

The comic became *Tales from the Crypt* with the twentieth issue but continued in the same vein. The Old Witch and a Vault-Keeper now narrated or introduced stories along with the Crypt-Keeper, each competing with the others to tell the most horrific work of fiction. "The Fatal Caper" has some people playing a trick on a fellow guest involving fake demons and spirits and a borrowed corpse, a trick which backfires on them when the man is inadvertently buried alive and the others discover that the corpse they've stolen has given them leprosy. "Rx ... Death" is a Lovecraftian-type tale in which a man takes a prescribed medicine whose deadly unknown ingredient begins transforming him both mentally and physically until he begins literally *digesting* himself.

But these stories were nothing compared to the grotesque "Last Respects" in *TFTC* 23 in which a man enters a mausoleum to pay respects to his child-bride, just placed in a casket after her funeral that afternoon, but winds up trapped inside the vault for weeks. The man, who had been a driver for his wife's wealthy uncle, has just murdered the old man, who objected to the marriage and refused to let him see his niece as she lay dying of pneumonia. To survive in the crypt, he catches dripping water in an urn—and eats the corpse of his beloved (this is not actually depicted). Unfortunately, he is killed not by hunger but by the poisonous formaldehyde in the body. In the following issue a man who goes out for a snack winds up chewing on a corpse in a graveyard ("Midnight Snack").

Tales from the Crypt really went beyond the pale with "Grounds ... for Horror" in the twenty-ninth issue, which has the brutal, abusive butcher who repeatedly locks his small son in the closet without supper winding up chopped meat in his grinder, his remains depicted revoltingly as piles of raw crumbling hamburger as the boy and his mother look on in shock and disgust. In a similar and better story in *TFTC* 32 "'Taint the Meat ... It's the Humanity," set during the rationing of World War II, butcher Zach Gristle gives in to greed, sells good meat to rich customers for much money, and horse and other poor quality meat to the poorer folk in town. Eventually he descends to selling these people tainted meat—and several die of food poisoning. When his own little son eats dinner at a friend's house and dies, his wife—who has just discovered what her husband has been doing and is furious at him—loses her mind to grief and anger. The story ends with her taking her husband's place in the butcher shop, and offering for sale—her husband, cut up into chops and steaks, with head and hands

Opposite: Gladstone began publishing classic EC reprints in the '90s.

on display and intestines laid out like sausages. While the first butcher shop story is memorable mostly for shock value, the second has a strong narrative flow and more satisfying impact. ("Mess Call" in *Tales* 41 was a far less effective tale about human meat being sold in a butcher shop.)

Some stories just presented gore for shock value. In "How Green Was My Alley" a happy bigamist named Bob only sees each of his two wives one week out of the month. The other two weeks he spends on the road as a salesman. The wives have each taken up a sport to fill their lonely hours: bowling and golf respectively. One week they are each competing in a different tournament at the same hotel, and due to a mix-up wind up sharing a room as they wait for their husbands to arrive. As they unwrap the gifts Bob gave them before starting off on his latest trip, the golfer finds bowling shoes in her package and the bowler finds golf shoes ... They compare notes and photos and then Bob shows up. The ending has one wife using Bob's eyeballs for golf balls while the other substitutes his head for a bowling ball. Not only is this literal overkill, but the story worked pretty well without the gruesome wind-up.

On other occasions the gore seemed to spring naturally from the story, such as in "Accidents and Old Lace" (43) in which Eric Holbein discovers that three old ladies in a rooming house create strikingly macabre and artistic tapestries every time they see a gruesome scene of accidental death. Greedy for the money a dealer pays him, only a percentage of which he gives to the ladies, he contrives to create more "accidents" that the women can witness. When the ladies discover what he's done, they reveal that they were responsible for most of the other "accidents" but insist they draw the line at murder, and advance on him with needles and the like. The next tapestry they bring the dealer has many small pieces of Holbein's corpse attached to it, which is drenched in his blood.

And there was gore, gore and more gore. Some was just suggested: An evil woman climbs up a magical rope taken from a murdered female, disappears into space and screams; then (non-bloody) pieces of her body tumble down on top of her husband. A man's voodoo doll is shattered into many pieces, and his new bride wakes up to find the same has happened to hubby (not depicted). On other occasions, nothing was left to the imagination: A nasty young fire chief, who let his old-timer partner die, runs to the fire pole when he learns his own house is on fire and discovers it's been replaced with a razor-sharp steel strip that slices him into fragments, the result of which is displayed in the final panel. An evil man who chopped up his wife is locked in a trunk, fires bullets through it, but when the trunk shrinks, his flesh comes out through the holes in gruesome ribbons. During Mardi Gras a man marries a woman whose face is hidden by a frightful witch's mask; the morning after he *tears* off the mask only to discover she wasn't *wearing* a mask.

Bad guys get their comeuppance: "A Sucker for a Spider" (29) has a man grinning with delight as he shows an employee how the vermula spider catches flies, paralyzes them, then injects a digestive enzyme into the bug so it can suck out all the juices inside. Of course, this fellow murders the employee, who tries to blackmail him, via the bite of a black widow, but when his plane crashes in the jungle he encounters a rather large vermula who does to him what its smaller cousin did to the fly. In "A Buried Treasure" (31) the carriage of a corpulent, callous duke runs over a little boy, killing him, and all he can do is complain of bloodstains on the wheels. When he has the hands of a man who tried to steal his jewels to feed the starving townspeople severed, the crowd has had enough. One man forces the Duke to eat dozens of his precious gems, then throws him to the people, who eagerly tear out his entrails to get at the booty (this is not graphically depicted). In a similar story in *TFTC* 34 a king who levies unbelievable taxes on his subjects—for instance everyone with a thumb must pay a "thumb tax" or have their thumbs lopped off—is axed to death, his stomach torn out in shadow.

In "Roped In" (32) three partners in a construction firm who have framed the fourth for shoddy jobs that brought them much profit but resulted in the deaths of innocent people, are flying down to another job when their plane is caught in the web of a gigantic spider that devours them. In "Last Laugh" (38) a yokel who plays an unbelievably cruel and wretched joke on some youngsters, causing the deaths of innocents, is put out of everyone's misery by a loved one of the victims. "Blind Alleys" (46) has the heartless manager of a home for the blind trapped in a razor-lined tunnel and ultimately fed to his starving, nasty canine, while "Success Story" (46) has a young husband turn and wreak havoc on the constantly nagging wife and in-laws who are making his life so miserable, probably a favorite fantasy for a lot of unhappy spouses of both sexes.

In "Food for Thought" (40) a man who has a mind-reading act with his wife murders her lover. Not much later he is believed to have been killed in an accident. But his wife can hear his thoughts and knows he is only paralyzed. She ignores his mental cries for help and allows him to be buried alive. The murderer hears someone digging up his grave and assumes it's his repentant wife, but it's actually a ghoul—who eats his "corpse" as he lies there in agony unable to fight off his determinedly hungry attacker. In "The Bath" (42) Senor Tobosa is an absolute monster who brutalizes the natives who work in his silver mine, denying them food, whipping them for alleged laziness, and even murdering one who inadvertently sneezes on him. The obese, smooth Tobosa has a horror of germs and the touch of "inferiors" and each day his servant draws him a warm, cleansing bath. One day Tobosa goes too far and kills a child that he insisted must work in the mines, then shoots the grief-stricken, furious parents when they attack him. They, however, happen to be his manservant's family, so the servant prepares a special bath for Tobosa, one filled with hungry man-eating fish. The last panel shows Tobosa with the lower half of his body turned into a very clean skeleton as the writhing creatures still feast. Tobosa is such an utterly loathsome character that the reader can't help but feel that even this horrible death is too good for him. In the same issue's "Hoodwinked" Leon cares and provides for his spoiled brother Chet who consistently takes terrible advantage of him. His financial demands—always with the promise of getting a job, a promise never fulfilled—prevent Leon from being able to marry his fiancee, Claire. Claire finally puts her foot down when Chet demands $100 for a fancy hood ornament for his car. When a drunken Chet rapes Claire and drives her to suicide, Leon finally snaps—and his brother's severed head winds up as a hood ornament on his convertible.

There were variations on werewolf and vampire stories. "Midnight Mess" (35) features a man, Harold, who comes to a small town to visit his sister and learns that several people have disappeared without a trace. He then discovers that his sister is a patron of a restaurant that caters only to vampires with various blood-related treats and libations. As she explains, "just like modern man, we (vampires) leave the hunting—and preparing—to the professionals." Then Harold is strung up, a tap put into his jugular vein, and a glass of blood poured for all the thirsty diners. "Concerto for Violin and Werewolf" (41) is a bizarre tale of an ambitious violinist, his old Transylvanian teacher, a priceless Stradivarius, a rapid-fire gun filled with silver bullets—and an entire town of werewolves busy stripping victims of every inch of their flesh.

Some stories had more than a share of dark or sick whimsy. In "The Den of Iniquity" (31) the editors and artists of the comic appear to explain why they turned to horror after sales of their romance comics plummeted. "Lower Berth" (33) shows how the Crypt-Keeper came into being from the unlikely union of two supposedly dead sideshow exhibits, an ancient female Egyptian mummy, and a two-headed freak in formaldehyde. In the amusingly cynical study of childhood callousness "The Funeral" (33), a cute little prince who becomes greatly attached to his nurse is heartbroken when she dies. To cheer him up his father says that candy and ice cream will be served at her funeral, and there will even be prizes, such as a pony. When the prince goes into the chamber where the nurse is lying in state, he discovers her awakened from a cataleptic trance. At first he is overjoyed until he remembers the funeral with the candy and the pony—and promptly bashes the old woman on the head with a candlestick, killing her for real this time.

Tales from the Crypt was not above lifting story ideas from other sources. In "The Living Death" (24) a man puts a rival into a hypnotic trance and tells him he cannot die. When the rival is hit by a car and killed, he continues to live, even though he's biologically dead. Ths story was "borrowed" from a tale by Edgar Allen Poe, "Facts in the Case of M. Valdemar." In 1952 *TFTC* 32 published a story entitled "Cutting Cards" in which two gamblers play "chop poker," in which the loser gets his fingers—then hands, feet and so on—cut off with a meat cleaver. This may have been influenced by "Collector's Item," a story by Roald Dahl about a man who bets his fingers in a card game that was published in *Collier's* in 1948. (It was dramatized on *Alfred Hitchcock Presents* in 1960 under the title "Man from the South.") There was an authorized adaptation of Ray Bradbury's "There Was an Old Woman" (34) about an old lady's ghost who demands her body back from the morgue, but it wasn't very well done. Bradbury's grotesque "The Handler" got excellent handling in *Tales* 36, however, a story about an embittered mortuary owner who gets his jollies desecrating the corpses given into his care. He pours cake and whipped cream into the empty head of one woman, burrows three old biddies in one coffin so they can continue to gossip, cuts off the head of a bodybuilder, puts parts of an elderly man in with an old maid (presumably hands and penis) so he can make "cold love" to her and so on. The dead get their revenge and distribute the man's body among every grave in the graveyard.

After adapting one of his stories without permission, EC Comics negotiated with Bradbury—whom they significantly called "America's finest horror writer"—to do authorized versions of his work. For whatever reasons many of Bradbury's stories, some of which were quite unmemorable, at least seemed to display a great deal of child-hatred. A school teacher is convinced that all little children are monsters and a bunch of them murder him even as a separate group of kids push another child out of a window; a couple are convinced that their adorable baby boy is a demon who steals about at night making mischief (apparently their fears are justified). In the sick (and rather ridiculous) "October Game" a man dismembers his own little daughter just to get even with the wife he hates and uses the pieces for a game at a children's Halloween party. (The adaptation was arguably better than the original story.)

Arguably the best cover was for *TFTC* 45, which had a man from a sunken ocean liner clinging to a floating beam as a humungous hungry rat, fangs bared, walks toward him. This was the penultimate issue of the series, and it contained two mini-masterpieces, the cover story, "Telescope" and "The Switch." In "Telescope" a man and a rat are the only survivors of a shipwreck and wind up on the same island, competing for what little food and water there is and eying each other hungrily. When a seagull with a fish in its mouth lands on the island, the rat pounces on the bird and flees into the ocean with it as the man pursues. Catching up with the rat, the man stuffs it tail-first into his mouth, just as a shark comes up and engulfs *him*. The natives capture the shark, and when it is brought up on the deck they see protruding from its mouth the man's head, from which emerges the rat, with the bird, and the fish, in turn protruding from the rodent, a macabre and gruesome "telescopic" tableau.

"The Switch" is the story of wealthy old man Webster, who has fallen in love with a beautiful young babe, Linda. Because he wants to be loved for himself, he hasn't told the woman that he's rich, but she confesses that she's turned off by all his wrinkles. Webster goes to a "quack" who switches his face with handsome young George Booth, who will be paid a great deal of money and says that his good looks never did him any good anyway. Linda likes his new face, but his body is so withered ... So Webster pays even more money to switch trunks with Booth. But Linda still isn't satisfied—she can't abide his spindly arms and legs, so Webster gives up all the rest of his fortune to exchange limbs with Booth. But when he turns up in his handsome and studly new form, Linda informs him that he's *still* not what she's looking for. What she wants is a man who's *rich*—and out walks aged, spindly, cadaverous George Booth, who now has all of Webster's money!

Other notable stories: "Madame Bluebeard" (27) is a French woman, brought up to hate men by the mother whose husband abandoned them, who murders all seven of her husbands in diabolical accidents In "Return" (27) a woman is impregnated by her husband when he returns from a long journey, only she later discovers that he died several months before. "Bargain in Death" (28) has two teams of young men who need money coming afoul of each other when their plots criss cross. In "A Corny Story" (28) an old man fired by a callous young employer who hates age sends him a voodoo plant that makes the man grow younger and younger until he's a baby, and then nothing. "The Ventriloquist's Dummy" (28) features a ventriloquist whose dummy is actually his own hand, which developed a head with its own consciousness instead of fingers, and which chews on victims with many tiny bites like a plague of rats. In "The Sliceman Cometh" (44) a distinguished headman during the French revolution has a devil of a time getting rid of the severed head of a man he condemned to the guillotine for money. Artists for the series included Jack Davis, Howard Larsen, George Roussos, Graham Ingels, Jack Kamen, and Joe Orlando.

The Vault of Horror

EC Turned *War Against Crime* into *The Vault of Horror* beginning with the twelfth issue. The first issue of the new series was a fairy standard horror mag with stories about a Frenchman who steals another man's artwork for money but winds up immortalized in wax; a man who fears he is a werewolf but is the victim of a hoax perpetrated by a greedy cousin; a hotel owner who has a premonition of murder; and a woman who fears her husband is trying to kill her but is really quite crazy. The next issue, *VOH* 13, was an improvement if only for the story "Doctor of Horror," about a doctor of anatomy who needs a steady supply of corpses for his classroom and doesn't care how he acquires them. *VOH* 15 has a story about scientists inadvertently creating a man-eating blob in the swamp, as well as a nifty revenge story with various people being "Buried Alive." The series began getting gorier with *VOH* 16's "Fitting

Punishment" in which an miserly old undertaker's miserable treatment of his nephew extends to not only crippling the boy with a blow, but cutting off his feet so he can fit in an unused coffin to save money. The wrapped up severed feet come alive, and the footless body manages to make its way back from the graveyard to have its way with its not-so-dear uncle. "The Grave Wager," in which a practical joke with an allegedly dead body backfires, and "Escape," in which a convict plots to escape in a coffin but doesn't realize the prison has just completed its own crematorium, were clever if minor suspense tales.

In the bizarre romance "Reunion" (19) young Lillian Ainsley is saddled with an invalid older husband even though she's in love with another man. She decides to do the right thing and stay with her husband and care for him. Her lover goes away for five years, but when he returns the situation is still the same. Then another five years, and another. Finally the husband dies and Lillian is free, but she discovers her lover has died in the interim. She goes to the spot where they were supposed to meet and to her surprise he shows up anyway—a rotting corpse determined to see the woman he waited for one more time. Lillian, her mind gone, reaches out for him ... and joins him in his grave. The story has an impact because Lillian, who faithfully cared for her husband when she could have run off with her lover, clearly doesn't deserve such a cruel fate. In the even more bizarre "Two of a Kind" (26) a female vampire and a male ghoul are actors co-starring in the same play, unaware of the other's secret. They go away for the weekend, each planning on feeding off the other, when they both realize they're in love and have no desire to do the other one harm. When they are trapped in a cabin by a blizzard, the two make up their minds not to prey on the one they love, so the woman drinks her own blood and the man eats parts of his own body to survive—to no avail.

There were, of course, mean-people-get-their-just-dessert stories in abundance. "A Stitch in Time" (23) features a truly odious and evil manager of a sweat shop who so abuses his female employees that they rise up in revenge, sew his lips together, and set him and his shop on fire. In "The Death Wagon" (24), two men who sell unsafe used cars that cause many deaths are confronted by the mangled corpses of their victims who use their body parts to "fix" and decorate one of the death traps on their lot. In "Collection Completed" (25) Jonah Tillman torments his animal-loving wife Anita by taking up taxidermy, capturing stray animals of all kinds and gleefully stuffing them. When he goes too far and kills and stuffs her beloved cat, Anita kills and stuffs him, a not unexpected resolution. Although you know that the haughty, cruel model in "Silver Threads Among the Mold" (27) will wind up a silver-plated statue the minute the homely sculptor who loves her talks of using the process on a likeness of her (and especially when he discovers how she was only using him), the ending—when her lover peals off the silver coating and sees the ghastly decomposing skull underneath—still makes quite an impression.

"A Grim Fairy Tale" (27) presents a portly and pompous king and queen who refuse to allow their subjects to kill off the aggressive rats that are eating their food and even babies because of the queen's affection for her pet white mice. The fed-up villagers storm the castle, stuff two especially ravenous rats down their mouths, sew up their lips, and watch as the king and queen dance around as the rodents eat their way out of their insides! Other revenge stories merely seemed an excuse to come up with shocking, super-gross endings, such as "The Chips are Down" and "For How the Bell Tolls" (both in *VOH* 28), the former having two men

Opposite: Gladstone's first compilation of material from EC's *Vault of Horror*.

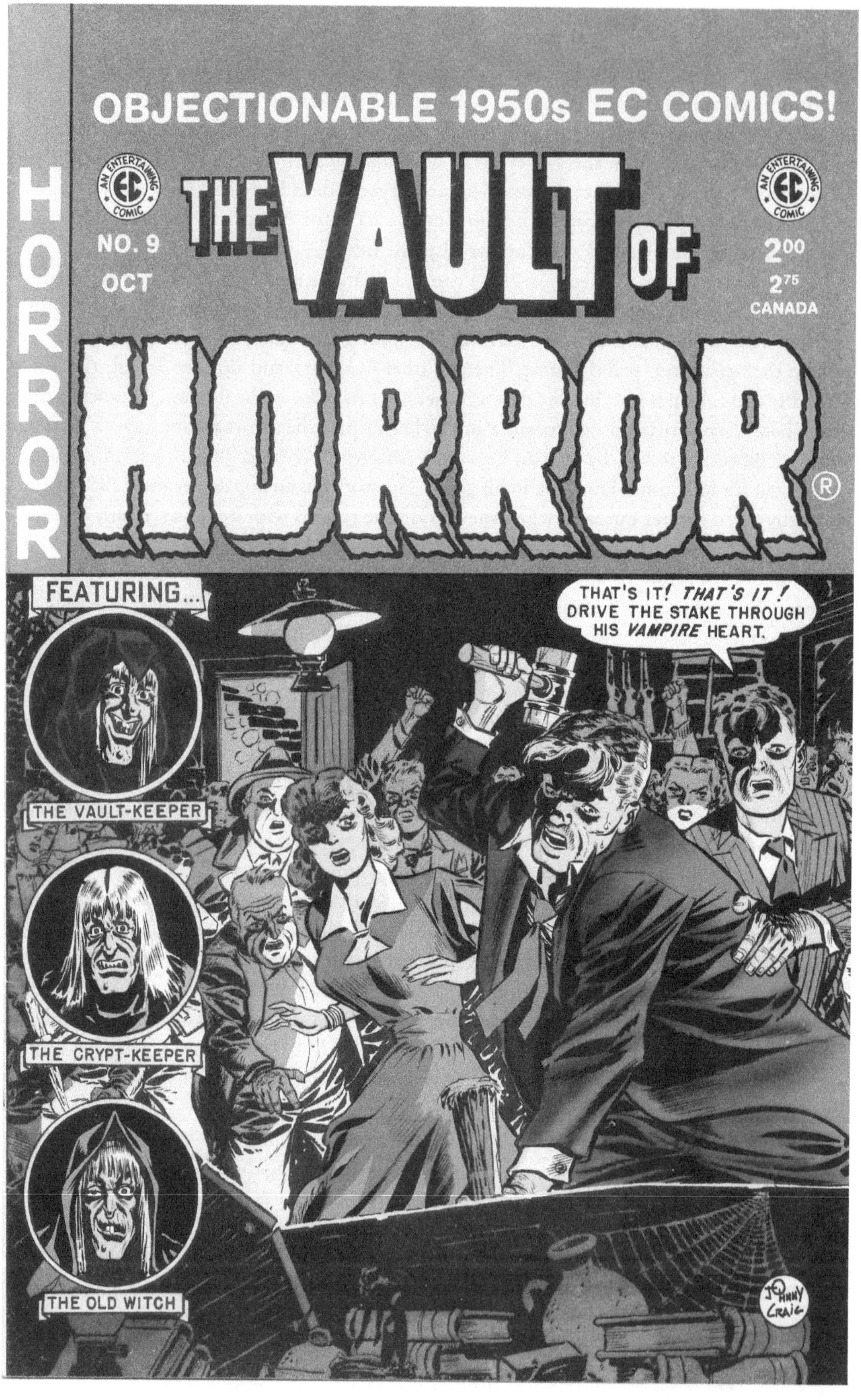

who caused a third's suicide pushed into a grinder that segments their bodies into small thin circular pieces, and the latter featuring a murderous bell-ringer whose bloody corpse is used to ring the bell all day long for the queen's birthday.

The gore quotient really began to go up by 1953, when the cover of the thirtieth issue showed a severed arm, with the bone showing, hanging on to an overhead strap in a subway car. Although some gore geeks would find the thought heretical, the fact remains that the gore shock ending was sometimes a mere substitute for good writing and for endings that were genuinely clever and surprising. For instance, "Split Personality" in *VOH* 30 has a highly interesting plot in which a con artist courting wealthy, eccentric twins pretends to be a twin himself in order to marry both and control all of their vast fortune. But he makes a couple of mistakes and is found out, enraging and mortifying the sisters. Naturally the almost obligatory "EC" ending has the gals taking an ax to the man, cutting his body lengthwise in half, and each cuddling up with one half of a husband. It's okay as far as it goes, but prevents the writer from coming up with something less predictable and formulaic. All that some stories, such as "An Ample Sample" (32)—in which a husband cuts up his wife into pieces in a box resembling the candy samplers she was addicted to—had going for them was the gory finale.

And sometimes bad things happened to good people in stories that were a shade sadistic in their lip-smacking telling of awful and ironic fates who envelope those who did nothing terribly wrong. In "With All the Trappings" (24) elderly trapper Pierre hates the idea of worms and decomposition getting at his or his wife Maria's body after death. When Maria dies, Pierre puts her body in an ice house to keep while he works hard to make enough money to buy a metal vault for her. He finally saves up the required amount, but discovers that a lynx who was caught in one of his traps and tore off a leg to escape, got into the ice house and has eaten most of Maria's body. In "Till Death" a man marries his sweetheart in Haiti where she dies of a fever. His manservant brings her back with voodoo, and at first the husband is overjoyed, until he realizes from the odor that she is still dead and decomposing. Her appearance worsens with every day but her affection for him is undiminished. He tries to destroy her completely but nothing works. He finally takes a fatal dose of poison, but wakes up to realize that he, too, has been turned into a zombie and his hideous bride will be with him *forever*.

"Tomb's Day" in *VOH* 35 was a good example of an EC horror story that worked up a lot of suspense without piling on the gore. A professor leads a number of people on a search through tunnels inside a pyramid for the members of the previous expedition, all of whom disappeared. As they get deeper into the pyramid, they explore different theories as to what might have happened to the others. One by one the members of this new expedition are killed off, their bodies disappearing, and the survivors react with very realistic near-hysteria. Although premiere EC artist Jack Davis' somewhat cartoony style is a little at odds with the subject matter, he does manage to provide atmosphere and the story is well-drawn. After all the build-up the ending is disappointing and rather generic, unfortunately.

Similarly, another Jack Davis mini-epic in the following issue, "Witch Witch's Witch" works up a lot of suspense over whether or not Eric Holbein's new wife Helena is a witch. As the people who hate her—her mother-in-law, the mother of Eric's old girlfriend, the head of the church ladies—die sudden deaths after unpleasant encounters with Helena, the whole town becomes stirred up and runs en masse to put an end to the witch—but Helena has

Opposite: Gladstone's ninth reprint issue of EC's *Vault of Horror*.

quite a surprise for them in a satisfyingly dark finale. Davis' intense "Chop Talk" in the next issue detailed the agonizing last days of a murderer who is facing the chopping block, the executioner being the bereaved husband of the woman he murdered, promising his "victim" that he will make his death as terrible as possible.

Like *Tales from the Crypt*, *Vault of Horror* was not above ripping off stories from other sources. "Island of Terror" (13) was borrowed from the classic short story and film "The Most Dangerous Game." "Baby, It's Cold Inside" (17) was an uncredited adaptation of H. P. Lovecraft's "Cool Air." "Voodoo Horror" (17) is a vastly inferior rewrite of "The Picture of Dorian Gray" in which a sculpted voodoo bust is substituted for a portrait. "The Thing in the Ice" (22) is a forgettable sequel to Mary Shelley's "Frankenstein" that ends just when it starts getting interesting. "Dead Weight" (23)—a man steals a pearl with the help of a native who wants his red-haired head as a trophy—was taken from John Russell's "The Price of the Head."

However, *Vault of Horror* also had plenty of memorably original tales to tell. "Terror of the Moors" (17) features a hideous creature, kept locked behind mansion walls, that only has a taste for decaying dead human flesh, and when it breaks out of confinement after his father's death, feasts on the old man's corpse. In "Dying to Lose Weight" (18) a doctor gives four fat people a weight reducing pill that costs 200 dollars and eventually leaves them emaciated and dead because it contains a tape worm that feeds upon them, and which breaks out, enlarged, from one woman's corpse and devours the doctor. In "About Face" (*VOH* 20) a disfigured woman, cruelly taken advantage of by a gold-digging suitor, wreaks a diabolical vengeance upon him. "People Who Live in Brass Hearses" (27) concerns a man who, unbeknownst to everyone in town, never gets out of the hearse he drives when he picks up supplies because he's attached to the decaying corpse of his dead Siamese twin.

In "Strictly From Hunger" (27) a man uses witchcraft to stay alive after he develops a malignant tumor on his arm but the cancer, needing a steady diet of healthy cells, turns him into a blob that devours people and leaves only bones behind. "Practical Choke" (30) has three callous medical students using parts of a corpse to play grisly practical jokes on people, until they are strangled to death by the dead man's creeping intestines. "Notes to You" (30) has a nasty man writing poison pen letters that drive several people to suicide, until some of his victims get together and inject him with "lye." "One Good Turn" (31) features a middle-aged woman who spends time making miserable people "happy" by killing them, including her bedridden husband who is horrified by the stories of her "good deeds." In "Smoke Wrings" (34) a lady ad exec steals an idea from a shy man but pays for it in the end. In "Where There's a Will" (34) two lawyers concoct a clever plot to secure a sick old man's wealth for themselves. "And All Through the House" (35) details a woman's attempts to get rid of the body of the husband she just murdered and which are hampered by the sudden appearance of a homicidal maniac dressed as Santa Claus.

"Shoe-Button Eyes" (35) is a disturbing story of child abuse and an alcoholic who winds up with very strange eyes. "Oh, Henry" (37) has a heartless cop put an old woman in jail for sixty days for shoplifting and refusing to check up her story about her invalid husband home alone with no food, until he finds out to his regret that he should have listened to her. "Top Billing" (39) has three competitive actors trying to land the same unusual role in a most peculiar production of "Hamlet" while "All for Gnawt" (39) is a darkly comic tale of a woman who answers a personal ad from a wealthy aging bachelor and discovers he has a serious rat problem to go with his moolah. "The Pit" (40) presents two sensitive men whose callous wives control their respective bloody dog-fight and cock-fight businesses, until the women are pitted against each other in the most gruesome final fight of both of their lives.

Johnny Craig offered some serviceable if on occasion hastily drawn art for many of the stories.

Crime SuspenStories

EC's *Crime SuspenStories* premiered in 1950. Although these were not always out and out horror stories, many had horrific elements to them. The lead story in the first issue, "Murder May Boomerang," was a variation of Samuel Blas' story "Revenge," which was later adapted in *Witch's Tales* and became even more famous as the first episode of *Alfred Hitchcock Presents* in 1955. In that story a woman is raped, points out her assailant to her husband—who kills the man—then points out another man as the rapist a while later. In "Murder May Boomerang" the couple become a father and son; the father is beaten by a runaway convict, points him out, the son runs him over, then the traumatized father points out another man ... "A Snapshot of Death," in which a dying women hires a hit man to kill her only to learn she will live after all, was also lifted from several sources. The best story in the issue, "High Tide," concerns a small boat whose several passengers learn that an escaped killer is aboard, as suspicion and paranoia become paramount in everyone's—almost everyone's—minds.

Crime SuspenStories began running a feature entitled "Haunt of Fear" in each issue—by this time EC had begun publishing a comic of that title—and these were more on the macabre and grisly side than the other stories. "Heads-Up" in *CSS* 4—a carnival worker who exhibits freaks in formaldehyde replaces the two-headed man destroyed by his wife with the heads of her and her lover—was lifted from Ray Bradbury's "The Jar." "Jury Duty," in the sixth issue, features a criminal who manages to survive a hanging and with his neck bent to the side goes about murdering the members of the jury who convicted him. The law cannot touch him since he is already legally dead. However, the surviving members of the jury get together and bury him alive, reminding him that it isn't murder because their victim is—as he told them—"legally dead." In "Partnership Dissolved" (8) a greedy meat packer murders the partner who came up with a fantastic meat tenderizer, but his body winds up being digested from the inside out when he accidentally swallows some of it. The "Friend to 'Our Boys'" (10) is a miserable slum lord who refuses to improve conditions in an apartment he rented to a serviceman and his family, and winds up a meal for the rats infesting the place. "Hail and Heart-y" (15) features a husband who gets out of every chore due to his weak heart—his wife has to work, rake the leaves, even shovel snow—who gets a surprise when she learns the truth about his condition from the doctor.

In "The Execution" (12) a man sits on death row because no one will believe that he was helping a man whose car was stuck in a snowdrift at the same time that a woman, his alleged victim, was being murdered. This man has never come forth and the condemned man has lost all hope. The story goes through the step by step process of his final day on earth, as he walks the final mile, and is killed in the electric chair. It turns out that the man who pulled the switch, who'd been on vacation and knew nothing about the case, was the man he'd helped in the blizzard. Under close scrutiny, however, the story falls apart, as surely a sensational murder trial based on circumstantial evidence would have lasted for months and received a major amount of publicity.

Ray Bradbury's "The Screaming Woman" is an excellent story in *CSS* 15 in which a little girl hears a woman screaming for help from under the ground. She tells numerous people, including her parents, about the "screaming woman" but nobody believes her. As the suspense builds, she has to endure a long supper with her family, then goes out to the lot and begins digging for the woman by herself, enlisting the aid of a little boy who simply thinks she's a ventriloquist. A man comes along and insists she fill in the hole, but he's too deaf to hear the screaming. The child runs around the neighborhood trying to find out whose wife is missing and hits pay dirt with Mr. Nesbitt, who tries to prevent her from leaving his house. Returning to the lot, this time the child hears the woman under the ground keening a song. When the child sings the song for her father, he recalls it as a ditty an old girlfriend once wrote for him and realizes what's probably happened to Helen Nesbitt. The story ends with the happy child watching as he and the other adults finally dig up the terrified woman beneath the earth.

Crime SuspenStories ran what they called "EC Quickies" in many issues. These were stories with more than one ending, or told from different points of view, such as a husband who wants to kill his wife's lover and the lover who'd like to murder the husband. In "First Impulse" (13), sort of a demented *True Confessions*-type story, a woman suspects that her boyfriend has fallen for her younger sister and vice versa. She hears them whispering together—"she's beginning to suspect," says the sister—and when she follows them finds them buying and engraving an engagement ring. Confronting them, she shoots the pair dead before they can speak, only to have a delivery boy ring the bell and hand her a package. Inside it is the engagement ring—engraved to *her*. In the alternate ending of the story, the couple manage to blurt out that the ring is for her, but she discovers this was a lie after the two run off together in typical "Broken Hearts" fashion. In *CSS* 14 one trio of "quickies" told what would happen if a wife and her lover were confronted by a husband who was, respectively, American, English, and French. The three men are sentenced to death by the electric chair, noose, and guillotine, but each escapes and ducks into the subway, underground, or Paris metro: The American runs onto the third rail and is electrocuted, the Englishman gets his tie caught in a door and is strangled, and the Frenchman is beheaded after he falls onto the tracks. Although it wasn't billed as a "quickie" to maintain the surprise, two of the stories in *CSS* 17—"One for the Money" and "Two for the Show" (separated by another unrelated story), although with different plots, were ingeniously connected, the corpse in the first story playing a major role in the second—but only in the final panel.

After awhile victims in the comic weren't just shot or stabbed, they were hacked to pieces or mutilated beyond recognition. After one character hacks up another and puts the pieces in the furnace for disposal, he relates how "I heaved convulsively into the wash tub, creating a ghastly brew with the jellied gore remaining." The cover of the *CSS* 17 shows a man blowing out his brains in front of his wife or girlfriend, bits of matter coming out of the back of his head. *CSS* 22 had a notorious cover with a woman's severed head being held up in a man's hand, the body lying below. The inside story that went with the cover would be completely unmemorable were it not for the ax attack that opens it.

Ironically the best story that ever appeared in *Crime SuspenStories* wasn't a gory shocker, murder mystery or man-hacks-up-spouse tale but an affecting heart-breaker entitled

"Mother's Day" (21). In this a woman favors her youngest son, Harold, because the older boy, Fred, resembles his father, the husband who walked out on her when she was pregnant with Harold, who looks like his mother. In spite of the fact that his mother gives all of her affection and attention to his brother, Fred still loves his mother and tries to please her, even going so far as to take the rap for a robbery-beating committed by Harold. During the five years Fred spends in prison, Harold shows his colors to his mother; when she tries to take a gun away from him he knocks her on the head with it. Harold is killed in a shoot out and Fred gets out of jail, coming home to see his mother and tell her the truth. He pours out his heart to her as she lies silent in bed, asking for her love and forgiveness, but when she doesn't speak he blows out his brains in regret and anguish. It turns out that the mother was paralyzed by the blow Harold gave her, and can't move or speak, only shed tears as she realizes she was never able to make up to her good son the miserable way she treated him. Frank doesn't deserve his fate, but his mother does. Even if one can't quite buy the notion that a brother would take the rap for his spoiled, unlikable sibling just to spare his mother's feelings, "Mother's Day" still packs a wallop.

Another especially notable story was "The Fixer" (26) in which police are called to the scene when a husband and wife are murdered with the only survivor being their ten-year-old son, Billy. A poor family in a snooty neighborhood, Billy and his parents had been treated like pariahs (almost as if they were a black family in a racist town, although they are white characters). Billy's father drinks to deal with the neighbors' rejection—the other children are even nasty to Billy—and fights break out between him and his wife over his behavior. When people in town begin to be slaughtered in their beds, suspicion falls on Billy's father; even his wife accuses him of the savage crimes and starts to call the police. When her husband tries to stop her and kills her, he commits suicide out of remorse. Little Billy tells the cops that he was fixing things, but now "I killed them all for nothing." Sociopathic children were certainly a fictional rarity at the time of the story's publication (1954); that same year William March came out with the classic *The Bad Seed*, which was a possible influence on "The Fixer."

Crime SuspenStories was a memorable series that could easily have been titled *Tales of Irony*, as it specialized in twists and ironic endings. Every issue had something of interest in it. Some of the more notable tales included: "Hatchet-Killer" (7)—a young wife becomes convinced that her maid is the notorious ax murderer who's been terrorizing the neighborhood; "Medicine" (9)—a wife who is jealous of her surgeon husband's relationship with his nurse poisons his medicine, but regrets it when she has an accident and he is the only man who could have saved her life; "Cut" (9)—an understudy murders the famous actor he resembles but his plans to take his place run afoul of a runaway lawn mower; "Rocks in His Head" (10)—a surgeon with a greedy wife and huge debts steals a diamond ring from a patient and hides it in the skull of another one during an operation; "Missed by Two Heirs" (10)—two brothers try to kill off their nasty, miserly stepfather but instead face a very ironic fate when he survives.

Also: "Snooze to Me" (12)—a wife thinks that she can win her philandering husband back if she fakes suicide with the help of her maid, but doesn't realize that the maid is her husband's lover. "Sweet Dreams" (14)—a man uses what he thinks are sleeping pills to kill off his wife but her doctor has quite a surprise for him. "Rendezvous" (16)—an embezzler who fears exposure puts a time bomb on a plane but winds up another of the victims when the aircraft crashes. "Fall Guy for Murder" (18)—a private eye hired to look for a missing wife believes her husband murdered her, but falls victim to an especially diabolical plot. "The Killer" (19)—a woman finds out her husband's secret profession in a most surprising manner. "This'll Kill You" (23)—a man murders the man who poisoned him but forgets what special date it is. "More Blessed to Give" (24)—a very unhappily married husband and wife each tries to bump the other off but have to change the script when they become wise to each other's plans. "Just Her Speed" (27)—a man confronts the former friend who stole his woman and his money in a late night diner.

Artists for the series included Al Williamson, Jack Davis, Jack Kamen, and Johnny Craig.

The Haunt of Fear

EC's *The Haunt of Fear* began with three issues in 1950, and then continued the following year as an on-going series. The first issue (actually no. 17) includes a tale of fraternity pledges who disappear forever inside of a haunted house; a mad magician who enjoys sawing people in half because he swears he can put them back together again; a swamp land blob that devours people; and a nagged husband who decides he can't put up with his wife and her beloved cat any longer. The following issue, which introduced the Old Witch, features standard tales of vampires, living mummies, shrunken heads, and a man who sneaks out of his coffin in a drugged state that resembles death to murder his wife only to be buried alive when his ill mistress is given a pill that makes her sleep for twenty hours. The third issue has one fairly memorable tale, "Television Terror," in which a television host takes his audience on a live journey into an allegedly haunted house, the comic panels serving as the television screen as the flippant host enters the house wherein deaths occurred, encounters the unknown, and winds up the latest victim. The gore started to pile on with the fifth issue, featuring a man who dreams his innkeeper is a vampire after his blood but wakes to discover he's really a ghoul who wants to devour his dead flesh; a troupe of sideshow freaks who use their blinded knife thrower to hack their nasty master into many pieces; and a man who murders his wife's lover only to wind up dismembered when he's thrown into the back of a sanitation truck.

In "The Irony of Death" (*HOF* 8) iron works owner Mr. Kreeger confronts his plant superintendent Jeff Slag over the former's daughter, and is outraged to discover they've been secretly married. Slag admits he only married the woman for her money, and to control the iron works once Kreeger is dead, which happens only moments later when Slag throws his boss into a ladle-car full of hot metal iron. Now boss, Slag insists the iron with Kreeger's remains inside it be treated the same as usual, turned into ingots, and turned over to him. During the next few months Slag turns the Kreeger-iron into a safe, lawn chairs, ash trays, and spittoons, every degrading thing he can think of; however some of the ingots turn up missing. His wife leaves him when he admits he never loved her, but he gets to keep the iron works. One day one of his employees suggests a publicity idea: an exhibit of the uses of iron down through the ages. When Slag goes to see how the exhibit is coming along, he jokingly steps into one of the iron objects on display, an iron maiden filled with sharp spikes. When the iron maiden closes on Slag as if by itself, and he is punctured to death, it develops that the torture device was constructed from the remaining ingots with Keeger's remains inside them.

"Wolf Bait" (13) was a suspenseful, tragic and nightmarish tale set in 1900 in which a group of people cross the Russian steppes in winter and try desperately to get to the next town before a pack of ravenous wolves can catch up to them. Each person thinks about the loved one waiting for them, and wonders if they'll survive to see them. Vanya holds an infant that her husband has yet to see; an old man has a package of meat for his starving daughter and grandchildren; soldier Netzka dreams of his lovely fiancee; and Ivan, the driver, just hopes he'll survive another dangerous trip for the meager payment he needs to buy milk for his wife and baby. Netzka shoots a couple of wolves, whose bodies satisfy the pack for only a time, but runs out of bullets. The old man throws the meat he hoped to give to his family to the wolves to keep them at bay a little while longer. The town is near, but the wolves are getting closer and will soon overtake them—there's no escape, until Ivan suggests that one of the other three sacrifice themselves for the rest of them; their being set upon by the pack will give the sled enough time to make it to safety. The passengers spring upon and throw one of their number out of the sled for the wolves to feast on—but you aren't told who it is. Did the young man and woman sacrifice the old man? Did the two men throw out the smaller female? Did they or the mother throw out the baby? Or did they throw out Ivan while one of the others took over the reins?

Horror comics published plenty of stories of people being buried alive; one of the most disturbing was "Chatter-Boxed" in *HOF* 15. Jacob Filbert wakes up in his coffin in the middle of his funeral and discovers that he's had a cataleptic fit that resembles death. Horrified that he might be buried alive, he has the funeral home prepare a coffin inside which is a working telephone. When he has a car accident, everyone assumes he was killed in the crash, not realizing that the accident was caused by another fit. The undertaker does as he was told, refuses to embalm him, and puts him in the specially rigged coffin. When Jacob wakes up, he first calls his wife, who is on another of her hours-long phone jags, then his brother, who is out as usual, then his doctor, who is, as ever, on the phone with a difficult patient. Then he calls the operator but can't get through, because Pearl Harbor has just been bombed and all the switchboards are overloaded. Poor Jacob suffocates in his coffin just as he feared. As noted, plenty of people in horror comics deserved their awful fates, but Jacob just seems like a perfectly nice and awfully unlucky fellow. The same is true of the hero of "Gorilla My Dreams" (17) whose brain is transplanted into a gorilla. Everyone assumes the ape killed him, and his grieving family come to the zoo to tell the poor fellow how much they hate him. Unable to make anyone understand who he is, he completely transforms into a beast.

Two stories in *Haunt of Fear* 21 neatly illustrate the two opposite approaches taken by it and other EC series. "Corker" is a depressing story of a woman, Janet, who believes she is possessed by an evil spirit, even though her boyfriend Peter thinks her problems are psychological. Janet insists on consulting a swami, who tells her that it sounds if she has been corrupted by a lamia, a demon who will drive her to self-destruction if it isn't exorcised. Janet witnessed a hanging in which the man was decapitated, and he believes this is how she was exposed to the unnatural force. Unfortunately, he tells Peter, there is no way of getting rid of a "decapitation lamia" and it will possess Janet until it breaks out of her body in an obvious manner. Not much later, Janet trips in the subway and is beheaded by the wheels of a train. The rising mist from her neck surrounds Peter, who starts laughing. While the story is strangely tasteful (neither of the beheadings are shown), it is also ugly in that there is absolutely no hope for the protagonists, who have done nothing evil to elicit their fate. Jack Kamen and Bill Elder did the art.

On the other hand, "The High Cost of Dying" in the same issue has *some* compassion for its characters, who don't ultimately suffer unjust miseries. Henri is a poor man in Paris in the 1860s. His wife dies of malnutrition and he is told that the Commissioner of Health has issued an edict that all bodies must be buried within 24 hours or taken away for medical dissection. Henri hates the thought of this happening to his beloved, but he hasn't enough money to feed his two young children, let alone pay for an expensive burial. An officer who comes to his hovel suggests that Henri bring his wife's body to the conservatory before it is forcibly removed so that he can at least claim the 75 francs paid for corpses for himself and his family. The officer explains that the Commissioner instituted the 24 hour rule not for health reasons but because he knows few people can afford burials and he wants to collect the money paid by the conservatory for himself. Henri takes the body away, gets his money, buys food and nice clothing for himself and his children, and even manages to give his wife a first-class burial. It appears that the corpse he delivered to the conservatory was not his wife's—but that of the Commissioner of Health! The ending is so perfect and satisfying (albeit a little incredible) that you're glad this particular EC protagonist didn't suffer a horrendous fate because of his murder. Reed Crandell's attractive art is a decided bonus.

Another story decidedly on the ugly side—bad-things-happen-to-nice-people—appeared in *HOF* 22: "Wish You Were Here," another "Monkey's Paw" variation. A once-affluent middle-aged couple, Jason and Enid Logan, are trying to figure out how they're going to survive now that they've gone bankrupt. Looking over old mementos she might sell, Enid happens upon a Jade statuette that is supposed to grant three wishes. Enid wishes for money, and she gets it when Jason is killed in a car accident and she gets his insurance money. She then wishes that Jason would return to the way he was just before the accident. Unfortunately, the accident was caused by his having a heart attack and he was already dead before the crash. His body in its coffin is delivered to the Logan home, and a desperate Enid wishes that he would just come back to life. Unfortunately, he was already embalmed, his blood replaced with formaldehyde, which is burning him up from the inside and causing him *agony*. Enid shoots him, but he doesn't die. She takes a knife to him, cutting him apart, hacking and hewing, but each piece remains alive as Enid finally goes insane.

There are two problems with "Wish You Were Here." If Jason and Enid were depicted as venal horrible people who'd made their money off the sweat and toil of others, their fates might have been at least a little justified (of course one could argue that then the story might be less horrifying to certain readers). A bigger problem is that Enid wished for Jason to be just as he was before the accident, so there wouldn't have been any embalming fluid inside him when she wished for him to return to life, making the whole ending ridiculous.

In each issue of *The Haunt of Fear* The Old Witch would introduce a new edition of "Grim Fairy Tales." These stories almost always ended with some sort of mutilation: a king who feasts while his subjects starve is turned into sausage links; a grouchy old queen having her portrait painted is beheaded, the front of her head sewn to the canvas; a princess cuts off her arm so an unattractive fiance can have her "hand" in marriage as she weds the man she really loves; a selfish prince swallows lead balls to make himself as heavy as possible since his father promised him his weight in gold as an allowance, but when he rushes to the weigh-in the balls burst bloodily out of his belly when the coach comes to a sudden halt.

Especially gruesome stories in *Haunt* include "What's Cookin'?" (12) in which the greedy owners of a specialty chicken restaurant murder the partner who made the business successful, but his horribly burned body drags itself to the restaurant where the police find one man drowned in the sizzling, melted fat of his obese and equally dead co-conspirator. In "This Little Piggy" (14) a British officer in Delhi, warned against killing the native boars, bags one anyway and winds up on a serving platter, his "hair boiled off ... flesh browned to a crisp" and a "juicy red apple" in his mouth! In "Garden Party" (17) a wife is so angered that her husband's guests have ruined her garden during a barbecue, that she dismembers him and roasts the pieces on the grill. In "Bedtime Gory" (18) a woman puts her miserable ambitious husband, who admitted he'd murdered her father, on a new bed which turns out to be a stretch rack, pulling him in two directions until he's twelve feet long. In "Indisposed" (25), a man dismembers his wife and stuffs the pieces down his new garbage disposal, but doesn't realize that the friend who installed it connected it to the well from where they get their drinking water and not to the waste pipe.

In the infamous and disgusting "Foul Play" (19), written by the prolific Al Feldstein, baseball player Herbie Satten uses poisoned spikes to kill star rival player Jerry Deegan (not even for his team but his own glory) so Deegan's teammates get even by dismembering Satten's body and using various body parts to play a midnight ball game with Satten's head, one eye falling out, as the grisly ball. Without the gore, of course, the story would be as forgettable as it is unlikely.

Haunt of Fear 28 was the final issue, and its four stories illustrated both the best and worst of the EC Tradition. "The Prude" was a splendid story in which a nineteenth century moralist, Warren Forbisher—who bullies the town into making adultery a capital crime and bans kissing or holding hands in public, among other idiocies—is himself guilty of having an affair and driving his mistress to suicide, the point being that most self-righteous types then or now are secretly guilty of the very things they condemn others for. Forbisher goes so far as to demand that men and women, even married couples, can no longer be buried together in the same cemetery. Although the women are dug up and put in their own cemetery, each night their spirits disinter their remains again and go join their loved ones. Convinced that the old caretaker is responsible for this, Forbisher hides out in the cemetery to try to catch him in the act, but instead sees the spirits, including his dead mistress, clawing out of the earth. The caretaker finds Forbisher's body entwined with the woman's in her grave and cries out, "Why Mr. Frobisher—don't you know there are laws about that sort of thing! *Shame on you*!" Frobisher is as dead as his mistress, but it's left to the imagination which position the two are in.

"A Work of Art" was another excellent story in which undertaker Jarvis Edwards, who takes pride in his work and feels most of his peers are mere butchers, tries to teach his new son-in-law, Andrew, the family business. Andrew is a cold, practical sort who thinks when you're dead you're dead, and can't understand why his father-in-law, who could make much more money, puts so much time and effort into his work when neither the dead folk nor anyone else would ever know. Jarvis argues that *he* would know. "All through life man suffers indignities," he argues. "At least, in death, he deserves the simple mark of respect ... a decent embalming." Jarvis realizes that Andrew will just never understand, and he is horrified at the thought of him or anyone else preparing his body for burial, so he puts his own death notice in the paper and builds a robot to embalm him before anyone else can get the chance.

The other two stories were more typical, albeit interesting, EC fodder. "Numbskull" presents a man who takes out on animals his disregard for the men and women, such as an unfaithful wife, who have filled him with bitterness and hatred. He delights in pouring oil in the anthill of large carnivorous ants and watching them burn. He especially likes to torture and kill gorillas, since their expressions remind him so much more of Man. It comes as little surprise when, tired, he falls into one of his own gorilla pits, and is devoured, his skull licked clean, by the survivors of the ant colony. The bizarre "Audition" concerns a 17-year-old girl, Ethel, who desperately wants to play in Phil Vitale's all-girl orchestra. Although he admits she is talented, Vitale turns her down, but Ethel won't take no for an answer. Literally stalking the man until he gives in, she finally gets her shot—only to learn that it is really an all-*ghoul* orchestra as the other musicians rush over not to welcome her to the band but to tear her apart and greedily devour her!

Also of interest in this final issue, published in 1954, was the "farewell" editorial which announced the death of the entire line of EC horror titles. "As a result of the hysterical, injudicious, and unfounded charges leveled at crime and horror comics many retailers ... throughout the country have been intimidated into refusing to handle this type of magazine... Magazines that do not get onto the newsstands do not sell... *We give up.* WE'VE HAD IT! Naturally, with comic magazine censorship now a fact ... we trust there will be fewer robberies, fewer murders, fewer rapes."

Other notable tales in *Haunt of Fear* include: "A Grave Gag" (6)—a man who plays morbid practical jokes at his family members' funerals winds up playing one gag too many; "The Gorilla's Paw" (9)—another "Monkey's Paw" derivative in which the title object immediately grants unspoken and often unconscious wishes of its owner, taking them, unfortunately, quite literally; "For the Love of Death" (13)—a morbid old man goes to funerals and wishes he could afford a lavish, dignified service and burial, so he murders one of the wealthiest men in town and takes his place in the coffin, hiring an acquaintance to dig him up afterward, but he gets a very hot and unpleasant surprise. "Fed Up" (13)—a woman sword swallower gets even with the obese husband who spends all of their money on food and more food; "Take Your Pick" (14)—a wife can't stand it when her husband's miserly nature and coldheartedness leads to the death of her dog and her mother on the same day; "Sucker Bait" (19)—a man conceives of a very clever way of finding a vampire that murdered his father by swallowing an isotope and making the bloodsucker radioactive, but his plan is undone when he learns the vampire's true identity; "Only Sin Deep" (24)—a gorgeous woman, thinking she's only letting a pawnbroker make a mask of her face, "sells her beauty" to him for a thousand dollars but discovers herself growing older and older and older; "The Light in His Life" (25)—snowbound in a cabin for months, a gluttonous woman eats up the oil her husband uses for light to read by, so he decides to put her fat to a good purpose; "Spoiled" (26)— two lovers find they can no longer stand to touch each other when the cuckolded husband anesthetizes them and switches their heads onto each other's bodies.

Shock SuspenStories

EC came out with the first issue of *Shock SuspenStories* in 1952. Each issue had one story each in the genres of crime, science fiction, horror and "shock" with twist endings The first issue featured a darkly comic story in which a woman with a pathologically neat and orderly husband finally can't take it anymore, kills him with an ax, and puts every piece of him in a separate jar with a label. Another story has a hunter, who wants a bearskin rug, cornered by a grizzly who turns him into a man-skin rug with head attached. Dismemberment remained the theme of the second issue—a man is picked apart by an alien plant creature in a macabre parody of "she loves me, she loves me not"—and children in an orphanage with a skinflint master use the monster's hollowed-out head for a Halloween pumpkin. However, the best story in the issue, "The Patriots," has a bunch of parade watchers murdering a "commie" who seems to be sneering at the soldiers and doesn't take his hat off when they march by, only to be told by his horrified wife that he's a Korean war vet whose disfigured face can no longer smile and who didn't take his hat off because he's blind. It was as if EC felt that running socially relevant stories would mitigate criticism over the gore, although these stories attacking prejudice and red-baiting were also controversial for the fifties.

The dismemberment theme continued in the third issue with one story about a man who throws a dinner party for all the people who wronged him and removes their heads, as well as one about a trapper who is pinned in his bear trap by a rival and chews his own leg off to get free so he can kill the guy before expiring. The socially relevant tale was "The Guilty," in which a black man is arrested for raping a white woman, the only evidence against him being that he was seen in the area. The sheriff is afraid civil liberties lawyers will get him off, so he sets him free only so that he can shoot him and claim he tried to escape. Then he learns that someone else has just confessed to the crime. The fourth issue had tales of a mean lumberjack boss getting axed to pieces by the younger man he blinded, and a greedy fight manager who literally loses his guts. Subsequent issues generally featured at least one gore story that often seemed to have no other *raison d'etre*. One of the most graphic was "Carrion Death" (9) in which a criminal handcuffed to a dead cop must lie there as vultures feast on the latter's corpse—flesh-torn rib cages graphically depicted—and then his own body, one bird popping his eyeball into its mouth.

The trouble with the dismemberment-of-the-month was that it quickly became tiresome and was, as noted, no substitute for good storytelling. For instance, "Well-Traveled" in the fifth issue is the story of a little man who has built an elaborate setting for model trains in his basement, but every time he saves up to buy the actual trains, his wife takes the money to go off by herself on another trip. It's not much of a surprise when at the end he finally gets his trains, says his wife has "gone traveling," and there are pieces of her rolling around the tracks in the little cars. The same issue has a story in which a man hacks up his wife and puts the pieces in his freezer, only to discover that his friend has used the meat for the dinner they're having.

Not every story relied on the often predictable shock-gore twist (eventually these were dropped in favor of fairly straight suspense stories). In "Dead Right" (*SSS* 6) Cathy is told by a fortune teller that she will marry a man who will inherit a small fortune from a relative and will die shortly afterward. Based on this forecast, Cathy goes ahead and marries a man she finds utterly repulsive. When she unexpectedly wins a large cash prize, she assumes the fortune teller made a mistake, and tells her corpulent husband she's leaving him in no uncertain terms. Her husband murders her, and the prediction comes true. He does inherit a small fortune—from Cathy's winnings—and does die shortly afterward— executed for her murder. In "The Bribe" (7) a normally honest fire inspector takes a bribe from a nightclub with only one exit, hoping to use the money to have a big wedding for his beloved daughter. Then a fire breaks out and hundreds of people are killed. This makes him feel guilty enough, but he sees a photo of his daughter taken in the club, assumes she's one of the victims, and kills himself. It turns out that his daughter had left the club with her fiance to elope and spare him the cost of the wedding. "Three's a Crowd" (11), in which a man is convinced that his wife and best friend are having an affair and sends the two off on a death drive, only to discover that they were really planning a surprise party to announce the wife's upcoming blessed event, also packs a punch.

In Al Feldstein's especially sick and even misogynous "Beauty and the Beach" (7) two attractive women with jealous husbands are given lucrative opportunities to get attention and make money, one with beauty contests and the other with advertising sun care products. True, the women are a bit self-absorbed and thoughtless, but not enough to deserve what happens to them. One husband pushes his wife into a tank of plastic liquid that imprisons her dead body like a fly in amber, while the other grills his sun-loving wife to a deadly shade of charcoal. In this appallingly sexist story the men seem to be angry that their pretty wives are not only getting opportunities that are unavailable to them, but are leaving them alone to do a little housework. *Shock SuspenStories* did stories that exposed racism, but they clearly weren't ready for feminist fiction despite all the stories of women offing terrible husbands.

There were also the socially relevant stories such as "Hate" in *SSS* 5, in which a man named John Smith helps some anti–Semitic neighbors harass, beat and finally murder a Jewish couple who moved in across the street, only to learn that he was adopted and his parents were Jewish. (*SSS* 13 had a similar, excellent story entitled "Blood Brothers" in which the victims were Black.) One of the most powerful of these stories was Al Feldstein's "In Gratitude" in *SSS* 11. In this a young soldier comes back to his home town from Korea with a hook where his hand used to be and discovers that his buddy, who threw himself on a bomb, sacrificing himself to save the protagonist's life and others, and who had no family, wasn't allowed to be buried in the town's cemetery because of his race. Giving a speech that night at the town hall, the soldier admonishes everyone and tells them how ashamed he is of them. He breaks down on the stage as everyone files out, all sheepish and silent. Of course next to stories like this, the pure-gore tales seemed like so much silly garbage.

There were also stories warning of the dangers of communist hysteria. In "The Hazing" (16) a college boy desperate to get into a popular fraternity accuses a hated professor of being a communist, manufacturing evidence, and sticking to his story even when it develops that the teacher has just married the student's sister. But the boy only ruins his own life along with those of two innocent people. "The Pen Is Mightier" (16) is a hard-hitting tale about the evil done by influential and corrupt columnists and opinion-makers who abuse their power. "So Shall Ye Reap" (10) is a brilliant story told from the opposite points of view of both a young man about to be executed and his stricken parents, who wonder where they went wrong. Although the parents are well-meaning, the story underlines the enormous gap between what they thought was right for their boy and his own need to be an individual, with tragic results. There was also the occasional tale of dark whimsy, such as "The Orphan" (14), in which a little girl with unloving and abusive parents gets a clever and final revenge on them when a triangle develops between her mother and father, and another man.

Other notable stories include: "The Sacrifice" (10)—a man who helps the woman he loves kill her husband has a highly unpleasant surprise in store for him; "Deadline" (12)—an alcoholic reporter desperate for another chance comes across a big story when he overhears a man murder his wife, but if she's not really dead it's not such a big story, something he'll need to rectify; "The Kidnapper" (12)—tragedy envelops a man and his wife when their only child is taken and completely disappears; "The Whipping" (14)—a racist man can't stand the idea of his daughter loving a Mexican and whips the neighborhood men into action by claiming he raped her, but the wrong victim is attacked; Raw Deal" (15)—the sole survivor of a plane crash who was picked up in a life boat screams over and over again that he "hates" his dead wife, until doctors realize she was with him in the lifeboat and the word he keeps repeating *isn't* "hate" but an explanation of how he survived after she died; "A Kind of Justice" (16)—a teenage girl is raped and warned not to tell anyone who her attacker was, and an innocent young man is framed by the true assailant.

Three

Prize Comics

Frankenstein

Mary Shelley's classic novel *Frankenstein* not only engendered a great many cinematic treatments, but almost as many comic stories. The novel itself was adapted for the twenty-sixth issue of *Classics Illustrated* in 1945 and became one of the very best in the series. Writer Ruth A. Roche was faithful to the spirit and basic plot of the novel, while the illustrations by Robert Hayward Webb and Ann Brewster, while lacking real compositional flair, had a nice old-fashioned flavor and flowed along adeptly. Norm Saunders did a striking cover painting for the reissue of the story depicting the Monster's climactic trek across the frozen wasteland. Decades later both Marvel and DC would have comics starring the Monster. In-between there was Prize's Frankenstein.

Frankenstein began as a feature in *Prize Comics* 7 from the publisher of the same name in 1940, probably the earliest continuing horror strip. In the initial eight-page installment, Mary Shelley's story was updated to the twentieth century and transplanted to America, where Victor Frankenstein creates a living monster from dead body parts. As in the novel, Victor can't deal with what he's done and the angry monster runs amok, throwing people out of the Statue of Liberty. He has a high forehead, pasty white skin, and a somewhat wizened lower face. The monster doesn't want to kill his creator; he wants him alive to suffer with the knowledge that he is ultimately responsible for the death and destruction caused by his creation. His size is variable; on one page he's able to lift two little boys *inside* his hands, making him much, much larger than he was in the novel. In the next issue the monster is consistently drawn as being about 20 feet tall. Victor goes to a carnival where a sideshow has an exhibit of a fake Frankenstein monster with dummies standing in for human victims. But it turns out that the real monster has taken the fake one's place and the "dummies" are the corpses of people he's killed. Victor, who is pretty stupid for a genius, decides to fight fire with fire by creating yet *another* dangerous monster, giving it the head of a crocodile. Unfortunately, the first creature is easily able to defeat the second.

In *Prize* 11 the strip was given a new direction as Victor takes it upon himself to become guardian to a small boy, Denny, who lost his parents and the use of his legs (temporarily)

Frankenstein nearly finds true love—with a corpse—in this (Prize) issue.

because of the monster's attack on a city. Ten years go by during which the monster continues to send Victor warnings of his future attacks, which the man can do nothing to prevent. Victor is now old and tired and Denny, a strapping young man, takes after the monster himself. He suddenly comes on like an athletic Batman, defeating the monster in one quick battle. He is christened "Bulldog" by the papers and the monster, as usual, escapes. In *Prize* 19–20 the monster is supposedly killed and put on display by an entrepreneur. But the monster's hunchbacked friend Nog substitutes a dummy for his "master" and successfully revives him. (By this time the monster himself was known as Frankenstein and Victor was no longer in the picture.) In *Prize* 21 Denny has a lively battle with Frankenstein at, of all places, the opera house, where the monster makes like the Phantom and brings the chandelier down upon the crowd.

In *Prize* 22 Frankenstein teamed up with Dr. Devil, a foe of the super-hero the Black Owl, who also appeared in *Prize* comics. Two issues later Denny rounded up all the super-characters from *Prize*, including the Owl, the Green Lama, and the costumed twins Yank and Doodle, and teamed them up against Frankenstein. (Decades later Marvel Comics would also incorporate their monsters into super-hero stories.) This was the first and last team-up of the Prize heroes. In *Prize* 27 Frankenstein crashes a penthouse society party (by improbably impersonating a playboy via mask and tuxedo) and is so disgusted with the snobby swells, one of whom refuses to acknowledge her own mother because she's poor, that he throws most of the guests off of the building. In *Prize* 30 the creator of the strip, Dick Briefer, appeared and said he hadn't heard from Frankenstein in a long time and had no story to tell, and a Frankenstein doll had misadventures in the monster's stead. It was sure signs of creator burn-out. By the thirty-ninth issue Frankenstein had reformed to a good guy, only he was hypnotized by the Nazis into working for the Fuhrer. Eventually the strip metamorphosed into a parody with Frankenstein getting a "ghoulfriend" named Zora, although their relationship was never exactly serious.

The new version of Frankenstein proved popular enough to get his own series, which continued as a crazy black comedy. The first issue told how a mad scientist, influenced by Mary Shelley's novel, created a man-monster to wreak terror and havoc, but the creature turned out to be gentle and good-natured. After the scientist is killed in a fire, Frankenstein is free to roam about having adventures. In one tale a town decides to send for him, hoping he can get rid of the plague of ghouls and vampires who have descended upon them. But when teenage girls see signs proclaiming that "Frankie is coming!" they assume it refers to "Frank Singatra [*sic*]." They rush en masse to the train station to greet their idol, although a caption asserts that it wasn't certain if they swooned because they thought it was actually "Singatra" who arrived or if they realized it was the Monster—in either case, they saw a pale, emaciated horror. Frankie gets rid of the vampires by innocently breathing garlic from his sandwich on them. Stories continued in that vein for the next two years.

With the eighteenth issue in 1952, however, it was decided to take a completely different approach. The series was completely rebooted as a serious horror comic and the title, on the cover at least, was changed to *The Monster of Frankenstein*. The monster is freed in modern times from the castle where it slumbers by two adventurers, and goes on a rampage. The townspeople contact the great-grandson of Victor Frankenstein in America in the hopes that he will have knowledge of how to stop the beast. Unfortunately Dr. Frankenstein's efforts prove futile, and the monster disappears. He surfaces on a ship bound back to the United States upon which the doctor is aboard. Two crooks take advantage of the monster's presence by killing passengers and stealing their valuables, hoping it will be blamed on the monster. When Dr. Frankenstein realizes the truth—the monster has no interest in jewelry or cash—the crooks try to kill him but he is saved by the monster simply because he wants him alive to suffer (the modern-day Frankenstein resembles his great-grandfather).

Frankenstein wanders the country looking for people to slaughter and hiding out wherever he can. There was no regular supporting cast and Dr. Frankenstein was never heard from again. The stories veered from sci fi action to outright horror stories. In "World of Monsters" in *F* 21 the monster arrives in Arizona and winds up on a mesa where a scientist has devolved some animals into prehistoric creatures, and turned a wildcat into a savage jungle woman named Kit. A reporter gets involved in a triangle with Kit and the scientist's daughter while Frankenstein keeps trying to smash into the enclosure where he can kill everyone, and hungry dinosaurs make periodic assaults. At one point Frankenstein even takes on a tyrannosaurus rex! In another interesting tale, Frankenstein encounters a ravenous werewolf in *F* 22.

Gradually the monster became more dimensional. In *F* 23 he encounters a pathetic giantess who had performed for a sideshow but lost her looks and mind in a terrible fire and has wandered about since the circus disbanded. Blinded in an attack by men who wrongfully believe her to be a witch and murderess, she is taken care of by Frankenstein, who at last has found companionship, as has she. But the townspeople catch up with them and kill the woman, whose life had been one long tragedy. In the following issue, Frankenstein is befriended by two little boys who play with him despite his hideous appearance. When their father finds out, he leads a posse against the monster but the children convince Frankenstein not to kill anyone and to leave town. In a moody story in *F* 26 Frankenstein is harpooned by a deranged captain of an abandoned whaling ship, then has to battle a real whale for survival.

The series was rarely concerned with continuity, but *Frankenstein* 27 picked up where the last one ended, with the monster adrift in the ocean. Now he's discovered frozen in a block of ice and given a world tour, still frozen, by some entrepreneurs, who make certain to keep the ice, now in a glass case, at the correct temperature to prevent disaster. The frozen giant is transported on a plane to South Africa for his next stop, but the plane crashes in the desert. As panic sets in and the passengers bicker, the ice melts and the monster wakes up. Most of the passengers want Frankenstein to drown inside the case so they can then drink the water, but a young woman feels sorry for the monster and smashes the case. The liquid turns out to be salt water. The excellent story was marred by a silly conclusion which has the monster battling living mummies who think the passenger who freed him is their long-dead queen.

Frankenstein 28 has an excellent, lurid tale in which an old scientist befriends the monster and makes him a mate from the dead body of an executed murderess. It isn't long, unfortunately, before she's back to her old ways, but Frankenstein won't let the old man kill her. After she kidnaps a baby, the scientist gives her a doll with a time bomb inside, and the suspenseful climax has the deadly doll going back and forth from the she-monster to some children she befriends and back again, until the female Frankenstein brings the doll right back to the scientist's house just in time for the explosion. Only the monster survives. The clever cover to the twenty-ninth issue depicts a terrified artist reacting to the sight of the monster pulling himself out of the painting he's working on—a sketch of the monster that comes to life—but the story inside actually concerns the monster's obsession with a beautiful woman with a sick child and the tragedy that almost develops because of it.

Frankenstein 30 is one of the very best issues in the series, featuring two stories in which the monster is allegedly befriended by two men who are only interested in using him. The sculptor in the first story uses the monster to drive his cousin mad, then maneuvers the trusting creature under a shower of hot bronze to create a life-sized sculpture of him, assuming all that will remain inside is ashes. But the monster isn't killed that easily, breaks out of the cooled metal, and pours gallons of the hot molten liquid down the sculptor's throat. In the second story, a doctor protects and feeds the monster and in return asks that he kill a few people as he needs corpses for his work. The town is terrorized as more and more people disappear, until the doctor only needs one more fresh corpse. Frankenstein shows up with the last body—the doctor's new bride! (The basic premise was used in other media.)

Frankenstein 31 is another outstanding issue with two stories. In the first, a strange tree develops a reputation for being "evil" when anyone who tries to chop it down or mar it in any way is attacked and killed—by Frankenstein, who knows the body of an old man who was kind to him is buried beneath it. The grotesque second story has three brothers—an artist, a singer, and an conductor—coming across the monster trapped in quicksand. Not only do they not rescue the monster, but they are so offended by his ugliness that they decide to sew up his eyes and ears and lips as he isn't worthy of seeing, hearing or speaking beauty. However, the monster is not killed in the quicksand and gets revenge by, respectively, destroying their eyes, ears and throat. The three men wind up in a mental institution where together they resemble the three "hear no evil etc." monkeys.

In the following issue the monster first steals a beautiful mannikin from the back of a shop, and sets it up in the empty house where he's taken shelter. When some thieves destroy the dummy, the monster retaliates by killing them. Later on, after being socked with electricity, the monster winds up in the morgue. Reviving, he sees another beautiful woman under a sheet, thinks she's another dummy, and takes off with her body. Going into town to get her more clothing and jewelry, he is spotted by people and in his flight from them winds up traveling from town to town. It is months before he makes his way back to his home, anxious to see his beautiful lady once more, only to rush inside and discover a desiccated corpse with a horrible skeletal grin.

In the thirty-third and final issue of the series Frankenstein finds himself assisting a nasty botanist who has developed a bizarre meat-eating plant. The plant's diet rapidly switches from flies to spiders to mice to cats before the botanist tries feeding it a living human baby. Frankenstein, who is as charmed by the infant as everyone else, puts a stop to this, and the botanist accuses him of kidnapping the child. Frankenstein escapes and the botanist decides to leave town with his plant before the monster can get revenge on him. However, Frankenstein comes upon the scientist just as the uprooted plant on its back gets hungry and uses its tentacles to pull the fellow into its rather large, and very toothy, maw. Ignoring the botanist's screams for help, the monster merely watches for two hours as the man is devoured by his creation. At the end, the plant's buds open and reveal the horrified face of its final victim. Any similarity between this macabre and fascinating story and the film *Little Shop of Horrors* that came out six years later is possibly *not* coincidental.

Frankenstein was a violent and gruesome comic with some great stories and serviceable artwork, mostly by Dick Briefer. There were back-up horror stories in every issue, most of which were not very memorable. "Clinging Corpse" (*F* 29) was a creepy tale in which a criminal who faked his death shoots the man who put him away for murder, but when he carries the corpse outside where he plans to dump it in the ocean, he discovers that rigor mortis has made the dead man's arms positively *lock* around his killer's neck—no matter what he does he can't get rid of the body. And then the tide comes in ...

Black Magic

Black Magic, a Joe Simon and Jack Kirby production, first appeared on the newsstands in 1950. The comic purported to tell "true, amazing accounts" of black magic, and "the strangest stories ever told."

"A Silver Bullet for Your Heart" (*BM* 3) is a fairly standard story of two hunters—one who falls for a beautiful white-haired young woman he finds in the woods, while the other warns him that she must be a werewolf—given an absorbing suspense and intensity due to Jack Kirby's highly adroit pencil work. "Satan's Sister" in the same issue, in which a man falls for a woman, Lisa, whose twin sister, Peggy, is a vicious amoral hellcat, has a predictable conclusion revealing that the "twins" were one woman, but it also has some vivid prose, such as this opening line: 'There is a certain street in New York City toward which the very dregs of humanity—those whose warped minds and depraved personalities have emptied life of all sensation—are inevitably drawn." The hero, Mark Kenyon, keeps trying to get Peggy to leave her life of sin and come back to her sister (naturally he never sees the two together) but aside from her occasional outbursts of physical violence, Peggy only seems to be a "bad girl" by strict, Catholic, middle-class standards. When she tells Mark that she doesn't want to come back "to people like you who haven't the nerve to live," back to a "sweet, make-believe world," you feel she has more common sense than the well-meaning Mark does.

Simon and Kirby generally had the lead story in each issue. "Choose a Face" (vol. 2, 8) presents the sad story of M. Josef Letoq, who is so homely that he has been unable to have a career as a concert violinist despite his great talent. An old woman selling flowers offers him a solution, and tells him to choose one of several masks she keeps in the back of her shop. Naturally he chooses a mask that turns him into a handsome devil. A kind and pretty woman named Mariette, whom Letoq had admired from afar, recognizes him through his mask, and convinces him to remove it, as she is not so superficial as to be alarmed. Responding to his essential good nature, the mask has remolded his features so now he is genuinely good-looking. Unfortunately, now that other women find him appealing, Letoq is unable to resist the charms of a wealthy patroness named Madame Daumier, who wants him for a husband and can do a lot for him. Neglected, Mariette leaves him a letter releasing him and wishing him well. But when Letoq goes to Daumier to tell her he is free, he discovers that his insensitive and selfish actions have turned him back into the frog-faced freak he was before, and everything is lost to him. The story is a very canny examination of how people are mercilessly judged by a physical appearance that can result in either fame and fortune or utmost despair.

Equally pathetic and of similar theme is "The Greatest Horror of Them All" (vol.4, 5) which takes place in Sanctuary, a refuge for horribly disfigured and malformed "freaks." A handsome man named Tom has come to the Sanctuary ostensibly to be trained as the head doctor's replacement, but is actually attracted to a beautiful woman named Elena who accompanied the doctor on a trip to New York. Tom reminds himself that these "freaks" have the same normal human feelings that he does, but they still make him sick to his stomach. He thinks the freaks avoid Elena, whom he assumes works with the doctor, because her great beauty makes them feel even more hideous in comparison. When Tom and Elena share a romantic moment, the doctor is unaccountably outraged, and Tom makes up his mind to leave the compound with Elena that very night. But inside her room he discovers a foam rubber appliance that resembles Elena, carelessly tossed over a couch—as the real Elena, a mottled gray, multi-limbed slug-like creature approaches him, tells him she loves him, and begs him not to run away. Tom fires at Elena and kills her. While the reader is clearly supposed to feel Tom's disgust and revulsion, it is impossible not to also feel sympathy for the lonely (if unrealistic) and tragically grotesque, Elena.

Simon and Kirby possible outdid this story with their "Head of the Family" (vol.4, 6) in which a woman, Francie, dates what appears to be the only normal member of a strange family that has been shunned by the town. Hugan is a handsome man with an odd older brother, a kid brother who barely speaks, a weird sister who does nothing but cook, and an Uncle Hugo who is never seen. Francie determines to meet Hugo, and discovers that the "head" of the family is literally that, a massive head sitting atop a withered, useless form that can hardly be called a body. Hugan explains that in their unusual birth one person was born with five separate bodies but only one mind, which resides inside Hugo. Hugan had a heart and thus was able to love; the older sister did the eating for all of them; the kid brother had the eyes, and so on. None of these "people" have ever hurt anyone but they have to be punished for their monstrous nature and are, of course, destroyed at story's end, like Elena.

"The Angel of Death" (vol.2, 9) was a huge, ancient insect that came to life and spread plague throughout a small town, a truly ugly and frightening creature as depicted in loving detail on the splash page by Kirby. In "Nasty Little Man" (vol.2, 12) Kirby creates a memorable portrait of a small fellow with magical powers who preys upon three tramps who have the temerity to enter the train car that he's chosen for his own, prefiguring the *Leprechaun* series of horror films by several decades. "Monsters on the Lake" (vol.3, 4) shows what happens when a flying saucer crash lands and the inhabitants of the nearby town fight over possession of it and its one living occupant. "Maniac" (vol.5, 2) presents the story of two brothers, one of whom, Harry, seems "touched" and is picked on by the children in town. His brother, Tom, doesn't want Harry to be committed, so he takes him to the graveyard and kills him. But what begins as an *Of Mice and Men* variation has a twist: when the men come to take the brother away, it is *Tom* they are after and not Harry. "He'll be locked up before he kills someone," says one of the men. Too late, alas.

There was a brief foray into EC comics land with the twenty-eighth issue (vol.4, 4) with a lead story in which a miserable, dying old man refuses to leave his eyes to a young man who's going blind. His assistant then claims that he changed his mind before expiring, but it turns out that he forged his employer's handwriting. The ghost of the old man purses the employee, gouges out his eyes, and places them in his empty sockets, a scene which is played up, albeit not too gruesomely, on the cover. Another story, "Screaming Doll," has typical EC gruesome irony in its tale of a man who murders his pretty daughter's persistent suitor, only to find the woman's corpse being torn and battered by his pet ape, who had previously witnessed the father doing the same thing to a doll. Even when the stories were forgettable, there was always Jack Kirby's incredible art. "Dead Man's Lode" (vol.2, 4) has a wonderful three quarter page panel showing a man entering a cavern full of numerous skeletons lying about in a grisly tableau. Other artists for the series included Bill Walton, Joe Kubert, and Joe Orlando.

Eventually Simon and Kirby left the series, and like other horror comics it presented less intense tales of irony, sci fi, and suspense. Many of the stories could be categorized as "anti-supernatural," in which supposedly magical devices—such as a typewriter that imbues the user with the famous former owner's writing talent, or an amulet that protects a Civil War soldier from harm—turn out to be fake. There were also some science fiction stories that often had compelling premises that were not very well developed.

The comic lasted for fifty issues until 1957. Some of the more interesting stories include: "A Curse on You" (*BM* 3)—a man tries to convince an old bookkeeper that he has evil powers so he can help him get rid of a rival; "Sleep, Perchance to Die" (5)—a dream shared by an egghead college student and the bully who torments him leads to tragedy for both; "Old Tom's Window" (7)—an ill man in a hospital commits murder to get the bed with the window view that he covets, only to get a bitter surprise; "A Giant Walks the Earth" (vol.2, 6)—two men hunt a gigantic humanoid creature in the interior of Asia; "You'll Die Laughing" (vol.2, 12)—a nasty producer dismisses a psychic's prediction that he'll 'die laughing' until he discovers that the joke is on him; "The Practical Joker" (vol.3, 3) encourages a nerdy friend to build a time machine but discovers to his ultimate regret that it actually works; "Buried Alive" (VG4, 4)—an Edgar Allan Poe pastiche of a cursed family and premature burial with its own special twist; "The Legend of Karnark" (vol.6, 1)—a huge miles-long stone serpent in France comes to life to slowly coil around a young couple who joined in on a sacred dance without permission; "The Hidden Doors" (vol.6, 1)—an elderly man who treasures his priceless artwork deals with a greedy and nasty niece when he discovers that a hideous modern painting she bought after discarding his beloved pieces has a three-dimensional quality one can literally get lost in.

In 1973, after Jack Kirby left Marvel Comics and collaborator Stan Lee for DC Comics, the latter company brought out a new *Black Magic* comic which consisted of many of the Simon-Kirby reprints from the Prize comic series. It lasted for nine issues.

The Strange World of Your Dreams, also produced for Prize comics by the team of Joe Simon and Jack Kirby, debuted in 1952, and was a different kind of supernatural comic, focusing on the meaning of dreams and dream-oriented fiction. The narrator was a "Richard Temple," who analyzed dreams allegedly sent in by readers, who were promised twenty-five dollars for their stories. There were also stories in which Temple was called in as a consultant when people had weird psychic dreams or inexplicable nightmares. The series, which only lasted four issues, was not very memorable all told, but there were some interesting moments.

In "The Dreaming Tower" (in which Temple did not participate) in the first issue, the narrator dreams that he is sole occupant of a tower in an old manor house, but when he sneaks out of the tower encounters a group of people in the parlor below who are startled by his appearance. No wonder, because he's horribly disfigured, and is usually kept in the tower under sedation to spare him emotional anguish. This is no dream—this is his reality, and this particular "dream" occurred when his medication ran out and he was awake and able to leave his tower room for the first time since his accident. His doctor advises his parents that now that he knows the truth of his condition, there is no point in keeping him sedated (as if there ever were).

In "Edge of Madness" in the third issue Temple helps a man tormented by a dream in which he sees his father burying something in the woods and he accuses his parents of being murderers. His mother is dead, and he has been estranged from his father for twenty years

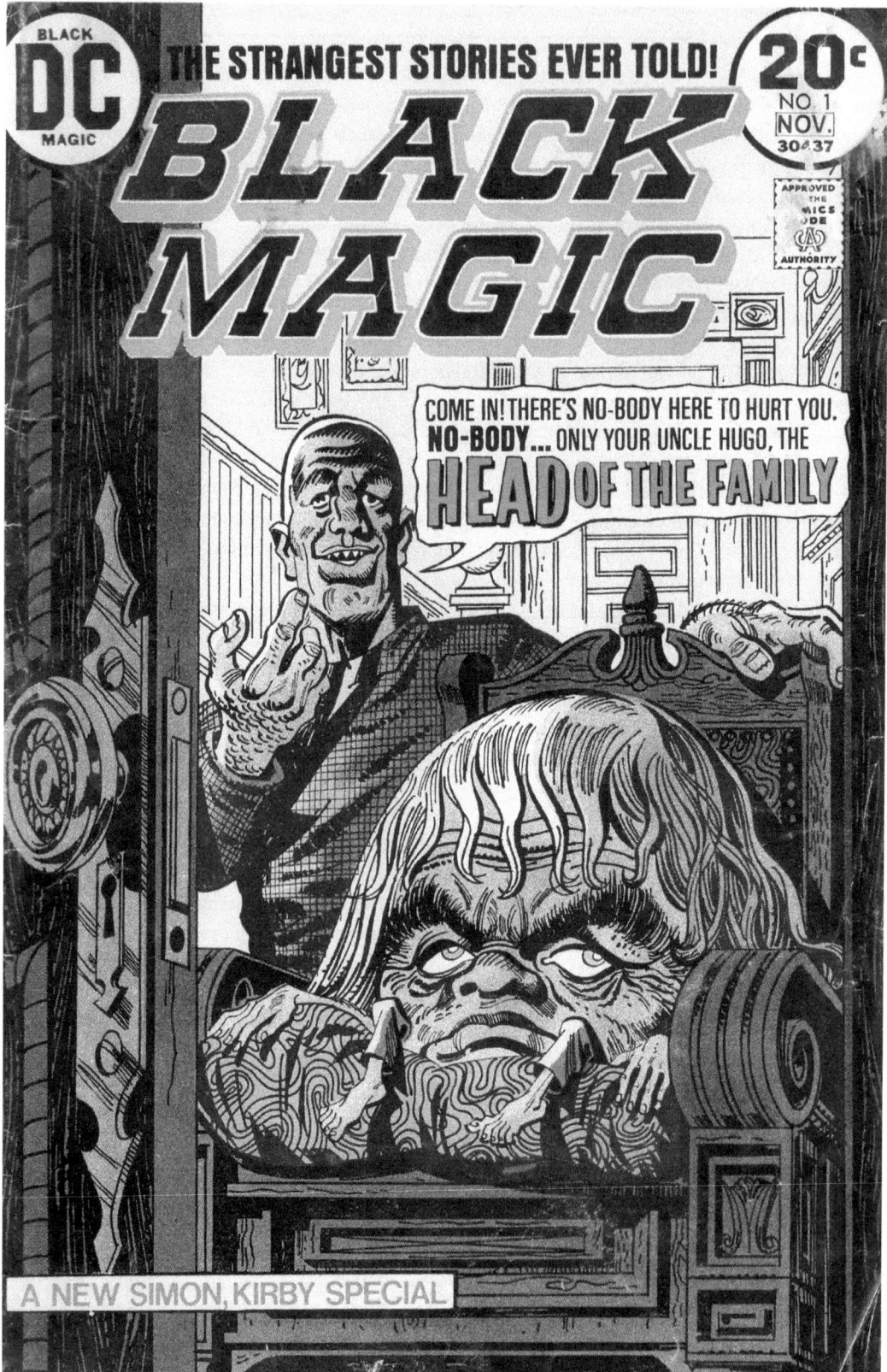

because he's subconsciously convinced he killed someone who was dear to him. Unfortunately, the story's suspense amounts to nothing when it is revealed that the father was only burying a beloved family pet! A one-page fill-in in the same issue is more interesting, as it depicts an old woman having a psychic flash of the bus she and her husband are traveling on hitting a train. She insists that the bus stop and let them off. The bus does hit a train minutes later, but only because of the delay caused by having to stop for the old couple to disembark, in effect making the woman the cause of twenty-two deaths.

The best story published in the comic's short run was "Show Your Face" in the fourth and final issue. A starving French artist named George Dumont dreams of coming across a corpse of a young woman in an alley, and wakes up just as the killer—whose face he cannot see—approaches him with intent to murder this witness to his crime. Upon awakening, George paints a very realistic tableau of the murder scene, and sells it for a thousand francs. Unfortunately, the painting exactly mimics a real-life crime scene and the police are convinced Dumont got all the details right because he was there—as the killer. After a lengthy trial that has all Paris talking, Dumont is convicted of the murder, and imprisoned to await his execution. Fortunately, at the eleventh hour he finally has another dream of the murder, but this time can clearly see the killer's face. After giving a description to the police, George waits desperately as they question this man who breaks down and confesses, saving George from the guillotine.

Opposite: DC brought out classic Joe Simon–Jack Kirby reprints when they re-presented Prize Comics' *Black Magic* in the 1970s.

Four

Atlas, Timely and Marvel

Venus

The now famous Marvel Comics went by more than one name in the golden and silver ages, such as Atlas and Timely. They were still one of the largest comic publishers and offered a wide variety of horror, supernatural, and science fiction comics.

Venus debuted in 1948 under the Marvel banner. Originally conceived as a humor/romance comic, it underwent a dramatic transformation. Venus, the goddess of love and beauty, is bored and lonely in Olympus, so she decides to come to Earth for some adventure. Spotted by publisher Whitney Hammond, she becomes a representative and editor of his magazine *Beauty*. The two fall in love, which does not sit well with Hammond's jealous, eternally scheming secretary Della, who wants both the editorship and the publisher for herself. Venus tells Whitney the truth about herself but neither he nor anyone else believes her—at first. In the third issue Apollo, the sun god, who loves Venus, visits the Earth and prevents nightfall from falling in frustration. Jupiter, King of the Gods, angrily tries to get Venus to return to Olympus in *Venus* 5. Beginning with the sixth issue the words "Romantic Tales of Fantasy" were emblazoned above the title. In this issue Venus encountered Loki, the god of evil, who also loved her, but managed to outwit him.

Gradually the humor was downplayed and the fantastic element was highlighted. In *Venus* 10, the goddess has to deal with the manipulations of Loki's son, Satan, who also desires her and threatens the earth with horrific storms and the like if she doesn't comply. That same issue Venus takes a trip to the moon with a lovesick inventor and battles monsters before returning to earth and reuniting the scientist with his neglected girlfriend. In "The End of the World" in the following issue another lovesick scientist endangers the planet by setting in motion forces that would push the earth closer and closer to the sun. Scenes depicted the oceans drying up, desperate people partying for the last time, sweat-stained wretches hoping for a last minute reprieve. Venus' intervention saves the day in the nick of time.

Venus now presented "Strange Tales of the Supernatural," most of them still starring the goddess of love. Often her antagonists suffered from unrequited adoration or something in the romantic arena to tie in with the love theme. In the twelfth issue Venus becomes a prisoner of the wretched sultan Khorak, who tires of his beautiful slaves easily and feeds them and others who've displeased him to hungry lions. She has the help of both Loki and Thor to defeat Khorak, but the reader is not treated to a scene of him being torn apart by the people he oppressed. In *V* 13 she faces a giant blob called "The Creeping Death" which threatens to completely smother the earth in twenty-four hours, but the creature is actually defeated by a lightning bolt from Thor. In the fifteenth issue there are hideous grave robbers and would-be conquerors from below who are stealing fresh corpses so they'd have human bodies to transform their souls into, as well as living dolls who turn out to have blood inside them. In *Venus* 16 the blond beauty faces a funeral director named Mr. Natas (Satan spelled backwards) who murders people just for the pleasure of incinerating them in his crematorium.

One of the better Venus stories, relatively speaking, appeared in the sixteenth issue and was entitled "Where Gargoyles Dwell." Venus discovers that the thirteenth floor of an office building has disappeared—the elevator man says there never was a thirteenth floor—but by climbing up from the twelfth floor she finds it—along with corpses and homicidal living gargoyles. She helps a secretary who survived the onslaught of the monsters escape, but when Venus returns with the authorities, once again there is no sign of a thirteenth floor, even when they take the stairs as she did. But she finds it again by climbing the elevator shaft, only to encounter a deranged woman who says that it was she who brought the gargoyles to life. The monsters pursue the villainess and she falls down the elevator shaft, her smashed body found among pieces of the now unliving gargoyles. Frankly, the story makes little sense, but the idea of an entire floor disappearing and reappearing again is nevertheless compelling.

Surprisingly the next issue of *Venus* managed to present not one but three entertaining macabre tales starring the plucky goddess. She investigates when a man claims his late stepdaughter haunts his castle and discovers a few interesting secrets; comes to the aid of a cartoonist when his creations pop out of comic book panels and make his life miserable; and intercedes when undersea titans of huge size, who first appear as statues, menace the entire planet. By this time the triangle sub-theme between Venus, her boss and boyfriend Whitney, and bitchy Della had been dropped. When Whitney asks Venus to marry him she declines, saying "our worlds are too far apart." Later she muses,"it's not in my nature to settle down and be domestic." With the ditching of the love stuff, there was a new intensity to both the stories and the artwork, and *Venus* decidedly became a horror comic.

In *Venus* 18 the goddess deals with a businesswoman named Deana Seacrest, who keeps building low-cost housing sites on the Atlantic coast that are completely obliterated—houses, people and all—by massive tidal waves not long after being inhabited. Venus unmasks Deana as Neptune's daughter, who wants revenge on the human race because her father has been killed by atomic testing in the ocean. The story was intriguing and had real suspense. Just when *Venus* was beginning to develop its potential as a horror series with an unusual heroine it was canceled with the following issue. Bill Everett of *Sub-Mariner* fame was one of the artists. Venus turned up twenty years later in a couple of issues of Marvel's *Champions* super-team comic.

Marvel Tales, Men's Adventures, and *Strange Tales*

Marvel Tales (the numbering began with 33) debuted in 1949. The comic ran fantasy and speculative stories until it also began presenting horror tales in the early fifties. By the 116th issue it was fully macabre, with stories about a man who imprisons people in a room with out-sized furniture to make them think they've shrunk; a man victimized by a werewolf who turns out to be his girlfriend's father; a little boy who can shoot people dead just by using his finger; and a nasty old skinflint who can't understand why no one will help him after an automobile accident until he makes his way back to the scene and sees a crowd staring at his decapitated head. "While Death Waits" (*MT* 131) is a well-written, uncredited story about miners trapped in a cave-in, waiting for an unlikely rescue, who talk about all the things they've regretted in life, all the things they haven't done. One fellow, convinced that they all will be dead in a couple of hours, contemptuously tells the others that he has no regrets, that knowing he might die young he lived life to its fullest and did *everything*, and then lists his crimes, which include payroll robbery and murder. And then the rescue team breaks through. "Oh, Baby" in *MT* 128 was a rip-off of a Ray Bradbury evil baby story published by EC. The comic switched back to sci fi/fantasy tales after the formation of the comics code, and lasted just a few more issues. Artists included Doug Wildey, Pete Tomlinson, and John Forte.

Premiering in 1950, *Men's Adventures* started out as an anthology comic of crime, war, suspense and adventure stores. The fifth issue had a science fiction story about the radioactive inhabitant of a flying saucer, and a ghost story in which a young man stays in a haunted house for the night. His brother shows up to keep him company, but the next day the young man discovers his brother was hit by a car and killed, and that the visit was actually from his ghost. The comic virtually became a war comic after that until it began presenting "weird" adventures with the twenty-first issue in 1953, which had one story about flying saucers shaped like clams that scoop up humans, and another one about a pretty female robot who electrocutes one poor fellow with a kiss.

Influenced by EC's horror comics, the comic then began running more gruesome stories with flippant introductions. In *MA* 24 there were stories about a "torture master" who runs a Nazi concentration camp and gets thrown to the prisoners who loathe him, and another about a disfigured hunter who winds up the blue plate special for ravenous baboons that strip him down to his bones. Then there were stories of shrunken heads with familiar faces, and hit men with vivid imaginations locked inside morgues. One of the only fairly memorable stories was "I Walked on the Moon" in *MA* 26, in which two successful, competitive men who hate each other build and fly spaceships to the moon separately and in secret, but their intense rivalry ensures that no one will ever know of their achievement. With the next issue super-heroes took over the comic and the horror and sci fi stories were gone.

1951 brought the long-lasting *Strange Tales*. In "Strange Game" (9) card sharp Lou Beltram plays and loses in a card game with some strange fellows who play for letters—cut outs of "A," "L" and "B" etc.—instead of cash. When he loses, Lou runs out but the other men swear they will collect what he owes them at midnight. Lou tells his story to a bartender as the clock approaches the witching hour. At midnight he screams in terror and the bartender looks down and sees only his head on the floor. Apparently the letters in the game stood for Arms, Legs, and Body. This would have been an EC type story but for the fact that it's oddly tasteful in spite of the gruesome denouement, as there's nary a trace of blood in the final panel and Lou's head, somehow balancing upright on the floor, looks more cartoonish than anything else.

"The Boy Who Was Afraid" (10) is little Terry, a child who prefers to stay inside and read because he says he is terrified of stepping on the cracks in the pavement. This infuriates his abusive father, an alleged macho he-man who thinks Terry is a sissy and drags him to a psychiatrist (one assumes the child manages not to step on any of the dreaded cracks). The shrink draws lines on his office floor with chalk and gets Terry to step on them but the child explains that it isn't the same as being outdoors and they just don't *understand*. Terry's father pushes him outside—the doctor accompanies them but doesn't try to stop him—and the two men force Terry to step on a crack even though he cries out in terror. As soon as his foot comes down on the crack, the earth opens up and both men and boy are swallowed up never to be seen again. While on the surface the story line is completely absurd, almost a bad joke, it can't help but remind one of painfully shy people who are terrified of life, their misunderstanding and often brutal parents (who helped bring about the shyness in the first place) and the eternal, heart-breaking battle between an athletic father and a bookworm of a son. A son of a different color appeared in "The Monster's Son" in *Strange Tales* 10. In this a man is convinced that the Frankenstein monster created his own offspring—whose deformed face he covered with a handsome mask—and he sets out to find him at the European castle where this horrific heir was created. It turns out that the original monster is still alive, and the man runs away from him in horror. He falls to his death, and the monster climbs down, pulls off a mask covering the dead man's face, and sadly says, "My son!"

Not all of the supernatural stories in *Strange Tales* were horrific. In "O'Malley's Friend" (11) O'Malley accepts two wishes from St. Peter and uses them to outwit the devil, then discovers that he is welcomed neither in Heaven or Hell, so he just sits in the back of a bar, tells his story to all who will listen, and orders another round of drinks. "The Poor Old Man" (27) is an old man who sweeps the back of a bar room and makes people wonder what he has to smile about. A year before, an imp appeared before the old man and granted him his fondest wish, the love of a woman, and brought this about via a series of events that made him rich, gave him a good position in the film industry, and attracted a woman who genuinely loved him and sensed his inner goodness despite the age difference; she eagerly agrees to marry him. Now wealthy, happy and loved, the man takes his fiancee and a producer to the bar where he used to work so they can soak up atmosphere for a new picture, but the imp—who can only be seen by the old man—appears once more, demanding payment. The price: the life of the woman he loves. If he does not comply, he will go back to his miserable old existence and no one will ever remember him. The choice is easy, which is why the old man smiles despite his heartbreak, knowing that the woman he loved and who loved him will be safe and happy, even if with someone else. (One can't imagine that this won't eventually begin to eat at him, however.)

"Come Share My Coffin" in *Strange Tales* 28 was not only one of the best stories the comic published but was featured on the excellent cover with the drawing of a terrified man struggling with a living skeleton in the confines of a cramped coffin. The story deals with a man, Chernak, who is conspiring with the commandant, Koslov, of a political prison camp, to find out by what secret route prisoners are escaping. Chernak pretends to hate Koslov because of his abuse, and gaining the other prisoners' confidence, discovers that they are escaping one by one inside coffins every time one of the prisoners dies. Chernak and Koslov hatch a plan, in which the former will hide in the next coffin, and Koslov will dig him up, after which Chernak will get the names of everyone helping the underground and Koslov will have them executed. The plan proceeds, but hits a snag when Chernak, who has been waiting quite awhile buried alive in his coffin, lights a match to see who is in the box with him and sees—Koslov, murdered by one of the members of the underground; no one will be digging Chernak up. A few years later, with a switch in locale and other changes, the same premise was used for the *Alfred Hitchcock Hour* episode "Final Escape" (and quite a few other horror comic stories with variations). *Strange Tales* continued well into the silver age when it presented mostly sci fi stories before becoming a super-hero title. Artists for the series included John Forte and Gene Colan.

Mystic and *Astonishing*

Marvel's *Mystic* hit the newsstands in 1951. The comic was not influenced overall much by EC but the 26th issue had a compelling cover of a man being served a human head on a platter by a ghoul waiter. The story inside, "Good Morning, Mr. Smith" had no such scene but was clearly the inspiration for the cover. With the aid of Paul, his more moral assistant, Dr. Festa removes the head from a recent corpse in the hopes of reviving it as scientists had done with canine heads. He succeeds in his awful experiment, but Paul is appalled and tries to disconnect the wires from the living head. But Paul's reward for his compassion is be decapitated by Festa, who is under the mind-control of the living head, which he calls Mr. Smith. Festa puts Smith's head on top of Paul's now headless body. In the satisfying ending, Festa awakes only to discover that he is now a disembodied head on a table, with "Smith"— his head on Paul's body—leaning over him and saying "Good Morning, Mr. Smith."

In the mid-fifties *Mystic* began running tales with twist or ironic endings: a man's plan to kill his wealthy aunt goes awry when she falls out a window and lands on him on the street below; a dead man told he can come back to life every Tuesday by a specter falls in love but is unaware that the lady he cares for *is* the specter and winds up killing both his benefactor and the lady he adores. In the black comedy, "Pain" (33), a man discovers that other things besides humans, such as trees, flowers and even rocks, can feel terrible physical pain and tries to convince a colleague of his findings, but after an argument winds up killing the other man with an ax. Strapped into an electric chair he is asked if he has any final words: "Yes," he says, "Tell 'em ... no flowers." *Mystic* became a sci fi/fantasy comic in the post-code and silver age eras. Artists included Vic Carrabotta.

Astonishing started out as a science fiction comic in 1951, but its resident hero, Marvel Boy, fought ghouls and vampires, and there was the occasional light horror back-up story. By the following year the comic had switched into a straight horror and supernatural comic with occasional sci fi stories while Marvel Boy went elsewhere. The stories in *Astonishing* certainly ran the gamut. "Accidents Will Happen" (*Astonishing* 24) posited the theory that inanimate objects such as stones and wood, as well as trees, flowers and grass, are not only sentient but furious at mankind for what they see as abuses at human hands. A reporter discovers this when he investigates the death of a man crushed by a falling piece of heavy masonry just as he prepares to enter the post office to mail a letter explaining his theory to a colleague. The reporter realizes the scientist, who seemed crazy and paranoid, had every right to be afraid: he was killed off by the inanimate life all around him because he knew their secret. In "Age Before Beauty" (*Astonishing* 28) a middle-aged man who keeps young through fitness travels to another planet where he falls in love with a younger woman who is horrified not of growing older, but of growing *younger*, a particular affliction on this alien world. As she slowly turns into a small child, an age transfusion makes her more mature, but turns her husband into a dead infant. "The Eyes" (*Astonishing* 30) begins as a credible and creepy story of gigantic eyeball creatures that emerge from the ocean and emit rays that turn any human they touch into mere puddles of water. Although it is never explained why this is happening, the creatures burrow into graves and make off with the eyes of corpses which under water grow into more of these giant eyeballs. A man comes up with an easy way of beating the creatures back: simply shine a flashlight into their pupils. But the story then turns into a bad joke when it ends with a radio report that there have been thefts of *dark glasses* all over the seaside city… In the darkly comical, slightly perverse "Transformation" a thug who was deformed when the acid he threatened a woman with wound up splashing his own face, forces a plastic surgeon to operate on him. When the bandages come off he does indeed have a new young face—of a female! In the clever "Brother Vampire" (*Astonishing* 35) one half of a pair of Siamese twins who work in a sideshow is a secret vampire who stalks victims as his brother can only watch in horror. One night the vampire goes too far and tries to attack a young girl, so his brother drives a stake through his heart. Surprised to find he is still alive, he discovers that he is attached to the vampire only with a kind of plastic, and that the vampire—who needed a unique hiding place—wasn't his brother at all.

The comic had a couple of memorable covers. *Astonishing* 12 depicted a man and woman imprisoned in a box with a ceiling of sharp spikes slowly and inexorably descending upon them and a litter of human bones on the floor suggesting their ultimate fate. *Astonishing* 30 had an especially grisly cover by Joe Maneely in which a man in a graveyard subjected to yellow rays from large evil bloodshot eyes has burnt clothes and melting flesh literally falling off of his horribly exposed bones (this was suggested by the aforementioned non-grisly story "The Eyes"). Artists included Louis Ravielli, John Forte, Don Perlin, Pete Tomlinson, Al Carenno, and Paul Reinman. The comic continued briefly into the silver age, wherein the stories were more in the fantasy and straight science fiction mold.

Adventures Into Terror

Adventures Into Terror also debuted in 1951. The fourth issue of the comic had the distinction of presenting what was probably the most unusual vampire tale ever, "Vampire Brats," in which a maternity nurse discovers that all of the infants on her watch have a thirst for human blood. Escaping from the hospital, she thinks the whole thing must have been a dream until she's asked to babysit and the infant bares its vampire teeth when she's alone with it. Unfortunately, the story was just as idiotic as the premise suggests. On the other hand, "The Man Who Was Death" in the following issue, about a man who discovers he's been transformed into a human bomb by alien invaders, but can't convince anyone of his sanity, was decidedly sobering with its utterly hopeless situation and bleak finale.

Otto von Schmittsder is a Nazi scientist who was executed, but whose head is kept alive by an associate. Thereafter the evil head is able to roll about in energetic fury emitting its evil thoughts and taking over decent men and women, forcing them to murder each other and betray countries. At the end of each story the Brain, as it was known—although it was actually a disembodied head—would look out at the reader and suggest that they might be the next person to come under the influence of … the Brain. Stories about the character appeared in *AIT* 4 and 6 but future episodes never materialized.

In "What Walter Saw" (*AIT* 10) a man with a telescope concession at Coney Island "borrows" an extra lens from every other telescope on the boardwalk and discovers that every one who looks into his now much more powerful telescope sees something so awful that they go crazy and have to be taken in for observation. He looks into the telescope and sees a bunch of the scariest, nastiest-looking aliens apparently surrounding and heading their way toward Earth. Despite the effective final panel the story doesn't work because it isn't clear exactly where the aliens *are* in relation to the planet, what size they are or even if they're invaders or some sort of weird microscopic life form; An interesting premise with a poor execution.

"They're Driving Me Crazy" in *AIT* 14 is a notable paranoia tale in which a scientist named Henry Johnson creates a form of life from inorganic matter. Johnson is to make the announcement of his discovery the following day, but when he arrives at his laboratory he is told the building blew up four years ago. Johnson goes to see his colleagues, but they both tell him he's crazy, and that "Henry Johnson" died in the aforementioned explosion. Johnson's own wife and children tell him he's dead, and the picture his wife has of her late husband shows a man who looks nothing like Johnson. The scientist, on the edge of despair, goes to a newspaper morgue and discovers that there have been other cases of scientists who claimed they were alive when they were dead, and who were accused of attempting an impersonation or considered mentally ill. Then a man hidden by shadows tells Henry what has happened. Earth's secret rulers are actually beings from another dimension who monitor the planet and take steps to erase the existence of anyone who develops beyond the point where they wish the human race to be. Henry was targeted for creating life. The story ends with the tragic figure of the scientist walking off, determined to find the other "erase" victims of the aliens and band together to fight back. A sequel would have been welcome but it was never published.

Adventures Into Terror 15 could have been sub-titled "animal horrors" as it presented stories in which a variety of critters cause death and dismemberment. There was a lion tamer whose act ends with him putting his entire head inside the lion's mouth and whose life ends when his wife—who is hated by both her husband and the lion—draws her picture on top of the headpiece he wears with predictable results. Another story has two thieves coming afoul of hungry gators who converge on them at the exact spot where they hid the money they stole. And a third has to do with giant vampire tarantulas who terrorize a town, and a group of looters who crash into one house only to discover the owner and his children are ravenous human-spider hybrids. This story was not only featured on the effective cover by Joe Maneely but had a horrific splash panel depicting one of the big tarantulas climbing over a helpless, terrified victim.

Adventures Into Terror also had its moments of pathos. In "It Can't Be Done" (*AIT* 16) Jed Dorish, an untalented clown at a third-rate circus, desperately wants to do a high-wire act and practices over and over again until he can balance high up in the air. Unfortunately, his boss finds his high-wire maneuvering just as mediocre as his comical escapades in make-up. Dorish is fired, and told not to come back until he's worked up an act that will really make the crowds sit up and pay attention. Amazingly, Dorish returns and proceeds to walk across the air high above the ring *without a wire* or assistance or equipment of any kind. Posters are printed up and Dorish gives the acclaimed performance he had previously only dreamed of. But there will be no encore. Dorish had committed suicide the night before and it is his ghost who is walking on air. In "The Girl Who Couldn't Die" (19), a man preserves the body of his beloved fiancee and spends years trying every possible way he can think of to bring her back to life. He finally succeeds, only to have the woman scream in horror at the "nasty, horrible old man" trying to embrace her. So many years have gone by that the man she once loved is now elderly practically to the point of desiccation. Another memorable tale is "Casper's Boss" (*AIT* 17), in which a mousy man with a dying wife gets a fitting revenge on his cruel and contemptible employer.

Adventures Into Terror generally avoided grisly EC type stories but there was the occasional exception. In "Don't Nod" (30) Chung Ku is a cruel head of the communist secret police. He has people machine gunned en masse, but prefers the more refined and less messy kind of death. He importunes his chief executioner, Li Po, to take up the ancient art of beheading and many victims are dispatched by sword on his chopping block. Li Po is so expert that there is little blood, and the victims are practically decapitated before they even realize it. One day Chung Ku's fortunes change and it is he who is marked for death at the sword of Li Po. Chung Ku importunes his colleague not to kill him—"my head must remain upon my shoulders!"—Li Po does as he is instructed. He then leads the deposed tyrant to a secret passage through which he can escape. Li Po, who has told everyone that he beheaded Chung Ku, is made the new head of the secret police, but over the phone "strongly advises" the man against nodding his head. Confused, Chung Ku lowers his head anyway—and it promptly goes kerplunk on the floor, as it was literally hanging on by a hair. Despite the subject matter, the story is not as intense nor as bloodily and graphically drawn as an EC version would have been.

Perhaps the most unusual story to appear in *Adventures Into Terror* was written by no less than William Shakespeare. *AIT* 27 presented a very well done adaptation of "Macbeth"—"Fire Burn and Caldron Bubble"—that was written as if Shakespeare were a modern-day writer for *Adventures Into Terror* and ended with a skeletonized, immortal Macduff slaying Macbeth and revealing that one of the witches was his mother. Writers for the series included Hank Chapman and Stan Lee. Artists included Russ Heath, Bill Walton, Joe Sinnott, Ogden Whitney, Tony DiPreta, Gene Colan, George Tuska, Dick Ayers, Cal Massey, John Forte, and Paul Reinman.

Spellbound and *Journey Into Mystery*

Spellbound debuted in 1952. The comic published black comedies and suspense tales with ironic endings. "Only a Rose" (*Spellbound* 16) featured a pathologically jealous wife, Helen, who discovers that her husband, Chester, is going out each evening, buying expensive bouquets of flowers, and giving them to one beautiful woman after another. Discovering the women's addresses, Helen sends boxes of poisoned candy to them, but is surprised when her husband has little reaction seeing news of their deaths in the paper. Any guilt she feels is dissipated by her feeling that the dead women should not have had anything to do with a married man. But it develops that Chester was simply delivering flowers for extra income so he could buy his wife an especially nice and expensive present for her birthday. He also gives her a box of candy, which she happily munches, not realizing that it was given to her husband by one of her would-be victims who didn't want the chocolate; like a great many characters in horror comics, Helen is undone by her own evil scheme.

In the undeniably perverse "Thing in the Mud" in *Spellbound* 22 a woman befriends an amphibian-like creature that comes from a world below a muddy canal and is lost upon our world. She hides the creature out in her home and, responding to her kindness, the thing brings her jewelry which it has stolen. The creature is captured by the police, who lead it away in handcuffs, but not before the woman tells it she will wait for as long as necessary, she's fallen in love with it. It's hard to say if this wind-up is meant to be heart-warming or disgusting and pathetic, as the mud-being is an entirely different species; it could be male or female, and the women even refers to it as "it." The creature's sex is less important than the fact that it isn't human, and the conclusion suggests that its benefactor must be mighty desperate for a companion or lover. The art is so matter of fact and bland that it doesn't do enough to underline the creature's repulsiveness, and the final panel when the woman kisses it is less repellant than it is comical. In the same issue's hard-hitting "13 Years" a man comes across a bag of fabulous jewels of all kinds and decides to chuck his life as a $40 a week clerk, leave his wife and child, start a new life under a new name, and wait several years until he feel's it's safe to hock or sell the jewelry. Of course it turns out that the jewels are paste. The man gets ten dollars in exchange for thirteen miserable, lonely wasted years and buys a gun and one bullet with the money, for obvious reasons.

The long-running *Journey Into Mystery* first appeared in 1952. "Now You See It" in the tenth issue was an EC-type story in which a magician, who regularly saws his wife in half in their act, *literally* saws her in two after she stupidly tells him she's running off with their business manager just before they go on stage. In the final panel the dead woman's body is in two boxes, several feet apart, but there is an absence of blood. (In the same issue another story has a hit man buried up to his neck in sand as the tide rolls in, an idea later exploited in the movie *Creepshow*.) In "We Don't Want Your Head" (13) an ambitious pianist who only wants to practice so he can go pro, kills off his nagging wife and winds up a captive of natives who don't collect heads but hands.

"The New Look" (*JIM* 11) is a disturbing story of a young, very ugly hunchback named Eric who calls upon the village witch, Nina, in hopes that she can give him a new face. Nina summons her master, Satan, who agrees to give Eric a handsome new countenance, which will appear at midnight. When Eric looks in the mirror at the appointed hour, he does see a very handsome visage looking back at him, but as he turns away senses something is wrong. The Devil gave Eric a new face, all right, but his hideous old face is *now growing* out of the back of his head, making him a bigger freak than he was before. The story is meant to be a black comedy throwaway, but instead it delivers a depressing wallop. True, Eric may have made a desperate deal with the devil, but he doesn't deserve an awful fate in which his future life can't possibly be anything but loneliness and heartache. One is reminded of people who have tough crosses to bear already only to have something even worse happen, as well as those who endure cosmetic surgery to improve their appearance only to wind up looking much, much more awful than before.

"Vampire Tale" in *JIM* 16 is an interesting variation on the usual vampire story. A man who is bandaged from head to toe is on trial for murdering a citizen; the motive, robbery. The defendant, however, claims that his victim is a vampire, that he had just murdered an innocent woman and got what he deserved. Neither the judge nor the jury believe the man's insane story, and he is convicted. Before he can be led away, the defendant removes his wrappings, revealing a desiccated face and skeletal body underneath. He knew the man was a vampire because *he* was one of his victims, and has been after him ever since; death was merely an inconvenience. He then collapses into a pile of ashes in front of the astonished courtroom.

Years before *Fantastic Voyage*, "The Human Germ" in *JIM* 22 presents a scientist, Harold Brant, who shrinks himself and enters the bloodstream of a rival who is about to publish his findings on "cellular shrinkage" and beat Brant, who is working on similar research, to the punch. Brant pours a poison into his rival's blood from inside his body, but is undone when antibiotics that the would-be victim takes to ease the pain caused by the poison surround and absorb the screaming Brant. If the story has any problem it's that it's hard to figure how Brant, once shrunken to microscopic size, would ever be able to make his way toward the other man's body or indeed even be able to distinguish it from its surroundings.

The cover of the eleventh issue features a truly frightening ghoul of giant size who has burst out of a tomb and is carrying off two screaming gravediggers as if for food. But by the mid-fifties the comic had switched from horror to sci fi and fantasy stories. Artists included Bill Walton, Mannie Banks, Vic Carabotta, and Gene Colan.

Adventures Into Weird Worlds and *Uncanny Tales*

Adventures Into Weird Worlds was another 1952 release. "Don't Bury Me Deep" in the fifth issue concerns an undertaker named Charles Beecher who finally gets to bury the town's richest and most hated citizen, old man Macomber, for a very hefty fee. When Macomber sits up in his casket and turns out to be alive, Beecher slams down the lid and listens to him pound on it for hours until the old man finally expires. When Beecher opens the lid, he accidentally falls inside, then gets locked within right on top of the corpse. Banging on the lid, he can't understand why no one can hear him. The trouble is, everyone thinks it's Macomber banging and no one wants to let the universally loathed man out of the coffin; Beecher is buried alive. "The Last Laugh" in *AIWW* 9 is an EC-type story in which a man's brother plays one practical joke too many, cackling how he'll "laugh his fool head off," thinking of his victimized brother's expression as he watches his beloved car fall apart. Naturally, the brother snaps and puts the laughing dead man's head on top of a scarecrow. The story was a fairly feeble imitation of the type of thing EC could do much better.

"Heads Will Roll" (*AIWW* 28) is more on the mark. In 1591 London, James Jurgens is entrusted to take the heads of executed criminals and place them on pikes for all to see on London Bridge. Jurgens is paid by the head, but when there are several slots—or pikes—to be filled, he condemns innocent people so that he can have their heads after death. One night he hears the severed heads talking to one another on the bridge, and one of them even shouts out that he's trying to burn it down. Guards rush forward, and Jurgens, acting crazy due to his fear, is decapitated by a sword's swift stroke. The story ends with Jurgens joining the other now lifeless heads on their pikes. Whereas an EC story would have showed dollops of blood, torn flesh, eyes falling out of sockets, "Heads Will Roll" was more tastefully, but less dynamically, drawn by Paul Reinman.

Weird Worlds also ran dark science fiction stories, most of which were unmemorable or downright hokey. "Indestructible" in *AIWW* 29 is somewhat more interesting than most, telling the tale of a time traveler who comes back to his ancestor, scientist Charles Cobart, in a booth made of plexi-thorium glass. The future has been beset with a plague of rapidly multiplying insects that wiped out everything in their path and Cobart's descendant hopes everyone can find refuge in the past. But there seems to be no way to break the futuristic glass and freeing the man inside. What's worse, there are two insects inside the case, and their ranks will multiply within minutes. Cobart runs to get colleagues to help him break through the walls of the booth, but by the time he gets back, his descendant and the booth have disappeared. However, Copbart realizes that something did indeed break the glass, as he looks down to see several of the horrible insects crawling up his leg. The final panel is decidedly creepy even if the story itself hardly stands up to close inspection.

There were many covers of ghouls, ghosts and corpses advancing on terrified living humans in horror comics, but one of the best of these was the cover to *AIWW* 5, which depicts a beautiful woman on a bed with the moon in the window behind her, while in the foreground there is the skeletal leg (in torn pants) of a fiend in muddy boots walking up the stone stairs from catacombs or a mine shaft below the stairs. The concept of something unspeakably evil and frightening emerging from secret underground chambers and marching up to the supposedly safe haven where you sleep creates an undeniable *frisson*. *AIWW* 29 also has a memorable cover of a man trapped under a descending metal press, a ghoul above him operating the machinery, and skeletons on incongruous pillows in a cavern below him; the man lies on a stone ledge between the press and the skeletons.

Artists for the series included Bill Everett, Joe Maneely, Joe Sinnott, Jim Mooney, Carmine Infantino, Jay Scott Pike, Sol Brodsky, Jack Keller, Paul Reinman, and Doug Wildey.

Uncanny Tales debuted in 1952. The comic published some monumentally stupid stories but now and then they came out with an acceptable tale or better. In "Crazy" (*UT* 2), very well-drawn by Jerry Robinson, a man thinks he's gotten away with a hit and run and is astonished when a lynch mob surrounds him, until they point out that the man he ran over is still sticking to the front fender of his car. *Uncanny Tales* 6 had two stories with good twists. In "He Lurks in the Shadows" a man steals and murders to get enough money for his wife—Paris vacations, a new house, and expensive presents in exchange for the ones she gives him—but one night he becomes a mugging victim himself, but it's hard to say if it's him or the mugger who's more astonished. It seems his wife has also resorted to crime to pay for those expensive presents. In "The Man Who Changed" a very homely man marries a pretty woman but just can't believe that she loves him for anything more than his money. He is upset by the constant stream of cruel remarks he overhears. Finally he goes away for a time and gets a handsome face via plastic surgery. But when he comes home to surprise his wife he gets a bigger surprise—she, too, went to a plastic surgeon to make herself *homely* and prove to him how much she loves him. It would be interesting to see if the now devilishly attractive man will stick around with his wife now that she's not so good-looking.

In the hilarious "Like a Chicken Without a Head" (*UT* 9) Dr. Feeney insists that his method of operating will save many lives. His plan is to cut off a person's head and have one surgical team work on the body and heart while another attends to the head. To demonstrate to a reporter, he cuts off a chicken's head, injects his wonder solution in the body, and shows the reporter a "healthy, happy, headless chicken" walking around the room. "If I can do that to a chicken, I can do it to a human being!" he insists as the reporter runs screaming out of the room. Sadly Feeney realizes that mankind is not yet ready for his radical surgery—and holds his own detached head in his hands.

"Don't Count Your Chickens" (*UT* 26), on the other hand, was a creepy sci-fi/horror tale with a fascinating premise: The earth and all the planets of the solar system are merely eggs inside of which gargantuan creatures are preparing to hatch. One ancient, formerly unknown planet between Mercury and the sun has already broken apart centuries ago, and astronomers not only discover the debris but see the fantastic, hideous and utterly huge creature that has emerged floating in space between the sun and Mercury. Scientists try to destroy the incubating creature sleeping inside the earth, but it is so gigantic that nothing can fatally wound it. To alleviate a panic, the lead scientist releases a statement claiming that only the demolished planet was close enough to the sun to hatch, but before his statement can be printed there comes a more momentous headline: "Mercury Hatches." Can the earth be far behind? In the same issue was a less interesting tale about a nutty professor who breeds two giant spiders in the hopes he can take over the world with their spawn, but as both arachnids are male his plot, of course, comes to nothing.

"The Hungry Jaws" in *Uncanny Tales* 11 was basically another rip-off of Carl Stephenson's "Leiningen vs. the Ants," but the tobacco plantation owner's deliberate sacrificing of native workers to the ants leads into an interesting final panel wherein the ants savaging the man have the heads and faces of the natives who died. In the grotesque "The Horse Laugh" (14) a nasty jockey double-crosses the mob and winds up in a mental ward riding a fake horse, now completely out of touch with reality.

Uncanny Tales lasted long enough to have a few silver age issues, mostly benign sci fi and fantasy stories. Artists throughout its run included Joe Kido, Bob Forgione, Paul Hodge, Mort Lawrence, Sheldon Moldoff, Gray Morrow, and Al Williamson.

Mystery Tales and *Menace*

Mystery Tales was another 1952 release from Atlas/Marvel. It ran a mixture of horror, suspense, sci fi and fantasy stories. "Marion's Murderer" (*Mystery Tales* 14) is a sophisticated tale in which a man, Eddie, is so bored with his perfect wife, who dotes on him, cares for him and cooks for him with nary a complaint, that he has come to despise her. He is particularly aggrieved by her perfect memory and the way she gently chides him for forgetting relatives' birthdays and the names of acquaintances. The ending, in which Eddie stabs Marion to death and carries her body down to the cellar, only to run into the hiding celebrants of a surprise anniversary party, was later borrowed for an *Alfred Hitchcock Hour* episode entitled "Goodbye George" that was written and broadcast ten years later.

"The Little Monster" in *Mystery Tales* 15 by an unknown author was a ghoulish little gem. Joe and Helen suddenly find a tentacled, beaked blob with purplish, blotchy skin squatting in their living room. Their first impulse is to shoot the thing, but it is impervious to bullets. It tells them that it comes from the star system Centaurus, and will give them anything they desire if he can merely stay and observe them. In the blink of an eye the couple find themselves with beautiful new clothes and furnishings, jewelry, and a handsome new automobile to replace the old jalopy. The alien tells them that he thinks humans are much nicer than he was told, and that he requires none of their food as he retires to their basement. As the days go by, Helen and Joe get any possession they wish for—mink coats, every modern convenience—and are never bothered by salesmen or other unwanted visitors. Finally the creature tells them that he must leave, but he will be returning with more of its kind. As they watch him float up to his waiting spaceship, alarming the neighbors, they wonder if he ever had anything to eat as the final panel, a long shot, shows the dozens of picked-clean human skeletons piling up out of the coal chute and tumbling into the couple's backyard.

In "The 13th Floor" (*Mystery Tales* 21) Hugh Carter, who has a weak heart, is worried about his wife, Mary, whose doctor suggests a change of scene for her own health problems. At work the elevator strangely goes up to a thirteenth floor, even though the building only has twelve. There Carter meets Death, who tells him not to worry, that he will adjust to his new state of being. But Carter, thinking of how much he loves his wife and how much she needs him, begs Death to let him go. As Carter was not supposed to die for another thirty years, and this was a special circumstance, Death has no choice but to comply. Down in the lobby, Carter sees his wife enter the same elevator, and realizes that Death was only showing compassion: his *wife's* time was up and Death figured Carter would want to be with her in eternity. Now Carter will have thirty long and lonely years ahead of him without Mary.

Although *Mystery Tales* tried to pretend it was still a horror comic in the post-code period, it concentrated more on sci fi and fantasy and harmlessly strange stories. The cover might promise a spooky tale about a mysterious locked door with something frightening and terrible behind it, but the story inside would be about a man who hides the pieces of a vase he broke and lied about in his youth, causing four of his parents' employees to lose their jobs, only to discover it has magically mended now that he's finally told someone the truth. "The House That Lived" wasn't about a diabolical house that swallowed its owners, but a non-supernatural tale about a house getting a fresh life (i.e., a coat of paint) when it gets young new owners. The stories were more sweet than scary. The sci fi/fantasy tales could be a little more downbeat. A premise *Mystery Tales* (and other comics) used more than once was of a homely man wearing a handsome mask to get a lady, then discovering that his face underneath has transformed into the good-looking mask out of true love or inner beauty. More original was "The Mystery of the Silent Fog" (*MT* 52) in which the citizens of a small town wake up after a terrible storm to discover the whole area is surrounded by an impenetrable fog and that they seem to be flying through space. Fearing they were snatched by aliens who wanted to study typical earthlings, they begin to behave in an unusual manner so the aliens, finding them atypical, will let them go; it works. Stephen King later used the idea of a town surrounded by a thick sinister fog in "The Mist." Artists for *Mystery Tales* included Paul Reinman, Gene Colan, Jack Abel, Martin Thall, Carl Hubbell, and Robert Q. Sale.

Menace, which presented "stories of maddening menace," debuted in 1953. Stan Lee and Russ Heath's "On With the Dance" (*Menace* 2) examined the case of dancer Stella Stevens, a loathsomely self-centered woman who covets the lead role when the main dancer breaks her leg. She is flatly turned down by the producer, who hires a plain but talented replacement. Stella is so evil that she allowed one poor smitten fellow to go to jail for three years in her place, but when he comes to see her after serving his time she blows him off, and lets him blow his brains out in despair. "I wish I could get rid of all my problems as easy as that," she says. So it's no surprise when Stella pays a call on the new dancer and threatens to shoot her if she doesn't resign. But the new girl has a secret: she's a witch, and she casts a spell that insures that Stella will dance and dance—and *dance*—all she wants to, until she turns into a thin wreck of herself and then drops dead as a literal skeleton on the floor.

"Men in Black" (*Menace* 3) was Atlas' contribution to the socially relevant, anti-bigotry stories of the horror comics of the type that EC ran on occasion, although it had significantly less impact. When Jim Horton is fired for fighting with his supervisor, his prejudice comes to the fore and he expresses hatred for all the "foreigners" working at the plant, which includes everyone from Italians to the Irish (although he later includes a Jewish man in his ire, significantly there are no references to Black people). Horton gets a group of like-minded individuals together to wear black hoods and take off after all the foreigners in town, beating and robbing them. The police break up this first attempt, and Horton manages to escape. Back at home, he takes off his hood only to find another hood underneath it—and another and another. When the police catch up with him, they discover he has literally torn his face off. While admirable, the story was not without precedent, as there had been anti-prejudice, anti-racism ads in comics going back to the forties.

"You're Gonna Live Forever" (*Menace* 3) was a creepy variation on a popular theme: a person who has gained immortality discovers they will indeed live forever but in prison or paralyzed or some other horrible, never-ending fate. In this instance a murderous crook comes across a scientist who has invented a solution that can prevent death by constantly revitalizing tissue and therefore healing wounds. The crook takes it and murders the scientist, then kills another man who leads him to a safe hideout in the swamp. The crook then steps in quicksand, and discovers that even while suffocating and becoming food for worms below the earth, he still cannot die and never will.

Menace 10 had three imperfect but interesting stories. In "Half Man, Half...?" Dr. Nostrum is a scientist working on a cobalt bomb. He only married his wife for her money and influence, thinks of his adoring young son as a "millstone," and is selling out secrets to a foreign power. Investigating reports of savage murders in the area of his lab, he discovers that certain emissions are turning humans into horrible monsters. Afraid that their existence will queer his traitorous deals, he kills as many of the creatures as he can. When he looks in the mirror and sees that he too is turning green and scaly, he commits suicide. His little boy hears the bang, which his mother tells him is a car backfiring. It turns out that as a joke the child cut out a picture of a monster and pasted it onto the mirror. The story is mediocre but what you're left with is the sense that the little boy will, however irrationally, blame himself for his father's suicide for the rest of his life.

"In the Cardboard Box" is in the tradition of a-maniac-is-on-the-loose-but-which-man-is-it? An old man named Winters, who has had a stroke and can neither walk nor speak, is disturbed when his regular companion has to leave to attend to her pregnant daughter. She hires a substitute, a seedy-looking man who arrives with a large cardboard box. In the meantime Winters reads in the paper about a series of decapitation murders that have rocked the city. The latest victim was a police sergeant who lost his head and his identification. Naturally a sergeant shows up and Winters tries to tell him about his new employee and his box. This leads to a tense scene when the two men confront each other and the real head-chopper is revealed. The one problem with the suspenseful story is that most readers will figure it out with ease.

"The Fake" is a black comedy about Agnes, an aged seductress who somehow manages to hold onto her youthful, sexy appearance via highly elaborate artifice. She has gone through—and financially drained—so many men that her pickings are slim, and younger men avoid her like the plague. She decides to settle for one last score with an elderly fellow, whom she manages to snare and marry. The ending—the husband is also a "fake," being a mechanical man—is terrible; the amusement is in the incredible disparity between the sexy siren and the actually hideous, incredibly ancient crone that she is without teeth, hair, make up and specially constructed outfits. The story spoofs the lengths people will go to to remain young and sexually viable in the days before botox, face lifts and collagen, While Agnes is hardly a likable woman, one can sympathize with her dilemma and even, to a certain extent, admire her brave battle against age and decay, a battle which goes on, perhaps even more ferociously then before, today.

"Locked In" (*Menace* 11) has an excellent premise. Jenifer Marlowe has gained quite a reputation as a woman who hunts down and explores the pathetic lives of hermits and tramps, especially once-wealthy people who walked away from fortunes to live in caves or hovels, and still-wealthy people who choose to live like paupers. She has even written a book on the subject. The beginning of the story presents several fascinating case studies, but there's a clever twist. Jennifer couldn't care less about these weirdos. Twenty years ago she and her husband Bill wiped out an entire wealthy family and made off with a million in loot. Or at least Bill did, and Jennifer has been searching for him and the money ever since. His disappearance had been so complete that she was certain he must have holed up in an out of the way place. Again, the wind-up is disappointing. Bill has not left the creepy old house that has been his refuge for two decades because the ghosts of their victims won't let him and they're not about to let Jennifer get away, either.

Menace, which had a very short run, was unusual because the early issues were full of the kind of hyperbole—"this is the greatest story ever!"—that Marvel (Atlas) Comics became famous for during the super-hero revival of the sixties. This was because Stan Lee wrote many of the stories for *Menace*, just as he later did for *Fantastic Four* and *X-Men*. Artists for the series included Robert Q. Sale, Seymour Moskowitz, John Forte, George Tuska, Joe Sinnott, and John Romita, the last three of which did much work for Marvel in the silver age super-hero era.

During the horror revival of the seventies, Marvel reprinted many of its golden age horror tales in such anthology titles as *Beware, Chamber of Chills, Crypt of Shadows, Dead of Night*, and others.

Five

DC, Fawcett, Charlton and Harvey

With Superman, Batman, Wonder Woman and other super-stars on its roster, DC Comics was the industry leader in the golden age, but it got competition not only from Atlas (who would become a more formidable competitor as Marvel Comics in the sixties), but from Fawcett, who published the extremely popular Captain Marvel, Charlton, who struggled on into the seventies, and Harvey, who published some of the most popular horror titles of the period. DC resisted the overtly gruesome EC approach, while the others embraced it to varying degrees.

DC's long-running *House of Mystery* first appeared on the newsstands in 1952. "I Fell in Love with a Witch," the lead story in the first issue, is a very entertaining and suspenseful affair in which a private eye gets engaged to a woman whose three previous fiances all met with violent deaths, and who wonders if the woman he loves is a murderous creature with supernatural powers. The only thing it had in common with the less successful "Wanda Was a Werewolf" in the same issue was that the heroines both turned out to be victims of sinister hoaxes. In that sense many of the stories in *House of Mystery* really *were* mysteries (or suspense stories) and not horror, although there were some generally supernatural tales as well as others that hinted at the supernatural without necessarily confirming it. Such a story was "The Tree of Doom" in the second issue, in which a man murders a wealthy cousin as he balances on a large beloved tree and said tree seems to be stalking the killer, even though there are also rational explanations for everything that happens.

In the brilliant, uncredited "Friday the 13th Club" (*HOM* 4) two disgruntled men who lose business due to their customers' superstitious attitudes form a club with thirteen members for the sole purpose of debunking superstition. A different person takes the chair each week and proceeds to smash a mirror. Then they confront any superstitions of their own by deliberately walking under a ladder or crossing the path of a black cat. Unfortunately, one by one the chairmen begin to die: a man walks *into* a ladder and causes a scaffold to rain bricks on him; another man walks into the path of a car after seeing a black cat; another is the third person to use the same match and falls in front of a commuter train. After five people are killed, the other members of the club angrily disband. Later it develops that the gavel each man used to smash the mirror had originally belonged to the Borgias and was coated with poison to eliminate any judges who ruled against them; the poison made anyone exposed to it dizzy, confused, and ultimately deceased. As the terrified members of the club die in terrible accidents, wonder if they're tempting fate and if there's something to superstition after all, the story seems like a forerunner to those *Final Destination* movies where people think they've cheated Death until Death catches up to them.

Sometimes it was hard to guess how the *HOM* writer would ultimately reveal that seemingly supernatural events were just elaborate hoaxes. When the Devil appears to a gambler in Europe and demands his past life in return for granting him stupendous luck at cards, said "Satan" turns out to be a lookalike gangster who controlled the casinos (hence the "luck") and wanted to go back to America in the gambler's identity. A man who claims that he can use the paintings of ancestors to siphon off their individual skills but also takes on their malevolent personalities as a by-product, murders his uncle and almost gets away with it due to insanity until someone proves he faked all the ancestral "skills" he displayed as well as his madness.

House of Mystery 7 (1952) introduced Mr. (later Dr.) Terry Thirteen, who investigates the strange case of split Siamese twins, one of whom uses mind-control to get his brother to commit robberies. He insists that neither of them can be arrested as he himself doesn't actually commit a crime, and his brother isn't in his right mind when he's robbing. Unfortunately for them Thirteen proves that not only were they never conjoined, but both of them are perpetrating a hoax, the unmasking of which gets them jail time. Thirteen later got his own strip in *Star-Spangled Comics*, but never appeared again in *House of Mystery* (in the golden age).

House of Mystery finally published a more macabre kind of story in, appropriately enough, its thirteenth issue. "Album of Fear" concerns a millionaire named Jasper Jennings who has a decidedly ghoulish hobby—he records the sounds of death. The reader first encounters Jasper as he stands at the side of a dangerous intersection along the highway, actually hoping for an accident to occur. When it does, he records the sound of the crash, including the screams of the passengers upon impact as well as their dying moans. Jasper has recordings of a man being hanged, eagerly acquires one of a man being electrocuted, and wants to record a madman's ravings at the very date and hour of the anniversary of a murder he committed. But Jennings is haunted by the ghosts of people whose last moments he intruded upon. It develops that the aforementioned madman's brother didn't want it coming out that he was poisoning the maniac for his money—he was afraid recordings might reveal the truth—so he drove Jennings crazy with ghostly projections. Instead of recording a madman's rantings, Jennings is admitted to the same asylum.

A similarly macabre story appeared in *HOM* 28. "The Spider-Man" concerns an old coot, Jasper Weems, who is convinced that people are reincarnated as insects, and has a huge collection of bugs whom, he believes, had once been people. There is always some connection between insect and person: a soprano who specialized in singing "Madame Butterfly" becomes a butterfly; a maker of honey comes back as a bee. This weird collector is obsessed with getting a spider that had once been human, and plans to travel to see a circus sideshow freak who resembles an arachnid. His hope is that the sideshow performer will kick off and come back as a spider, which he can be on hand to snare. Unfortunately after Weems boards a boat to take him to France to see the freak, he dies in a freak accident—a horse falls on him after a cable snaps and both plunge into the ship's hold. As dead horse and sprawling dead man are pulled from the hold they resemble a certain eight legged creature ... and soon a spider appears.

Generally the stories which truly involved the supernatural were more memorable than the hoax stories, however clever the latter. Sometimes, however, the hoax stories were *so* clever and surprising that it didn't matter that the supernatural element was a crock. "The Ordeal of Roger Black" (*HOM* 17) concerns an executioner who is cursed by a condemned man and discovers he is unable to successfully perform his duty. An electric chair malfunctions, a hanging rope breaks, a man in a gas chamber fails to expire. In a fine example of mis-direction, it turns out that Black himself was responsible for these incidents just so he could earn a fat pay out from a murderer slated to die and whose survival he planned to blame on the non-existent "curse." When said murderer tries to cheat Black of his payment, he gets shot for his ingratitude and Black winds up hiding out—and getting locked in—a cold storage unit. Hacking at the walls to get free, he releases a poisonous gas which kills him as if he were in a "gas" chamber.

Occasionally a hoax story was too clever for its own good. In "The Giant Out of Nowhere" (*HOM* 33), numerous people see hallucinations of a weird giant man tearing up the city. A Hindu healer named Handar says he can heal these people of their hallucinations. When a scientist pretends that he is one of the victims, Handar tells him he knows that he is faking. The reason is because all of the people having hallucinations are Handar's agents, and the whole thing is a bizarre plot to flush a president who suffers from visions out of hiding so that would-be dictator Handar can kill him. The "giant" was a complete fabrication in more ways than one.

Many stories in *House of Mystery* have excellent premises and build-ups but come to unfortunately abrupt and flat conclusions. For instance, in "Hangman's House" (*HOM* 29) a man is horrified to learn that he is descended from a long line of state executioners. He is told that he must follow tradition and kill people for a living or there will be terrible consequences, but he'd rather drive a taxi. Then a man runs in front of his cab and is killed. Some days later he accidentally backs into a man in a crowded metro stop and the latter falls in front of a train. His uncle tells him he will kill people whether he wants to or not and must accept his fate as executioner. The story is riveting so far but it ends only a page or so later with the protagonist refusing to back down from a bully on top of the Eiffel tower, and going to death row for the latter's murder when he falls off the tower during the fight. Not only is it unlikely that he would be charged with first-degree murder in such a scenario, the ending is rushed and lacks invention.

As the silver age approached, *House of Mystery* concentrated more on fantasy and sci fi stories—many of these remained tales of hoaxes, of course—and generally eschewed horror and the supernatural altogether when the sixties began. Eventually the series featured an array of weird, often extra-terrestrial monsters. It wasn't until 1968 when *House of Mystery* went back to being a horror comic. The main artist for the series in the golden age was Ruben Moreira, who turned in attractive, more than competent work issue after issue.

Other notable stories of the golden age included "Partners in Fear" (*HOM* 9)—a man who is jealous of a braver and more successful friend tries to kill him but only winds up losing his mind; "The Bewitched Clock" (11)—a man uses a clock to go one day into the past so he can amass a fortune by knowing future events, but eventually winds up living the same day over and over; "Nine Lives Equal Death" (11)—another story in which a man who gets nine lives uses this ability to do evil and winds up outwitting himself; "The Curse of the Deadly Dolls" (14)—a doll maker hatches an ingenious scheme to torment a former partner whom he felt cheated him.

Also: "Dance of Doom" (14)—tragic accidents that befall dancers are blamed on a curse that hangs over a ballet but the real cause is an ambitious member of the troupe; "The Bravest Man Alive" (17)—an American and a Frenchman dangerously try to outdo one another to win acclaim as the most courageous man in the world; "Enter the Ghost" (29)—an actor must fend off the attack of a jealous rival who plans to kill him in the guise of an angry spirit who objects to the play being performed, which portrays him in a negative light; "Diary of a Nightmare" (32)—a tragedy in which a decent man agrees to become a guinea pig so he can have money for his wife's operation but is turned into a monster his wife doesn't even recognize; "Mr. Misfortune" (33)—a sad sack claims that ever since he violated a sacred tomb he has had nothing but miserable luck; "The Fatal Superstition" (5)—a man conceives of a plot to murder his partner in a town where having any mirrors, ladders, umbrellas, or black cats is against the law.

Dr. Thirteen and *The Phantom Stranger*

Star Spangled Comics, which had been running the solo adventures of Batman's boy partner, Robin, and other heroic types for years, had a brand new cover feature beginning with the one hundred twenty-second issue (1951): "The Ghost Breaker," also known as the aforementioned Dr. Thirteen. When Terry Thirteen was a boy he entered a forbidden room in the family mansion—Doomsbury Hall—and saw paintings depicting the violent deaths of his ancestors, all victims of the "thirteen curse," burned at the stake for witchcraft or similar grisly ends. The elder Thirteen was convinced that these ancestors had actually been geniuses who were so ahead of their time that they were convicted of sorcery. He begs his son to shun the supernatural: "You must never believe that your life is governed by other than natural forces." After his father's own violent demise in a fiery car crash, Terry moves out of the mansion and devotes his life to debunking phony psychics and other alleged instances of the supernatural. Before his accident his father told him to memorize five questions and ask them in Doomsbury Hall on the fifth anniversary, and see whether or not his ghost will answer. Terry is shocked when he hears his father's voice intoning the answers to his questions, but discovers it is only a voice on a tape recording made some years before. As his fiancee Marie explains, his father wanted him to realize that there was always a natural explanation to ghostly events.

In *SSC* 123 Dr. Thirteen has a puzzling case in which people die in ways that correspond to injuries made to dolls in their likenesses. In SSC 126 he investigates when a strange phantom appears as singers are murdered during performances at the Paris Opera. In *SSC* 129 he exposes a greedy botanist's human orchid hybrids—big green flower people—as fakes, although the real man-eating cactus that swallows its creator whole and has a huge red tongue in its maw was almost as strange. SSC 124 features an especially good story in which Thirteen investigates a cursed tower in Mexico which has claimed the lives of everyone who climbs it for centuries. It's assumed by many that the victims were merely suicides but few of the people who died had any reason to kill themselves. Thirteen climbs the tower himself and uncovers the clever and tragic secret behind the many deaths. The series lasted until the 130th and final issue of *Star Spangled Comics*. Dr. Thirteen would come back in the silver age.

An interesting aspect of the character was that although Dr. Thirteen always uncovered the rational truth behind weird occurrences, he was still never entirely convinced himself until he came up with the solid proof. Still it seemed questionable in *SSC* 127 when he wondered if a voodoo doll had something to do with a crime boss's sudden death when he'd already completely debunked voodoo doll deaths four issues earlier. Apparently Dr. Thirteen was always afraid that there would come a time when the supernatural would prove real— which might mean that he, too, would fall victim to the gruesome "thirteen" curse that killed off virtually every one else in his family.

The Phantom Stranger appeared in 1952 and lasted six issues. The title character was a mysterious dapper figure in a hat, suit and tie who came in and out of the darkness like the Shadow and seemed to have similar powers, although there were hints that he was a supernatural being, maybe even a ghost. Sometimes he would be on hand for genuine cases of the supernatural and in others debunked phony situations like Dr. Thirteen, such as a story in which a man uses electronic devices to create magical illusions or one in which a greedy fellow makes it look as if an amusement park he covets is haunted. In one story in which three men are killed in a plane crash, he exposes a fourth man who is pretending to be the ghost of all three for his own purposes. At the end another character sees a picture of the passengers on the doomed flight—snapped before take-off by a photographer who then exited the plane—with the Stranger in it and wonders how he could have survived the crash when everyone else on board was killed. The Stranger would team up with Dr. Thirteen when the former's title was revived in the late sixties.

Sensation Mystery

Sensation Comics, which had featured the exploits of Wonder Woman since its inception in 1942, turned into an all fantasy and horror comic with the one hundred seventh issue in 1952; the title was changed to *Sensation Mystery* with the one hundred tenth issue. "The Sinister Jack-in-the-Box" (107) is found in a pawnshop and either grants you a wish or kills you. In "The Wheel of Fate" (108) an archeologist who discovers an ancient series of drawings discovers that the actions of thousands of years ago which the drawings depict are somehow forecasting events in his own life. In "The Phantom Enemy" (116) a man discovers that another painter is turning in artwork that is exactly the same as his own and ruining his career; tracking him to his studio, he replaces his pills with poison, then discovers too late that he and his rival are one and the same person.

The best story ever published in *Sensation Mystery* was the superb "Fingers of Fear," the cover story for *SC* 109. Albert Tisdale murders five men for diamonds, escapes through the "cursed waters" of the River of Black Death, and discovers back home that along with his riches he has acquired five highly unusual finger tips: the tiny arms and faces of the men he killed, holding miniature versions of the instruments of their death and cackling how they're going to kill him as soon as he lets his guard down. Tisdale wears a glove on the affected hand, and goes about his business, but whenever he is forced to remove the glove or it is torn, exposing the sinister digits, his five victims do their level best to kill him (employing one of the methods he used to murder them) until after several tries they succeed. (Years later, in a very different type of story, the idea of fingers tapering off into tiny human fingers was used on the cover of a classic issue of *Justice League of America*.)

FAWCETT

Fawcett comics published several horror series during the golden age, the first of which was *This Magazine Is Haunted,* debuting in 1951. The stories were introduced by Dr. Death, a grinning skeletal corpse in a top hat and old-fashioned cloak with a high collar. Eventually Dr. Death would appear in some stories or act as instigator of the plot such as when he mischievously encourages a bunch of complaining townspeople to put their troubles in a bag and exchange the bags with one another in *TMIH* 10; one young man exchanges bags with his wealthy boss only to discover he now has a deadly heart problem to go along with his fabulous new-found wealth.

"The Weirdest Corpse of All" is an effectively intense tale about a nervous exterminator, haunted by the eyes of all the creatures he's killed, who shrinks in size and is victimized by illusions of spiders and mice feasting on his body, until his wife finds his tiny corpse, which has taken on rodent-like characteristics. (*TMIH* 2). "The Man Who Saw Too Much" (7) concerns a man who invents a camera that can take pictures of long ago events as well as the long-dead, but he gets more than he bargained for when he photographs the scene of a decades-old murder and homicidal spirits think he's seen too much. "The Phantom of Disaster" (10) appears to engineer Roger Ellis—and to him alone—just before there's some terrible tragedy, and he's afraid the bridge he's just toiled on for months will be destroyed by the phantom. Roger gets a medium to summon the phantom and the latter is able to imprison it in a bottle. But as Roger celebrates the completion of the bridge, one of his employees, "celebrating" with alcohol, finds the bottle, thinks it's liquor, and unleashes the phantom ... In "The Wall of Flesh" (12) a mad doctor feeds his pretty, non-compliant nurse to a literal wall of flesh he has growing in a room (a "flesh bank" instead of a blood bank), but before it digests the woman her fiance pulls her out and saves her. (In an EC comic he would probably have pulled her out only to find that all that's left is half-eaten bones!) "Death Fish" (14) is a fifty-foot marlin that keeps the bodies of the luckless fishermen who hunt it as trophies in an undersea cavern.

"The Aged Curse" in *Haunted* 8 is a little gem on a familiar theme. Horace Lowry is the young and miserable head of an old folk's home wherein he allows his charges to wear rags and go without needed blankets. An old man comes to the door seeking shelter, but is cruelly turned away by Lowry. "Would you treat yourself this way?" the old man asks him as he goes off into the cold night. The next day everyone notices that Lowry seems older; he is turning gray and getting wrinkles. By the end of the day he is so aged that the staff assumes he is a senile new patient and puts him away in the proper wing. Lowry breaks out, hoping to convince someone of who he really is, and he encounters the old man he turned away the night before. Showing him much more kindness than Lowry did him, he gathers him up and takes him back to the nursing home. Lowry, now just wanting rest and warmth and kindness, is brought before the new headmaster, who is, of course, himself, and he experiences his own callousness and hatred from the other side of the desk as the old man, Father Time, vanishes and reminds him of what he said: "would you treat *yourself* this way?"

"The Greatest Secret on Earth" (*Haunted* 14) posited the fascinating theory that human beings are all controlled by gigantic beings called "ids"—literal manifestations of our subconscious—that use invisible energy strings to force men and women to behave the way they do as off-screen the ids use their "puppets"—people—to play out dramas they fabricate for their entertainment. They see humans as nothing more than mindless marionettes who exist only for their amusement. Steve Drummond learns the truth after he feels compelled to commit suicide, but manages to survive a fall from forty stories. Thereafter he can see the strings that are attached to everyone's bodies, but no one will believe him. He resists further inclinations to kill himself, confronts the ids face to face (more or less), and manages to survive his encounter with them, but in the end he must submit as everyone else does, although before he expires he convinces another man that what he's saying is true....

"The Slithering Horror of Skontong Swamp" and "The Ghost of Fanciful Hawkins," both in the fifth issue, were fairly standard script-wise—the first had a convict escaping into a swamp full of demonic creatures while the second had a murdered man's ghost getting even with his killer and paying a nightly call on his beloved for decades after—but were beautifully drawn (the first by George Evans, the second by Bob Powell), the art well-composed and dramatic, with atmosphere to spare.

The cover of *This Magazine Is Haunted* 7 depicts a chemist looking on in astonishment as an ghoulish imp materializes out of a beaker. The cover of the tenth issue was a bit more grisly: a fisherman netting an ugly severed head that is dripping much blood from the neck yet is grinning as if still alive. The eleventh issue had a highly dramatic cover in which Dr. Death looks on as a man is confronted by a skeleton holding a noose in its hand. The thirteenth issue showed men hacking a head out of a block of cement as the headless owner, its neck a gruesome red circle of blood, advances into the room behind them, Dr. Death cackling under the logo.

The magazine lasted 14 issues, then an additional seven issues were published by Charlton comics in 1953. In the first Charlton issue, *This Magazine Is Haunted* 15, there was no sign of Dr. Death, but there was a "Black Cat" derivative in which a man puts his rival inside a cement mixer and then plants his body in the ceiling of his new house, only to be driven crazy by alleged sights and sounds caused by the corpse, culminating in his confession. Much better was a mini-masterpiece called "Monsters of the Deep." In this some unfortunate sailors encounter sea creatures that have fed on humans for so many years that, while still green and scaly, they have taken on a human appearance. What's worse, immediately after feasting on a luckless person, the monster's face takes on the characteristics of the person it ate—future victims are then attacked by a creature that resembles one of their friends! Some thieves come aboard the ship, throw the surviving sailors overboard, and then are set upon by hungry monsters that look just like the men they killed. Meanwhile, Dr. Death returned for the sixteenth issue and was eventually joined, however briefly, by other hosts such as the Mummy.

Haunted began to publish stories that were obvious imitations of the EC Style, but while the stories were often gruesome, they were never quite as repellant or graphic as EC could be. Some of the stories were mere scripted puns—a woman who always tells her husband that his face could stop a clock winds up dying because a clock literally stops as his dead face stares at it—or had endings that made you groan, such as one in which an evil hunchback builds a monument to show the city that he is really straight and upright on the inside, only the building turns out to be the Leaning Tower of Pisa.

Occasionally there was an interesting new story: "The Curse of the Odyssey" (*TMIH* 20) presented a crew of adventurers who discover the lost treasure of Ulysses, but ignore the curse on it. While taking it back to the States they discover that somehow they've gone through a time warp and must face all the dangers that bedeviled the Greek hero and his men—Lotus eaters, who drug men and consume them raw; giant cyclopes; Circe; and Scylla and Charybdis. The idea was good but the art too mediocre to make it that memorable. In "Tunnel of Terror" (*TMIH* 21) amusement park visitors are chopped up by the exhibits and ground up inside a giant demonic statue. Each Charlton issue would feature at least one reprint from the earlier Fawcett issues.

Charlton brought out a second volume of *This Magazine Is Haunted* in 1957. The company would typically substitute one title for another and continue with the numbering of the original title, so the first issue of volume two was actually the twelfth. The stories were now introduced by a weird figure in a green hat and cloak called Dr. Haunt who sometimes appeared in them as well; in fact he became quite intrusive, and his appearances, which seemed like padding, often slowed down the pace of the stories. Like the later Marvel Comics' character the Watcher, Dr. Haunt claimed he could only observe events and tell about them later, although, like the Watcher, he did tinker with things from time to time. Steve Ditko did much of the artwork for the series, and probably worked on many of the scripts as well.

The fourteenth issue had a couple of stories that aimed for minor pathos: a lonely man who's always been different—he could go months without food—discovers that he is a plant-based life form and is completely alone in the world; another man wastes his life and grows old waiting for a re-appearance of a beautiful mermaid he fell in love with—but the final story was little more than a rip off of *The Incredible Shrinking Man* or the Richard Matheson novel it was based on. The following issue had a bizarre story, "Past Imperfect," about a scholar who is determined to prove that Alexander the Great was no hero but a hated monster, and he entrusts his wayward son to a colleague's care while he travels for further research. His son admires Alexander and the times he lives in, so when he enters a time machine to get away from police who want to arrest him for murder, he winds up back in those ancient days. What's more he *becomes* Alexander the Great, the very man his father most despises, although the older man mercifully remains unaware of the conqueror's true identity. This second volume of *This Magazine* was largely mediocre and didn't last past sixteen issues. Other artists for both volumes of the Charlton series included Dick Ayers and Mike Sekowsky.

Worlds of Fear

Worlds of Fear, Stories of Weird Adventure hit newsstands in 1952. "City of Fearful Night" (*WOF* 2) was a satisfyingly creepy tale about a man, Frank Thompson, who misses his flight, takes a train, and winds up in a strange small town which turns out to be purgatory, where dead souls who died too soon due to accidents or murders await the opportunity to move on to the next level. But Thompson is different from the other people there, who develop demonic forms at night, and they believe he has somehow cheated death. They chase after him, tearing at him for the "secret" and he barely manages to make it back onto a train at the depot. He discovers that the plane he was to have taken crashed with no survivors, and he was supposed to have died; his entry into the town of the dead was simple error. "The Devil's Prize" in the same issue concerned John Dirge, who has himself committed as a way of covering up an act of embezzlement. But three of his associates have conspired to let him rot in the asylum while they merrily spend the money he stole. To get even with them, Dirge makes a deal with a satanic stranger to get out by occupying the bodies of other men but he can only do it three times. As he enters another person's body he is temporarily taken into an alternate dimension where horrible shadowy forms wait to get their hands on him. He does manage to kill his three betrayers but he is unable to leave the last possessed body and winds up back in that eerie dimension which, of course, is Hell. Both stories had familiar themes but were done with enough panache and good art to make them stand out from similar stories. A third story in the issue, a more standard tale of a kind man who becomes a werewolf, had especially fine artwork by Sheldon Moldoff.

"The Metamorphosis of the Gkmloooms" (*WOF* 3) was an early study of radiation mutation with an escape artist named Commanger, doing an exhibition in Japan, winding up in an undersea world below Hiroshima where mutated survivors of the H-bomb explosions have gathered together and plan to transform the entire human race into misshapen blobs. Commanger is experimented on but manages to escape, but when he reaches the surface he discovers that he's already undergone metamorphosis, causing his fiancee to go into understandable shock. It wouldn't be long before countless movies, comics and TV shows would go into the grotesque horrors of atomic radiation and mutation.

"The Dead Lover Returns" (*WOF* 4) was the story of Ted Femur, who is killed in a boating mishap shortly after seeing a lovely woman on a ferry. In the afterlife, he complains that he died too young to experience love, and asks to go back to the real world and romance the woman from the ferry. He is told that if he finds the right woman she will see him as he was in life, but his true, hideous decomposing form will become more apparent to her as she falls in love with him. If they are meant to be together, however, the woman will also wither and die and take her place beside him. After scaring many possible females with his grotesque appearance, Ted finally locates the object of his desire—as promised, she sees him as he used to be—and there is an immediate attraction between the two as there was on the ferry. A man named Bud has asked the woman, Helen, to marry him, but she puts him off after meeting Ted. Ted appears to Bud in the latter's car, to try to talk to him about Helen, and causes a non-fatal accident. Helen goes away to think, Ted follows, and the two embark on a whirlwind romance, culminating in Helen agreeing to marry Ted. But as they drive off to get married, Ted sees that Helen is beginning to take on the look of death, and realizes that if he allows her to become a ghastly spirit he is only being selfish. He lies and tells her he was just stringing her along and has no intention of marrying her, and urges her to go back to Bud, who is in the hospital. Helen finally sees Ted as he really is, and he goes off to his dark domain unfulfilled and unloved. The suspenseful story is moving as well as grotesque and can be taken as a metaphor for the kind of all-consuming, self-centered desire for love that can and often does destroy both the loved one and the lover.

In contrast, "The Resurrected Head" in the same issue is a wild, lurid tale of a mad scientist who keeps the severed heads of animals alive and is dying for a human subject. A gangster arranges for his boss to become the doctor's subject so that he can take over the rackets and use the unlucky man's brain to plan capers. Unfortunately, things don't quite work out the way anyone intended. In "The Fleshless Ones" (*WOF* 10) a man uncovers a conspiracy by living skeletons, who have a society beneath the earth, to infiltrate and take over mankind by kidnapping humans, completely skinning them, and then using the skinned flesh to cover a skeletal creature so he can take the dead person's place.

Strange Suspense Stories

Strange Suspense Stories also appeared in 1952. The first issue certainly lived up to the title as it presented three very suspenseful and macabre stories, two of which were especially noteworthy. "The Man Who Warmed the Bones of the Dead" concerned an old man who has been hired to tend the furnace of a forbidding mansion in the woods, and who gets locked inside the house with a broken leg, painfully climbing up from one floor to the next as he tries to avoid ghastly unseen spirits who are after him. Bob Powell's art for this was quite evocative and effective, with the man's panicked expressions perfectly delineated. In "He Bartered His Head" a nasty man is given a statue that can bring luck, but is told that there is a price to be paid: after a year the statue will lose its head and so will the one who possesses it. What follows is a tense roundelay as the man tries desperately to outrun his grisly fate after he sees that the statue no longer has a head.

The second issue presented a bizarre piece entitled "Aieee! The Teeth!" about two rival dentists, Stanley and Arch. Stanley hates and is jealous of the more successful Arch, and finds him so patronizing that while he is under anesthesia—the two treat each other's teeth—he pulls out all of his pearly whites. A distraught, furious Arch chases after Stanley and falls to his death, which is ruled accidental (even with a mouthful of missing teeth!) Stanley fashions the dead man's teeth into a dental plate as a macabre souvenir, but like the usual disembodied hand, the teeth follow him around everywhere, biting him, and ultimately driving him into a nut house. Stanley needs to have all of his teeth extracted, and winds up choking to death on his new dental plate, convinced he is wearing his victim's teeth inside his mouth.

The startling cover of the third issue pictured a headless man running across a bridge towards a screaming woman. The inside stories boasted high-quality art by Bernard Bailey and George Evans: "Brother Volcano" deals with a village that is saved from a greedy developer by the spirit of a dead man who lives inside and controls a volcano; and "Port of Terror" concerns a crook who is pursued by the headless man of the cover, who was beheaded by the villain and now wants to exchange his murderer's head for his own missing cranium, which he does with the aid of a boat's propeller.

Charlton took over *Strange Suspense Stories* as it had *This Magazine Is Haunted* and began the numbering with sixteen in 1953. The lead story was a oddball concoction in which a husband and wife, both of whom are surgeons (but apparently *not* transsexuals), fascinated by a recent sex-change operation (one assumes Christine Jorgensen), decide to perform surgery on each other so that each resembles his/her spouse. The wife, who now looks like the husband, murders the husband, who now looks like the wife, but when circumstances dictate that she reveal the truth about herself, no one will believe her (simply stripping would have revealed the truth as artificial penises were still quite a bit in the future). The story had an intriguing premise but was developed without logic or intelligence. The rest of the issue was filled with crime double-cross and retribution stories. A gimmick of the comic was that the endings of some of the stories were deliberately left out and readers were invited to send in their own wind-ups, the best of which would be illustrated in a subsequent issue.

Strange Suspense Stories 21 finally presented an out and out horror/supernatural story with "This Bite is Sweet," a vampire tale whose blood-sucker, writer Peter North, has a conscience, which hasn't prevented him from amassing a number of victims in a town in the Pyrenees. He has fallen in love with Monique, but is horrified to realize that there is something especially tasty about her family's blood. Knowing that he won't be able to avoid succumbing to his unnatural desire and will eventually kill her, he contrives to have her drive a stake through his heart, sacrificing his own life for hers. North is a "modern" vampire in that he can go about by daylight and his affliction has none of the Dracula-like trappings of the more old-fashioned bloodsucker. The rather tasteless "Killer's Arms" in the following issue presented the one-armed Professor Morton, his daughter, Anne, and her fiance, Jonathan, who happens to be her father's assistant. The trio trek into the jungle with the plan of using a gorilla's arm to replace Morton's missing limb, Jonathan assuring the uneasy Anne that after this he will marry her, retire and write a book. They have the misfortune to be attacked by a ferocious man-killing ape, who tears off Jonathan's arms. (We see blood at the joints under the man's clothing but not the torn off limbs.) The father attaches the dead gorilla's arms to Jonathan's body, but Jonathan can't control them and they attack Morton, who throws his grafting serum into the younger man's face. The solution gives Jonathan a bestial appearance and affects his mind so that he runs off with Anne in his arms, reminding her how he planned to marry her and retire, the implication being that the woman will spend whatever life is left to her being ravaged by an ape-man.

The series continued well into the silver age, but stories like the above were no longer included. Artists included Dick Giordano, Artie Cappello, Joe Shuster, and Steve Ditko.

Beware! Terror Tales

Beware! Terror Tales also came out from Fawcett in 1952. Stories were introduced by a grinning mummy in a hood. During its short run *Beware! Terror Tales* was an entertaining comic with some suspenseful and well-drawn stories, even if most were unspectacular. There were a few notable items, however. In "Death's Round Trip" (*BTT* 3) Dr. Albert Carlton has decided to gain fame by exploring the after-life as he stops his heart for fifteen minutes. An older associate, Dr. Clode, will then start a machine that will pump blood through Carlton's veins and bring him back to life. Carlton "dies" and winds up in a bizarre purgatory in which assorted ghouls and demons attempt to stop him from leaving. Suddenly, their efforts cease and Carlton finds himself free to run toward the mystic ferry boat that will take him back to the land of the living, as he chortles at his triumph over Death. But as the passengers on the arriving ferry boat disembark, Carlton sees Dr. Clode, who had tried to warn him that he had a weak heart and who died during the previous fifteen minutes; Carlton had simply arrived a quarter of an hour before he was scheduled to. Now both men are truly dead. While Carlton is an arrogant person in some ways, you can't help but feel he got a raw deal.

"Horror at the Lighthouse" in *BTT* 6 is an effective horror tale that employs a time-honored sea monster but adds an extra dimension of terror. This huge, tentacled monstrosity is intelligent and telepathic and demands that a light house keeper deliberately steer ships onto the rocks so it can have human victims to feed upon. The new keeper, Lester Junes, is horrified to learn what the old man he is replacing has been doing to save his own skin, but after the latter is consumed by the creature—not being the keeper anymore he serves no useful purpose other than as food—Lester finds he has no desire to wind up in the beast's belly either and complies with its terrible wishes. After the people on board four boats are devoured, Lester fears he will either be accused of murder for directing them onto the shoals, or they will be seen as accidents and he will be replaced. The story ends with him realizing that no matter what happens he will wind up as food for the monster as soon as his usefulness is ended....

The seventh issue had two interesting stories: "The Man Who Defeated Death," in which a chess master plays chess with Death and tries to beat him at his own game; and "The Walking Cadaver," in which a man rents out the bodies of the recently departed into which he transfers the minds of his clients. The eighth and final issue featured three compelling, well-paced tales concerning a man who transforms townspeople into a legion of large, deadly eagles; a junk dealer whose interest in a ouija board leads to his demise; and a young railroad station master who comes afoul of a demonic whip-wielding figure who causes one disastrous train crash after another.

Fawcett's *Strange Stories from Another World* debuted in 1952. "To turn the cover is to pry loose the lid of musty coffins and unleash eerie and terrible beings beyond all imagination" read ad copy for the comic. "The Rain, the Deadly Rain" (*Strange Stories* 5) was an interesting variation on the old formula of a god strenuously objecting when jewels, in this case a pair of diamonds set in the eyes, are taken from its statue. This deity is a rain god and it pursues the offending party throughout the world using water—shipwrecks, quicksand, heavy rain fall and so on—in one attempt after another to murder him. Finally the thief acquires the statue itself and installs it in his basement, hoping to somehow appease it, but the god is furious at being blinded and will not relent. The thief tries to sacrifice a young woman to the rain god but her husband prevents this, and the thief runs out into the rain, which dissolves his flesh like acid. In "The Flaming Witness" in the same issue a man pushes his partner into a molten vat in their steel mill and is plagued with a series of attacks by a fiery creature that contains the dead man's soul. The murderer orders the ingot containing his victim's remains flattened into sheets. Unfortunately, these sheets are used in the construction of a train car, in which the murderer becomes a passenger, being incinerated when the fire-being reappears for its ultimate revenge. *Strange Stories* did not have a long run.

Worlds Beyond, Stories of Weird Adventure was a 1951 one-shot with three entertaining stories about a painting with a curse on it; a man who encounters death and his own ancestors in a mental trip inside his own body during a dangerous surgical operation; and a pilot who abandons his plane and passengers when the ship catches fire and has to deal with some voodoo justice when he boards the very same plane some time later. *Unknown World*, another one-shot, came out in 1952. In the creepy "The Sea of the Dead" a sailor jumps aboard what he thinks is his new ship only to discover it's been abandoned—except by the ghosts of those who drowned when the ship hit a reef thanks to the sea man's carelessness. This ghost ship has come back from the deep to claim the captain who abandoned all the passengers, with nary a warning, to save himself. "The Serpent Queen" was a wild tale in which adventurers climb a mountain to encounter a hundreds-year-old queen with a beautiful body and a mask over her face, some skeletons whose heads are oddly preserved with the flesh still on them, and a gigantic serpent that slithers out of a cave with demonic hunger. The craziest story in the book, however, was "Footprints on the Ceiling," in which a dog that has definitely died remains "alive" and animated (and in agony) and becomes a vaudeville attraction even as hordes of the undead chase after its owner attempting to claim the pathetic animal as their own.

Horror and borderline horror was also featured in some of Fawcett's crime comics. *Suspense Detective* (1952), for instance, had a strong element of tension and terror along with the suspense. The first issue was a winner, with three excellent stories. In the first, three small criminals try to escape a prison by winding their way through a pipeline that makes its way to the river, but first they kill an old convict who knows too much about their plans. On the appointed day they decide to stick to their plans despite a bad storm. Crawling through the pipe, they are nearly at the end and freedom when they discover that the storm rains have washed the old con's body from the pump house into the pipe and it's completely blocking their exit as the water in the pipe rises and rises. Another story has an old man discover the identity of the person burning down tenements, but he's attacked by the felon and left paralyzed in the hospital, unable to speak, before he can tell anyone. The firebug comes to see him and promises to burn down the hospital that very evening. Desperately the man tries to alert the authorities by using his eyelids to telegraph morse code. The third story has a woman racing against time to find the true killer responsible for the murder for which her husband, sitting on death row, was convicted.

The second issue maintained the high quality. One story has a murder victim and the witness to the crime, a mute, walled up in a building under construction as the mute's father tries to find him and the mute struggles to escape his confinement before he runs out of air. Another story features a desperate chase as a man who had hid a time bomb in his business partners' car races after them when he discovers his wife is in the same car. With the third issue there seemed to be a change of direction, with the more intense tales downplayed in favor of more standard crime stories. However *SD* 4 has an interesting story about a sinister nursing home that has its own "Torture Room" where inmates are killed for insurance, and *SD* 5 has an intense tale wherein a woman who witnesses a man murder her wealthy employer winds up in a coffin with him, about to be buried, as her boyfriend rushes about on a frantic search for her.

CHARLTON

In addition to *This Magazine Is Haunted* and *Strange Suspense Stories*, continued from Fawcett publications, Charlton had another golden age horror title: *The Thing* had an auspicious debut in 1952 as three of the four stories in its premiere issue are memorable. The stories in each issue were introduced by an unseen person or creature billed as "The Thing." "Grunwald" is a harrowing piece about an attack on a lighthouse by hordes of voracious and aggressive rats that have jumped off an abandoned ship that floats up to the island of Grunwald. At one point the men trapped inside the lighthouse are confused by the fact that it's still dark out even thought it's morning, until they realize that the rats *have completely covered the windows* and are blocking out the sunlight. "Nightmare" is about Hiram Crane, a timid man with disturbing dreams who is afraid he is being followed on the subway. He lifts up the hat of a man sleeping on a seat nearby and discovers he has been beheaded. There is a headhunter on the loose but police have kept it out of the papers (their blasé attitude towards the deaths adds another chilling dimension to the story). Hiram turns out to be the (amnesiac) killer, and when he is cornered by the cops lifts off his head to explain why he wasn't electrocuted by the subway's third rail during the chase: he's already dead. "Hellfire of Doom" is the name used by an unknown person who blackmails a city by using infra-red rays to cause spontaneous combustion among several innocent people. The villain, unmasked as a reporter, is so loathsome that he reminds one of the fiendish monsters fought by the masked character, the Spider, in the old pulp magazine stories. The fourth and lead story, "The Creature," is about a monster pulled to earth from another dimension as it takes the place of an ape pushed into this other world. Albert Tyler and Bob Forgione did all the art.

The stories in *The Thing* 2 were not as effective but were nevertheless entertaining. The lead story was basically a borrowing of Poe's "Masque of the Red Death'; the rest had to do with a man with the face and horns of a bull; a scrawny scientist who beats up his sadistic lab assistant after taking a growth formula but comes afoul of a hungry white rat who sampled the same solution; and an unnecessary sequel to "The Creature." Subsequent issues generally maintained a steady quality of mediocrity in story and art, although the comic remained entertaining. Things got a bit grisly in *The Thing* 11 with a reworking of "Hansel and Gretel" in which the old woman tries to eat a married couple but they turn the tables on her and turn out to be flesh-feasting ghouls themselves; and "Beyond the Past," in which an old professor summons a hungry demon from (Lovecraft's) Necronomicon and in the final panel winds up a terrible stew of bones, fluid, and a half-eaten head (with the glasses still on it) for his poor daughter to find.

The Thing definitely entered EC territory with another perverse and gory fairy tale, "Cinderella," in the twelfth issue. In this Cinderella's step-sisters and step-mother are vampires who murdered the girl's father. Their plan is to bewitch the handsome prince at the ball, thereby gaining them access to the richest blood in the kingdom. Cinderella goes to the ball and tries to warn the prince, but the clock strikes twelve before she can do so. At home she is murdered by her angry, blood-drinking "relatives." The prince tries to find the woman who fits the slipper, but only discovers Cinderella's corpse. He invites her step-sisters to try on the slipper, and tells their mother that each of them was a perfect fit for the shoe—then reveals their corpses, with the ladies' severed legs wedged into multiple slippers. It seems that the prince is also a blood-drinker and is furious that the gals deprived him of his prey. Despite the black comic tone of the piece it is depressing because, unlike the real fairy tale, it offers absolutely no hope: no matter who she turned to Cinderella was doomed from the start; even the prince was no prince but a monster. Also in *The Thing* 12 was "The Mummy's Curse," in which a murderous female mummy, of huge size and overbearing ugliness, is revived and goes on a killing spree; and "The Sound of Death," in which a wealthy and completely untalented violinist uses deadly sound waves to kill off the critics who dared to tell the truth about him, but winds up undone by his own manipulations.

The Thing 14 had an even more gruesome story entitled "The Evil Eye." Warren Cairo tries to kill off his crippled Indian wife Gerda, but she survives the accident he plans, enters the cabin he hoped to occupy during a cruise, and uses a mystical device to brand his forehead with a red hot searing symbol, the pain of which can only be eased by sea water. As Warren lies helpless, a horde of rats attack him and chew off most of his arms and legs. Somehow he manages to push himself overboard, but he is unable to rise to the surface. A smiling Gerda makes the identification of his mutilated remains.

The Thing 15, besides having a memorable cover depicting gigantic, slobbering worms destroying a metropolis, featured an above average monster story entitled "The Worm Turns." In this a scientist creates one of a unique worm-like species that is impervious to disease or injury and with which he hopes to discover ways to make humans equally invulnerable to death. But when his girlfriend objects to the horrible, hungry creature he's been growing, he murders her and feeds her to the worm. The worm monster breaks out of its containment, multiplies, and takes over the earth, becoming one gargantuan creature spreading across continents feeding on what's left of the vegetation. But this is not the end of the human race, as some survivors have hidden *inside* the worm, and destroy the monster from within, creating deadly tumors, finally breaking out to begin life anew. The story had nice art by Steve Ditko. Other artists for *The Thing* were Lou Morales, Dick Ayers, and Anthony Tallarico.

"If Looks Could Kill" in the same issue features a man, blinded by an opponent whom he kills, who manages to transplants the dead man's eyes into his own (apparently the opthalmologist to end them all) and discovers they can emit a burning ray that takes care of all his enemies, including an unfaithful wife, before he makes the mistake of looking in a mirror. "Family Mix-up" is a dark gem in which a fat wife and her skinny husband, who have grown to despise each other as well as each other's appearance, take out life insurance policies and scheme to kill one another, with botched and gruesomely comical results. "Nothing He Couldn't Do" (*Thing* 16) is a depressing tale of four men, captured by cannibals, who figure they won't all be killed at once because human flesh spoils very quickly. Unfortunately, three of them wind up in the pots at the same time because the fourth has been tortured into telling the natives how to keep meat fresh in cans. The panels depicting this poor man—the only one of the four who is decent—numb from terror and agony, with a nail driven straight through his head, are quite disturbing, not to mention the whole idea of people being boiled for dinner while still alive.

Charlton's *This is Suspense* (1955) presented a fairly well done and faithful adaptation of "Dr. Jekyll and Mr. Hyde" in its first issue (the numbering began with 23), although this was not touted on the cover; there were only the words: "To what extent would a brilliant young chemist go to win his love?" In subsequent issues of the short-lived series, however, the comic presented no further horror tales but rather well-done if standard mystery and suspense stories.

HARVEY

Harvey's The Black Cat was a popular super-heroine who was an actress by day and a crime-fighter by night. As the popularity of costumed heroes began to wane, her comic took a dip in sales, and it was decided to rechristen it *Black Cat Mystery* with the thirtieth issue in 1951. The Black Cat herself introduced the stories in that issue, claiming she would be appearing in some of them, but she wasn't seen again for quite a while. Of *BCM* 30's stories, "Gateway to Death" has two men using a machine to venture into an alternate dimension, only to realize they are apparently in the scalp of an enormous alien creature, while "The Werewolf Must Kill" was a standard if suspenseful tale of a man-wolf who stalks his own brother and the brother's fiancee. Sales of the comic increased enough for it to go back on a monthly schedule. Most of the covers were done by Lee Elias. There were a few grisly covers —a rotting severed head in a beaker; a desiccated skeleton—but the most notorious was for the fiftieth issue which depicted the lower half of a man's face gorily disintegrating due to a blast of "White Heat."

Black Cat Mystery had its share of gruesome stuff on the inside pages as well: "Satan's Suit" (32) had a man down on his luck buying a suit to wear to his college reunion, but the suit, which had been worn by a dead man, sucks away his life and literally makes the poor fellow's flesh fall from his bones. In "Army of Scorpions" (33) a deranged man orders a horde of cat-sized scorpions to attack anyone who harms insects, but when he throws one at his horrified girlfriend and it splatters on the wall, the little devils interpret it as an attack on them, swarm on the man, and leave behind a nibbled and desiccated corpse. "Rotting Demons" (36) features two treasure hunters who come upon the ruins of an eighteenth century pirate ship in the Louisiana swamps, as well as a bevy of corpse-like pirate demons in various, graphic stages of decay. The two men outwit the demons and manage to escape from them—the demons collapse into puddles of putrescence if they try to leave the area of the ship—only to discover they have been infected with their decay, and will also dissolve into grisly slop if they try to flee; they commit suicide instead. "He" (38) is a story of a deranged innkeeper who eats human flesh and carves up his victims with a sharp swinging pendulum in his basement. "The Body Maker" (39) is an ugly man so desirous of a mate that he decides to build one by removing body parts from different women. First he amputates and carries off the legs from a woman purported to have the most beautiful gams in the world. Then he acquires hands, torso, and head, but his seeking tresses of perfect blonde hair proves his undoing as the stolen hair gets caught on a swinging signpost and strangles him in a freak accident.

"Doomsday" (40) is a mini-masterpiece in which a reporter tells how he was assigned to interview a weird old scientist who insisted that the earth was facing calamity. He had been contacted by a monstrous humanoid alien creature who was coming to earth to replenish its food supply: people. The gargantuan creature surprises the authorities and military by actually bursting up from the bowels of the earth and immediately begins snatching up people and popping them into his jaws. The army can not stop him, and he lays waste to city after city as he literally devours the population of the planet over the next couple of years. At the end the reporter tries to dodge the monster's gigantic hand and it seems that he has managed to escape—until we learn that he has been giving his report from *inside the belly of the monster* where he now resides with the remnants of the human race. "Man is a tenacious creature," he writes. "He lives anyplace if given half the chance." While in some ways similar to the aforementioned "The Worm Turns" in *The Thing* 15, this was a little more intense.

Black Cat Mystery, like many horror comics, began to imitate the very popular EC comics, presenting tales of "impact," in 1953. "The Old Mill Stream" (51) has a husband and wife team luring men into their trap and grinding their blood and bones into pinkish flour. "Punch and Rudy" in the same issue has a rejected punch-drunk fighter using his ex-manager's head as a literal punching bag (the panel that was to depict said head in all its gory glory was left blank, however, but the idea still came across). In several issues the comic also presented black comedy parodies of movies such as *High Noon*, *Mogambo*, and *Come Back, Little Sheba* in tales collectively known as "The Silver Scream." But the comic wasn't that great and none of this was enough to drive up flagging sales; the crackdown on horror comics didn't help. The fifty-third issue consisted of reprints and the comic became *Black Cat Western* with the fifty-fourth issue, featuring mostly reprints of old Black Cat adventures. After six issues of this, the comic was then turned into *Black Cat Mystic* which lasted three issues, presenting benign fantasy stories, many of which were reprints.

Black Cat Mystery was not an outstanding series, but it did publish its share of notable stories. In addition to those previously mentioned there were: "Trick the Devil" (35)—a man agrees to give Satan his soul when he dies but asks to live forever, which he does, even after he is beheaded for murder and Satan makes off with his head so he can neither, see, speak

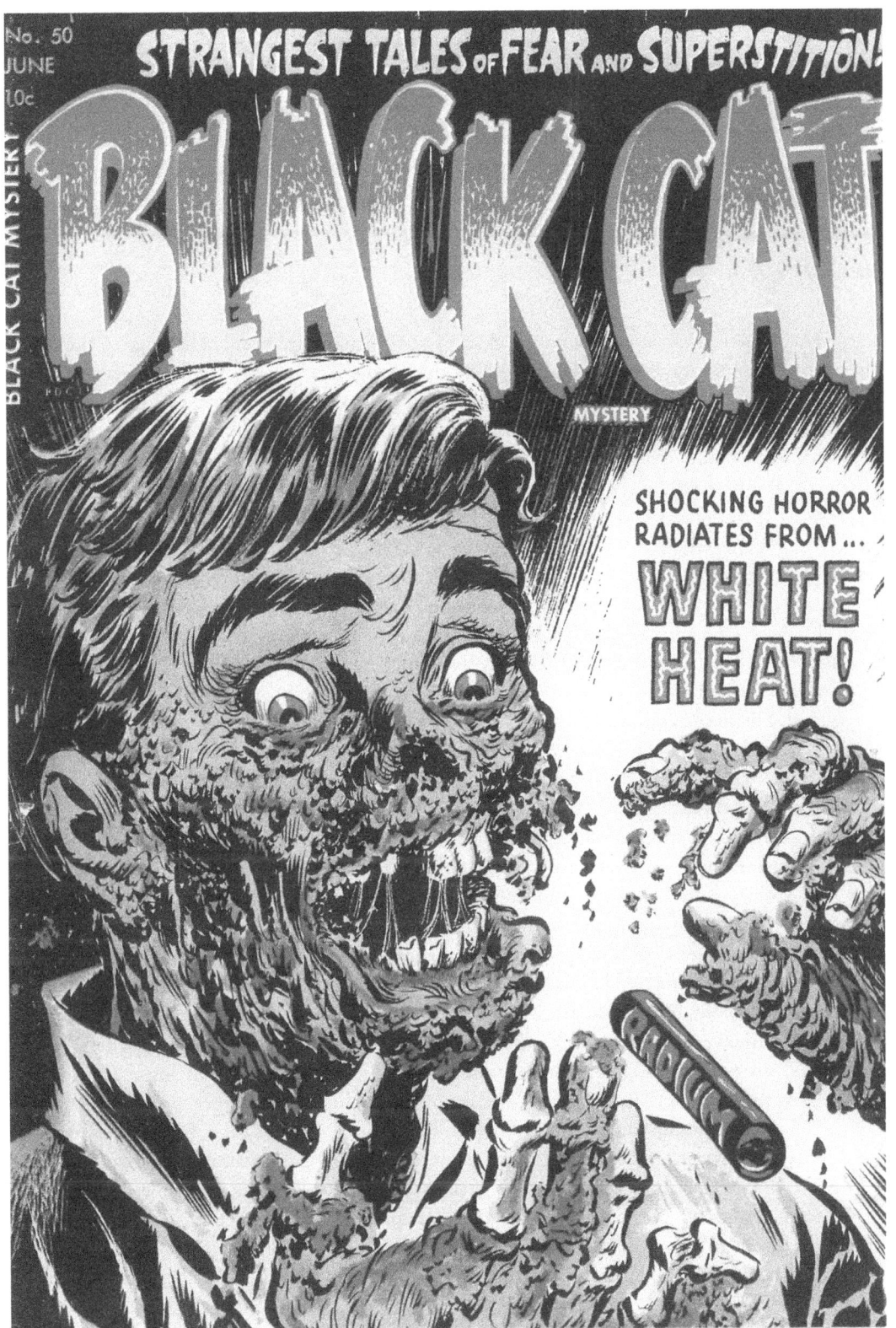

A classic gore cover from Harvey's *Black Cat Mystery* 50.

nor eat for an eternity; "The Visitor" (42)—a scientist brings a creature from another dimension into our world then discovers he must deliver human minds to it to feed on or he will have to sacrifice his own intellect instead; "The Lonely" (48)—a man murders another by throwing him overboard but when he winds up alone on a deserted island the man's rotting corpse becomes his very best friend.

Witches Tales

Harvey's *Witches Tales* debuted in 1951. (The title may have been an homage to the first horror radio show, *The Witch's Tale*.) The third issue boasted an excellent story entitled "Tombstones to Tibet" about an ill-fated expedition to a temple on top of a snow-covered mountain. The members of the expedition are after an idol that will reportedly grant three wishes, but before they arrive at the top they must contend with one man's falling to his death, ghastly zombie-like creatures who come out of a cave, grotesque vulture-eagles who claw away one man's eyesight, and walls of ice that drip blood when attacked by pickaxe because they hold the bodies of men frozen inside. Once inside the temple there is a desperate struggle to gain the idol and its precious wishes, which it is suggested, are only the stuff of legends, and wouldn't do dead men much good in any case.

In "Art for Death's Sake" (*WT* 15) Artist Paul Chambre is told that his morbid paintings lack reality because they are painted only from imagination. He decides to terrorize a pretty young model and paint her in realistic poses, which greatly improves his work. He keeps the woman a prisoner, and subjects her to a variety of horrors all for the sake of his art, until she is mad and looks almost elderly. When the model's brother tracks her down and realizes what Chambre has done to his sister, he pushes him into a cauldron of molten bronze. The artist manages to pull himself out, but is covered with rapidly hardening and agonizing red-hot bronze. Ironically, the resultant statue inside which is Chambre's body is hailed as the missing artist's finest work. "He finally caught the right expression of realistic horror," declares a critic.

The comic featured plenty of monsters: Invitation to Doom" (*WT* 7) features a remarkably stupid scientist who, impressed with the longevity of certain tree species, injects himself with their fluid and turns into a malevolent tree creature, snatching up people and crushing them in his branches. Uprooting himself (or itself) the killer tree goes on the rampage, until the well-placed blows of an ax finally end its reign of terror. In "Demon Flies" (*WT* 8) a crazy scientist discovers a breed of unknown fly that can wipe out spiders, and uses them to feast upon his peers, who laughed at him, leaving only skeletons behind. Realizing that the flies are growing larger and may become difficult to control, he breeds a larger spider to take care of them, but winds up caught in its web. (Disappointingly, he isn't eaten but burns to death when he knocks into a chemical beaker on a table.) "It" (*WT* 10) features another mad scientist who creates a protoplasmic blob that has an insatiable desire for human blood, for which he brings it many living specimens to feast upon. He lets loose a host of these creatures on the university from which he was fired, egging them on to devour student, faculty member, and board member alike, until he, too, is consumed when his creations' hunger gets the better of it. In "The Web of the Spider" (*WT* 12) yet another loony scientist creates a serum that turns men into giant spiders. He uses the serum on himself and terrorizes the city, walking off with payroll trucks and the like. When he catches his secretary spying on him, he throws her into a huge web where his spider-men close in for the kill, but before their jaws can close on her he metamorphoses, springs on the web, and decides to finish her off himself. But before he can do the deed he begins turning back into a man, having built up an immunity to the serum. The secretary, who has already become unhinged due to the slobbering horror she has been exposed to, laughs hysterically as she realizes her boss is going to be devoured right along with her by his own creations.

There was occasional gore in the comic but not too much of it: A man is picked up by a giant bird and fed to the babies in its nest, his arm bloodily torn off in one bird's beak. (18). In "A Matter of Taste" (19) a wife is fed up with the way her glutinous husband mistreats her so she feeds him a special dish, which he loves, which turns out to be his equally unpleasant mother—or so the reader is led to believe. But it turns out Mom is alive and well, but after the traumatic experience junior may never be the same. It was like a gruesome story done by EC if EC had been kinder and gentler. Similarly, "Mother Mongoose's Nursery Crimes," a one-page strip in two parts, was a much milder imitation of EC's grosser nursery tales.

Witch's Tales was not always influenced by EC in the more obvious ways, but the influence was there. "Mutiny on the Boundary" (24) was meant to be a horrific parody on "Mutiny on the Bounty," with a lisping Charles Laughton as Captain Bligh treating his men in abysmal fashion, but the ending wherein he gets his comeuppance completely lacks the visceral gut-wrenching impact of an EC tale. "Eye, Eye, Sir" in the same issue was a more successful private eye parody, with the detective's client, who wants him to find her husband, a gorgeous babe who wears glasses. Throughout the story every man comments that she'd be really hot without the glasses "but isn't bad as she is." No one can figure out why the husband would run away from such a beauty. At the end the husband turns up dead and the private dick finally has his chance with the lady, during which she takes off her glasses. Instead of eyeballs she has sockets, empty except for little candles. "Now you see why my husband left me," she says. The final story in the issue has no horror in it at all, but details the career of a young man who hopes to become a football great so that he, too can be commemorated by one of the statues at the edge of the field. He dies in an accident, but a statue is erected in his name. EC would occasionally run stories like this, but they were generally not as mediocre as this.

One story that EC might well have been proud of was the suitably grotesque "Ali Barber and the Forty Thieves" in *WT* 25. Ali is an extremely unsuccessful, inept and unhappy barber who is behind on his rent, losing all of his customers due to too many nicks, and his wife is nagging him to buy her a new hat. He decides to close up his shop and take his business to conventions, but at the first hotel he goes to he overhears conversation making it clear that there is the largest assemblage of racketeers ever gathered under one roof. He decides to forget about shaving anyone and collect reward money instead, so he goes from room to room under the pretext of giving a shave or haircut and proceeds to use his razor to cut throats and collect the heads of all the gangsters in a basket. Happily he takes his booty downstairs, only to realize that the hotel is actually sponsoring a policeman's convention and he has just beheaded forty *cops*!

In the weird, slightly perverse "Honeymoon" (19) a young couple have a meal in a Chinese restaurant and are given an almond cake that they are told will help them to love each other more. After some silly experiences in a weird netherworld below the subway, they discover that they have switched bodies; because of this they are able to more fully understand each other and therefore do indeed love each other more. The wife declares that they were now "the happiest couple alive—for we had gained what so many couples had hoped for—we were *each other*." A psychologist could probably make much of the wife's—and writer's—assertion that what couples want most of all is to *be* each other; the story doesn't even get into the fact that two presumably heterosexual people, whatever bodies they may be in, will live out their lives with partners who are the same sex and look exactly like them (before the switch); they will be, in essence, making love to themselves. Rather than a story of a husband and wife discovering what it's like to be their spouse, it's more a parable of ultimate narcissism.

The twenty-first issue of *Witch's Tales* had yet another rip-off of "Revenge"—wife points out assailant, whom husband attacks, only to have wife point out yet another assailant—which even appropriated the title. The same issue had a story with a couple inadvertently dragging a corpse of a blackmailer into a surprise party, an idea, as noted, done in other comic stories and later on television. The last two issues of *Witches Tales* consisted of reprint material.

The thirteenth issue had a great cover of a weird creature lowering a hungry rat into a glass jar with terrified tiny people inside it, but the story that related to it on the inside, "The Torture Jar," was poor and hadn't much to do with the horrific cover image. *Witches Tales* had other memorably gruesome covers. The twenty-fourth issue depicted a strange man or ghoul waking up in the city morgue and watching with alarm as two men in the background work on a corpse, while the following issue featured a decomposing severed head hanging from inside a bell that is being rung by a sinister fellow far below at the bottom of the rope.

Chamber of Chills

Chamber of Chills began with an inauspicious twenty-first and twenty-second issues, the numbering apparently continued from another series, in 1951, then came out with a fifth and several subsequent issues the following year. "The Vault of Living Death" in *COC* 22 recounts in grim detail that last hours of a man buried alive after taking an anesthetic, but the other stories were not memorable.

However, "The Shrunken Skull" (*COC* 5) was a minor masterpiece in which a man, Michael, buys a box at an auction, brings it home excitedly, and opens it to discover a shrunken head. Worse, this head speaks and puts him in a trance. The head explains that it belonged to a high priestess who was considered so evil that she was put to death and beheaded, but not before she put a curse on the natives so their flesh would fall off their skin while they slept. The priestess tells Michael that she will grant him success and riches if he goes out and gets a body for her to use. Initially repulsed by the idea, his greed gets the better of him and he decapitates an innocent woman and carries her body back to the priestess. He places the shrunken head on the dead woman's neck—she uses her magic to blend both parts together—and shrieks at the result: "I've never seen anything so horrible!" (Actually the sight of the tiny shriveled head on top of the body of the smartly appointed corpse is rather comical.) Wearing a veil, the priestess accompanies Michael to Africa, where they arrive at her village. The priestess is pleased to see that her curse came true, and all of the natives are now skeletons, which she uses her magic to reanimate. Michael is so repulsed by this, that he cuts the woman's head off, but the skeletons, still alive, come together to slay him. At the end the priestess' head is discovered, sold at auction, and a new man runs home happily with the box.

Chamber of Chills 7 offered a quartet of interesting stories. "Pit of the Damned" deals with a carny owner who dabbles in sorcery in order to populate his chamber of horrors with highly unusual and fearsome ghouls. But he winds up on a disturbing tour of the pits of Hell: people scorched by fire but who can never die; living human heads on pikes crying out in terror. "Garden of Horror" is a semi-comical tale of a man whose garden develops the ability to *instantly* turn anyone who steps into it into a skeleton, be it servant, horticulturist, or interested passers by. "The Seal of Satan" is one of the better stories dealing with the popular theme of a gambler making an unholy pact with the devil for success at cards and in the casino, but who discovers that there's no way to get out of his end of the bargain. But the highlight of the issue was the grotesque "Crawling Death," in which two couples land on an island infested with giant crabs with strangely human qualities. Bill kills one of the crabs, who utters an oddly human cry as it dies. As if in revenge, another crab attacks and kills Bill's wife, Janet, and Bill and his two friends are forced to leave the island as more crabs converge. Bill wants to get even with the crabs so he dives overboard, to discover that the crabs are now feasting on Janet's corpse (depicted quite graphically). As the other married couple watch from the boat, they see the crabs converge on Bill and somehow transform him into one of them, then watch in utter disgust as the Bill-crab rushes forward to *devour the rest of his wife*. This story undoubtedly had some influence on Roger Corman's *Attack of the Crab Monsters*, in which giant crabs eat humans and absorb their memories and thoughts, made several years later.

"The Dead Sleep Lightly" in *Chamber of Chills* 10 is a disturbing and inventive horror tale that takes place in the coalmine area of the Appalachias. Dr. Les Miller finds it hard to believe it when miners tell him that living dead men are attacking them down in the deep shafts, but one man he visits has definitely been clawed and bitten. Miller descends into the mine and discovers that the stories are true; the dead men are led by a hulking brute who resembles Bull Moosse, a miner who was killed in a cave-in ten years before. Miller barely manages to escape, and in the mine office looks at a photo of Bull Moosse, and indeed recognizes him as the leader of the ghouls. Miller believes that these "dead" men are actually alive, and decides to open up Moosse's grave. He is not surprised to find the grave empty, but he is surprised by the presence of a trap door and tunnel at the bottom of the coffin. Suddenly Moosse himself reaches up to snatch him into the underground. Miller is told that the dead miners have risen because a new mine shaft is to be dug directly below their graves, disturbing their sleep. One dead miner argues that Miller should be let go so he can convince the owners not to continue the shaft, but Moosse thinks he will only tell them to move the graves, which is not acceptable. In one of the most chilling panels in horror comics, we see Miller in the grave with Moose, who lies beneath him, a comparative giant, holding him down in his arms, one giant hand covering Miller's mouth. Up above, people are preparing to shovel the dirt back over Moosse's coffin, but Miller can neither move nor cry out, as the bigger man's arms are stiff with rigor mortis. Thus, this perfectly innocent man is buried alive in the unloving arms of a monstrous unliving ghoul.

Chamber of Chills 13, presented "The Man Germ," another story that reminds one of the later *Fantastic Voyage*. An arrogant safari head named Darcy arrives at a lost city and is warned to stay away from a gigantic humanoid statue that the natives tell him is alive. Determined to see what's inside the statue, Darcy digs a cavity in the idol's massive foot, noting that the material reminds him of skin. Inside the hole, which closes behind him, sealing him in, he discovers a river of blood and a network of veins, as well as insect-like corpuscles that chase him into an artery where he is finally crushed inside the statue's huge and pulsating heart.

Caleb Wainwright drinks an elixir that will keep him alive for 500 years in the uncredited "The Wax Man" (*COC* 16), only he is unprepared for the fact that he will still age and look older and older. Full of energy, Caleb doesn't care, but people object when the 300-year-old Wainwright, looking more like a decomposing odorous cadaver than anything else, struts around town. To prevent being locked up, Wainwright has the owner of a wax works fashion a skin-like coating for his face and body. Wainwright not only murders him, but also the wealthy man, Stephen Winters, whom he now resembles. But Winters likes a good hot steam bath every morning, and when Wainwright, trying to avoid suspicion by sticking to the dead man's routine, gets a dose of steam it not only melts his wax but his entire over-aged body into a puddle on the floor. The panels where people object strenuously to Wainwright's exaggeratedly elderly appearance remind one in equally exaggerated fashion of the fear of aging and subsequent/concurrent elder-hatred that permeates our society.

Chamber of Chills definitely ventured into EC type territory—and almost outdid them—in a macabre little gem in the twenty-first issue, "The Choir Master." Carlo Furelli is an aging, unemployed choir master behind in his rent who finally hears from an employment agency, but when he arrives at the theater is told that he was hired to be a janitor, not to handle the chorus. Disconsolate, he seeks help from several former pupils, many of whom have become famous soloists, but they either refuse to see him, rebuff him cruelly, or give him a buck out of pity when all he wants is a job. Finally driven mad by the extreme mistreatment, disappointment, and sense of betrayal, he goes about at night paying a call on all of these ingrates when they are not surrounded by sycophants. Once through with this grisly mission, the details of which are kept secret, he carries a large valise into a studio where in a few moments the show that is currently broadcasting must halt due to weird music coming from next door. In the adjacent studio, Furelli sits at an organ, joyously playing, while atop of each pipe sits the severed head of one of his former pupils. Beneath this rather masterful gruesome set piece is a ferocious story that illustrates the utterly miserable treatment accorded the elderly and forgotten, Furelli almost becoming a sympathetic maniac.

"I, Vampire" (*Chamber of Chills* 24), drawn by Howard Nostrand, presents a sympathetic bloodsucker who argues that humankind has never tried to see things from the vampire's point of view. He relates that they decided to take cash from their victims so they could pay for blood at special blood banks and build up a huge supply—contained in a huge reservoir in a special chamber with pipes leading to faucets—that would last for years without their ever having to attack anyone ever again.

Other macabre and gruesome set pieces from *Chamber of Chills* include: a necklace of rubies that turn into tiny heads that gnaw into the neck of the man who murdered the witch doctor to whom the necklace belonged (6); aliens disguised as people who use heat waves to literally melt the flesh off of anyone who sees them as they really are (6); a tree that spouts finger-like buds that resemble the hands of the murdered wife buried nearby, as well as fruit that has the shape and faces of both her and the husband who killed her (12); cannibal ants who use the fleshless bones of two men they quickly devoured as a bridge to get to the dead men's partner, who slew the men in hopes they alone would satisfy the rapacious insects (13).

The most unusual story published by the magazine appeared in *Chamber of Chills* 22. "The Ugly Duckling" is a tragic story with horrible aspects but not really a horror tale; rather it deals in fairly realistic fashion with the effects of disfigurement on a man's life and soul. Much, but not all, of Jed Barnes' face is bandaged due to an industrial accident involving sharp blades. Although his financial needs have been met, Barnes is shunned by most people, turned away by fine restaurants, and is desperately lonely (even while admirably trying to keep up a brave, positive front). He contemplates suicide, but as he heads for the river he sees a young woman trying to kill herself and prevents her. The aspiring, unsuccessful actress finds Jed sympathetic, and the two begin a romance and eventually get married. But partly out of curiosity and partly out of concern, the wife, Ruth, nags him to remove his bandages, "You mustn't hide behind those bandages the rest of your life," she pleads, "they'll have to come off some day." One night she goes so far as to take a scissors to the bandages and Jed, furious, finally rips them off. He reveals that underneath the bandages—there is *nothing*, the blades cut so deep that there are only wedges of bone and raw flesh (the colorist makes these fleshless strips all pink instead of white or red, somewhat blunting the effect). While it delivers a certain shock, the ultimate effect is pathos, for it is clear that Jed will never be able to live without his bandages, and Ruth may no longer be able to live with him now that she knows the truth.

Other notable stories include "Green Killer" (8), in which a man thinks he has gotten away from a devilish tree out to kill him but flows right into the branches of his nemesis during a flood; "The Face of Horror" (10), in which a brother and sister who move into an old house see an awful, smirking ghoul staring out at them in the night; "Cave of Doom" (10) wherein two men wind up in the mouth of a huge idol that turns out to be alive in a tale that borrows heavily from Lovecraft; and "Cycle of Horror" (16), in which a man kills his partner, then sees his corpse with its rotting feet —a very gruesome image—in every hotel room he goes into, because it turns out that he is also deceased.

Covers were generally drawn by Lee Elias. Among the more notable were for the tenth issue, which depicts two arctic explorers standing in the maw of a living ice giant about to bite down on them; and the nineteenth, upon which a skeletal hand raises a toast to a beautiful woman, only the portion of her face that can be seen through the glass is also desiccated and skeletal.

Tomb of Terror

Harvey's *Tomb of Terror* debuted in 1952. It was as if the editorial department at Harvey saved up all the best stories for *Chamber of Chills* and *Witches Tales*, for *Tomb* almost exclusively offered incredibly mediocre fiction and generally wretched art with few exceptions. Even the better stories weren't that great, such as "The Closet" (*TOT* 11), in which a little girl gets even with the cruel aunt who practically starves her by locking her in the closet with an imaginary friend. *Tales of Terror* occasionally ran science fiction stories and switched to that genre beginning with the thirteenth issue. Oddly, the best horror/suspense stories the comic ran were in its sixteenth and final issue (after which it metamorphosed into *Thrills of Tomorrow* for a subsequent four issues): in "All Keyed Up" a beautiful and unfaithful wife lusts for her old husband's secret treasure which he keeps in a vault in a dark cellar. She poisons the man, but before he dies he swallows the key to the vault. Her lover digs up the man's

Harvey's *Tomb of Terror* joined *Chamber of Chills* as one of their most popular comics.

grave and cuts the key out of his belly, but when he uses it in the vault he is killed by an explosion. The wife rushes over his body into the chamber, only to discover that the "treasure" is a million worthless match books.

In "Tag.... You're It" a couple have a scare when their little boy is chased by a frightful man while he's out playing in the backyard. "He wanted to ... eat me. Don't let him catch me!" cries the terrified child. A series of vampire murders then rock the community, with husband and wife both coming to suspect the other of being the vampire. It may not come as a shock that the actual vampire is the boy, who clearly did not get away from the strange man in the first scene, but the story has resonance beyond its simple plot, such as intimations of child molestation. Assuming the couple survive their own child's blood-lusting assault in the final panel, one can imagine the grief and shock that reverberates throughout them when they realize the truth. One contrasts the ending to a panel on the second page, in which the mother hugs their beloved child as the father stands by, which the artist does in long shot, the three figures surrounded on all sides by a grayish-red, isolating background. A subtly disturbing note is that the less concerned father is not touching his sobbing son, offering comfort as the mother does, but simply has his hands in his pockets.

As the golden age gave way for the silver, Harvey brought out two more short-lived nominal horror/fantasy series: *Man in Black* and *Alarming Tales*. The Man in Black was a caped man, meant to be Fate, who appeared in and narrated would-be ironical stories with his female associates, Venus, and the Weaver; it lasted four issues. *Alarming Tales,* which lasted six issues in 1957, was essentially a weird story mag with more emphasis on sci fi than horror.

Six

Ace and Ajax-Farrell

Ace publishers took a comic entitled *Men Against Crime*, whose sales were indifferent, and turned into it the more successful *The Hand of Fate* beginning with its eighth issue in 1951; included was an exciting tale in which a serum not only reawakens a sleeping corpse but turns it into a destructive giant. The theme of the comic was how your life could change—generally for the worse—when "The Hand of Fate" intervened. By the ninth issue a cloaked Fate himself began to appear in the stories, either narrating, interfering, or commenting on the action. *HOF* 9 featured a story of a chess match with Death in which the chess pieces were portrayed by living people who were killed when they were moved off of the chess board. *HOF* 10 featured a silent film director who made what amounted to snuff films—the victims in his films really died—and who comes out of his grave to make one last movie with a terrified aspiring actress.

Fate became a major character in "The Final Curtain" in *HOF* 11 in which he tries to warn off a Shakespearean actor from killing off his rivals for the lead role in Hamlet. The evil protagonists of the stories always ignored or poo poohed Fate's warnings of dire doom because they were either arrogant or thought he and the future-visions he conjured were mere figments of their imagination. Frankly Fate's nagging presence in many stories became a tiresome device that generally just interfered with the narrative flow. He was like a spoilsport importuning the characters to stay on the straight and narrow when of course the reader wanted to see all the skulduggery that the bad men and women could come up with before they met their ultimate "fate."

In "Dead Ringer" in *HOF* 15 a man, Hubert Newton, meets his double, Vic Morrain, on an airplane. Newton faces an uncertain future as a "second-rate nightclub singer," while Morrain has just become enormously wealthy due to an inheritance. When the plane crashes, Newton is the only survivor, and decides he might as well take Morrain's place and get the money the dead man will now be unable to spend. But when Newton arrives at the Morrain castle he meets only ghosts, and then discovers he has to take Morrain's place in his grave and *be conscious* until his ordained death date arrives *in twenty years*. The story is especially disturbing because Newton is not a murderer or truly horrible person, but—while his actions may be morally wrong—dares to do what many otherwise decent people would also have done if they had the chance.

"The Sorcerer's Spectacles" (*HOF* 17) presents a truly loathsome individual, Vernon

Hutchins, who steals a pair of glasses from his grandfather, who warns him against wearing them. As he explains it: "if a good man looks through the glasses, he sees only the benevolent spirits —but if an evil man uses them he activates the evil spirits who walk the earth seeking the ruination of souls." Vernon promptly puts on the glasses so that the evil spirits will come forth to murder his grandfather, which they do, enabling him to inherit all of the old man's money. He then uses the evil spirits to kill off athletes during games he has bet on so he will win, and to cause a train crash with tremendous loss of life so he can carry off some bags of money during the ensuing pandemonium. His comeuppance doesn't occur until he puts on the spectacles and accidentally looks into a mirror, calling the evil spirits down upon his own head. If there is any problem with the story it is that Hutchins' death isn't nearly horrible enough.

The protagonist of "To Behold His Doom" (*HOF* 22), Stanley Timor, is just as evil. Down on his luck, the poverty-stricken Timor chances upon a mirror that forecasts disasters whenever someone looks in it during a full moon. Timor first learns that there will be an explosion in the House of Horrors at the fairgrounds at Luna Park and initially considers warning people to prevent the many deaths. Instead he decides not to say anything and, after the explosion and before rescue workers arrive, sneaks among the dead and dying stealing their money and other valuables. The next time he peers into the mirror he sees a ship sinking with all hands, so again decides to keep his mouth shut and insure some boxes full of junk for $100,000, which he collects when the mirror's prediction comes true. The next mirror-vision shows a deadly plague in the city, with Timor himself one of the victims. Timor desperately contrives to get out of New York on a boat, but everyone on it, including Timor, winds up dying of smallpox.

More misguided than evil is state executioner Philip Spayne, the protagonist of "Shattering the Time Barrier" (*HOF* 23), who accidentally discovers a way into a dimension of spirits, including the angry souls of every criminal who died in the electric chair. Spayne threatens to destroy the spirits unless they follow his orders for them to hunt down and kill evil men who have eluded the law. But both Fate and a pretty female spirit who falls for Spayne argue that the men *he* executed had been tried and convicted of their crimes, which is not true of the men on his hit list. It all ends badly.

There were other interesting stories. A count snares souls of hopeful opera singers, turns them into stars, and calls them forth from their graves to serenade him as he tries to snare a pretty new aspiring and clueless singer (*HOF* 14). "Long Shall the Undead Wail" in *HOF* 20 is a bit of fanciful fiction combined with fact which shows how Isabella of France, aka the "she-wolf," and her lover Roger Mortimer, murderers of Isabella's husband Edward II, are turned into literal ghouls after their deaths. "Invitation to Your Wake" (21) presents a writer who receives a note inviting him to peruse the rare occult book the "Necronomicon" (invented by H. P. Lovecraft); when he arrives at the appointed house early he overhears a group of ghouls, vampires and demons talking about how they plan to wipe out him and other occult authors to keep them from spreading their secrets. Also notable were "Orchids from the Dead," "Mirror Macabre" (*HOF* 17) and "Web of the Spider Woman" (18).

Baffling Mysteries

Ace's *Indian Braves* comic was transformed into *Baffling Mysteries* beginning with the fifth issue in 1951. *Baffling Mysteries*—which included a series of one-page fill-ins under that title—published horror stories, not mysteries. The cover promised tales that were "weird," "fantastic," and "astounding" but in the first issue at least, were pretty awful. A woman transformed into a tiger—or did she? A cult of goat people lived inside a mountain. The ghost of a dead miner popped up on a highway. None of the stories were especially well-written or had interesting twists. The following issue, however, was an improvement, with two memorable stories. "Fatal Rendezvous" has a man being called to the afterlife too early, being sent back, and discovering he's developed clairvoyance—he can tell when deaths and disasters are going to occur, only no one believes him and he is tormented by his visions. "Black Magic in a Slinky Gown" presents a beautiful brunette who can transform into a giant black widow spider and kills anyone who is "mean" to the more ordinary and helpless eight-legged arachnid.

The comic slowly became quite intense and rather gruesome. "House of the Screaming Fiends" in *BM* 12 wasn't a great story, but it has a memorable splash page (drawn by Dick Beck) depicting an old house and nearby trees that have gaping sinister mouths on them as well as baleful eyes. In "Never Bargain with a Spirit" a gambling baron down on his luck buys a talisman once owned by Caesar Borgia and which is reputed to have magical powers. He is warned that he must get rid of it before he dies, even if he has to sell it for less than he paid for it, or he will be doomed to eternal damnation. The talisman makes him rich, but as the time approaches when he realizes he ought to pass it on, he has a devil of a time finding someone to buy it, leading to a tense and suspenseful climax (12). In "Greed's Grisly Treasure" (13) Barton Frost follows a stranger's advice to seek treasure in an inn populated by ghosts and demons. Discovering that he can virtually knock off the heads of these fiends—one panel depicts a head flying off revealing the spine inside the flesh of the neck—he discovers that he himself was decapitated during the battle and didn't even know it; the final panel depicts his headless body with the head nearby in a pool of blood.

"The Dead Are Never Lonely" (14) is an excellent tale in which a femme fatale named Nolita attempts to leave her husband and is murdered by him, but absolutely refuses to stay dead. She strides angrily away from the cloaked figure of Death after he kills her husband and returns to the states, trying to take up her old man-killer ways, but discovers that while the spirit may be willing the flesh is weak—or rather beginning to decay, as overnight her beautiful face turns into a hideous wizened skull. The spirits of men who killed themselves out of unrequited love for her begin to pursue her, and doctors tell her there is nothing they can do for her condition—she has the appearance of life, yet her body is *dead*. She winds up reunited with her husband for eternity. In "Prowl of the Stalking Terror" (14) a handsome professor is turned into a particularly unpleasant-looking and ghoulish vampire by his undead uncle.

"Slaves of the Orchid Goddess" (14) is another story that presents a man-eating plant in a shop gobbling up writhing animals and people in one gulp years before the film *Little Shop of Horrors*. "Kill My Minions of Death!" (17) is a wild story in which a madman named Buloff murders many people, cuts off their hands, and then uses a formula to make the severed hands do his bidding, going so far as to blackmail the prime minister with mass death-by-hands if he doesn't turn over half the public treasury. Buloff, like many maniacs, outwits himself and winds up being throttled to death by a legion of disembodied fingers.

In its short run, *Baffling Mysteries* had several other memorable stories. A woman combines a vulture and a bat into a "vulbat" which bites her and turns her into a grotesque vampire (9); a giant thing made up of protoplasm engulfs screaming humans and spits out fleshless skeletons (9); a man who kills and beheads a tiger doesn't realize that the animal was a were-tiger and is stalked by his mate, a princess who can also turn into an animal (12); a woman can turn into a gigantic python and crushes, strangles or drowns her rivals for a handsome guy (15); a ballerina gets a pair of demonic slippers that turn her into a dancing star but ultimately destroy her (21); a fiddle inhabited by a demonic gypsy turns everyone who plays it into a murdering maniac (22); a man uses pills to feign death for insurance money, but after he's buried he discovers that his wife and best friend have other plans which don't include him (22); a woman blackmails a wealthy count who is a werewolf into marrying her and then tries to get rid of him (23).

The Beyond

Ace's *The Beyond* also debuted in 1951, and delivered similar material to that in Ace's other horror titles. The first few issues had a number of creditable terror tales: A woman kills her fat rich husband, gets acquitted, then marries a slender young bum who slowly begins to resemble her first husband, driving her nearly insane (*Beyond* 5). "Horror Blown in Glass" in *Beyond* 9—an average story about a glass sculptor who turns into a ravening beast— boasts some superior and beautiful artwork by Ken Rice. In the same issue are "On the Other Side of Death's Door which has a somewhat similar plot to that of Lucille Fletcher's "The Hitchhiker" (which debuted on radio ten years earlier) with a male lead, and "Vampire of the Opera," in which a soprano who is a vampire and was walled up a century ago in the basement of the opera house is disinterred and causes more deadly mischief.

Beyond 12 had two notable tales. In "Trail of the Phantom Gypsy" a mean old man is subjected to a gypsy curse, but his compassionate son is the one who suffers for it. In "The Bedeviled Battalion" a woman searches for her missing fiance and discovers he was killed and is being forced to serve in a legion of the undead. "Game for a Mad Huntress" in *Beyond* 13 is another lively variation of "The Most Dangerous Game" with a woman on an island and her undead servants hunting a castaway from a ship. In "The Ghost on Television" (*Beyond* 16) a woman and her lover, who poisoned her husband, see him appear on television, then his corpse shows up in person and presses his moldy, decomposing lips against his widow's in a very gross kiss. "Black Coffin of the Voodoo Jinx" (19) has a man using voodoo dolls to kill off his enemies and securing his own doll in a safety deposit box, but he forgets that whatever happens to the doll happens to the real person—and he winds up being buried alive. "Lair of the Spidery Fiend" (20) features a witch who can not only transform into a beautiful woman but into a giant man-eating spider with a hideous human head.

The Beyond 21 featured three compelling stories. "Red Shadow of Abbadon" has a ballerina making a bargain with a stranger—guess who?—who promises her twenty years of fame, after which she must sit and watch performances in the audience, made up of the dead who made deals with Satan. The ballerina tries everything she can think of to outwit and escape from the devil, but in the end her fate catches up with her. "Werewolf Blood on My Hands" has a file clerk in the police station go after a promotion by deciding to bring in the werewolf terrorizing the city. He injects himself with wolf's blood during a full moon and becomes a werewolf himself, then sets out to hunt his own kind. Unfortunately, he doesn't bargain with the fact that his animal instincts may take over ... "If Flesh Could Crawl" is the story of Darrel Thomas, an unsuccessful and unpublished horror author who is about to kill himself when manifestations of the creatures in his manuscripts appear and importune him not to do so. These demons tell him how to amass wealth and power, which he does, but whereas the creatures first appear only at his bidding, they then decide to stick around no matter who he's with or where he goes. He decides that death would be preferable to this and kills himself.

In "Swirling Mist of Doom" (*Beyond* 22) John Courtney, while attending a carnival, happens upon an interesting exhibit which he suspects is not a fake: a bottle housing a demon who can grant wishes, and who feeds on human minds, the first of which belongs to Courtney's best friend, Bill. Courtney is only interested in wealth and power and Bill's fate only disturbs him for a second. But as the demon sucks away more and more minds and grants Courtney's wishes, he not only gets more powerful but amasses a small army of mindless slaves, more than enough to force Courtney to take his place in the bottle—and become the exhibit at the very same carnival where he first spotted the bottle inside which he will reside for eternity. "Prey for the Vampire Horde" in the same issue has a sound engineer being targeted by an aging living vampire who wants the man to record an invocation that would bring the latter back to eternal undead existence after his mortal life is over. The engineer defeats the vampire and his human-bat hordes of silent flying horrors by cooking up a device that "blinds" them by affecting their radar. "The Unsleeping Dead" (23) presents an incredible invention: a movie camera that when focused on a murder victim will record the corpse's spirit naming its killer as well as the image of the crime itself. A TV producer uses the camera to get a top-rated series but when he inadvertently focuses it on the grave of the inventor, whom he murdered to get the device for himself, his doom is sealed.

"These, My Hands of Doom" (24) is the story of a disfigured sculptor named Cosmos whose equally grotesque statues, although beautifully crafted, earn him the scorn and enmity of the art world due to their hideous nature. A dark messenger grants him the means to gain vengeance by giving his hands the ability to turn all of his numerous enemies, male and female, into statuary, but he is warned he must never touch himself or he'll suffer the same fate; therefore he wears gloves at all other times. He meets a pretty and caring young woman who can see "the beauty in ugliness," admires him and his work, and asks to study with him. Unfortunately, after Cosmos suffers an accident she kneels beside him in concern, takes his hand in her own, and becomes a solid statue. Horrified by the fate of the only person who was ever kind to him or understood him, Cosmos puts his weeping face in his hands and ... The figures of the crying man and kneeling woman are put on exhibition as brilliant examples of sculpture but the unknown artist never materializes. In the gruesome "Lair of the Black Widow" in the same issue a man takes a formula which turns him into a half-human/half arachnid hybrid, and he sets out to snare his enemies in giant webs, until a large female black widow sets her sights on him for her latest meal. Artist Sy Grudko's panels depicting his terror as the she-spider slowly advances upon him are unsettling.

The cover of *The Beyond* 25, like most of the series' covers, had nothing to do with the contents, but it was memorable. A stewardess is being assured by the pilots that the plane will weather the storm and the passengers will "have a very long sleep"; the pilots faces are death's head skulls. The issue also boasts one excellent story "From the Graves They Crept," whose author is unknown, in which a coffin salesman named Richter, with his own factory, is taken to task by townspeople for charging for the best mahogany coffins while actually

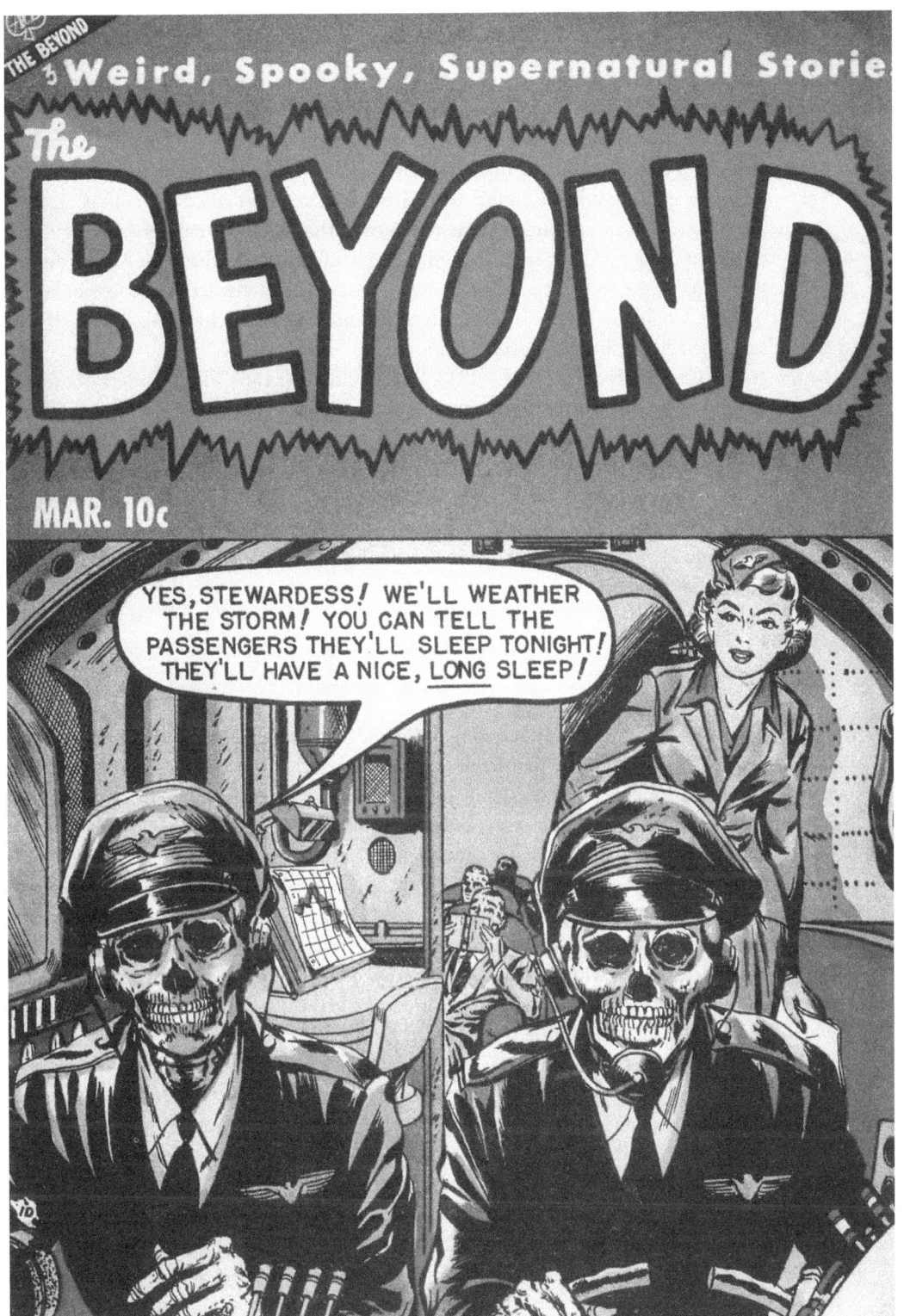

The Beyond 25 from Ace had a splendidly macabre cover exploiting the almost universal fear of flying.

burying everyone in cheap fruit crates. Too cheap to pay for special medication for her, he lets his own wife die. When he puts *her* in a fruit crate, even his well-paid staff are dismayed and quit en masse. When a flood in a nearby town results in thousands of corpses, Richter has nobody to help him fill the demand for coffins, but his dead wife's spirit enlists the aid of everyone in the graveyard to fill in for the missing workers—provided the coffins are of the highest quality. Richter puts out all of his cash buying the necessary materials, but figures he'll get the money back and then some in coffin sales. Unfortunately, the spirits of the dead use the coffins they make to *replace* the ones they were buried in that let in the worms and have fallen apart. Unable to fill the record orders, and now broke, Richter hangs himself— and winds up buried in a sheet in potter's field.

In the grisly "Candles for the Dead" (29) a Balkan chandler can't fill his orders because of a cattle plague so he substitutes human corpses in his tallow vats and fashions his candles from the result. Unfortunately, once lit these candles give off a foul odor and also emit the spirits of the dead criminals whose bodies were used to make them. When the chandler's ex-fiancee discovers what he's done, he strangles her and throws her into the vat as well, but an out-of-control fire puts paid to his future schemes.

The Beyond ended with its thirtieth issue, but during its relatively brief run it presented some very clever and interesting stories.

Web of Mystery

Web of Mystery—"Weird! Eerie! Startling!" was the cover slogan— was yet another Ace title that debuted in 1951. In the first issue one (uncredited) story stood out amongst the tales of mummies, vampires, and ghosts of pirates: "The Lamenting Voice of the Bell," In this a sinister bell-maker uses a secret ingredient to create the special tones with which his bells reverberate. He has kidnapped most of the children in town and thrown them into the cauldron with which he boils the metal for his bells (this is not depicted, however). Discovering that an old friend is dying and that he is his sole heir, and unable to get at the remaining carefully guarded children, the bell maker throws the friend into the cauldron. But this creates two problems. First, without a body he cannot collect the friend's money for a decade, and second, the friend's spirit haunts him each time the bell tolls, until, nearly driven crazy, the bell maker confesses and is hung.

There are two notable stories in *Web* 6: "Gargoyle's Revenge" and "The Mad Beast of Monaco." In the first story master stone craftsman Dorion Joost of Bosnia is commissioned to create some gargoyles but the town elders find them too hideous and order Joost to destroy them. He not only refuses to do so but is unable to come up with any alternate designs. When townspeople attempt to shatter the statues, the gargoyles come alive and begin attacking and killing everyone they encounter. Joost discovers that the only thing that will end this curse is his life, and although he fights to stay alive at the end he winds up a stone statue himself. The second story is a variation of Pushkin's "Queen of Spades," with Count Duclos, who has lost his fortune and fiancee due to his gambling, murdering an old duchess who has the Secret of Numbers (Cards) after she refuses to divulge it, claiming that despite her winnings she has led a miserable life. After the murder, Duclos again begins to win at cards, but the twist is that he turns into a werewolf every night. He tries to murder the woman who jilted him after first killing her husband, but winds up destroyed in her stead. The next issue ripped off no less than Oscar Wilde with a derivative of "Dorian Gray" in which a man's evil deeds are reflected in the decaying, hideous form of his statue. Another story, the oddly titled "Quest of the Never Ending," presents a man who keeps repeating the same dark deeds over and over again, with him assuming that he is either dreaming or seeing a possible future, but the truth is far worse.

"Prophecy of the Frightful Image," the cover story in *Web* 10 is the saga of Felicia, the "most beautiful woman in Monte Carlo" and one of the greediest. She dumps her poor boyfriend and takes up with a wealthy Arab who wants to marry her. On a lark they visit a fortune teller who suggests she look into the "mirror of destiny" to see her future. The mirror reveals an ugly, twisted visage; this image tells her that this is how she really looks inside and will eventually look on the outside unless she mends her ways. Naturally, Felicia pretends she is unaffected but the Arab potentate is scared off. Felicia steals the mirror from the fortune teller so no one else can see it. Felicia cuts a swath through several more wealthy, loaded bachelors, but they all dump her when they realize her only interest in them is satisfying her desire for glittering objects to showcase her beauty. When she refuses to give money to the poor uncle who raised her when her parents died, the ill man commits suicide. The image in the mystical mirror is now even more hideous, and this scares her. Felicia decides to pay for an expensive funeral for her uncle, but the mirror knows that even this act of generosity, besides being too little, too late, is really being done for herself. Almost overnight Felicia turns into a wretched, ugly hag, but continues to haunt the casino hoping to make money, until they throw her out into the street, now just an object of pity and derision. The story is remarkable in that it manages to evoke some pity for a heroine who arguably doesn't deserve any. While it, too, may have been influenced by Wilde, it takes off in its own direction.

Web 12 has two absorbing tales. In "The Carpenter's Cursed Creature" a man disfigured in an accident inadvertently brings to life an equally hideous giant wooden statue that follows him everywhere on a killing rampage; "The Silver Bell of Doom" features a man who falls in love with a witch who was executed but didn't *quite* die, only to discover that marriage to her is not the bliss he'd imagined. *Web* became a bit more gruesome and sadistic with its thirteenth issue, especially in one story when a man angers a spirit, has his flesh picked at by "vengeance vultures," and shows up dead, disfigured, and with his ribs exposed. In "The Beast of Skeleton Island" a shipwrecked man eats his companions (the cannibalism is not depicted, however) and becomes a werewolf, attacking and eating people once he's back on land. "Syr Darya's Death Song" features the preserved, decapitated head of an evil woman who is still causing mischief decades after her death. In "Spell of the Devil Dancers" a young ambitious dancer makes the mistake of wanting to view some forbidden dances, and becomes a slave to Siva. When she escapes, she discovers that years have passed and she is now old and unrecognizable to her family, so she returns to Siva, whereupon she is cast into a fiery pit, a tough price to pay for merely wanting to see some dance numbers for a projected specialty act.

Web occasionally ran monster stories, such as "The Moon Was Red" (18), in which sailors are beset by a gigantic humanoid sea freak who comes up from the deeps out of hunger. This frightening monstrosity has a shaggy mop and beard, tiny green eyes, a mouth filled with sharp, pointy teeth and a mottled face and body with ugly oval spots. In one panel he picks up a man in his outsized hand and squeezes him to a pulp, much, much blood dripping down from the completely squashed corpse. The cover of *Web* 21 depicts a giant, hideous spider to whom people are sacrificed, but there is no sign of the creature in the inside pages, unfortunately. A giant spider finally showed up four issues later in "Lair of the Silken Doom," about a beautiful woman who ensnares, captures and devours men, using their substance to spin webs of the finest and rarest silk, which she then offers to greedy entrepreneurs who eventually wind up on her dinner plate themselves. Evil women who could transform into giant spiders were apparently legion in horror comics.

There were also the usual complement of stories about mummies, werewolves and an inordinate number of tales about female vampires. *Web* 22 presented a female were-tiger who is raised from a cub by the hunter who killed her mother. The man's original intention is to exhibit the she-tiger for profit, but after she grows up he falls in love with her. She is tricked by him into revealing that she can turn human, and tries to stay in that form after she kills some people in her tiger form. Alas, their attempts to have a happy life together are doomed to failure.

Web of Mystery 20 was a superlative issue of the comic, with three notable stories. The heroine of "Out of the Black Night" is a sweet elderly school teacher who is concerned about vampire attacks in the small town she lives in. The reason for her concern is that *she* is a vampire and another bloodsucker has moved into town and is trying to take over her territory. She ferrets out his identity and he invites her out to his isolated home where he intends to spring upon her, but she surprises him and kills him instead. Guilt-wracked, afraid she might have broken some vampiric code, she starts for home and is startled to see a bunch of ghouls in swift pursuit, causing her to panic and fall to her death. But they are only some of her school children wearing costumes and trick or treating for Halloween. "What Was It?" has a scientist contacting an alien life form just as his shrewish, neglected wife destroys his equipment, causing him to murder her. The evil, goblin-like alien comes to earth, but needs the damaged device to be rebuilt so he can return to his home planet. When the scientist refuses, the alien enters and resuscitates the corpse of the dead wife, leaving the man no choice but to blow himself, his lab and the evil alien to pieces. "Crimson Hands Against Him" has the large, severed hands of a criminal preserved down through the ages until they come into the possession of a modern-day doctor. The ghost of the condemned criminal comes to demand his hands back, but the doctor throws the ghoulish creature down an incinerator. He then unwisely grafts the man's hands onto the arms of a magician who is losing the use of his own hands. The patient is appalled that he now has these clumsy, ungainly mitts, which against his will strangle the life out of the doctor. The ghost, who can't be killed as he is already dead, appears again and chases after the magician trying to get his hands back. When the magician falls out of a window, his dead arms stretch across streetcar tracks and his new hands are severed, whereupon the original owner comes along to take back his hands and go peacefully to his grave.

The last couple of issues presented mostly reprints, and with the twenty-eighth issue there was a change in format. A mysterious hooded figure now introduced "Strange Tales of Retribution." Judging from the very old-fashioned and very poor art it is likely that these stories were also reprints from another comic. *Web of Mystery* disappeared for good with its twenty-ninth issue.

Other notable stories in the series include: "Corpses on Cue" (18), in which a stage magician uses a zombie in his act, billing him as "the man who cannot be killed," but while the audience is amazed at the man's ability to survive bullets and knife thrusts, he eventually gets the better of his master. "The Night the Statues Walked" (19) has an old watchman in a museum discover a parchment from Pygmalion that tells how to animate statues, which the old man then uses to destroy his enemies, but not before first testing the statues by tearing one poor man to pieces and beheading a suspicious policeman. In "Bondage in Stone" (21) a thief and murderer releases evil ancestors whose souls were placed inside gargoyles and gains a treasure, but discovers that having four ghouls for companions has its shortcomings. "Long Arm of the Undead" (23) features a neurotic, evil actress who comes back from the dead to destroy any woman who tries to replace her in her last unfinished movie.

Ace decided to turn its *Love Experiences* into a horror comic beginning with its 6th issue and came out with the one-shot *Challenge of the Unknown* in 1950. Among the ghost stories and a story of brain transplants, there was an interesting tale of an evil snake cult that transforms men into serpents, and an amusing story of a vampire haunting an Italian villa that has been transplanted to the U.S., where the ghoul unwittingly frees a young bride from the unhealthy influence of her domineering mother.

AJAX-FARRELL

Ajax-Farrell publishers had several magazines devoted to horror, and they were among the best of the comics that imitated the EC style. Ajax came out with *Haunted Thrills* in 1952, produced by the Iger Studio, which lasted eighteen issues. The cover depicted a corpse standing on a doorstep—watching a pretty woman who sits inside the house—and thinking: "Ten Years is a long time to be away. Helen should be pleased to see me." Unfortunately, the contents of the issue, tepid horror and mystery stories, were not as interesting, although the comic would rectify that in the future. One of its most grotesque stories, "Out of the Grave," appeared in the eleventh issue and took place in a Nazi concentration camp. Colonel Eric Von Grimm is shown his wife Helga's proud new possession, a lampshade made of human skin, and is annoyed that because of the dearth of leather his boots have holes in them. The lampshade gives him the idea of making boots out of skin as well, so he has a camp inmate shot specifically so he can send his skin to Antonio, the cobbler. Antonio realizes that the "leather" he has been given is really human skin and is horrified to see the tattooed numbers which he last saw stamped on his own son, a prisoner in the camp. He gets even with Von Grimm by making him a fine pair of boots with his dead son's skin and planting a bomb in the heel so that when the colonel salutes and clicks his heels—BOOM!

"Terror Below" (*Haunted Thrills* 12) features a heartless Governor of Tortuga who feeds pirates and other enemies to ravenous crabs that come out of the sea at the same hour every day. His pretty wife has come to hate the cruel man and fallen in love with his kind and handsome male secretary. The governor tortures a maid until she admits she knows about the affair, then captures his secretary and forces his wife to watch as he is tied to a stake and fed to the crustaceans. But after a sea battle with pirates, the governor winds up on shore with a large piece of timber crushing his legs. He realizes that it is almost time for the crabs to emerge from the sea to find dinner. He importunes his wife, who arrives on the beach, for help, but neither she nor anyone else will come to his rescue. And the crabs come out and begin their feast.

Haunted Thrills 13 boasts the memorable "Experiment in Terror." In this grotesque mini-masterpiece a wizened, stooped old anthropologist named Chadwick tells a pair of young lovers that he will give them money if they agree to be his test subjects in an experiment proving that hunger is stronger than love. He puts the couple in a cage and starves them, watching as they nearly come to blows over a loaf of bread. When a colleague, Horton—who has surmised that Chadwick hates the lovers because of his own deformed appearance— protests that he's gone too far, the old man locks him in the cage as well. From atop the cage the old man proffers a raw beef steak to the desperately hungry trio, and in his sadistic eagerness allows the lower half of his body to fall into the opening —upon which his three victims begin to greedily gnaw upon his legs as he shrieks in agony.

Ajax-Farrell's *Strange Fantasy* came out in 1952 and lasted about twenty issues. "Death Holds an Auction" (*SF* 2) presents the bizarre sight of a man who can change into a giant octopus, still retaining his human head above the tentacles. In "Fate Has a Thousand Faces" in the same issue a man falls in love with a beautiful ventriloquist but can't stand her wizened, unattractive female dummy, only it turns out the real dummy is the beautiful mannikin and the ugly dwarf is the mistress. In the harrowing "Death on Ice" (6) a party climbing Mount Everest not only have to contend with frigid temperatures and hard-to-scale ice, but the angry ghost of a man who died on the ascent years before. "Nightmare Merchant" (7) features a couple who move into a new house where they keep finding bottles filled with blood; these are delivered, like milk bottles, to the vampire rental agent, who delivers the couple to the supplier as "payment." "Bloody Mary" (10) is the nickname of an adopted little girl who goes about murdering people à la "The Bad Seed," only this "child" is really a midget. When her stepfather is arrested for murdering his wife, he can't get anyone to believe the truth about the girl and is executed. In "The Murder Pool" (13) a nasty, corpulent man fills his new pool with acid and invites his enemies to swim in it one by one until his wife gives him an unpleasant surprise.

1952 also brought *Voodoo* from Ajax. Jungle, war and crime stories were sometimes mixed in with the horror (the first few issues emphasized zombies) as if Ajax were using the mag to get rid of some inventory, but there were a few memorable shockers as well. "Plantation of Fear" in the third issue takes its cue from legends about the poisonous mandrake plant, whose roots often resemble human figures, and fashions a tale of mandrakes that pull themselves out of the earth, grow to man-size with nasty eyes and teeth, develop sentience, and advance upon a manor house to slay the owner before disappearing forever. In the gruesomely satisfying "Corpses of the Jury" (*Voodoo* 5) a Nazi commandant uses the skin of a young woman's hands for gloves, and still wears them years later after the war and he thinks he's safe, but she appears with a host of ghosts of others he killed in the camps—slowly they skin him alive until all that's left of him is a "grisly red dripping thing" on the wall.

In "Ghoul for a Day" (*Voodoo* 5) a woman marries a man without knowing that he's an undertaker. She's so horrified by his profession and the dead people lying about that she wants to leave him immediately but her husband cowers her into submission. After years of abuse at his hands and of being forced to be his assistant with the corpses, she snaps and poisons him, burying him in the basement. She resists all attempts to get her out of the house so that no one will ever find the body, and becomes the town's only female undertaker. After a fire her husband's body is discovered and she's sentenced to life imprisonment—and discovers she's been assigned to the prison mortuary, causing her to break out into hysterical laughter. "The Weird Dead" (6) features a gigantic, man-eating snake guarding a treasure and a greedy man who arranges to get the treasure by feeding the serpent several screaming human sacrifices. In "Killer Lady" (6) a beautiful jungle princess seemingly falls for a handsome vain reporter and is especially impressed with his beautiful blond hair. She takes him back to her land to be her king but he learns to his regret that she's really just interested in his head—preferably severed (another story influenced by "The Price of the Head").

In "Horribly Beautiful" (*Voodoo* 11) an ugly and jealous woman throws acid in her beautiful sister's face, disfiguring her. The once-pretty sister studies witchcraft to find out who did the deed, and learning it was her own sister, visits upon her "the curse of beauty." The ugly sister discovers that she has indeed become a stunning beauty, and can hardly find it a curse—until she realizes that her head with its beautiful face has grown to grotesque size while her limbs and trunk have become disproportionately spindly. "Horror Comes to Room 1313" (11) tells of a series of deaths as people jump out of a hotel room window because of some ghastly thing they see when they are alone in the room. "Skulls of Doom" (12) tells the story of a doctor who has the ancient, still living and super-wise brain of Vishnu transplanted into his brain—how the doctor could retain his own memories, knowledge and personality is never explained—but the angry skeleton of long-dead Vishnu saws off the top of his skull to get his brain back.

"Heads of Horror" deals with a doctor who discovers that his wife has a boyfriend, and uses a special formula to shrink their heads while they're *still attached* to their bodies. But the despairing couple give him a dose of the formula and then commit suicide, while the now babbling doctor winds up an exhibit in a freak show. (This story was sort of the reverse of "Horribly Beautiful.") "Nightmare Island" (15) has a man and his wife trapped on an isolated island with a huge rat created by a mad scientist who becomes the mutant's first victim. Aware that the rodent has tasted human flesh and will be wanting more, the couple set a trap for it but are still unable to stay out of its claws. Arguably the best cover for the series was for *Voodoo* 14, which depicted a line of beauty contestants being checked off one by one by a skeletal judge.

Ajax's final golden age horror series was called *Fantastic Fears,* which debuted in 1953. The eighth issue had two especially memorable tales. In "Fiends from the Crypt" Roman Police Commissioner Renzi, chasing a criminal in ancient catacombs, comes across flesh-eating creatures that nibble away everything down to the bone except the head and shoulders of humans, leaving behind especially grotesque corpses. He enters into a sick bargain with these creatures, agreeing to direct them to groups of victims on the streets above if they give him whatever booty they come across. Before long Rome is terrorized by a plague of monsters as Renzi, above suspicion, gets richer and richer. Living in splendor with his wife and little girl, Renzi decides to end his bargain with the monsters, who respond by kidnapping the other members of his family. Renzi pursues the monsters into the catacombs, only to see the nibbled-to-the-neck corpses of his wife and daughter (graphically depicted in a nauseating panel), after which he is easy prey for the still ravenous and angry underworld creatures. "Carnival of Terror" has an Indian snake charmer turning a man and woman who try to murder him and steal his fortune into snakes with fangs and human heads. The transformed couple bite the snake charmer to death, but then realize there's no way they can ever become human again. Another story in the issue, "Careless Corpse" (1953), about a man who's horribly disfigured in a car accident but doesn't realize he's dead, was a blatant copy of an EC Story.

The most unusual story published in *Fantastic Fears* appeared in the fifth issue: "My Coffin Must Wait." Seth Bates is told that his wife Martha is dying and nothing can be done for her; she has been given a pill to make her more comfortable and it won't be long. Remembering a promise he made to her, Seth gathers her up and puts her in the passenger seat of his car, then drives hurriedly out into a storm. Time is of the essence, as he must fulfill his promise to her before she dies. Bank robbers on the lam try to commandeer his car, but he drives right through them, as well as through a road block set up by the cops. Finally he makes it to his destination and bangs on the door frantically until the proprietor opens up. All along the reader is wondering what sort of horrible promise the man might have made—this is, after all, *Fantastic Fears*—but it turns out that Martha only wanted her picture taken before she died so that Seth would have something to remember her by. The photographer snaps her picture just before she expires.

After the comics code came into being *Fantastic Fears* underwent a name change to *Fantastic Comics* and it published stories of supernatural adventures. Even in a story where a reporter goes to track down an alleged ghoul, said ghoul turns out to be very weird but *not* an eater of human flesh. The post-code *Fantastic* did not last long. Ajax had a few nominal horror comics in the early years of the silver age, but they didn't last long, either. *Strange* and *Midnight* debuted in 1957 while *Dark Shadows* came out the following year. Often these comics reprinted golden age stories that were not too gruesome (and had no vampires, ghouls or werewolves) or went so far as to rewrite certain stories, redrawing a few panels, to make them less objectionable. Thus "Out of the Grave" from *Haunted Thrills* 11 was turned into the more benign "Fair Exchange" in *Strange* 5. Instead of wanting a pair of boots made from human skin, the Nazi steals boots and wants the cobbler to repair them. Instead of putting a bomb in the heel of the boot, the cobbler simply puts in a loud time piece that (inexplicably) makes it seem as if the Nazi is mocking his superiors and he is imprisoned instead of being blown to bits.

Another story, in which a jealous man shoves his wife and her lover off a snowy cliff and they are frozen together forever, was rewritten for *Midnight* 2 so that the man wasn't married (hence no adultery), the falls are accidental, and the ending is more tragic than sinister. Another story in which a woman predicts her own death ends with her falling through the ice as before, but a caption explains that she survived whereas in the original version she doesn't. Another story about lovers from feuding families who are killed and come back from the grave to murder everyone else was turned into a happy fairy tale in which said lovers convince the two families to love one another as they do! What few new stories appeared were unmemorable. "The Girl No One Really Knew" (*Strange* 1) seems to be about a movie star, desiring a simpler life, who wills herself into becoming a chicken! Ajax-Farrell went out of business in the late fifties.

Seven

Avon, Better/Nedor, Comic Media and More

Avon's *Eerie* debuted—initially as a one-shot—in late 1946 (cover dated 1/47), the first all-horror comic book on the market. The cover illustration depicts a ghoulish-looking man or vampire with a knife in his hand descending a staircase amidst Gothic ruins and approaching a supine frightened female in a slinky red dress. Nothing like this actually happens on the inside pages, which consisted of an interesting mix of terror tales. In "The Eyes of the Tiger" a man winds up the victim of his pet tiger when during the night the animal becomes intrigued with his owner's blue-veined feet and begins licking them ... tasting blood for the first time. "Dead Man's Tale," narrated by a corpse in the morgue, is a dare-to-twist-fate-and-suffer tale in which a man appropriates an elixir from an old man, whom he murders, that can grant wishes to anyone who imbibes it, but then discovers there's bit of a problem once the liquid is all gone.

"The Man-Eating Lizards" (written years before movies like *Attack of the Crab Monsters* or *The Giant Gila Monster*) presents downed fliers who wind up on the menu as sacrificial offerings of some very unfriendly natives who worship giant, voracious lizard-gods. In an interesting if silly twist some of the ladies of the tribe find the boys fetching and initiate a revolution, making sure that they can escape with the fliers, and their oppressors themselves wind up the blue plate special. "Mystery of Murder Manor" is a tale in the "phony ghost" tradition, as visitors are attacked by a maniac who pretends to be a spirit. "The Strange Case of Henpecked Harry" is a revenge-against-a-hateful-wife tale, with the vengeance going awry as it usually does in stories of this type. Harry's wife is an especially loathsome specimen, and Harry doesn't seem to deserve her literally physical fury. Discovering he's the beneficiary of her life insurance policy, Harry pushes her in front of a train. (Although the actual moment of impact and the aftermath is not shown, we can see the woman splayed out on the tracks with the heavy wheels about to dissect her, and an oddly composed train man saying in a later panel: "I never seen anyone so mangled to pieces before in my life! She ain't a woman anymore—she's a *mess*!" Harry is so haunted by the crime that he thinks he sees his wife's bloodied body and winds up falling from the roof to his death to escape the specter. The trouble is, Harry's wife isn't dead—she lent her coat to a perfectly innocent co-worker who died a dreadful death in her stead. She and battered Harry are the true victims of the tale.

Eerie 2 didn't appear for another five years. Aside from a fair-to-middling story about a man who walks into a radio station and announces people's deaths minutes before they happen, it is unmemorable, as is *Eerie* 3. The fourth issue, however, has some reasonably compelling tales, such as "Cremation of Evil," in which a young wife who has died comes back to life moments later as a demonic, murderous creature; "The Ship of Death," in which a model ship plays a fateful part in the lives of another young couple; and "The Puppet Pulls the Strings," in which a ventriloquist builds a man-sized puppet who may have too many human qualities. The stories may not have been the most original or sophisticated, but the artists gave each story a suspenseful pace.

In "I Painted Only Terror" (*Eerie* 5) an artist has secured his reputation painting scenes, often from real life, of frightened people, but it's taking a toll on his psyche. When his psychiatrist suggests he switch to lighter and happier subject matter, the artist can only laugh. He decides to create his masterpiece by luring a pretty model to his home, terrifying her with a trick, taking her snapshot with a hidden camera, then painting the portrait of her agonized face at his leisure. Unfortunately, the woman is so scared that she dies. He buries her body and proceeds to paint, but the woman's ghost appears. The artist's final portrait, his masterpiece, is of his own face distorted by abject terror. In "Green Grows the Grass" (10) a man murders his scientist employer so he can steal a seed he created that can grow in anything and doesn't require soil. But as he dies, he fires the seed into his murderer's body, making him eventually sprout green growths and then turn into a plant form that takes permanent root in the ground.

The twelfth issue of *Eerie* is easily the best ever published. It features an excellent, very well-drawn, full-length adaptation of Bram Stoker's "Dracula" that seems quite faithful to the novel; the credits are lost. *Eerie* lasted for a few more issues but published mostly reprints. Harry Lazarus was the chief artist.

Avon's *Witchcraft* hit the stands in 1952 and lasted a mere six issues. The book was mostly full of crudely drawn and instantly forgettable tales of witches, zombies, and vengeful spirits but there were some exceptions. "The Monster of Sarno Gulch" in the final issue features a reporter who meets a young woman while tracking down stories about a hulking man-demon terrorizing the countryside. The woman has personal knowledge of this creature as it turns out to be her husband after he swallowed a voodoo potion that made him bestial. The story wasn't that special but the art by Nodel and Alascia was quite effective. "The Northern Horror" (2), in which men come across an ancient Viking ship filled with frozen corpses and dangerous spirits, manages a small *frisson* or two. The book was poorly edited. One issue contains two stories in which a man throws a woman off a cliff and is haunted by her ghost, while another has two stories in which a man drinks a native potion and turns into a beast.

Diary of Horror was a 1952 one-shot with a trio of standard horror tales; *Night of Mystery*, a 1953 one-shot, had four stories but was also unmemorable, as was *The Dead Who Walk*. *City of the Living Dead*, another one-shot, featured "Death Has Many Tongues," in which a vicious captain and slave trader develops bumps on his arms that turn into the heads of two of the native witch doctors that he killed. Avon also came out with an adaptation of Sax Rohmer's novel *The Mask of Fu Manchu* in 1951, which was probably more faithful to Sax Rohmer's novel than the film with Boris Karloff. It did not feature much horror, however.

BETTER/NEDOR

Better/Nedor/Standard publications unleashed three horror comics in 1952: *Adventures into Darkness, Out of the Shadows,* and *The Unseen.* Monsters figure in a few of the stories. "The Fangs of Fate" (*Shadows* 7) has a scientist cornered by a man who threatened him with deportation, resulting in the latter's murder. Desperate to get rid of the body, the scientist feeds it to his pet python. This not only makes the snake grow to alarming proportions, but gives it an insatiable craving for human flesh. It eventually breaks out of confinement and is destroyed by authorities as the scientist falls prey to his other normal-sized snakes. "The Hungry Lodger" (*Unseen* 5) deals with a man who asks the proprietors of a coffee shop to bring him meals, left just outside his door, every two hours, and who turns out be transforming into a gigantic, carnivorous caterpillar.

"The Corpse That Came to Dinner" appeared in *Shadows* 9. Newlyweds Dan and Joyce read in the paper that their friend Henry, who also loved Joyce, has committed suicide. They go out to the grave to pay their respects, where they are confronted by Henry's revolting corpse as he pulls himself out of the ground. He tells the couple that he intends to spend all of his time with them, and that they had better not complain considering what happened to him. Dan and Joyce importune Henry to return to his grave, to no avail. They invite no one over for fear they will see Henry lying about, and one night during dinner the ghoul informs them that the meal they are consuming consists of human flesh. Disgusted and infuriated, Dan manages to secure a voodoo potion that will make the dead *really* dead. Unfortunately, it also paralyzes the *living* as (improbably) the whole thing has been a nasty prank and hoax perpetrated by Henry, in heavy make up, who now wishes he'd just let the happy couple alone as he is entombed in the graveyard once more and unable to even cry out for help as the air runs out.

Out of the Shadows 13 had two especially grotesque and effective stories. In "The Recluse" lovers Gladys and Phil cook up a scheme to steal the $40,000 that homely recluse Ezra withdrew from the bank years before, Gladys going so far as to marry the old man. Deciding it would be easier to find the money if Ezra were out of the way, they murder him as he cries: "I'll haunt you—my face will be with you forever!" They finally find the cash, but one of them upsets a kerosene lamp which not only burns up the money but puts both of them in the hospital, wrapped in bandages. Released from the hospital, the two are depressed by losing the money but make hopeful plans, until they remove their bandages. Phil cries out in disgust when he gets a load of Gladys, although he doesn't realize that he looks even worse: both of them are ugly and wizened, resembling old dead Ezra.

In "The Cannibal" a series of horrible murders rock London, the victims picked clean of all flesh by human teeth. During the state of paranoia in the city, pretty waitress Libby is warned against going out with the cultured and strange Mr. Darrow, a customer, but Libby does what she wants and refuses to listen. She and Darrow are followed by a handsome cop, Alf, who loves Libby, as well as other waitresses and the concerned proprietor of the restaurant, but Libby always returns safe from her dates. However another waitress—and even a cop—are found stripped of skin. The restaurant's owner is deeply alarmed when he sees Libby take Darrow up to her flat, and calls on Alf for help. Alf arrives at the apartment and is told by a smiling Libby that Darrow is gone. Alf asks Libby if she'd like to go out for a bite, but as she invites him inside she says "I can't even think of food. See, I told you Mr.

Darrow was gone, every last bit of him." As Alf screams at the sight of Darrow's skeleton lying in Libby's living room, she adds "I simply couldn't eat another bite." One assumes that despite her feeling bloated, Alf was next on the menu, just as one imagines Libby was some kind of mutant if she could consume an entire human being in such a short time. But stories like "The Cannibal" aren't meant to be closely scrutinized.

In the infinitely depressing "Eerie Glen" (*Unseen* 6) Joe comes home from work and tells his mother he isn't feeling well. He goes to bed but wakes up feeling refreshed and okay. Suddenly his dead father appears and asks him to take a walk with him into the forest where they used to spend many happy hours. Joe's father, who died ten years ago, shows him a dark and haunted glen deep in the woods which has a strange but ominous beauty. Joe admits that it frightens him. He tells his father he hopes to see him again and goes home, wondering if it were all a dream. People he runs into, including his girlfriend, ignore him, as do a crowd of people outside his house. He sees a coffin in the living room and is terrified that his mother must have died. But, no she sits besides the coffin crying, but even she, his own mother, won't acknowledge him. Then he looks in the coffin and sees why—it is his own body in the coffin. In the final panel Joe slowly makes his way back to the glen and his father. One could easily dismiss the story as trite and predictable, argue that it's been done a thousand times, but it has an undeniable power, in no small measure due to the atmospheric art by George Roussos. One can't help but sympathize with Joe, dead at such a young age, and his mother, who's now lost the second person who mattered the most to her. Joe will have the company of his father in the glen, but one can't imagine this will be any substitute for a lifetime of light and love and laughter, and although the father wears a sweet, kindly smile, the sunken, haunted quality of his eyes make it clear that death has not been an especially wonderful experience for him, and that he almost welcomes his son's demise so he'll have someone with which to share his comparatively bleak existence.

Joe was a complete innocent, undeserving of his fate, which is not the case for the venal characters in "The Sealed Coffin" (*Unseen* 11). Movie stars Jeff and Myra have finished making a film in Africa, and are off for a two month honeymoon. Speeding to make the boat on time, they run over and kill a native boy. Jeff insults the boy's father by offering him money, and Myra says "a human life means nothing to these savages." The father sends another native to the actors' hotel room and Myra is pricked in the arm with a poisoned thorn. As her arms and face swell, she is told by a doctor that she has contracted an incurable and fatal case of acromegaly. She and Jeff hide away as the disease progresses, but Jeff now finds his wife so hideous that he can't stand to look at her and carries on with a beautiful actress, Valarie. Not only does Jeff break his promise to stay with Myra until the end, he's in such a hurry to be with Val that he suffocates Myra. Seeing ghostly images of his dead wife causes Jeff to snap and kill Valarie in a rage. Desperate to see if Myra is still alive, Jeff rushes to her tomb—and gets locked in, sharing her fate for the rest of eternity. In "A Shroud of Vengeance" (*Unseen* 13) the protagonist, a disfigured factory worker named Abel, is so horribly mistreated by people that you're almost cheering him on as he comes back from the dead and gets vengeance on certain cruel souls.

In the grotesque "Flowers on Deborah's Grave" (*Adventures into Darkness* 9), a witch-like old woman named Annie is in love with a sexton named Long Jeems. Each day Annie brings him a bouquet of flowers, but she's infuriated to discover that he takes these flowers and puts them on the grave of a young woman named Deborah. Annie is savagely jealous of her rival, not even caring that she's dead. She opens a hole in the grave and allows crawfish to enter it and feast on the corpse, then displays the skeleton for Long Jeems to see. Suspecting her of desecrating Deborah's tomb, the sexton has already called the authorities to take her away, but the shock of seeing the skeleton kills him as he reveals—too late and to Annie's dismay— that Deborah was not his lover but his daughter.

"The Man Who Could Not Die" (*Adventures into Darkness* 10) concerned a hit man, Mike, who is hired by a shadowy figure to murder a man named Ankar. But the latter seems to have extraordinary luck, as Mike tries again and again to kill him to no avail. Mike trips as he's about to stab the man in his bed; when he throws Ankar off a balcony his clothing gets caught on an overhang and saves his life. When Mike sets fire to Ankar's house, it starts to pour, putting out the fire, and so on. Ankar finally approaches Mike and tells him that he is under a curse. Five thousand years ago, when he was a pharaoh, Ankar summoned Death and asked what he could do to become immortal. Death told him that no less than ten thousand other souls could be exchanged in order for him to be forever bypassed and live forever. Ankar put ten thousand slaves to work on a pyramid, then collapsed the structure so they all died screaming. But five thousand years later, as a wizened, elderly man, Ankar is haunted by the dying screams of the ten thousand slaves, and only wants to die—but Death refuses. Mike meets up with the man who hired him, who is, of course, Ankar himself. When Mike tries to shoot him, the bullet bounces off and kills Mike instead.

There were many stories in horror comics about people who have seemingly cheated time and death only to discover that this was not the case, as well as stories inspired by the ending of "The Lost Horizon." For instance, in "The Frozen Death" (*Adventures into Darkness* 14) Paula falls off the slope of the Matterhorn during her honeymoon, causing her husband to commit suicide. Fifty years later her body is found frozen in a block of ice by Mack Lane, who is smitten with her (literal and figurative) glacial beauty. To Mack's surprise, Paula comes back to life once she is thawed out, but he can't convince her that if she gets too warm she will decay. Paula can't bear the thought of being cooped up, constantly cold, with this old man, so she importunes a stranger seeking directions to take her with him. The stranger complies, and they get a room in a hotel, but the next morning Paula is nothing but a desiccated skeleton.

Artists for Better publications' horror comics include Ruben Moreira, Mike Roy, and Mike Sekowsky.

COMIC MEDIA

Comic Media's *Weird Terror* debuted in 1952. The first issue contained stories about a group of Nazi survivors being tormented by Hitler's manic ghost; a bitter actress who employs a curse against her enemies; a man who murders his wealthy older wife only to encounter a demonic beauty who proves his doom; and a rip-off of H. P. Lovecraft's classic story "Pickman's Model," about a man who paints monsters from real life. While *Weird Terror* could never be considered one of the more memorable horror comics, some of the "ghostly tales of spine-chilling horror" were at least entertaining.

In "The Evil Ones" (*WT* 7) a man is convinced that accidents are not really accidental, and uncovers the cause, a race of underground gnomes only he can see who run about pushing people into the paths of trucks and the like. They also like the taste of human flesh. In "The Improved Kiss" (8) a barbarian who falls for a monarch's beautiful daughter murders her beloved. The woman, wearing a mask over her face, allows the barbarian to kiss her, only to reveal that the lower half of her face has decomposed due to plague and is spewing forth dozens of deadly blue flies. "Witch Girl" (10) is the story of four sisters who all fall for the same man, a handsome lawyer named John. The plainest of the sisters is determined to snatch this one man away from her siblings and uses demonic spells to do so, making one sister old and ugly so that she kills herself, and sending large flying bugs after the sister who's overly proud of the buxom figure they feed upon. She herself is killed before she can knock off the third sister by blasting her brain with her magic. Artist Don Heck did many covers for the series as well as much of the inside artwork.

Comic Media's second horror series was entitled *Horrific;* it debuted in 1952. "Final Warning" (*H*6) was an EC-type story in which a woman objects to her husband's constant bowling until she plays the game one night and gets hooked herself. It isn't long until the sport becomes the most important thing in her life as she neglects her husband, their two children, and the house; finally her husband snaps. It's no surprise that the next time he goes bowling he uses her severed head as a bowling ball. The seventh issue, besides having an effective cover depicting a guillotine blade rushing down towards a screaming victim, featured more severed heads in "Shrunken Skull." The greedy protagonist kills and beheads an unsuspecting acquaintance, then prepares the head to make it seem as if the man were the victim of headhunters. At the end of the story he falls overboard into some propellers, and his own head shows up in a box just like that of the man he killed.

Horrific 8 introduced "The Teller," a host-character whose origin is recounted in the lead tale. He had been a young chemist who was caught in a blast that gave him psychic abilities and a new purpose in life, that of observing evil events. Unlike the ugly, grotesque hosts of EC's horror comics, the Teller was a dapper, handsome man with a mustache. He had four more ghoulish friends to assist him. "Beneath the Grave" (10) told of Lars Swenson, a gravedigger—and grave robber—who discovers that a recently buried corpse, whose jewels he'd hoped to obtain, has disappeared. He follows a tunnel leading from underneath the grave and discovers that huge rats have stolen this corpse and many others; dark gods from Below have given the rodents the decaying flesh to feast upon after snatching the souls of the departed. The rats, who are bloated, clawed monstrosities that can walk on two legs, espy Lars spying on them and give chase, but poor Lars winds up in the wrong grave and is dragged off to his death and the rodents' supper. *Horrific* only lasted 13 issues and this was arguably the best—and best-drawn —of its stories; the art was by Rudy Palais while the story was unarguably "borrowed" from Henry Kuttner's "Graveyard Rats."

Fiction House

Fiction House publishers was best known for its popular aviation comic, *Wings*, and its science-fiction series, *Planet Comics*. *Rangers Comics*, which eventually starred a red-headed "frontier queen" and adventuress named Firehair beginning with the twenty-second issue, ran two horror features in the back pages. First came "The Werewolf Hunter," which debuted in the mid-forties. The elderly Professor Armand Broussard, who had knowledge of black

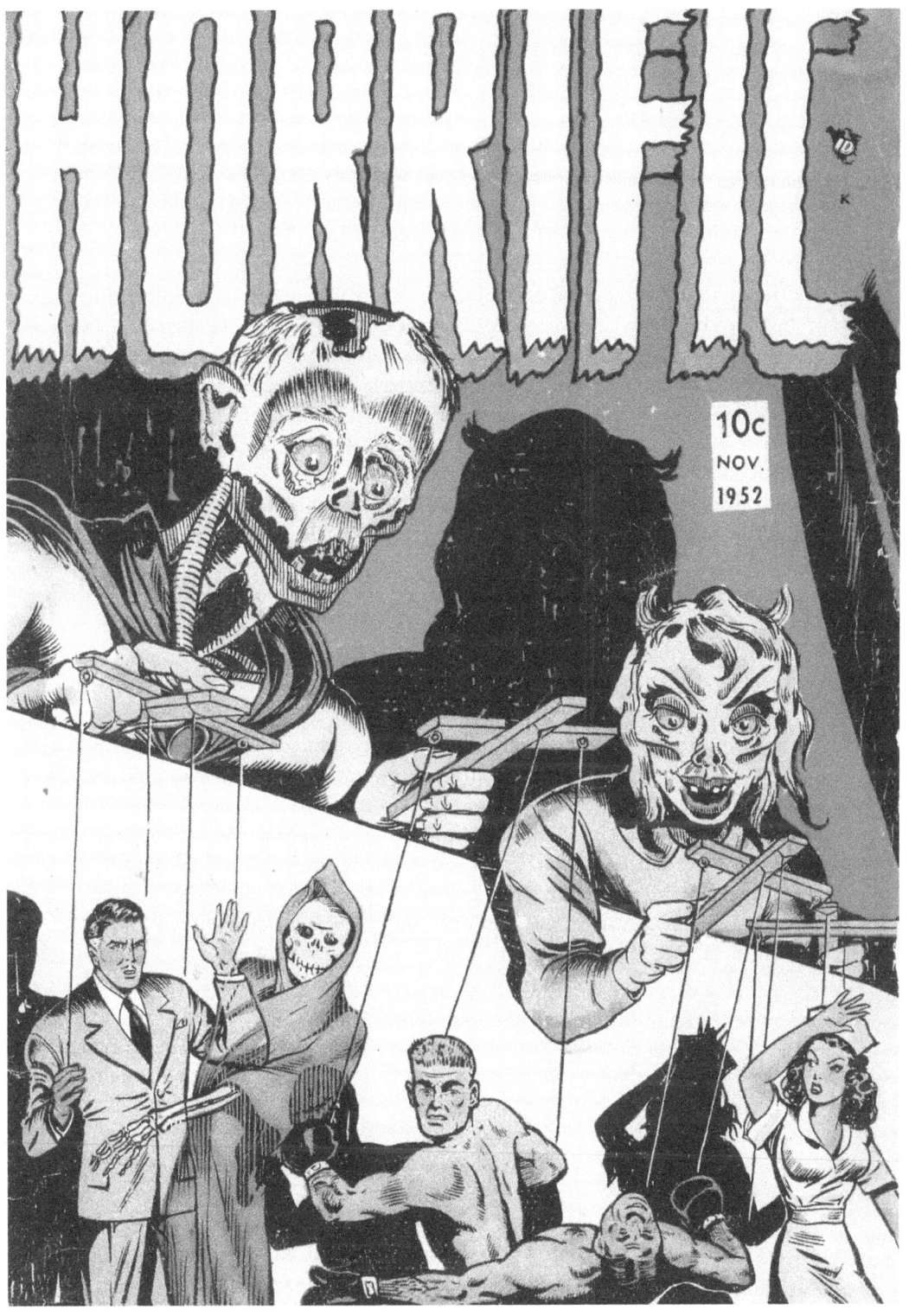

Comic Media's *Horrific*.

magic, was involved in cases of the supernatural, not limited to werewolves. The writing of the strip was first attributed to an Armand Weygand, and then to "Armand Broussard," while the art was by L. Renee. The professor battled an evil woman who put human souls into tiny dolls, and another evil dame who cuts off dead men's hands and uses them to murder, steal or play the danse macabre (via the hands of a famous pianist). Broussard had a great number of female antagonists, including Madame Dante, who uses a machine to turn little children evil and commit murders and thefts (*Rangers* 38). In another story Broussard is shrunk down into a microscopic world on the surface of a diamond. After awhile Broussard did not appear at all, and the strip consisted of a stand-alone mystery or supernatural tale.

"Werewolf Hunter" was eventually replaced by a feature entitled "The Secret Files of Dr. Drew," Investigator of the Unknown, beginning in the late forties. Drew lives in a castle on top of Bone Hill and still uses a horse and carriage in the twentieth century. These strips were drawn by Jerry Grandenetti in a cartoonish style that nevertheless credibly portrayed the action and suspense of the best of the stories. In early stories Dr. Drew was so nondescript in appearance it was hard to get a handle on him. In later stories, he was drawn more as the standard handsome comic hero with graying temples. In one adventure, Dr. Drew helps an elevator boy discover what happened to some people who got off on the non-existent thirteenth floor. In another tale a gypsy witch returns from the dead to dispatch descendants of her enemies with a poisonous kiss. There was a secret mystical underwater city, and a bunch of "fetish rags," or beautiful Parisian gowns, that adversely and horribly affected the women who wore them. In an untitled story in *Rangers* 50, Drew takes on no less than Satan himself in the form of goateed Mr. Nicholas. Satan was to take the soul of Paolo Vincenti, a violinist-composer, when the latter finished his 30th composition, but he died after only writing 29 pieces. But his soul has entered the form of Paul Vincent, an American composer, and the Devil does his best to get Vincent to play opus 30 so he can collect *his* soul, but Drew manages to outwit him. The series was not bad, although the art was often uneven, and Dr. Drew was a completely one-dimensional character. *Rangers* ended its long run with the 69th issue.

Ghost Comics debuted in 1951 with four stories from the "ghost gallery," including one in which a victim of a car accident winds up on a bus with the phantoms of the recently deceased, including his girlfriend, who was a passenger in the car. Some of the stories in the first few issues were narrated by a blandly handsome blond guy who was some kind of psychic investigator, and there were a few Werewolf Hunter stories as well. Spy stories and crime tales with restless ghosts were interspersed with tales that were purely supernatural, as well as many Gothic stories and, rarely, science fiction. The ghosts of innocents would rise up against those responsible for their deaths, while on occasion an evil spirit would try to get vengeance on the innocent descendant of an alleged tormentor. The stories were all tasteful—and dull.

With the ninth issue there came a change in editorial direction. Instead of mediocre ghost stories there were genuine horror tales and speculative fiction. There had been many stories about man-eating plants in horror comics, but "The Devil Seeds," the lead story, is one of the best, very well drawn by Johnny Bell. Two archeologists discover preserved seeds inside a temple devoted to Isis, and are warned about removing them. Back in the states, they importune a farmer and his wife to let them plant the seeds on their property, as the soil is similar to that from which they took the seeds. The seeds grow into large, unusual plants, which begin snacking on birds, the family dog, a cow, and finally the farmer's wife (and the scientists) before the farmer destroys them with gasoline and a match, overlooking some new seeds that escape the conflagration.

In "The Thing that Walked By Night" a childless couple adopt a little girl who transforms into a creature that goes out at night to slaughter animals. Afraid she might start in on people next, they draw lots as to which of them should perform a mercy killing before the child is cornered by an angry mob. The wife contrives to get the short stick, but instead of shooting the girl, she shoots her husband, explaining that the girl is actually her biological child. "She really isn't dangerous," she says, as the girl picks up a branch to beat mommy with. "The Monster of the Sea" is actually a heart-warming fantasy tale about a little boy who uses one of three wishes to turn his negligent, criminal father into a real and loving dad.

The tenth issue features "The Ghost of the Gorgon," who comes forth on an island to turn men to stone and is supposedly destroyed, until she turns up again on a ship heading for America, whereupon the captain uses a mirror to finally end her reign of terror. In "The Ghost of Dr. Renick," another heart-warmer, the title character quits his profession after losing his own wife on the operating table, but her spirit guides him when he decides to take a chance and operate on a small boy who desperately needs similar surgery. The eleventh issue has two fairly interesting tales—one about abominable snowmen that turn men into zombie slaves and live in a prehistoric world behind the ice, and another about cursed objects that bring death to a group of co-eds—along with some Dr. Drew and Werewolf Hunter reprints that seemed quite out of place. This was the final issue of the series.

Fiction House then came out with *The Monster* in 1953 which featured "all new stories of weird terrors" but only ran for two issues. There was one memorable story: "The Dark Abysmal" in *The Monster* 2 is an excellent tale, quite well-drawn by Johnny Bell, that relates how a young boy finds a weird but cute animal at the bottom of a pond, freeing it from a hook. The animal's strange appearance frightens many of the townspeople, but there are some who are hoping to exhibit it for cash. The creature is sensitive and picks up the emotions of the people around it, causing it to become much, much larger and more dangerous. It sprouts many tentacles and is able to cast realistic hallucinations. As it begins to cause destruction, becoming larger and more terrifying, the townspeople attack it to no avail, and the army is called in. The youngster who rescued the creature suspects that it means no actual harm and is able to calm it enough so that it retains its usual cuddly size. The creature turns out to be a friendly alien visitor who was only reacting to the psychic distress and fear it was inadvertently causing. The story is unusual in that it has a happy ending, and there are no deaths, gruesome or otherwise.

HILLMAN

In 1939 speculative writer Thomas Sturgeon wrote a memorable and influential short story entitled "It." In the story the decades-old bones of a man combine with vegetation and earth to form a sentient, shambling, faceless monster that comes alive and kills, more out of curiosity than anything else. The story deals as much with the trauma suffered by a farm family due to the monster's appearance and actions even more than it does the monster itself. Three years later, in Hillman's popular comic *Air Fighters* (vol. 1, 3) a strangely similar character appeared in the Sky Wolf aviation strip. The story relates how during World War I the ship of German flying ace Baron Emmelmann is shot down in swamps in Poland, where his body merges with vegetation to form a creature that would become known as the Heap. The Heap is a large shuffling monster whose malleable, nearly indestructible body seems composed of seaweed and grass. The Heap feeds by getting oxygen from the bloodstreams of the humans and animals it squeezes to death. The story then advances to World War II where a Nazi commandant hopes to use the Heap to kill off Sky Wolf and his comrades, but instead the Heap is defeated and presumably destroyed. The Heap seemed influenced not only by Sturgeon's story but by Frankenstein and other Germanic horror tales.

It was four years before the Heap made a second appearance in the Sky Wolf strip. By this time *Air Fighters* had been rechristened *Airboy* after its most popular lead feature—a uniformed teen who had adventures in his plane—and "The Return of the Heap" appeared in the fourth issue of the third volume in 1946. In this a crazed Professor Kringle, who somehow knows the former identity of the Heap, brings the creature to the United States where he manipulates it into killing his shrewish wife and other enemies. Sky Wolf blows up a plane with the professor and the Heap aboard, but wonders if the Heap can truly die. Apparently not, because the Heap got his own strip five issues later.

The Heap

In his new series the Heap makes his way to the small town of Lawndale, where his simplistic attention is attracted by the model of a German airplane owned by a teenager named Rickie Wood. Not knowing of the creature's origins, the boy befriends the monster, but later becomes aware of its destructive potential. Because the model airplane reminds him of his flying days, the Heap has affection for Rickie and never harms him. Thus follows a series of misadventures of the boy and his monster which today remind one of the Hulk and his boy pal Rick Jones, although both of those characters were much better developed than the Heap or Rickie. (The Heap—and "It"—also spawned such other swamp monsters as DC's Swamp Thing and Marvel's Man-Thing many years later.)

Now and then The Heap would be reminded of his past—although always in the vaguest of ways—such as a story wherein some crooks try to steal pearls that once belonged to the Emmelmann family (*Airboy* vol.4, 1). Another story takes place in the Emmelmann castle, which has been transplanted to America by a wealthy man who wants to disinherit his sons, both of whom accuse the other of his murder (*Airboy* vol.4, 7). A more memorable story had Rickie, his girlfriend Winnie, and the Heap encountering a man named Lustig whose voice is able to hypnotize and sway people to do his bidding. In this the Heap's memories of his country are awakened by strains of German opera! Then the Heap takes care of a rival who slanders the late, great (von) Emmelmann within his earshot to his ultimate regret (vol.5, 8).

A new direction for the strip began in *Airboy* (vol.4, 9) when it is revealed that years before the gods had decided to make the dead baron a test case. The goddess Ceres was determined to rid the Heap of past influences and turn him into a force for good, while Mars, the god of war, hoped to do just the opposite. Rickie, Winnie, and Lawndale were all gone the following issue. Instead the Heap is discovered in the South Pacific by the naturalist Dr. Drake, who takes him to South America where they encounter man-eating plants and other nefarious characters (vol.5, 1), but not before the Heap battles his second big octopus and shows Ceres that he can fight for the angels as she hoped (vol.4, 11). Later on the Heap's rebirth is attributed not to Ceres but to Mother Nature, depicted as a nun-like being in a cloak.

Gradually the Heap seemed to become a guest-star in his own strip, which was turned into mini- morality plays featuring people who did evil things and faced retribution at the hands of the Heap, even if inadvertently. An ugly man taken advantage of by a beautiful woman who only wants his money goes on a killing spree of ugly people to spare them his misery, and goes crazy when he comes across the even uglier Heap (vol.5, 6). A self-styled queen of the underworld tries to make the Heap her invincible bodyguard but he strands her in an isolated pit with no way to get out or get help (vol.5, 7.) In a bizarre story that takes place in The End of the World Cafe in South Africa where a Hollywood actor has come with his girlfriend, the Heap battles a big trained ape who has the temerity to sit in the honorary chair put out for the late, absent Von Emmelmann by a group of fliers; the dying ape than strangles the actor's girlfriend. (vol.5, 9). The Heap could turn up in any country or city in the world with no explanation for how he got there.

The Heap was eventually given more to do in his strip, and more stories were tied into his background. In *Airboy* (vol.5, 12) he not only saves a boyhood friend from being murdered but prevents the destruction of a village, which he saw another friend's father destroy years before by opening a water gate and flooding the area. After a sabbatical of several issues the Heap returned in a story in *Airboy* (vol.6, 6) which took us back to his days as von Emmelmann. A jealous rival named Bocke contrives to have von Emmelmann killed so he can claim the Belled Goose Emmelmann was awarded, which is said to have mystical properties and which Bocke believes is responsible for Emmelmann's glory in the air. Although only Bocke himself can see the goose after Emmelmann is killed, he is given life everlasting—and eventually only wants to die. For a time most of the subsequent stories took place in the Polish village of Wasau. The goose was forgotten.

One could argue that the guts had been taken out of the Heap, but occasionally there was a story that was reasonably horrific. In *Airboy* (vol.7, 3) the Heap initially befriends Hugo, a young man who is an outcast from a nearby village. But Hugo in turn befriends all the outcasts of the animal kingdom, including rabbits with fangs, dogs as fierce as wolves, and other frightening creatures, using them to attack the town. The Heap smashes into the menagerie and what he doesn't destroy winds up getting caught in quicksand, along with the demented Hugo.

In *Airboy* (vol.7, 5–6), the Heap discovers that the swamp that gave him life has been drained of oil, apparently now a vital ingredient in his continual resurrection. But in the dim recesses of his brain he remembers that when he was von Emmelmann he had discovered the secret of eternal life was hidden in Egyptian pyramids, so he slowly makes his way across Europe. He is pondering how to voyage over the Mediterranean when he rescues a fisherman from a hungry octopus (the third and largest that the Heap fought in his career) and the grateful man gives him a ride. They manage to make their way to the proper pyramid and the Heap discovers the right beakers, but the fisherman is killed by some angry Egyptians who object to the desecration of their tomb. In the next issue, which seems only vaguely related to the aforementioned story, the Heap travels back to Egypt only to encounter Bocke, the man who was responsible for his death. Bocke hopes to put an end to his miserable life with the Egyptian Book of the Dead, but instead sees the Heap as being Death Personified, and now wanting to live, runs away until he is attacked by crocodiles. Although it's implied that he's still not dead, he never appeared again.

One of the best Heap stories appeared in *Airboy* (vol.7, 8) in 1950. Eric von Emmelmann is visiting his Italian friend Rudolf Sienna just before the outbreak of World War I to watch the annual spectacle of seals migrating into caves nearby the estate. Eric and Rudolf exchange pendants and vow to remain friends no matter what happens. Eric is, of course, betrayed and shot down and metamorphoses into the Heap, while Rudolf—due to his friendship with Eric—is branded a traitor by his conniving stepbrother, Pilastro, and locked away in a dungeon for a great many years. A high-living Pilastro, who's taken over the castle and the community, allows a chained Rudolf out each year to see the seal migration and taunt him with past glory, but this year the Heap interrupts the festivities, during which Pilastro and Rudolf are left alone. Rudolf chases his stepbrother into the caves just as the mass of heavy seals begin to pour inside, presumably crushing them. But the Heap rescues Rudolf, who sees the pendant hanging from the creature's chest and realizes it's his old friend, Eric, whose fate was even worse than his own.

Another memorable Heap tale began in fifteenth century Spain where a blacksmith is outraged by how the evil Duke of Manchez abuses people, especially the blacksmith's young son, whom he nearly runs over in the road. The blacksmith challenges the Duke but is defeated and subjected to torture on a windmill. The Duke falls into the mechanism of the windmill and is crushed to death, only his hands remaining untouched. Down through the centuries the duke's hands appear from behind a curtain and continue to dole out cruel orders to his subjects. Now the hands want a bullfighter to throw a fight. When the Heap intervenes it is discovered that the disembodied hands of the duke were merely a hoax perpetrated by his equally malicious descendants (*Airboy* vol.7, 12).

In future issues of *Airboy* the Heap's wanderings (which were rarely depicted; he just showed up wherever the story took place) took him everywhere from the Congo, the Irish Coast, and Mongolia, to Cyprus, New Mexico and India. He got involved with a horror movie filmed in a German castle (vol.7, 11); aided an orphan with a cruel miser guardian who has gold pieces, the boy's heritage, hidden in a tree (vol.8, 1); and helped a deserter regain his honor when he came up against a mad count and his giant lizards (vol.8, 3). The Heap was frequently pitted against similarly grotesque menaces such as "The Green Peril," a monstrous man-eating plant that grows to tremendous size after being planted in the soil of the Wasau swamp (vol.8, 9); a giant mold from Uranus that stowaways on a spaceship to Earth (vol.9, 2); and a somewhat more prosaic but lively and monstrous sea serpent (vol.8, 11). Other antagonists included everything from wild boars and rogue elephants, to an ape trained to strangle men, to giant vampire bats, and a spider-like sea monster with a tentacled nose, scaly body and big bright red glowing eyes.

The Heap got the cover to himself for the first time on *Airboy* (vol.9, 3) in 1952, and again two issues later. The cover of the next issue showed the Heap and Airboy together fighting a monstrous phoenix. A gargantuan Thunderbird did appear in the Heap story, but Airboy and the Heap did not appear in the same story together. They appeared together again on the cover of *Airboy* (vol.9, 8) but not inside the magazine. Whether or not the Heap appeared on the cover, there was always a blurb announcing his presence inside.

There were two notable stories during the series' last year. One dealt with a young Chinese couple torn apart by an insidious war lord and a battle between a mechanical dragon and a real one (vol. 10, 1). In the following issue the Heap intervenes when a girl sent to beg for a loaf of bread from wealthy players in the San Remo casino is caught with the others when the whole building crashes through a fissure into the caverns below. The Heap descends into the caverns to save her. By now the once fearsome and monstrous, even evil, creature of its first appearances was positively benign and incredibly kindly (vol. 10, 2). Two issues later *Airboy* was discontinued and the Heap was gone from the comics scene in 1953.

"Airboy and the Rats"

As the *Airboy* comic neared its conclusion there were a few back-up horror stories. The two most memorable were "The Crown of Cort" (vol.9, 5) and "The Answer of the Maelstrom" (9, 8), which would have been a standard ironic revenge tale were it not for the art by George Evans and the intensity of the storytelling. Another of the more memorable horror stories that appeared in *Airboy* wasn't in the Heap strip or a back-up, but appeared in the main Airboy feature in the eleventh and twelfth issues of volume 5 (1948). "Airboy and the Rats" has organized rodents, who had existed unchanged for thousands of years and were biding their time, deciding to wipe out humanity in mass attacks. The best scene has thousands of rats descending on the town of Webster Heights, New Jersey, gnawing through phone lines, chasing terrified people through the streets, and then viciously assaulting and devouring the populace. "Less than an hour later, the people of Webster Heights were no more," reads a caption that shows a street that is bare but for a skeleton with torn clothing and a rat standing on top of it. The rodents than attack Manhattan in such droves that it seems impossible to beat them back until Airboy comes up with the idea to pour oil onto them: "blinded and half-paralyzed by the clinging, overpowering black blanket," the rodents drown by the millions. Rats are repulsed by marines with flame throwers in the subways, and Airboy wipes out battalions of bats—the rodent air force—by leading them into a storm. "The rats have only been repulsed," says Airboy, "they have not been defeated."

In the next issue the rats seem to disappear from their usual haunts in major cities and some think the threat is over. Actually, billions of rodents have come together from every corner of the world to convene in the gorge of the Grand Culvert Dam. As they gather together, certain rat strike teams attack prominent politicians and bring down planes with important scientists aboard. Trains and experimental bombers are sabotaged, and Airboy allows himself to be captured to learn the rat army's location. Scenes of the head rat addressing his teeming soldiers in their rat language and rodents scurrying through a network of underground tunnels are creepy. One has to take it all with a grain of salt—it makes no sense that the rats would want to keep Airboy alive, nor that they would choose to convene near a dam which Airboy explodes to drown them all—but the story is nevertheless entertaining and eerie. Airboy knows the rat army still isn't quite finished.

Airboy had other fantastic opponents in subsequent stories. In *Airboy* (vol.6, 7) he comes up against a crook who used a scientist's growth formula—which had already turned an ordinary salamander into a freak the size of an alligator—to turn himself and others into dangerous giants. In *Airboy* (vol.7, 3), the young hero descends into the ocean depths for research in a bathysphere but unknowingly brings up a small cancerous-like creature that grows to such tremendous size it threatens the entire world with destruction. Timmy, a boy whom a sailor thoughtlessly called a coward, takes Airboy's place and sacrifices himself by parachuting down to the creature to report on its physical properties, whereupon he is devoured after relaying the required information. (You imagine that the kid will turn up alive once the beast is defeated, but no such luck.) This was almost as good as the rat stories.

In a two-part story in *Airboy* (vol.7, 4–5) the lad investigates when the waters of the world begin to rise to dangerous levels. He discovers that a villain has planted a certain device in a volcano, now frozen over with ice. Airboy smashes the device, but the resulting steam thaws out all manner of prehistoric creatures that had sought warmth in the volcano and were trapped in ice instead. A pterodactyl carries off the villain of the piece, while a platoon of seabees use tractors to force a herd of thundering mastodons off a cliff, and Airboy himself evades the hungry jaws of a large tyrannosaurus rex. In *Airboy* (vol.8, 10) the hero leads the fight against large insectoid aliens who arrive on a meteor and develop a society under the earth. More aliens with huge tentacles which they use to snatch away scientists, and Airboy, appear in *Airboy* (vol.9, 6). The next issue depicts a lively full-scale invasion of the slimy monsters in pyramid-like spaceships, but Airboy and the armed forces are able to beat them back. A spooky story has Airboy investigating a ghost plane that appears each night on a closed-down runway even though the real plane crashed, killing everyone aboard, some time ago. It develops that the pilot survived and flies the "ghost" plane, filled with dummies in place of passengers, to try to freak his business partner, who planned the crash for financial reasons, into confessing (*Airboy* vol.9, 8).

Eight

Key, St. John's, Story, Quality, Smaller and Canadian Publishers

KEY COMICS

A Dapper Dan in an opera hat, mask, and cloak introduced "Tales of Horror and Suspense" in *Mister Mystery*, which debuted in 1951. The first issue has one story, "Hand," in which a man, who has already lost one evil twin to illness, is strangled from *within* his body by the late-developing hand of another twin who was never born. The compelling "Death à la Carte" tells of how guilt eats away at a man who feels responsible for the death of an imbecilic, nearly vegetative young cousin that he's forced to take care of. Other notable stories in the series included "The Brain Bats of Venus" (*MM*7) which features title organisms that attach themselves first to Venusians and then humans and take over their minds; and "Capsule" (10), in which a man tries to escape from jail by taking a pill that shrinks him to tiny size but hasn't reckoned with a mouse that shares his cell and has him for dinner; the last panel shows the rodent gnawing on a tiny human skeleton. "After Death" (15) features a mousy man who rebels and murders his wealthy wife, but she is reincarnated as an animal and gets a diabolical revenge. There were also the occasional EC-style story such as "Modern Design" (9) in which an unfaithful wife keeps nagging her designer husband to "put something of me" in his work, so it comes as no surprise when his next lamp consists of her dead, twisted body with a shade on top of it. In "The Immortal Brain" (16) a man has the top of his head sliced off with an ax so it can be a receptacle for the title object and some prisoners devour the fat pig of a jailer who eats food intended for them in "Hunger" (16). In "Hen Pecked" (17) a man with a loathsome wife and daughters who have nothing but contempt for him kills them and places their heads atop sculptures. "Intelligence" in *MM* 9 was simply another rip-off of "Leiningen versus the Ants."

Weird Mysteries debuted in 1952 and lasted for twelve issues. The third issue introduced a witch-like, wart-faced narrator called the "ghoul teacher," and also had a gruesome cover with a specter holding up a human head while the man who severed it stands over the headless corpse in shock. The lead EC-style story, "While the Iron Was Hot," features a hen-pecked tailor who finally turns and uses his wife's armless, headless body as a clothes dummy. The

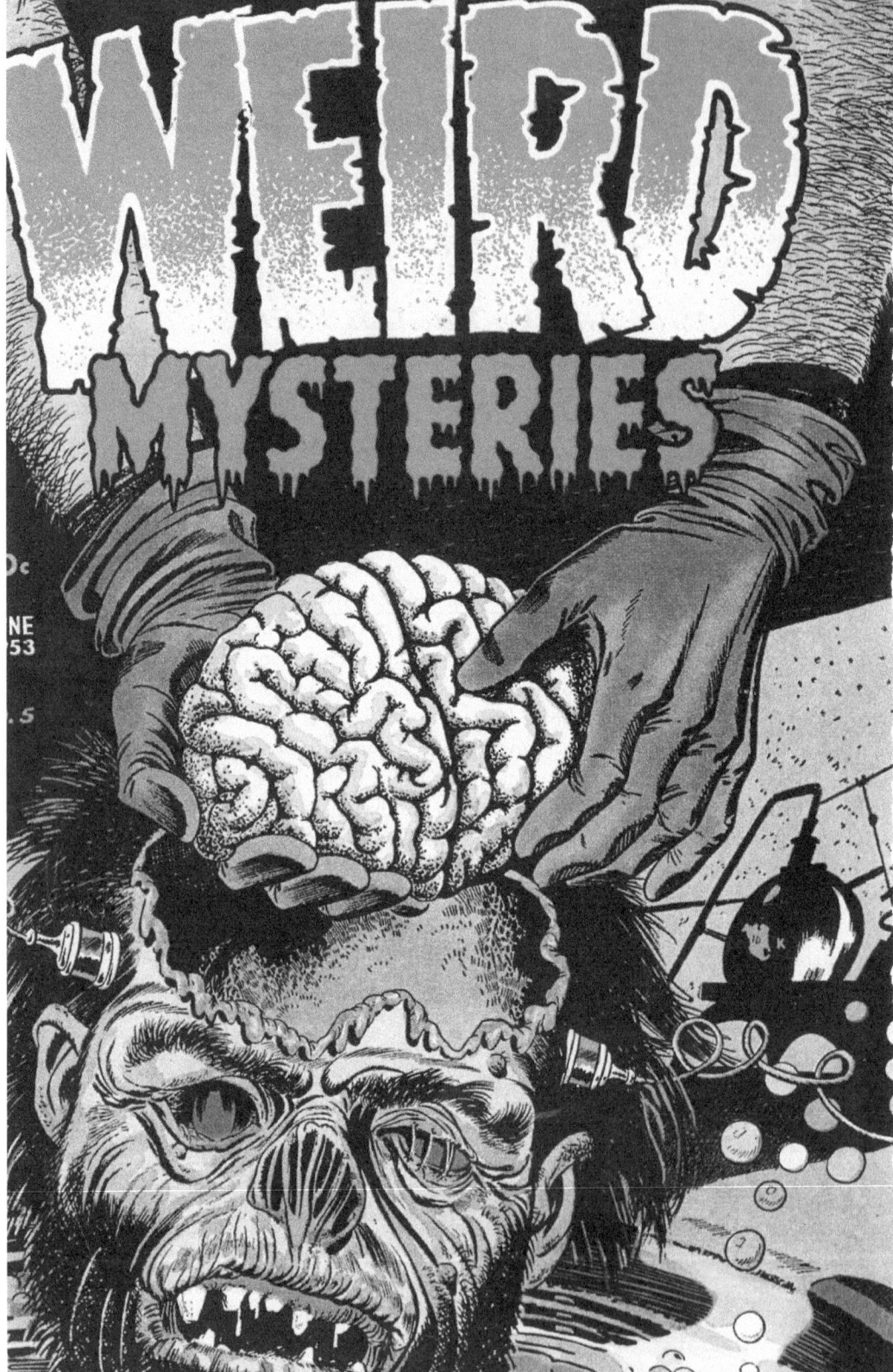

series tried to outdo EC Comics with its covers: On the fifth issue, a brain is lifted out of a desiccated cranium attached to electrodes. A severed head with its lips sewn shut was pulled up out of a magician's top hat on the cover of *WM 6*.

While never a first-class series like its sister publication, *Weird Mysteries* had a few entertaining stories. "Turnabout" (2) has space explorers bedeviled by a giant ant-like creature who has them scurrying like earth ants to stay out of its hungry pincers. There were more giant ants in "The Disbeliever" (3), about sewer monsters who eat their victims down to the bone, after which the skeletons somehow turn into more giant ants. In "Epitaph" (9) ghosts come out of their cemetery graves to etch the unpleasant reality of their lives with spectral fingers on their gravestones, thus the protagonist learns that his recently deceased and beloved wife was unfaithful and died in her rush to meet her lover. In "Life Insurance" (11) a man buys a policy from a firm that assures him their "business is to prevent death" and soon discovers this is literally true, that he cannot be killed, a situation that brings him joy until he is in an accident that leaves him paralyzed, burnt, and unable to see or speak—but hopelessly *alive* until the policy runs out in many years, another variation on a popular theme in horror comics.

In "Eternal Death" (*WM* 10) 72-year-old Professor Pierre Caron falls in love with a much younger woman, Lydia, who admits she loves his mind but needs a younger man. Caron comes up with a fascinating scheme to get a young body. He searches for a handsome man who accidentally died while young and presumably in good health. At this point most stories would have Caron digging up the younger man's grave, but instead the wise old professor contacts a medium, and with the aid of a machine, is able to put his mind into the physical and intact body of the dead man. Unfortunately, this man turns out to be Lydia's late fiance, who had a heart attack while driving to see his specialist. A distraught Caron also succumbs to heart disease, but while he appears to be dead, he is still conscious even as he's being buried, wishing he'd told someone to turn on his machine and reverse the process.

On occasion *Mister Mystery* and *Weird Mysteries* would present very similar stories with different artwork, probably because the editors had commissioned two different artists to bring the same script to life; there would then be some adjustments made to the dialogue so the stories wouldn't be exactly alike. Sometimes a story would be turned into a new one by switching or adding a few panels and changing the ending or combining panels from two different stories, a cost-saving device. Some stories in both comics also utilized a bit of business where some panels depicting thunder and lightning, the moon, or something similarly portentous would appear in the story just before a murder took place.

Key came out with one issue of *Weird Chills* in 1954. In "The Last Supper" a man feeds his friend, whose wife has become his lover, a pill that is supposed to kill him without leaving a trace, but instead it literally blows him to pieces, then causes a chain reaction that wipes out him and the wife as well. "Hallucinations" has a man coming to realize he is haunted by an invisible presence that, when covered in flour, turns out to look just like him. He gives this alter-ego his own bedroom, then discovers that the alter ego has his *own* alter ego, and so on, driving his psychiatrist bonkers. "The Gorilla" is the tender tale of a wife who meets a big ape at the zoo and falls under the beast's spell, going so far as to prepare to marry the animal before her husband comes in with a gun and breaks up the ceremony. *Weird Chills* was, indeed, quite weird.

Opposite: Key's *Weird Mysteries* series: brains were always popular.

QUALITY

Quality comics published a lot of super hero comics but did only one horror series, *Web of Evil,* beginning in 1952. "Custodian of Death" in *Web of Evil* 1, drawn by Jack Cole, concerns an undertaker, Horace Vennery, who helps himself to the belongings that the deceased have buried with them by robbing their caskets after burial, and has special plans for a beautiful stick pin worn by Egbert Madison, an elderly man of his acquaintance. But Madison doesn't trust Vennery, and tells him he's going to another undertaker. When the gravediggers go on strike, however, Madison winds up in a receiving tomb with many other bodies awaiting burial, and Vennery breaks in to steal the goodies; Madison's corpse gives him trouble, however, as it seems a little too animated. Vennery tries for the stickpin again once Madison is properly buried, but discovers that a horde of rats have other ideas when it comes to Madison—and Vennery. This story, and many others like it, owes a debt to Henry Kuttner's classic tale "Graveyard Rats," published in the thirties.

In addition to suspense stories of evil spouses and greedy business associates or treasure seekers plotting murder, *Web of Evil* ran a few monster stories, including one about a King Kong–like prehistoric ape and another about an irradiated scientist who grows into a mad giant desperate for atomic energy. There was also a thirty-foot giant Zombie named King Zog and a rip-off of *The Beast from 20,000 Fathoms* in which a scientist can't convince anyone that a sea monster is on the loose. One of the best creature stories to appear in a horror mag was the cover story in *Web of Evil* 4, "The Monster of the Mist."

In this Dr. Mornay, a scientist, is out in a boat with his daughter, Beth and her fiance Dick, when a sea monster attacks their boat. The young couple manage to escape and make it to shore, but they assume Mornay was devoured by the beast, their tale of which turns them into laughingstocks. But they discover Mornay is alive when he contacts them and tells them to meet him at a small coastal town where someone has been killing and carrying off numerous sheep. Mornay explains that the monster only nudged him to shore, and he wanted to keep it near land so he could study it. Figuring if he fed the creature it wouldn't leave, he brought it sheep, but the beast wouldn't eat the sheep until Mornay cut their throats and the creature smelled blood. But Mornay discovers that because of its very large gills, the monster can actually come ashore whenever there's a mist, and it is now going after its own sheep. Afraid it might munch on people by mistake, Mornay puts explosives inside a sheep and is trying to feed it to the monster when a bunch of angry sheep owners arrive. The creature takes after them and gobbles them up, now developing a taste for human flesh. Dick manages to destroy the blood-hungry creature, but before he dies Mornay confesses that there is a smaller one in the sea that he already fed meat to. Whenever there's a mist this creature may come out and walk on land in search of food.

Web would frequently run "fake" supernatural stories with twist endings. An adopted woman who is hated by her entire family pretends to commit suicide, then "comes back" from the grave to murder all of her relatives. In "The Uninvited Corpse" (*Web* 12) a woman preoccupies her husband as her lover rushes up behind him to push him off a cliff, then both of them have to contend with his living corpse, which shows up and drives them crazy. As they walk to town past the spot where he fell from the cliff, they begin to bicker, battle, and fall to their deaths. At the end it is revealed that the husband survived his fall, put his identification on the body of a drowned sailor, and made himself up to look like a cadaver. (It's a question if he could be prosecuted for conspiracy to commit murder even though he never laid a finger on the dead couple.) In "Scared to Death" (*Web* 18) a young student is laughed at because of his belief in ghosts and the like and becomes the victim of a practical joke involving a corpse, a joke which leaves him dead and disfigured. His ghost comes back from the grave years later to get even with the jokesters, leaving them deformed in various ways as he crows that he has proved the supernatural exists. But it turns out that he only faked his death (using the aforementioned corpse) but once he gets his revenge has to be put in a nuthouse. (*Web* published an inordinate number of tales of actual spirits coming back to extract brutal vengeance.)

Web of Evil rarely if ever went the extremely graphic route of EC comics, and in general, wasn't even that gruesome. A rare exception was "The Shrunken Heads of Dr. Death" (*Web* 12), in which a mad doctor in Brazil kills the surviving passengers of a DC-6 crash, decapitates them, and adds them to his collection of shrunken heads. When one passenger's sister and friend come looking for him, they encounter this Dr. Death, who denies all knowledge of the crash. But the woman sees her brother's ring on the doctor's finger. Dr. Death tries to kill both of the them, but his pet chimp discovers that he also shrunk his mate's head, so he turns on the doctor and throws him into a lime pit. Despite the grisly goings-on the depictions were tasteful as compared to the EC product.

Web of Evil was often quite entertaining and had good story ideas that weren't always developed with enough elan or skill. It was, however, one of the best-drawn horror mags on the market. Artists included Jack Cole, Sam Citron, Sheldon Moldoff, and Charles Nicholas.

St. John's

St. John's publishers came out with both *Strange Terrors* and *Weird Horrors* in 1952. The covers for the former were unusual in that eventually they looked like magazine covers with illustrations instead of comic book covers; *Weird Horrors* followed suit. This was done to make the titles stand out on the over-crowded newsstand, but it may have backfired as the covers weren't dramatic or horrific enough to attract attention. The fifth issue of *Strange Terrors* has one fairly interesting if predictable story in which a man falls for a young lady who is to be sacrificed to a mammoth, flesh-hungry minotaur on her twenty-first birthday. The last two issues of *Strange Terrors* were 100 pages each. There was an improvement in the art in the new material (some reprint material was included), but the stories—a mix of horror, fantasy and sci fi—were standard fare without originality or clever twists.

The one exception was "Wrong-Way Taxi," which appeared in *ST* 7. The story begins with a cab suddenly appearing on the roof of a hotel during a parade. The taxi plummets to the street and the five passengers are killed. A reporter who was assigned to discover their identities goes to a medium, and winds up in a trance in which he becomes a sixth passenger in the cab. The other five people are all dissatisfied with life—one old woman is afraid her children will put her in a home, and another man is a gangster on the run, while the remaining three passengers have much more frivolous reasons for wanting to escape reality. When they arrive at the other dimension—whatever it is—where the cab is heading the driver is told that they have to take the extra passenger, the reporter, back before they can disembark. The driver turns the car around and explains that whenever he returns the taxi to the real world it can wind up in the oddest places—like, for example, the roof of a hotel; he is unable to stop the momentum and the car plunges to the street. The reporter wakes up back in his chair at the medium's home, and returns to work. But he doesn't want to know the names of the passengers. "People who can't face up to things any better than that these days, should be forgotten," he says. (Which is an odd thing to say considering he was in some bizarre metaphysical way responsible for their deaths in the first place.) While this allegorical look at suicide was at least original, like most of the other stories in the series it wasn't as well developed as it could have been.

Early stories in *Weird Horrors* often seemed like standard mysteries or adventure stories with some supernatural stuff thrown in at the end. *WH* 5 has a science fiction story entitled "Invasion from the Past" in which a scientist invents a window through one can see events and creatures from long ago, but his jealous idiot assistant brings these creatures—including a giant man and a dinosaur-like serpent— into the present, where they cause much havoc before being dispatched with sonics. More interesting is "The Phantom Guillotine" in the following issue, in which Fowler, an American businessman, gets rid of a French rival, Michaud, by giving false testimony that convicts the Frenchman of murdering his business partner. Sailing back to America with his daughters after Michaud's execution by guillotine, Fowler gets a telegram stating that someone else confessed to the crime, and ordering him back to Paris to stand trial for perjury. Instead Fowler jumps overboard and is beheaded by the boat's propellers (this is described but not shown). His daughters want to make amends for their father's evil deeds, but Michaud's brother, Henri, is convinced they were in on the plot to destroy his sibling, and follows them to the states with plans to exact revenge. The two women are tormented by constant dreams and fantasies of grisly decapitation, until at last they are confronted by Henri, but he is dissuaded from his plans by his brother's spirit, who assures him that the ladies are innocent. (If this had been an EC story both women would probably have lost their heads.) Despite the lack of graphic bloodletting the story still summons up a certain *frisson*.

The ninth and final issue of *Weird Horrors* had a more traditional cover drawn by Joe Kubert, who also did the art for the issue's excellent lead story, "Map of Doom." A newlywed couple named Bev and Carl come to an old mansion inherited from Bev's dead aunt. Inside a secret room they find a coffin inside which is an ancient atlas. Oddly, the atlas looks old but its maps are completely up to date. Not only that, but when Carl puts his finger on the map of Manhattan, he swears he can *feel* the buildings, as if the map were alive. Bev touches a map of Hawaii and her finger comes up dripping wet. They later hear on the radio that downtown Manhattan has been wiped out with thousands of deaths, and the Hawaiian islands just sank without a trace. Reeling from the news, Carl decides on another test and smashes a hammer down on Iceland; it, too, is destroyed in a flash. Drunk with power, the evil couple call the authorities and threaten to obliterate Chicago if their demands aren't met, but no one believes them, which means the end of the Windy City. Eventually more cities are wiped out by the nasty pair until the world leaders capitulate, but now Carl decides he can now do better than Bev and decides to murder her. Bev realizes what he's up to and uses the map to get rid of him when he's in town, literally tearing up the streets—and Carl— with a knife. But in her haste and fury she brings the knife too close to the mansion where she is sitting and....

St. John's *Nightmare* came out in 1953. The comic presented such tales as "The Werewolf of Washington Square," which is merely a standard wolfman story despite the promising title, just as "The Quivering Brian" is a pallid imitation of "Donovan's Brain," although it at least offers a closing panel of the evil brain being tossed in a garbage can where it gathers flies; both stories were in the third issue. Then *Nightmare* took over *Weird Horrors* so that its third issue was followed by its tenth. The comic presented everything from sci fi stories similar to DC Comics' (and with DC artists like Murphy Anderson on art) and Poe adaptations such as a well-done version of "Hop-Frog," in which a dwarf gets even with an evil king and queen, in *Nightmare* 11. "The Mouse" in the same issue is a fascinating tale of Albert Small, a put-upon man who during one unusual day is the sole survivor of several terrible accidents—on a bus, in an elevator, etc.—that each claim the lives of five other people. Albert wants to kill off the two old aunts he lives with who control the family fortune, so he invites three hated co-workers to dinner to make up a party of six, hoping the other five will be killed, but in the comparatively flat wind up to an intriguing story Albert is crushed by a grandfather clock that reads six o'clock as he goes to answer the door.

"The Horror on the S.S. Malabar" (*Nightmare* 12) is the true story of Ann Saunders, one of several crew and passengers on a ship wrecked in 1826 who later admitted that they resorted to cannibalism to survive and that she drank the blood of her own fiance, the ship's cook, after he expired. The story is told without sensationalism or gore, with matter-of-fact artwork, but it certainly doesn't have the impact it might have had in an EC Comic. With the fourteenth issue the title was changed to *Amazing Ghost Stories*, which reprinted stories that had already appeared in Ziff-Davis' own *Nightmare* series.

St. John's came out with one last horror-fantasy series in 1957: *Do You Believe in Nightmares?* The first issue was entirely drawn by Steve Ditko, but the stories are unmemorable, to say the least. There were a number of artists in the second issue, but the stories were just as poor and that was the final issue. The one-shot *House of Terror* in 3D presented reprints from St. John's other series.

Story

Story comics came out with *Mysterious Adventures* in 1951. The lead story in the first issue, about a Civil War vampire, features the startling sight of a bat flying about with a normal-sized human head on its winged body, but is otherwise forgettable. In "Terror of the Ancient Skeleton" (*Mysterious Adventures* 4) anyone who carries off a piece of a skeleton from an ancient race winds up losing the same piece—be it finger or leg—from their own body. The protagonists of "The Pool of Eternity" (*MA* 5) imbibe a liquid that makes them immortal, which is a decided problem when both are beheaded by Jivaros and wind up shrunken heads on poles—still alive *forever*! "The Absent-Minded Fiend" (7) is a wealthy woman who thinks her husband is trying to drive her out of her mind by convincing her she's turned into a cannibalistic ghoul. There were lots of half-eaten bloody limbs strewn about this story, but even more gruesome is the final panel of another story in the issue that depicts a man who'd been skinned alive when his assailant "took back his tattoos." In "The Vultures of Doom" (12) a man gains control of a large vulture that does what he commands, including killing enemies and stealing jewels, but when the woman he loves refuses to marry him the vulture goes off and returns with her head in its claws. Disgusted, the man screams that he never wants to see the bird again, whereupon it pecks out his eyes.

Eventually the series added nameless horror hosts who were modeled on the EC comics hosts, similarly called the readers "kiddies," but had little personality. The comic, which had generally featured art that could best be described as wretched, hired artists who could deliver visuals that were more attractive and yet also had more "impact." The gruesome EC style continued with such stories as "A Dead Ball" (*MA* 14) in which a young man who blames the gruff football coach for his brother's death apparently puts the man's severed head inside the football that's kicked around in the next game. (This came out the same year as EC's "Foul Play" and was presumably a copy of it.) Then there was the astoundingly sexist "A Pound of Flesh" (*MA* 16) in which Herbert, whose wife has become grossly fat after fifteen years of marriage, builds a slender robot that resembles her, but can't find the right kind of material for her skin—until he takes a knife to his wife and uses her own skin for the robot. In "Paralyzed" (17) a man has been caring for his wife—and going broke doing so—out of guilt because he was driving drunk when she was a passenger during the accident that paralyzed her. But he discovers that she has been faking her injuries, and carrying on with her doctor, and that both of them hope he'll have a fatal heart attack from overwork and they can collect his insurance. When the doctor comes around the next day, he discovers that the husband has indeed succumbed, but not before chopping off his wife's legs and letting her bleed to death. "Chef's Delight" (20) has a woman with a pig of a husband, a famous French chef, taking an ax to him and leaving pieces of him in his kitchen as various not-so-succulent dishes.

"The Iceman Cometh" (*MA* 16), with no apologies to Eugene O'Neill, takes place in 1926 and deals with a man who runs an ice business but who is losing money because more and more people are buying refrigerators. His greedy wife falls in love with the hunky guy who delivers the ice, and they decide to lock hubby in the walk-in ice closet so they can collect his insurance (never mind that this would probably *not* freeze the man to death). But hubby overhears the plot and outwits them; his wife discovers the dismembered frozen pieces of lover boy's body in the ice closet before she gets locked inside by her husband. "Bottoms Up" (18) has a woman who supports her constantly drunken husband going over the edge when he lets their little boy walk to school by himself and the child is run over. To pay for the funeral she returns the last case of rye that her husband bought from his bootlegger, but the latter is unaware that the alcoholic husband is distributed evenly inside each bottle in gory shreds after the grief-stricken and enraged wife took an ax to him.

Also like EC comics, some of the stories were more interested in the gruesome ending than in telling a well-constructed tale with a satisfying conclusion. For instance "The Hunter and the Hunted" in *MA* 15 presents what today we would call a young sociopath who tortures and kills animals at an early age and grows up to become a famous hunter with a huge menagerie of trophies. He is easily flattered and talked into hunting down legendary prehistoric beasts in isolated territory that no other hunter has been able to capture. The story is compelling thus far, but it completely loses its reason when our anti-hero finally encounters these dinosaurs, who are intelligent, speak perfect English, and love bowling as much as the protagonist loves hunting—only they use severed human heads, including you-know-who's, instead of bowling balls. The story didn't even work as a black comedy.

There were mothers who went to monstrous lengths to control their sons lives, and jealous husbands who dispatched their wives for alleged misdeeds but who were often innocent. A man who puts acid in his wife's drink winds up getting the liquid thrown in his face while two "normal" circus men who murder a midget get turned into a two-headed freak when the head of one is sewn onto the neck of the other. Now and then there would be the usual vampires and werewolves to go with the avenging husbands and philandering gold-diggers, such as "Ghoulash" (*MA* 20) in which two brothers court the same pretty woman unaware that she's a vampire who has plans for both of them, just as she is unaware that they are werewolves whose designs on her are equally unhealthy (variations of this plot appeared quite often in the horror comics). The last few issues of *Mysterious Adventures* in 1954 underwent an editorial switch from gore and mutilation to fantasy and supernatural tales. The series was gone with the twenty-fifth issue. Artists for the series included Doyle Cohen, John D'Agostino, Doug Wildey, Hy Fleischman, and Richard Doxsee.

Story's second horror comic was entitled *Dark Mysteries* and also debuted in 1951. In the disturbing "Dead Man's Chest" (*Dark Mysteries* 8) a man named Ted has a skiing accident which leaves his body twisted and deformed. Fresh bone is the only thing that can be used to repair his body, so he opens up the grave of a recently executed killer named Lefty and his doctor uses Lefty's bone for a successful graft. Unfortunately a smaller version of Lefty's head begins growing out of Ted's chest, growing larger and larger, and it causes Ted to attack and murder women the way the vicious Lefty did. Ted winds up in an insane asylum, still sticking to his story, but Lefty's head still grows out of his chest even after Ted's death. Despite his forgivable grave-robbing, poor Ted really did nothing but have a bad accident. In "A Murderer's Mask" (12) a sculptor named Roland Adams loves to be shown to the scenes of a recent series of gruesome murders, so he can make death masks showing the grotesque facial contortions of the victims, for whom he seems to have little pity. The police have no idea what the murder weapon could be, until Adams discovers it's a sculptor's chisel when he becomes the maniac's latest victim.

Eventually, like *Mysterious Adventures*, *Dark Mysteries* ladled out the gore in the EC manner. An angry mystic who helped a man make money and was cheated out of the half he was promised, takes his money and *half* of the man's sweetheart and kills the man, leaving the police to find one and a half bodies. The cover of *DM* 13 depicts a convict's severed leg, bone protruding and chain attached, walking the corridor of a prison. A story on the inside was entitled "Horror of Mixed Torsos" and had a crazed mortician's assistant murdering two men and mixing up the four pieces of their bodies. Another story in the next issue has a man feeding his shrewish wife to a cement mixer which grinds up all but her vengeful hands.

"Time to Die" (16) was a rare relatively sensitive story in *Dark Mysteries.* A dead father comes back from the grave when he hears his little boy cry out in terror as he's beaten by the man who was supposed to take care of him. The father takes the now dead boy back with him to his grave. The story is meant to be moving but with no real characterization or context it falls flat. "Some Die Twice" in *Dark Mysteries* 18 is probably the best story published by the series. Barney, a miserable slave trader, captures cannibals who refuse to eat dead people. When Barney learns that his gentle wife, Marna, who's just discovered his profession, has taken a lover, Blair, he brutally murders him. So Marna gives Barney a paralytic drug that makes him appear to be dead. The story ends with the cannibals about to feast on Barney as he lies completely conscious but totally unable to move.

Story Comics' *Fight Against Crime* gradually began adding graphic horror elements to its stories of murder and mystery, blazing the words HORROR AND TERROR under the logo. The seventeenth issue (1954), in which all of the four stories are winners, boasts a visceral crime tale called "Trapped" in which two men who have robbed a bank and inadvertently

A cleverly ghoulish cover for Story's *Dark Mysteries* 13.

murdered a small boy wind up crossing a desert while handcuffed to each other, until the first one to die of thirst and exhaustion becomes food for vultures, his skeleton picked clean, while the other waits his turn, which isn't long in coming. (This was, of course, not the only vulture/desert story published in the fifties.) "Heartless" deals with a miserable soul in the hospital who tells the doctor how he ruined the life of an innocent woman who once worked for him, only to learn she killed herself and the doctor was her husband—and he has special plans for his "heartless" patient. A story about a man who murders his wife and thinks he'll get away with it, and another revenge tale of a woman who gets even with the man she thinks is responsible for her husband's lynching, round out the issue.

Fight Against Crime 20, in an obvious bid to get EC's readers, features a notorious cover of a man stuffing a woman's body down through a manhole while he holds her severed (if bloodless) head in his hand and a cop car drives up in the background; this scene doesn't appear in the issue itself, however. The contents were good in any case. The lead story "Smoked-Out," in which a husband murders his cheating wife only to discover that he was tragically mistaken about the whole situation, is hardly a new premise, but the ending still delivers a punch. The man she was supposedly having an affair with was a doctor treating her for terminal lung cancer, a condition she wanted to keep from her husband. The doctor knew that she couldn't have died from smoking in bed—arranged by her husband—because she'd given up smoking two months before her "accident."

"Double Trouble" is a James M. Cain pastiche of lovers who murder the woman's much older husband with graphic scenes of him being bloodily crushed by a truck. "The Thief" is an ironic tale of a middle-aged man who takes desperate steps when he is prematurely let go from the firm that has been his whole life. In "Two-of-a-Kind" a spinster daughter and her boyfriend take an ax to the woman's hateful old mother, but are done in themselves when the dead woman's equally nasty dog runs in with her severed arm in its mouth just as a cop comes calling for a promised ten dollars for the policeman's ball. If there's any problem with this otherwise excellent crime-horror story it's that one can't imagine why the daughter didn't manage to get away from the awful mother long before.

SMALLER PUBLISHERS

Holyoke publishers had some macabre tales in their publication *Suspense Comics* in 1945. In "The Man Who Murdered Himself" Harvey Smith is terrified that Elias Green, a man he sent to prison but who has served his time and is now free, will come to kill him. When a crook on the lam tries to hide in Smith's home, the latter notices how much they look alike and conceives a plan. This man will pose as him in his opulent mansion, and hopefully Green will kill *him* instead of the real target. But when Green shows up at the mansion, the imposter is able to subdue him and has him arrested. A relieved Green goes back to his home whereupon the imposter insists that *he* is Harvey Smith and Smith is an imposter. An outraged Smith kills his double, is arrested, and executed for—as he ironically realizes—murdering himself, as the police still believe the dead man to be Smith.

Some stories in the comic were narrated or otherwise observed by "Mr. Zero," a lackluster Phantom Stranger type (that actually pre-dated the DC character), although there were on occasion some interesting tales, such as "The Double-Cross Coffin," involving a harried housekeeper and the miserable old man she works for; "After I Murdered Sandra," in which a bored, psychotic writer plots and executes the perfect murder; and "Snare of the Spider" in which two cousins who hate the idea of sharing their dying uncle's wealth plot each other's murder. A particularly interesting tale appears in *Suspense* 10, "A Matter of Text," in which a beautiful woman in the Golden Scorpion cafe hands a man a letter written in Arabic. When the protagonist asks a series of people to translate it, they either become outraged or terrified but in each and every case they die within moments of reading the letter. This story would be a bizarre little gem were it not for the fact that the writer was unable to come up with a satisfactory ending, let alone an explanation. *Suspense* also featured a mediocre series in which Satan changes places with a gang leader and walks the earth in human guise.

Star comics took over the super-hero comic *Blue Bolt*, which had previously been published by Novelty Press, in 1949, beginning with the one hundred second issue. Blue Bolt appeared with such supporting players as Target and the Targeteers and Rick Richards. But as with most other comics companies, super-heroes were on the wane and the Blue Bolt comic eventually started running horror and supernatural stories, the title being changed to *Blue Bolt Weird Tales* in the early fifties. The chief writer-artist, Jay Disbrow, would contribute two or three stories each issue. Most of these were not memorable, but there were exceptions. In "The Black Room" (*Blue Bolt* 113, reprinted in *Eerie* 15) Hector Thorg murders his brother with a guillotine which their father kept in a locked room and used to dispatch his political enemies. The crazy Thorg sees everyone as conspiring against him and leads so many people into the black room and death that townspeople eventually invade his domicile and wall him up in the room to suffocate. Years later his ghost breaks out but is finally destroyed during an encounter with the current resident. "The Ghoul of the North" recounts an unfortunate reporter's investigation into a gigantic creature in an Alaskan gorge that can change into different, equally terrifying shapes. Two issues later "The Return of the Ghoul" tells how explorer Jeff Charteres decides to follow the reporter's trail and comes across the same enormous creature, but is able to destroy it without discovering all of the secrets it was guarding.

Star comics debuted *Startling Terror Tales* in 1952. The tenth issue (vol. 1) has a very well done adaptation of Stevenson's "Dr. Jekyll and Mr. Hyde" that was almost as suspenseful and exciting as the original. "Love from a Gorgon" in *STT* 13 (vol. 1) is a bizarre Jay Disbrow concoction in which a horrified man discovers he is the object of a massive and aggressive crush by a hideous female alien who wants him to be her mate but who completely repulses him. Unfortunately for its second volume *Startling Terror Tales* became a true-crime comic with a nominal lead horror story, which itself was eventually dropped. During its brief run the comic also ran a few jungle stories, functioning as a kind of loose story dumping ground. Star came out with *Ghostly Weird Stories* in 1953; its first issue was numbered 120. The comic was a strange, indifferently drawn melange of sci fi, horror, super-hero, and jungle stories. In five issues there was only one halfway decent story: Jay Disbrow's "Death Ship" (122) is an interesting study of a spaceship captain reflecting on his dissatisfaction with life despite his love for his life and child back on Earth, his continual quest for something wonderful and different in the stars, as he and his crew burn to death as a star goes nova. Star also took *Spook*, which had presented crime and detective stories, and turned it into a semi-horror mag in 1953, although it continued to run a few "true" crime stories and a lot of reprints along with poor stories about mummies and swamp monsters.

Sterling Comics debuted *The Tormented* in 1954; it lasted only two issues. "The Girl Who

One of Star comic's entries in the horror sweepstakes was *Ghostly Weird Stories*. The only halfway decent story was in this issue, 122.

Wasn't There" (*T* 1) is a creepy tale in which a jealous actress who covets a leading stage role turns out to be a witch who is able to wipe out all traces of the starring actress's existence, as well as anyone who dares to remember her. In "Dinner for One," also in the first issue, a nasty hunter and his reluctant bride come afoul of a man in the woods who serves the woman a plate of meat that has her husband's bracelet in it, then pulls out a knife to make her another main course or two. "Design for Death" (*T* 2) is the comical story of mad Leopold, who makes special platters in his kiln that incorporate flowers and birds that are somehow still alive after the process, as is the startled severed head of the chubby patroness who dares to order Leopold out of her house. "Honeymoon Horror" is yet another rip-off of the classic story "Revenge," in which a woman points out her attacker as one man, and then another man, after her husband has killed the first in retaliation.

Toby/Minoan introduced *Tales of Horror* in 1952. The first issue presented a mix of horror, crime, fantasy and science fiction, none of which were very memorable. Some of the tales in the comic were introduced by an unnamed and uninteresting host who often wore a hat and cloak. *Tales of Horror* 3, however, has a smashing story entitled "The Big Snake," in which a crazy scientist develops a formula that grows animals to giant size. A gargantuan snake escapes and devours him, absorbing some of his personality and hatred. The snake attacks Manhattan island, wrapping itself around the Empire State Building (this scene illustrated the cover when the story was reprinted in *TOH* 8), until another brave scientist sacrifices his life to get the creature to eat a formula that brings it back to normal size.

In "Who Shall Inherit the Earth?" (*TOH* 4) another crazy and embittered scientist uses a formula to make rats super-intelligent, resulting in the biggest rat-human war since the stories in *Airboy* in the forties. The Army drops a hydrogen bomb on the rat-besieged European city, but some of the rats manage to make their way shipboard. "Sisters of the Witch" (*TOH* 5) features a plain and jealous woman who uses witchcraft to horribly kill off her rivals for a man's affection—her own sisters, not the first time this plot was employed. "The Beast from the Deep" (7), about a sea monster who responds to a foghorn as if it were a mating call, is a "borrowing" of Ray Bradbury's story 'The Foghorn," filmed that same year as *The Beast from 20,000 Fathoms*. In "Pool of the Skeletons" (8) a very wealthy man who was picked on in school, invites three of his attractive tormentors to dinner at his estate, then invites them to swim in his pool. Unfortunately, they are unaware that he has filled it with a formula that strips them down to skeletons in a matter of moments. He then pushes in his horrified, protesting butler, but as he walks away he trips on the dead female guest's bathrobe and becomes the fifth skeleton in the pool. A character called the Purple Claw (referring to a mystical glove he wore), aka Dr. Jonathan Weir, briefly took over *Tales of Horror* after his own series was discontinued. He investigates a couple who can turn into giant man-eating, black widow spiders; a were-snake; a ten-foot giant; and a man who can transform into a gigantic man-eating flower. The thirteenth and final issue of *Tales of Horror* is one of the most interesting. It features a murdered gypsy who comes back as a bull and mauls the matador responsible for his death; a ghost who stands by and lets her philandering husband be murdered so he can join her in the afterlife, only he continues to be a cheating dog even after his death; and a man who comes to believe that his adorable adopted son is one of several demons who are disguised as children and blowing up factories. Artists for the series included Myron Fass and Sal Trapani.

Trojan comics came out with *Beware* in 1953, continuing it after Youthful publishers dropped the series. Stories were introduced by a "Nameless One" in a hood that revealed only the narrator's eyes. In "The Thing from Beyond" (6) an ugly hunchback and cemetery caretaker is shunned by everyone and seeks revenge, cutting off the hands of one tormentor and killing several others, then combining body parts to fashion an unliving creature that he torments mercilessly and discards, but that comes back to life to get revenge on him. In "Almost Human" (6) robots murder people and steal their tongues, the only part of their anatomy that cannot be duplicated by science. In "The Life of Riley" (7) a robber hangs out in a sinister house in the swamp with strange characters until it's safe for him to leave, but discovers human body parts in a food locker and realizes too late that the real reason he's there is to be the next item on the ghouls' menu. "The Black Death" (8) has two young lovers try to escape a city in the midst of a plague despite warnings that they must not leave, but their plans involving a coffin with a princess' and plague victim's corpse only lead to awful tragedy.

"The Bell Tolls Death" (10) details how a young couple dive for pirate's treasure off a lonely atoll but discover that the corpses and ghosts of the pirates aren't about to let them steal their hard-earned booty. In "His Own Funeral" (11) a man uses the blood and fluids of bums to make an embalming solution that makes corpses seem alive and in the peak of health. "Appetite for Death" (12) is an amusing story of a giant man-eating Voracia plant that a botanist brings home with him and which proceeds to eat everyone and everything that comes near it, including the botanist. Like the ending of the film *Little Shop of Horrors* made six years later, the plant's buds open to reveal the heads of its victims (as noted, this also occurred in a story in *Frankenstein*). "The Clutching Hand" and "Give Me Back My Head," both in the fourteenth issue, have some graphic dismemberment panels in stories of, respectively, a crook who cuts off the hand of a robbery victim to steal his ring, and two men who come afoul of headhunters and greed. Artists for the series included Art Gates and John Forte.

Trojan also did a series entitled *Crime Mysteries*. "Susan and the Devil" in the ninth issue tells the story of a beautiful temptress who leads many men to their doom, murders her rival, but is acquitted of the crime by the all-male jury and judge. When one of her rejected suitors kills her, she gleefully goes to Hell in hopes of vamping Satan — only the Devil turns out to be a woman!

Youthful Comics came out with *Chilling Tales* in 1952. Most of the stories were badly done fantasy-supernatural tales, but there were exceptions. "The Secret of Life and Death" has a man coming to an old house to serve as secretary to a scientist who warns him never to enter a certain room. Of course he does, only to come across a collection of dismembered corpses. Cornering him, the mad doctor tells him he needed the bodies to derive an elixir of life, upon which the corpses get off of their hooks and surround the professor as he screams. There was also the occasional Poe adaptation, and even reprints of his prose stories. The comic had some incredibly crude art. Youthful's *Beware* comic was taken over by Trojan comics, as noted above.

Ziff-Davis publishers came out with three issues of *Nightmare* in 1952. The editor clearly chose material with care, as the comic generally has interesting stories and attractive artwork. "The Corpse That Wouldn't Stay Dead" (*Nightmare* 1) is the tale of two brothers, robust Jeff, who looks after his less athletic and somewhat whiny brother Tom, who resents and even hates him for it. The two are trapped in a cabin during a blizzard and go out to hunt for food, when Tom's gun accidentally goes off and kills his brother. Tom buries Jeff in the snow, but Jeff keeps appearing in the cabin the next day. Tom buries Jeff again and again but he keeps re-appearing. Although Jeff's death was an accident, Tom is wracked with guilt because many times he wanted his brother dead, and he realizes that he still needs him. Tom is eventually rescued, but his mind is gone, and he has to be institutionalized. One night during a storm he breaks out and dies while searching in the snow for his brother, his guilt and his feeling of loss—"I need you Jeff, I need you"—giving him a fatal heart attack. Underneath the supernatural elements was an interesting examination of sibling rivalry and its often contradictory psychological results.

Nightmare 2 is full of good material. "The Devil Dolls" features a criminal mastermind who temporarily places his gang members into dolls that are able to play dead one minute, and jump up and steal—and even commit murder—the next. A police officer assigned to the strange case is trapped in one of the dolls when the crime boss figures out who he is, after which the boss is murdered by the cop when he refuses to switch his mind back into his own body. The grim story ends with the cop pleading with his superior to kill him instead of leaving him as he is, but instead he's locked away in a room for a lifetime or more of loneliness. "The Devil from the Deep" has a man, Robert, falling in love with a beautiful mermaid and trying to make his home adaptable for her even as his best friend, John, warns him that he's becoming enraptured with a freak. The mermaid doesn't like the seafood his houseboy prepares her, so lovesick Robert feeds her some meat. She loves the taste of meat so much that she devours the man's dog, and then goes to work on the houseboy. After burying the houseboy, a distraught Robert takes poison. Discovering the dead body of his friend, John determines to murder the mermaid, especially after he sees that she's gnawed off one of Robert's arms—but this is her undoing, as the poison in his system rapidly puts an end to her hunger and her life.

"Dream Girl" in the same issue concerns a pianist who comes upon a life-size "doll" of a woman in a shop, and discovers that she can come to life and be anything he wants, responding to his innermost thoughts, his ideal woman. She becomes the greatest accompanist he's ever had, but when she responds to another man's desire to paint her, his jealousy and subconscious thoughts make her murder said artist. The woman is put in prison, and the musician thinks that it would be better for her if she were dead—upon which she dies, and he takes her place in the shop, waiting inertly until someone comes along to make *him* do whatever they desire. The issue was rounded out with a fair adaptation of Poe's "Pit and the Pendulum." *Eerie Adventures* was a one-shot from Ziff-Davis that appeared in 1951: A pasty-faced visitor from Venus breeds vampire plants that feed on blood and can uproot themselves to chase after human victims; a sore loser at chess has Death play a rematch in his stead; and a gangster escapes into the 4th dimension and discovers too late that it's Hell.

Master Comics came out with *Dark Mysteries* in 1951 and it ran for 24 issues. In "Cannibal's Revenge" (*DM* 6) a racist who murders a native and accuses his ancestors of eating "long pig," or humans, winds up on a lonely island where he and his girlfriend wind up on the menu. "The Vampire with the Iron Teeth" (15) certainly has a novel twist. When a duchess must have her teeth removed and replaced with iron teeth (because wooden teeth clack terribly), her husband demands that her dental surgeon get her a complete set of ivory teeth pronto because of the laughter her new teeth engender. The surgeon hits upon the idea of using the beautiful teeth of a young woman who recently died. Unfortunately, this lass was a vampire, and the simple act of replacing the duchess' false teeth with the dear departed's turns the duchess herself into a blood-drinker. Art was not the comic's strong point.

Mysterious Stories (Premier, 1955) certainly did its best to resemble an EC Horror comic. The stories were introduced by a Keeper of the Graveyard and a Gravedigger and there was even a feature called "Grandma Gruesome's Deadtime Stories." The comic was not as graphically grisly as the EC product, however. The second issue has at least one somewhat memorable story, "Fate Plays the Violin," in which a concert violinist, Morty Jenks, learns that his Stradivarius will only produce truly breathtaking sounds if hair from the newly dead is used for the bow. Unfortunately the sweet sounds turn sour if the hair isn't replaced on a regular basis. First Morty steals hair from freshly dug graves, then snips it off a person just hit by a car, then goes so far as to frighten a young woman to death. He decides that hair from someone who was a singer should make the violin produce the loveliest notes, so he pays a man to get the hair from a recently departed songstress who performed at the circus. But the man hates the idea of desecrating someone whom he cared for, so he substitutes long fine hair hidden in the folds of an elephant's hide. Monty doesn't know the difference, until he gives a concert and a herd of elephants crash into the hall, trampling him underfoot!

Premier also came out with the one-shot *Horror from the Tomb* in 1954. In "Absent-Minded Professor" a co-ed falls in love with her older college professor and eagerly agrees to marry him. When they arrive at their honeymoon cottage high on a cliff, the professor reveals that he is so accident-prone that most of his parts—arm, foot, ear, hair, teeth and just about everything else—are artificial. Recoiling in disgust, his bride falls out the window to her death as he is revealed in all his featureless and gruesome glory. In "The Bone Man," a paleontologist who is responsible for boiling and cleaning all of the assorted white skeletons in a museum, gets even with a rival, the man's daughter, and indeed the entire board of directors by chopping them up, putting their pieces in his pot, and then dressing the skeletons and featuring them in a special display.

Spook Comics (Bailey Publishing, 1952) was a one-shot with the cover feature of "Mr. Lucifer," who is released from his prison after centuries by some small-time hoodlums whom he "thanks" by pitting his devilish imps against them. Satan then goes on a rampage, he and his imps attacking a boat and killing those on board and diving under the water. They are accidentally locked in a block of stone, however, and never seen again. The other features were cartoons with "horror" themes with the exception of the final story, which concerns a nightclub singer named Caresse who can raise the dead when she dances. By and large, *Spook Comics* was pretty awful.

Canadian Publishers

The writers of *Strange Mysteries* (Superior Publishing, 1952) often seemed to be influenced by famous literary works: one story about a condemned man reviewing his life, and his reason for murdering his father, in the second it takes for him to die from hanging is reminiscent of "Occurrence at Owl Creek Bridge," while another about a manufacturer of inferior airplane parts being haunted by his victims reminds one of Arthur Miller's "All My Sons!" The comic did publish a few more original stories, however. In "Death Deals a Hand" (*SM* 18) John Manning advertises for members for his "Doom Club" for bored souls seeking excitement and adventure. When he gathers a group together, Manning explains that every night they will draw cards, and whomever draws the Ace of Spades must be killed by whomever draws the Club of Spades. Each member agrees to sign over their worldly possessions to the club in the event of their demise. As the game proceeds, some who draw the ace protest in terror while others bravely go to their fate, but no one knows that John Manning is a card sharp who always decides which member is to die—until the ghosts of all his victims get even with him. "Tomb for a Werewolf" (*SM* 18) has a unique spin on the typical werewolf yarn. In this the werewolf is a maker of tombstones, and he prepares the headstones for his victims *before* he even murders them, cleverly combining pleasure with profit.

Superior also came out with *Journey Into Fear* in 1952. Similar to its sister publication, it ran stories in which: a man has his dead wife stuffed and takes him with her everywhere he goes; a voodoo curse turns a man into a midget who has to hide inside a dummy of himself; a man marries a 3000-year-old mummy; a man's life becomes a nightmare after he acquires a crystal ball that foretells terrible events of the future, including his own death; a corpse comes back to life but discovers that the living can't put up with a living *skeleton*; and a gossip columnist gets stories from a typewriter that works by itself but undoes himself when he mistakes something his secretary wrote for a hot tip. Arguably the best story in the series is the genuinely creepy "Doorway to Death" in *JIF* 19. This features a painting of a door—the insane artist mixed human blood from numerous victims into the paint—that is so realistic that the owner of a gallery isn't surprised that he can open the door and walk into a new dimension, the inner rooms of a sinister castle. Each time he enters he feels as if something is behind him, and sees the mark of a huge claw upon the wall. He sets about killing everyone he dislikes and hides their bodies behind the door, where their bones are picked clean by vultures. But after he deposits the body of a police inspector who suspected him (although he could never find the bodies) he discovers that the now-mutated artist who painted the door is waiting to make a meal out of *him*.

The most grotesque story run by *Journey Into Fear* is undoubtedly "The Flat Man" (*JIF* 19). Harry Meekins is accidentally run over by a steam roller but survives, and feels better than ever—although his body has been crushed completely flat. His wife is horrified by his appearance and divorces him, and he uses his new shape to slide under bank vault doors and steal money. He advertises for a new wife, and marries a pretty applicant who plans to murder him for his money. When he uncovers the plot, he ties her up, puts her in the middle of the road, and fires up a steam roller. When she wriggles out of its path, he gets out to move her, but his leg is caught and both husband and wife wind up "a red sludge in the road, no one can ever part," as we can see in the final repulsive panel.

Superior also came out with *Mysteries Weird and Strange* (as the cover read; its actual title was simply *Mysteries*) in 1953. There were interesting stories about a man who commits every sin imaginable but siphons off his guilt and evil into a jar; a man who pretends to be the personification of the Black Plague; a husband fed to cannibal fish who manages to survive to get even with his wife and her lover; and a thief who uses a shrinking formula to commit crimes but discovers he's stuck at six inches.

In "Swamp Horror" (*MWAS* 2) Gabriel Leffert hears a knock on the door of his shack and sees an old crone outside begging to come in. He is repulsed by the old woman, shoves her into the dirt, and threatens to kick her teeth in. The woman wanders off and dies in the swamp. Shortly after her body is recovered, Leffert receives a letter from an institution saying that his mother has been released and is on her way to see him. He realizes with shame and horror that he is responsible for the death of his own mother, whom he did not recognize after so many years. The old woman's ghost comes back to the shack, wanting an embrace from her son, but Gabriel runs off into the swamp in horror—until the old woman catches up to him and her touch from beyond the grave brings instant death.

Part II

The Silver Age, 1956–1969

Nine

Marvel, DC and Charlton

MARVEL

Journey Into Mystery

Stripped of extreme horror and graphic bloodletting, horror comics in the silver age had to go underground—at first. Horror was to be found primarily in monster stories in a variety of sci-fi fantasy mags, although eventually some legitimate horror titles began to appear on the newsstands. Tales of marauding, giant or grotesque animals *could* be classified as science fiction, but as most concentrated on the creature's horrific size or terrifying appearance, they were decidedly of the horror genre as well if not primarily.

Journey Into Mystery, which had begun in the golden age, continued as a sci-fi/fantasy/monster comic for several years before turning into a super-hero title headlining The Mighty Thor. Before that there came "The Beasts" in which a man teaches animals to speak but his talking spider is swatted before he can prove it (*JIM* 46); "The Strange Secret of Henry Hill" (40) in which a jealous man discovers a town favorite may come from another dimension and plots his ruin to his own regret; and "I Spent the Night in the Haunted Lighthouse" (56), an atmospheric tale of a man temporarily shipwrecked on an island when the lighthouse in which he's taken shelter gets a visit from specters off of the infamous "Flying Dutchman." "I Don't Believe in ... Ghosts" (77) is a clever, if confused, variation on the ghost story in that the protagonist, a ghost breaker who debunks haunted houses, turns out to be a ghost himself, whose mission is to convince people that houses aren't haunted so that the domiciles won't be torn down and the spirits will still have a place to reside.

Some stories feature a narrow-minded bigot or condescending twit who winds up the prisoner of a "superior" race, sees the error of his ways, and develops a new love for his fellow human creatures. An amusing story in *JIM* 75, "The Magic of Mordoo," has a different moral. The protagonist, Franz, a middle-aged man, falls for a widow, Katrina, who is "intelligent and charming" but as old as he is, and he wants a younger, more glamorous wife. He takes the woman to the magician, Mordoo, who casts a spell that turns her into a teenager. Unfortunately for Franz, Katrina is appalled at the thought of being with a man old enough to be her father and goes off with a younger man—Mordoo!

Journey Into Mystery features a great many stories about monsters. Often the monsters would turn out to be a little more complicated than the typical sea monster on the rampage found in 1950s creature features. In the interesting "I Brought Zog Back to Life" (56) a hairy, thousand-foot-high creature is found in a block of ice with the word ZOG on it. Mankind is so frightened at the thought of the gargantuan creature getting loose, and of what it could do when it does, that people just give up and begin to act as if the end of the world were near. One man decides to free the creature and end mankind's collective terror, figuring things could hardly be worse, and is arrested for treason. But before he can be executed it develops that the creature has refrozen itself and is waiting for rescue from its alien brothers—"zog" is just another word for S.O.S.

"I Planted the Seeds of Doom" in the same issue is a clever story of a man who brings back plant life from an otherwise inhospitable planet filled with very large and dangerous carnivorous lizards. The plant produces a great many seeds, which are sold to the public in great quantities, as everyone wants to own an alien flower. Unfortunately it turns out that what emerges from the large bud is not a extraterrestrial poinsettia but one of the lizard monsters. No one had reckoned that on other planets flora and fauna could be combined into one life form. Luckily the plants are recalled before they can all hatch, which undoubtedly would have spelled doom for mankind.

In "I Found the Giant in the Sky" (55) a homely and lonely professor discovers the famous magic beans of legend, and uses them to climb to the sky where he discovers a kingdom presided over by a giant. Although the big guy is friendly, he won't allow the professor to leave because he fears the actions of the human race. But there's a small princess there who has little knowledge of men and thinks the professor is handsome. Lonely no more, he agrees to stay in the miles-high kingdom forever. The story was very well drawn by Steve Ditko. "There is a Brain Behind the Fangs" (62) concerns a man, Frank, who is convinced that dogs have secretly evolved as men have and are surreptitiously plotting to take over the world when the time is right. His friend, John, a psychiatrist, tries to convince him that he's only being paranoid, and hypnotizes Frank's dog to get at the truth. Under hypnosis, the dog proves to be just a harmless pooch, and reassured that dogs pose no danger to mankind, a grateful Frank leaves. Only it turns out that the dog didn't answer truthfully because it was under a stronger hypnotic command—of John's cat, biding its time with other animals to take over.

In the two-part "Brute That Walks" (*JIM* 65) a scrawny scientist who thinks his girlfriend would prefer a he-man, drinks a solution meant to increase his brawn but which turns him into a three-story-tall hairy monster that smashes through the streets and pursues and terrorizes the lady he's in love with. When the solution wears off, his girlfriend thinks he somehow defeated the monster, and the jerk lets her believe it, not only accepting a reward for "destroying" the creature but avoiding criminal prosecution and a zillion dollars in lawsuits! The story is entertaining nonetheless and very well served by Jack Kirby's dramatic artwork. An especially good half-page panel shows the monster's head ripping up through the floor of the room directly above the scientist's laboratory. The cover, in which the monster, looking a lot more like King Kong than it does on the inside pages, tears the walls off a building with screaming people inside, is also quite effective.

"Gruto, the Creature from Nowhere" (*JIM* 67), is a large, shaggy alien who lands on earth with a case of amnesia. A reporter who's been told by his editor to get a hot story or he's through, comes across the alien while out with his girlfriend, and decides to build him up into a menace, an advance scout in an invasion fleet, so it will make a better story and win him a Pulitzer. His conscience-stricken girlfriend convinces Gruto to take off before he can be harmed, and out in space the creature regains his memory. Of course he had been sent to share his species' great wealth of knowledge, but decides mankind isn't ready—and the reporter is shunned by everyone, including his *ex*-girlfriend. "Spragg, Conqueror of the Human Race" (*JIM* 68) becomes a menace after an earthquake in Transylvania. A scientist traveling in Europe investigates, and discovers a frightened townspeople and a walled off area where people are working around a very large mound or hill. It turns out that this hill, which has eyes and a mouth, is actually alive, a malevolent creature from inner-earth that has hypnotized the villagers into building a device that will increase its mental power and enable it to take over the whole planet. The scientist bravely enters the conclave in secret, reconfigures the equipment, and blasts the nasty monster out into space. In "The Sandman Cometh" (*JIM* 70) a man is afraid that his son, a bright, bespectacled lad who is always reading, is a sissy, although his wife tries to explain that he's just sensitive and very smart. On a trip to toughen the boy up, the family accidentally unleash an malevolent invader who is comprised of sand, who threatens to overrun all the earth. The macho father does his best to pummel the alien, to no avail, the army uses all of its might, but its the boy who uses simple science to finally defeat the creature, showing his proud father that brains are as good as brawn any day.

Other monsters include Orogo, a gigantic alien invader; Shagg, a walking sphinx; Bombu, the Witch Doctor; Gomdulla, the Living Pharoah; Goliath, the Monster That Walks Like a Man; Rorgg, King of the Spider Monsters; Korilla; The Glob; Lo-Karr, Bringer of Doom; and Kragoom. Some stories published in the 1960s were probably inspired by creature features of the previous decade, such as a tale about a giant bird called the Roc, which reminds one of the 1957 film *The Giant Claw,* and "The Spider Strikes," a tale of a humungous spider that was modeled on 1955s *Tarantula,* although the comic story also made the spider intelligent and able to speak English; ditto for "The Scorpion Strikes" in *JIM* 82, possibly inspired by 1957s *The Black Scorpion.* Another good story sans monster was "The Genie with the Light Brown Hair (*JIM* 76) in which a hobo enslaves and humiliates a genie who only wants to return to his bottle, but who outwits the hobo in the end. Other artists for the series included Richard Doxsee, Al Williamson, Don Heck, and Paul Reinman.

Strange Tales, Tales of Suspense and *Tales to Astonish*

Strange Tales, Tales of Suspense and *Tales to Astonish* were silver age science fiction/fantasy titles that eventually changed into super-hero books, but before that they each had their share of memorable monster-horror stories. "Grottu, King of the Insects" (*Strange Tales* 73) is an irradiated Army ant who grows to giant size and leads huge armies of ordinary soldier ants on the march across Africa. The big guy is defeated by pouring sugar over him, after which masses of his minions crawl all over the sugar and smother him to death. "Fin Fang Foom," a huge Chinese dragon that can talk (but, oddly, does not breathe fire) and decades later appeared in Marvel's super-hero mags such as *Iron Man,* first appeared in *Strange Tales* 89 in 1961. The protagonist, Chan Liuchow, lives on Formosa with his brother, who has joined the army to fight the Red Chinese. Chan has come up with his own novel way of destroying the invading armies, by awakening the sleeping Fin Fang Foom of legend and maneuvering him into chasing after him and smashing through the would-be conquering hordes. Jack Kirby's pencils for the story got across both the unwieldy bulk of the monster as well as its formidable strength and speed. Other monsters who appeared in *Strange* Tales included: Gargantus, a beast from the depths of the ocean (two appearances); Grogg, another fire-breathing dragon (two appearances); and Mechano, a giant robot.

The "monster" in "The Worm Man" (78) is actually a normal-sized rat. The title character is a spy who takes a pill to shrink himself to doll-size, making him one of the most sought after seller of state secrets in the world. He finishes his latest caper successfully but on the way back, still in reduced size, encounters a hungry rat that he manages to maneuver into a deep hole. Unfortunately his enlarging pills have fallen in with the rat; if he fails to take one within a certain time he will remain minuscule. He has three choices: go down to retrieve the pills and face almost certain death at the teeth of the rodent; remain at his tiny size forever; or go for help and be arrested as a spy and traitor. The story ends with him desperately trying to figure out what to do, but one imagines the rat will be picking its teeth with tiny human bones in short order. The story was beautifully drawn by Steve Ditko. Later on Marvel would create a pint-sized hero called Ant-Man who would take over *Tales to Astonish*.

Before that, however, *Astonish* featured horror and sci fi/fantasy stories along with plenty of monsters. "Groot, the Monster from Planet X" is a giant wood creature that can draw wooden objects to itself to add to its already formidable bulk, as well as command the trees of the forest. The story utilizes the popular theme of a mousy man of science conquering the frightening creature with smarts instead of firepower, and as usual, the man becomes a hero to his formerly contemptuous wife, who constantly derides him as weak and who dreams of muscle men. These stories rarely ended with the husband telling his nasty wife to get lost, but there were exceptions. "Trull the Inhuman" (*TTA* 21) is about an engineer who helps save the day when an evil alien consciousness takes over a steam shovel. The hero's fiancee has dumped him and become engaged to another man after he quit his job when one of the bridges he designed collapsed due to a flaw. She and her new boyfriend cruelly taunt the man, but when he saves her life after the boyfriend refuses to confront Trull, she decides she wants him back—to which he tells her to forget it in no uncertain terms.

"I Created Krang" (*TTA* 14/December 1960) is one of the all-time best of Marvel's monster stories. A scientist theorizes that giant insects can be used to tow ocean liners and be used in place of airliners, but although his peers scoff at him he creates a growth formula using an ingredient from the Krakow trees in Europe. Unfortunately his jealous assistant tests the formula on an ant—wanting to see if it will work before bothering to steal it—and uses too much, resulting in a gigantic insect that has human intelligence (and gives itself a name as well). After "Krang" tears the castle laboratory and nearby town apart trying to grab the scientist, from whom he wants the formula to create an insect army, he is defeated when the professor creates a giant ant*eater*. The artwork by Kirby and Ayers is so good that it makes the fairly formulaic story remarkably exciting and even scary.

"X, the Thing that Lived" (*TTA* 20) is a four-part, nearly full-length tale in which a comic book writer discovers that every time he writes about a monster the government tells him that such a creature not only actually existed, but was destroyed the very way he detailed in the story—how did he come into such classified information, they wonder. They ultimately decide that in each instance it was pure coincidence, but then the writer creates "X," a giant monster from another dimension that can change its shape at will. Our hero is afraid that nothing will destroy this new monstrosity he unleashed on the world. The writer finally figures out that his typewriter brought the creature into being via magical means, and the last few pages feature a desperate race as he tries to rush home to write a new ending on the machine as the shape-and-size-shifting monster pursues him down streets and into sewers, all vividly brought to life by Kirby and Ayers. Another exciting tale with Kirby-Ayers artwork is "The Crawling Creature" (22) in which an intellectual high school student, held in contempt by the jocks and their girlfriends, volunteers to descend to the depths of the earth in a new machine and struggles against a voracious carnivorous lizard that he finally defeats using his wits and courage.

Tales of Suspense continued the tradition of monster stories that were influenced by fifties creature features but which had their own unique twists. "Monstro ... The Menace from the Murky Depths" about a gargantuan octopus attacking a seaport behind the Iron Curtain (*TOS* 8), was clearly influenced by the 1955 film *It Came from Beneath the Sea*, but adds an American scientist who figures out that the radioactive creature will shrink to normal size in 24 hours along with a warning for the Reds to stop their dangerous nuclear testing. The story is skillfully penciled by Jack Kirby and engendered one of the best creature covers ever, as the horrific form of Monstro rises from the ocean, eyes glaring, its tentacles flailing about causing destruction. The effective cover of *TOS* 11 features the giant amoeba, Sporr, but the story itself is forgettable.

"Gor-Kill, the Lurking Demon" (*TOS* 12) is an alien energy form that comes to life as a huge destructive and hungry mass of water. After it dives into a damn after its first rampage, no one believes the town bum when he observes that the creature doesn't merely hide in water, but *is* water, and that if it escapes into the ocean as they hope, it will only come back at a much, much larger size. The bum essentially saves the world by using dynamite to blow the creature to pieces, but only winds up in jail for stealing the explosives! Another hero who is excoriated instead of celebrated appears in "Titan, the Amphibian from Atlantis" (28), who pops up out of the ocean as an advance guard of his gigantic undersea race. When Titan offers a fortune to any human who will betray his species and tell him of mankind's weapons, John Cartwright volunteers and becomes the most hated man on the planet. But Cartwright lies to Titan and tells him of imaginary advanced weaponry that could reduce all of Atlantis' inhabitants to dust—and is killed, with the world still despising him and knowing nothing of his sacrifice. "Bruttu" (22) is another scrawny scientist who inadvertently transforms into a gigantic menace and has some harrowing misadventures before returning to normal and learning that the woman he loves, whom he feared only pitied him, is in love with him too.

Amazing Adventures debuted in 1961. Like *Journey Into Mystery* it often ran monster stories with a little extra twist. Torr (*AA* 1), a huge, malevolent alien, takes over the mind of a scientist, John Carter, and causes his colleague, Paul Ramsey, to be put on trial for murder after shooting Torr in his more susceptible human form, Carter's body. A device Torr has affixed to Ramsey's wrist prevents him of telling anyone of his existence. Fortunately, Carter is not dead, and upon awakening, shows up in court to exonerate Ramsey, while Torr, back in his own body, simply remains dead. In the very satisfying "I Led the Search for Manoo." (*AA* 2) a poor high school student who is mercilessly razzed by his wealthy classmates gets embroiled in a war between a good alien and a bad one, but has to uses all of his wits to figure out which is which. The aliens had a distinctly unique and interesting appearance thanks to the pencils of Jack Kirby.

"We Were Trapped in the Twilight World" (*AA* 3) presents a young student who is convinced that the present, past and future all exist simultaneously in different dimensions, at which his professor scoffs. Wouldn't you know that that very afternoon young Harper and his girlfriend drive through a mist that handily takes them into the prehistoric past where they must confront cavemen and monsters in a silly but harrowing tale well-served by Kirby and Ayers' artwork. "Monsteroso" (5) is a gigantic alien who turns out to be a mere infant and "Sserpo, the Creature Who Crushed the Earth" (6) is a lizard-creature who ingests a growth formula and grows so huge that his sheer size threatens to unbalance the planet. The latter story was probably influenced by an episode of the radio show *Lights Out!* entitled "Chicken Heart" in which a formula enlarges the title object to positively humungous proportions. Both stories, especially "Sserpo" were entertaining and well-drawn, again by the Kirby-Ayers combo.

Marvel comics brought out a few more horror/sci fi/suspense mags at the start of the silver age, including such short-lived series as *Mystical Tales, Adventure Into Mystery* and *World of Suspense*. *Mystical Tales* ran everything from stories about astronauts teaching aliens how to play baseball to supernatural tales in which an artist who makes a deal with the devil winds up being trapped inside his own painting; there was little originality. *Adventure Into Mystery*, which also debuted in 1956, was somewhat better, although it didn't last much longer. "The Hex" (*AIM* 4), which was reminiscent of Fritz Lieber's "Conjure Wife," concerns a man who removes all the hex signs on his farm over his wife's objections. His health fails without explanation, the crops burn, the whole farm is flooded, one disaster after another, and his wife implores him to hire someone to paint a few new hex signs. He thinks her attitude is just superstitious nonsense. One morning he wakes up and finds that he has not only recovered his health, but has won money in a lottery. "Do you still believe in those hexes?" he asks his wife. "I still do," she says atop the ladder where she's just finished painting a fresh new hex sign. (In "Conjure Wife" the woman used black magic to advance her husband's career, then watched in horror as his luck turned sour after he destroyed her assorted fetishes.)

In "The Day of the Wreck" (*Adventure Into Mystery* 6), which pre-dates Stephen King's "Christine," a boy's hot rod, upon which he lavishes a lot of time, attention and loving care, tries to run over and kill in other various ways the boy's terrified girlfriend—the jealous car doesn't want a rival for the lad's affections. "The Watcher" (7) is a scientist who can instantly traverse space by simply sticking his hand through a portal he developed, transporting it thousands of miles away to, say, save a car from falling off a cliff by catching it in his enlarged mitt. While the idea is intriguing the story really goes nowhere. "The Man Who Couldn't Be Killed" (8) features a Devil's Island prisoner, Henri, who is due to be hanged on a Monday. He escapes and threatens the island's native witch doctor with a gun, forcing him to give him a magical potion that will insure that from that moment on Henri will not exist on Mondays, only during the rest of the week. Unfortunately for Henri, the potion is retroactive and since he was born on a Monday, he has ceased to exist. This begs the question of how the warden or anyone else can even remember him. Also, the story hinges on the notion that Henri can only be legally hanged on a Monday, a dubious idea at best. In "Effigy" (8) a man paints a portrait of his rival, who bested him in everything, planning to shoot at the picture and once and for all get over his hatred of the man. He also paints a gun in the other man's hand—with which, of course, the man in the painting shoots the artist. Seems he'd been dead for years and his spirit couldn't resist some mischief. The effective cover for the eighth and final issue depicts a man on a crowded subway platform being backed up to the edge just as a train comes in, but this scene is not presented in any of the stories.

Like the other Atlas comics *World of Suspense* presented a mix of horror, sci fi, fantasy and supernatural stories. The best story it ran was "The Face" (*WOS* 7) about a major domo named Roy Farnum who is hoping to inherit millions from his grumpy and wealthy employer, Wallace Lawson. When he discovers that Lawson has a son, Andrew, whom he has not seen for years, but still loves, Farnum panics, figuring all of Lawson's money will go to his flesh and blood. Through an intermediary, he is introduced to a scientist whose machinery can instantly change a person's face to anything they desire. Roy asks to look like Andrew Lawson, while the scientist asks if he might have Roy's rather handsome countenance as long as he's not using it. The scientist agrees to take over as butler for a while and is therefore present when old Wallace finally dies and at the reading of his will. Wallace has left only one dollar to his son, Andrew, and *all of his fortune* to Roy Farnum! The scientist, of course, turns out to be Andrew Lawson.

DC

For about ninety issues beginning in 1952 *Star Spangled War Stories* presented well-drawn heroic escapades of a variety of military men. Eventually it introduced pretty French resistance fighter Mlle. Marie, who added a feminine, but still-tough, dimension to the comic— but she didn't last. But by the late fifties sales had declined enough for DC to introduce an entirely new and unexpected element to the series: prehistoric *monsters*.

The concept, decades before *Jurassic Park*, was an intriguing one. An island known as Island X—later on it was called Dinosaur Island or Monster Island—experiences an earthquake which revives hundreds of dinosaurs that were in suspended animation under the earth. During the next forty or so issues a variety of heroes would battle against a wide variety of carnivorous prehistoric beasts. This series-within-a-series was eventually called "The War That Time Forgot." Not all of the stories took place on the original island, however. The first dinosaur issue was *Star Spangled War Stories* 90.

In "Last Battle of the Dinosaur Age" (*SSWS* 92)—which it certainly wasn't— the men try to escape from the island in their sub, but various monsters put paid to that scheme, and the survivors find themselves trapped on Island X with a horde of rampaging beasts heading right toward them. In subsequent issues frogmen, paratroopers and others all came afoul of the revivified dinosaurs, either in the ocean or on Island X or some other area. At times the site of dinosaur infestation would be called a time-lost spot where time stood still, as if the news of the earthquake reviving the dormant monsters never made it back to civilization. In other issues, such as "The Island of Thunder" (*SSWS* 108) the action apparently takes place on another island altogether, one which is destroyed by a volcano at the end of the story. In *SSWS* 102 one soldier with a robot partner is swept through an underwater cave that leads to a "secret underground world" full of dinosaurs. And in *SSWS* 106 three soldiers pass through a cloud that they're convinced conceals a time warp that's sent them back to prehistoric times.

In "The Guinea Pig Patrol" (*SSWS* 95), there's a great scene when the men wind up on an island the size of a matchbox and a dinosaur begins to tear chunks of it away, reducing its size in an effort to get at the man-sized morsels. "The Sub-Crusher" in *SSWS* 97 has many harrowing moment as a PT Boat goes down a river and is besieged not only by "rocks" that turn out to be dinosaurs with hungry, gaping maws, but a pterodactyl overhead who dives at them with a live torpedo in its mouth.

Some of the dinosaurs in the comic had actually existed and were accurately rendered and identified, while others looked like no dinosaurs that had ever walked the earth, hideous monstrosities of enormous size, bizarre physiques and voracious appetites. "The Monster Who Sank a Navy" (SSWS 127) features a slithering sea monster of Godzillian proportions with huge rows of teeth and a seriously aggressive attitude, taking on a Japanese battleship after tearing apart American planes and subs. (In the same story a frogman is swallowed by another, smaller, though still monstrous fish, and has to blow himself out of its belly, although by that time he's gone mad from the experience.) A giant ape that appears in *SSWS* 97 is about ten times the size of King Kong. Another big ape—not as large and as white as snow—shows up in *SSWS* 111, where he proves friendly to humans and saves them time and again from dinosaurs. In this story the soldiers fly through that same white cloud that takes them to "the island that time forgot." The time-warp cloud reappeared in *SSWS* 125's "Tidbit for a Tyrannosaurus" wherein a robot G.I. sacrifices itself to save some human soldiers.

In some stories the Pacific island full of monsters was left behind and dinosaurs would show up in other locations. In "Doom Came at Noon" (*SSWS* 114) three skiing brothers who are looking for a secret Nazi sub-pen in the Arctic, of all places, come across a crevasse full of awakening dinosaurs. Like most of the protagonists in these stories the brothers are scared by the monsters but keep up a slap-happy banter throughout. As the series progressed, characters became less and less impressed by, or curious about, the existence of prehistoric creatures in the modern world.

Because the dinosaurs had no real personalities, writer-creator Robert Kanigher would attempt some characterization for the soldiers in certain stories. In "Battle Dinner for Dinosaurs" (*SSWS* 115) a pilot named Mickey flies off to rescue a macho old pal named Ace Waller, whom he finds unconscious, floating on some wreckage in the vicinity of Monster Island. What follows is one harrowing escapade after another as Mickey manages to save the both of them time and again from one horrendous creature after another. Mickey remembers that in childhood Ace was always saving his life and then sneering at him that he should stick with the boys instead of men. Mickey fears he'll never be able to "wipe that sneer off his face" because Ace wasn't awake and aware of what was happening. But it turns out that Ace, although unable to move, heard everything and makes sure Mickey gets a medal. As interesting and thrilling as the story is, it has two troubling aspects. Despite the snickering he had to endure, Mickey doesn't seem particularly grateful for all of the times Ace saved his bacon as he attempted one foolish action after another. He doesn't fly off so much to save an old friend as to prove something to himself and to Ace. And the point is never made that not every man can be a warrior—it takes all kinds to make a world.

SSWS 116 introduced "The Suicide Squad," specifically two members—Morgan and Mace—on another Arctic mission with improbable dinosaurs. The two men despise each other. Morgan's brother was killed during a two-man toboggan run at the Olympics, and he blames Mace—his brother's partner on the run—for panicking and for preventing the U.S.

from winning a medal. When the two wind up in The Suicide Squad, described as "a French foreign legion—American style"—an especially tough division of the armed forces consisting of men only too happy to volunteer for missions they probably won't return from—Morgan decides he'll accompany Mace on every mission and shoot him with his .45 if he begins to panic again. Morgan's brother's death was an accident, Mace is by no means a coward, and Morgan is pretty much a complete jerk. He is definitely courageous and not without intelligence, but his hatred of Mace reaches pathological proportions. It was an interesting idea for an odd couple, although it would have been unlikely that the two men would ever have been sent on missions together in the first place, considering that the whole world knew of their history. Their conflict was never resolved.

SSWS 117 and 118 feature not only Mace and Morgan, but Dino, a baby pterodactyl whom Morgan saves from becoming another dinosaur's supper. Dino has an incredibly long memory and great intelligence, and he comes to the aid of the two men more than once. He has an especially charming habit of tapping on Mace's helmet with his beak as a show of affection. Morgan, however, is convinced that as soon as the flying monster is hungry they'll just wind up on his dinner plate. The term "dinosaur island" is employed for the first time in *SSWS* 118. Other members of the Suicide Squad were employed in stories, but they were always two men who had a reason to hate each other or had a serious conflict of some kind. The Suicide Squad did not appear in every issue.

"My Buddy the Dinosaur" (*SSWS* 124) is a strangely compelling if illogical tale in which a soldier addicted to stories of werewolves, vampires and the like, begs his buddy to promise to kill him if he starts changing into some kind of dangerous creature. On Dinosaur Island, although no explanation is offered for it, he changes into a hulking dinosaur and begs his buddy to kill him; the friend complies and he reverts to human form. *SSWS* 129 and 131 feature an Army pilot who, unbeknownst to his comrades, has grown up on Dinosaur Island, been raised by pterodactyls, and can actually communicate with the huge flying reptiles. His mother was an aviator who died when she crash landed on the island. In both stories he uses the pterodactyls to attack the Japanese. Despite nice art they are not especially memorable and the character did not catch on.

"Divers of Death" (*SSWS* 122), which showcases scuba-diving quadruplet brothers, has especially wonderful art by Russ Heath. It not only features a grotesque underwater spider snaring subs in its web, but has a great scene when the brothers put bombs on a reef that turns out to be the spines of an enormous saurian. "Secrets Die on Monster Island" (*SSWS* 130) also had some striking scenes of monster mayhem and cliffside sunsets in a story about an American and a Japanese temporarily joining forces to help each other survive the forbidding isle. (A similar if more suspenseful story about a Japanese and American pilot on the island, "Save My Life and Kill Me," appears in *SSWS* 135.) An even more uneasy truce occurs in "Big House of Monsters" (*SSWS* 132) between a cop and a criminal who got away from him during a train wreck on the way to the penitentiary. This story also had very attractive art by Russ Heath.

One of the best-drawn and most memorable of the "War That Time Forgot" stories appeared in *SSWS* 133. As usual, "You Owe Me a Death" adds an emotional battle between men to the basic dinosaur formula. A young G.I. named Buster despises his corporal because he believes the man was responsible for his brother's death. The two team up to survive the dangers of the island, but the corporal is unable to convince the younger man that his brother's death was an accident, until Buster inadvertently trips and his gun goes off, hitting the corporal. Realizing that accidents *do* occur in war time, he goes to the corporal's rescue and the two become friends. In the meantime they are not only besieged by dinosaurs in some harrowing episodes, but humongous snakes and giant bugs as well. As usual, Russ Health's artwork is splendid.

"The War That Time Forgot" was pretty much wrapped up for the silver age in *Star Spangled War Stories* 137, the final dinosaur issue. Joe Kubert's artwork for the lead story, "Fight to the Last," was exceptional. There were the usual harrowing episodes with enormous, genuinely frightening monsters, and the typical sub-plot about a rivalry between two childhood enemies. It wasn't a bad way to go out. The striking covers for the series were magnificent, showing a wide variety of horrendous creatures and frightened if defiant fighting men in grotesque situations, although on occasion they were cheats. The "plane eater" that wraps its tongue completely around an aircraft on the cover of *SSWS* 118 is only seen in two panels inside.

CHARLTON

In the silver age, Charlton made its mark with some comics based on popular monster movies, as well as a few horror anthology titles. *Gorgo* (1960) was based on the British film in which salvage men capture a sea monster and exhibit it in London, only to have its much larger mother show up to get Gorgo back, completely smashing the city in the process. The first issue of the comic was a fairly faithful adaptation of the movie, except for the fact that the scenes of mass destruction and the deaths of thousands of Londoners were eliminated, effectively stripping the comic version of a bravura climax. The comic was well-drawn by Steve Ditko. Bill Montes and Ernie Bache were among other artists who worked on *Gorgo* and the rest of Charlton's monster line.

Several months later the comic resumed, presenting further adventures of Gorgo and his mother. In *Gorgo* 2 (Joe Gill and Steve Ditko), the two beasts inadvertently foul up the Atlantic cable and the huge communications network it serves. This leads to a playful Gorgo following a boat back to New York, where he's again captured. When Mama wakes up, she follows and manages to destroy half of Manhattan. The animals are injected with a drug in the hopes it will kill them, but they only go to sleep at the bottom of the ocean. *Gorgo* 3 features an excellent, suspenseful story in which a South American dictator forces one of his scientists to capture and tame Gorgo, which he does via the use of painful electrical shock. Eventually the scientist overthrows the dictator and places himself in power, but Gorgo manages to summon up the energy to conquer his fear of the pain and fight back. Defeating but sparing the life of the man who'd been torturing him, Gorgo returns to the side of his still-hibernating mother. The scenes depicting the scientist desperately trying to get away from the wrath of the hulking Gorgo are especially exciting.

In *Gorgo* 4 a man comes back from space only to have his capsule land right near the mother and son team of sleeping monsters. Gorgo sort of adopts the man as a pet; his mother soon loses interest and goes back to sleep. The armed forces do their best to rescue the astronaut with boats and planes, but they only succeed in annoying Gorgo. Finally the astronaut manages to communicate his desire to go home to Gorgo, and he's carried to New York atop the beast's massive head. Once again, Gorgo is treated as a sympathetic creature (his mother was responsible for most of the destruction to New York). In *Gorgo* 6 the theory is posited that Gorgo and his monstrous mom are not prehistoric survivors, but actually a more-or-less immortal species of saurian throwback that were left behind in caverns in the depths while other sea creatures evolved into land animals. In "Graveyard of Lost Ships" in *Gorgo* 8 an aspiring documentarian, his wife, and two no-good-niks travel to a warm spot in the Arctic where, according to them, lies the "legendary" Sargasso Sea (which is actually located in the middle of the North Atlantic). Gorgo and his mother are romping in the area and inadvertently save the lives of the filmmaker and his spouse when the other two men, who want the treasure they find on the lost ships all to themselves, try to kill them. An interesting story is bolstered by some excellent artwork.

Oddly, in some stories the authorities and others express disbelief at tales of sightings of Gorgo and his mother when it was already established that the creatures were seen by many witnesses as they attacked major cities. It makes no sense that their existence would be called into question. But then everyone seems to have selective memory in *Gorgo*. In *Gorgo* 10 Gorgo and his mother help defeat gigantic Venusians that attack the planet. Two issues later the Venusians are back with another plan but the Earthlings don't seem to remember them and the Venusians don't remember Gorgo. In *Gorgo* 15's "Land That Time Forgot," wherein an expedition finds living dinosaurs in Africa, none of the white men seem to recognize or even to have heard of Gorgo. You would think a creature that had ravaged London and New York and other cities would have had its features etched immutably upon everyone's consciousness.

In some issues Gorgo and his mom manage to save humanity by beating off aliens, devouring mutated plant monsters (16), or attacking communist bases during the Cuban missile crisis while somebody or other ranted that *they* were the world's greatest menace. The irony of this was gotten across with little subtlety while the human toll of their attacks on cities and towns was always glossed over. Surely those who'd lost loved ones as the creatures tore through London or New York would not feel so kindly toward them. And Gorgo's pro-human actions were mostly accidental. Still, it made the big lugs a hell of a lot more sympathetic.

In *Gorgo* 11 the monster accidentally becomes a movie star when a film crew with a has-been director and stars arrives on an island full of headhunters to film an epic—only the director hasn't told the actors who their gigantic co-star is to be. "The World Shaker" in *Gorgo* 19 features an embittered mad scientist who experiments with gigantism in animals and winds up growing to Gorgonian proportions himself. While he manages to defeat the baby monster, he has a harder time with mama, who, as usual, comes to her mischievous son's rescue. The story wasn't helped by a somewhat campy approach and uneven artwork. One of the best Gorgo stories, however, appears in *Gorgo* 23, "The Land of Long Ago." In this, a scientist sends Gorgo back in time to the age of the dinosaurs, figuring mankind will be free of him and the big little guy will be a lot happier. Unfortunately the scientist is dragged back to prehistoric times along with Gorgo, and what follows is a series of charming adventures as Gorgo becomes the man's protector, much like King Kong continuously battled monsters to save Ann Darrow. But the time experiment doesn't work. Each day both man and monster wind up several eons closer to the present day; eventually they're right back where they started.

Possibly the strangest issue of the series is *Gorgo* 20, "Monsters for the Moon," in which red scientists create duplicates of Gorgo which they plan to send to the moon to scare off

American astronauts. However, Gorgo, nestled in a space capsule which he finds comforting, winds up accompanying one of the duplicates. On the moon they encounter aliens who dispatch the duplicate easily but have problems with the real item. Stilted scripting and below par artwork did not do much to aid the story's veracity.

What's amazing isn't that *Gorgo* managed to last for about 25 issues, but that so many of those issues are as entertaining as they are. The characterizations of the humans rarely rise above a soap opera level, and the art is uneven on those issues not penciled by Steve Ditko, but *Gorgo* is a more memorable series than anyone could have expected.

Konga

Konga, based on another British horror film, was Charlton's next big monster series. In the movie Konga was a chimp that had been blown up to Kong-size by a crazy scientist. At the film's end Konga went on a rampage in London and was shot to death by police, whereupon he reverted to his natural state; the scientist was killed. The first issue of the series retells the story of the movie, but the scientist protagonist is turned into a nice guy instead of an evil sociopath, his live-in female assistant is turned into his wife, and the assorted deaths and murders are seriously downplayed (this story was reprinted in *Fantastic Giants* # 24). In the next issue of the comic book, acquaintances of the dead scientist, Sandra and Bob, inject another chimp with the same formula, creating a new menace. As the enormous beast has assorted adventures, they try to revert it to normal, and believe Konga is dead at the end.

The big ape has survived, however, to become embroiled in a marital drama between a yachtsman, his captain and his wife, as well as some natives and a bunch of crooks who are after uranium on the natives' island. Konga also has a fight to the death with an enormous, slithering sea monster. In *Konga* 4 Sandra and Bob arrive at this island, where Konga is revered as a god, in the hopes of injecting their former pet with shrink formula. Instead it winds up in the veins of a group of neo–Nazis who, reduced to doll size, go running off in hysteria. The next issue Konga finally gets the serum, but the shrinking effect is only temporary, and he winds up nearly getting caught in an H bomb explosion on another test island. Once again Bob and Sandra assume Konga is dead, but he's actually been blown far away to Africa.

In *Konga* 6 the ape has a delayed reaction to exposure to the H bomb and shrinks down to the size of a gorilla. He is captured by hunters, but when he begins to grow again, they put him on display à la King Kong in circuses throughout Europe. Bob and Sandra learn of his appearance in London and tell the management that Konga is a scientific experiment and they intend to get a court order to take him away. Seeing the couple attacked by thugs employed by the manager, Konga breaks out of his chains, smashes his way out of the city, and is presumed killed by depth charges. Actually he winds up on an island near the equator where he basically saves humankind by obliterating the advance guard of 15- foot-tall aliens intent on taking over the earth (*Konga* 7). In *Konga* 8 the ape discovers a lost world of dinosaurs under the Arctic ice, but is so busy fending off attacks from hungry creatures that he beats it post haste. In the next issue Konga outwits the communists with the aid of a prisoner in a Siberian labor camp who has a wonderful rapport with all animals. These stories were graced with some effective Steve Ditko artwork.

In *Konga* 12, our hero travels around the world seeking friendship and being rebuffed, then winds up in Switzerland where he causes an avalanche that encases him in snow up to his neck. Bob and Sandra are called in, and take him away to an island off the coast of Africa to resume their studies. This seemed like a happy ending for the giant chimp but the series continued without any mention of what happened to Sandra and Bob and the idyllic island situation—perhaps Konga got bored and wanted to go out to play. He encounters a power-mad dictator, and some more aliens, then was briefly bewitched by an embittered Russian scientist in a Siberian prison camp who wanted Konga to get revenge upon the world for him. In *Konga* 17 he saved a blind man from giant crabs, then helped the fellow unite two warring tribes. Konga seemed to be able to communicate empathically and telepathically with certain humans, and supposedly could recognize good people from bad. He was becoming a champion of earth in much the same way that Godzilla did in the movies.

The point was made time and again that Konga just wanted to play, have friends, and be loved. Unlike Gorgo and Reptisaurus, who had been born as mighty and aggressive animals, Konga was just a cute chimp who had grown to giant size through no fault of his own. He took care never to harm any humans, because he loved Sandra and she loved him. *Konga* 20 is a study in pathos as the giant, lonely, misunderstood beast dreams of how happy he'd been when Sandra had taken him from his cage in the lab and adopted him as a pet; she and Bob made him part of the family. "I wonder if I can sue an ape for alienation of affections?" muses Bob. (In this issue he was correctly drawn as a chimpanzee instead of a monkey, as he had been depicted in some earlier stories.)

Konga ran for 23 issues then returned as *The Return of Konga,* in which he finally gave vent to his anger and began smashing cities à la Gorgo's mother. In the next issue, retitled *Konga's Revenge*, another scientist manages to reduce him to the size of a squirrel, wherein he learns what it's like to be small. Returning to giant size, he seems to be the playful, friendly fellow of before.

Reptisaurus

Reptilicus, based on the monster movie of the same name, had two issues in 1961. The first issue recounted the story of the movie, how a drill unearths some tissue which eventually grows into a prehistoric monster that ravages Amsterdam. The creature is blown apart at the end, but for the second issue of the comic a piece of it expands into another monster with the ability to fly (and without the acid-spitting talent of the movie version). The creature shows up in Africa, where Peter Blinn of the State Department, who has come to the continent to convince a reclusive scientist to work for the government, helps the natives defeat it. It was nothing special.

For the third issue the title was changed to *Reptisaurus*, and there was a new lead character—two of them, in fact. Atomic testing reawakens two hibernating mutant pterodactyls, Reptisaurus and his mate, just in time for them to scare off an alien invasion of Earth. His mate and their little ones disappear from the storyline; in fact, in the fourth issue the fickle beast gets into what appears to be a big battle with another flying reptile but this other creature turns out to be female and the fight is just "billing and cooing." In the fifth issue Reptisaurus falls in love with an Oriental robotic dragon to the dismay of the Red Chinese. Broken-hearted to learn that its sweetheart is phony, Reptisaurus flies away to rest for another million years. Alas in *Reptisaurus* 6 the communists capture the beast for propaganda purposes, purporting to show via the creature's defeat that communist forces are stronger than democracy. To counter this, American paratroopers land near the monster, feed it protein, and incredibly, set it free. By this time people had affection for Reptisaurus as if he were nothing more than an especially big, friendly puppy—or Gorgo.

The approach was completely changed for *Reptisaurus* 7. The redesigned beast was back with his sleek, pregnant mate, making a nest for their eggs in Africa. A scientist, his bickering wife, and a crude guide go into the jungle to find the nest; the scientist steals one of the eggs for research purposes and supposedly destroys the others. *Reptisaurus* was once more considered a menace, and the free world tries to find a way to destroy him once and for all. In *Reptisaurus Special* # 1, which followed the seventh and final issue of the series, a mad scientist tries to control the monster with sound waves, but he's bombed out of existence. Reptisaurus and his mate escape and fly to Central America, where a tribe of hidden, renegade Aztecs believe the beast to be their ancient god, Quetzacoatl. Most of the story was actually taken up with a love triangle consisting of a megalomaniac hunter, his ward and fiancee, and a guide who comes between them. The art in the brief series was adequate if uneven for the most part, but Bill Montes and Ernie Bache's work in these final issues was quite good. (Reptisaurus made a brief guest appearance in *Gorgo* 12, rising from the sea to attack Venusian monsters trying to invade Earth; he did not have any scenes with Gorgo or his mother, however.)

Charlton Anthologies

During this period Charlton also published some "regular" horror/supernatural comic books. *Tales of the Mysterious Traveler* debuted in 1956. The colorless, generic traveler in his gray hat and overcoat who told the tales was, if anything, a rip-off of DC's Phantom Stranger, who'd debuted four years earlier, although he had much less personality. Most of the times he just watched from certain panels as the story proceeded and he narrated; on occasion he would enter the action. (Able to transcend time and space, in one short-short he rescues a dog who is placed inside a satellite.) Few of the stories in the short-lived series were memorable and most were fairly lame. For instance, an unseen person that a trapper keeps up a dialogue with and verbally abuses throughout the story turns out to be his dog. The partner that a stage entertainer keeps wanting to get rid of turns out to be his dummy. And so on. Some of the ideas were good but they were not well-developed. Still, there were some modestly intriguing moments. "And the Fear Grew" (*TOMT* 7) concerns a man who discovers an adorable and unusual pet that belongs to a species that has yet to be discovered. Natives tell him that it is an evil creature, and while he initially scoffs, he can't understand why he and everyone around him are having such a run of bad luck. Discovering that no naturalist has ever seen such a creature, he comes to think it may be an alien bent on destruction and shoots it dead, after which he is ashamed of his actions. But the final panel, in which the creature seems to be alive, suggests that perhaps there was something to his fears after all ... or not. (When the same basic story appeared in Marvel's *Adventures into Fear* 7 as "Beware ... the Brimm" the ending left little doubt of the creature's evil nature.)

In "The Valley of Eternity" (11) four low-lifes in India come across a stranger who tells them he wishes to pass along the secret of immortality and eternal peace, and they will be his emissaries. Afraid that the world that will result from these good works will have no place for them, the foursome carry him out of the valley planning to wrest his secrets from him. Of course, like something out of Hilton, he crumbles to dust as soon as he leaves the valley.

The series was gone with its thirteenth issue; Many years later in 1985 there were two additional issues consisting of reprints. Art was contributed by Steve Ditko, Matt Bakerino, and Rocco Mastroserio.

Dr. Graves

In 1966 Charlton discontinued its Blue Beetle super-hero title, kept the old numbering, and turned it into *Ghostly Tales (from the Haunted House)* beginning with the fifty-fifth issue. The host and narrator was a cloaked, pasty-faced devil with warts named Mr. L. Dedd. The first issue also introduced a "ghost-fighter" named Dr. Graves, who later got his own comic. L. Dedd narrates and appears in most of the stories, usually not as a character but hovering in the background out of sight of the protagonists as he comments on the action. There were times when he interacts with the characters, however, such as a story in *Ghostly Tales* 69, "Labor Problem." Tybalt Tyson has come up with a transmogrification machine that can change ordinary metals into gold, but a side effect always causes the person who operates the machine to be killed. When he runs out of living operators, Tyson gets ghosts to do the job, until the union objects. Then L. Dedd appears and suggests to Tyson that with his great force of will he should be able to operate the machine safely—with predictable, if amusing, results. Generally Dedd was a fairly obtrusive and sometimes irritating presence.

Ghostly Tales seemed to take its cue not so much from the old EC horror comics, but from *The Twilight Zone*, which it often resembled. Case in point: "Dream, Dream Go Away" (*GT* 69), which Rod Serling could have written. Airline pilot Tom has a recurring dream in which his plane keeps hitting a mountain. He calls in sick day after day until a psychiatrist suggests he rest for a week and then get back to work. Tom comes to the conclusion that it isn't him in the cockpit during the dream, but his friend, Don, who is also a pilot for the same airline. Realizing that Don has a flight that very afternoon, Tom races to the airport, nearly crashing his car in his haste to stop him. When Don refuses to let Tom take his place, Tom knocks him out. Even as the plane approaches the spot where the crash occurs in the dream, Tom is confident that he's changed the outcome, even as Don contacts the plane's captain and warns him of Tom's strange behavior. But when the captain turns to look at his co-pilot he discovers that Tom is *gone*, later learning he was killed in the car crash.

Some of the more memorable silver age stories include: "A Promise is a Promise" (*GT* 57)— a dead soldier guides his buddy through war torn Asia and keeps him out of harm; "The Flying Dutchman" (58)—a man investigates rumors of a plague ship full of greedy mutineers that can never land and discovers the rumors are true, to his ever-lasting regret; "The Curse of Miller's Cave" (59)—a man who killed his wife and her lover hides out in a cave from whence his ghost periodically emerges to attack any romantic couples who chance to wander nearby; "Up on the Mountain" (63)—a college student can deal with being picked on by other students but it bothers him that even his professors enjoy doing it, so he builds a special

Horror began creeping back into comics in the silver age in such series as Charlton's *Ghostly Tales from the Haunted House*.

A Jim Aparo cover for *Ghostly Tales* 72.

snow sculpture and leads the teachers inside for a big surprise; "The Legacy" (66)—a man becomes tragically obsessed with locating a treasure chest that was originally found by his late father. However, Gary Friedrich's "If I had Three Wishes" (60) is a blatant borrowing of "The Monkey's Paw," while "Abandoned Ship" (61), a tale of man-versus-rat at sea, would have been fine had similar stories not been done so much better in the golden age. Artists for the series included Steve Ditko, Jim Aparo (who did much better work for DC Comics), and Pat Boyette.

The Many Ghosts of Dr. Graves debuted in 1967. M. T. Graves, who sometimes appeared in the stories, presented and investigated cases of the supernatural, some of which were hoaxes or had logical explanations while most were genuinely spiritual in nature. Graves believes that the dead have no place among the living and should not influence the living in any way, making him seem callous when lonely, newly dead spirits reach out to their still-living loved ones. In the twelfth issue Dr. Graves began to more resemble Marvel Comics' Sorcerer Supreme, Dr. Strange, using his astral form to fly into the nether world and weird dimensions to combat a gargantuan entity come to conquer the earth; the story was even drawn by Dr. Strange artist Steve Ditko.

Among the more notable Dr. Graves stories were: "The Perfect Crime" (*MGDG* 2)—a man uses astral projection to commit a perfect murder but is undone when his victim's ghost enters his body and forces him to confess; "The Name" (9)—Dr. Graves investigates to find out why a ghost in a haunted house keeps repeating the name of his aunt, Beth; "Charming Girl" (9) —a college student who uses a spell to win back his girlfriend discovers they both must pay an awful price; "The Lost Chord" (10)—rock musicians innocently incorporate ancient chants in a song that summons demons; "The Last Sacrifice" (25)—a man who plans to steal an emerald from a Mayan temple reckons without the interference of an unknown priestess; "Don't Lose Your Head" (43)—when the servant of a man who helped the poor condemns him to the guillotine, a curse insures that he and his descendants will all lose their heads in one way or another; "The Things in the Subway" (43)—a nurse assures a man that he only saw monsters in the subway due to a concussion but she may have other reasons for saying so.

The fifth issue features tales that "borrowed" from "The Picture of Dorian Gray" and even "Moby Dick" and some stories had absolutely nothing to do with ghosts, such as "The Enemies," a harrowing tale of a new insecticide that turns ordinary cabbage caterpillars and moths into giant and highly aggressive monsters.

Dr. Graves began publishing reprints with its sixty-third issue, but it kept going for another twelve issues before expiring in 1985. Writers included Steve Skeates and Joe Gill, while Pat Boyette, Jim Aparo, Don Perlin, and Sanho Kim took care of the art chores.

Ghost Manor

Ghost Manor debuted in 1968. "A Matter of Grave Concern" in the first issue is a taut and suspenseful piece about a convict in a Devil's Island-type prison who hopes that his friend—whom he turned into the police and who is dying—will be able to help him escape. A plot unfolds involving the convict hiding in a coffin, being buried, and waiting to be dug up hours later. Yes, it was yet another tale in which a man hoping to be dug out of a grave discovers that his fellow occupant in the coffin is the very man who was supposed to dig him up. As noted, a similar plot was the basis for "Final Escape," an episode of *The Alfred Hitchcock Hour* that aired in 1964, although even that was not the first time the premise was used.

"The Devil's Cauldron" (*GM* 5) is a full-length story about a married couple who wind up back in 1891 helping the husband's great-grandfather battle a plague of pasty-faced ghouls that have come out of a mine after being killed by a deadly gas issuing from fissures far below. Joe Gill's story is effective and while Sanho Kim's art is quite crude, it manages to get across the horror of the situations in atmospheric fashion. Kim's artwork was somewhat improved by the following issue, especially in a story about a cat who gets even with a lawyer trying to fiddle around with its owner's will; this would have been fairly worthless without Kim's fluid portrayals of the feline in question and the stylish lay-outs of the piece. In subsequent issues Kim's work was less effective, often amateurish, like the worst of golden age art, yet he did display occasional spurts of imagination, such as when he depicted a man who had crushing gambling debts literally crushed beneath a giant pair of die.

Ghost Manor 13 introduced the shapely Winnie the Witch as the new hostess. An intrusive narrator, Winnie, who was dressed like a super-heroine with a mask and cape, appeared in nearly every other panel of the stories, spouting witless jokes and failing to disguise the dreadfulness of the mostly fourth-rate material. There were some exceptions: In "When Johnny Comes Marching Home" (*GM* 16) a couple's son goes to war, leaving them at the mercy of his evil foster brother. The parents are beside themselves when they get a telegram telling them of Johnny's death, but the good young soldier comes home anyway, as a ghost who lives on in his brother's body. In "Safe Behind Bars" a convicted man can send out a deadly living force that repeatedly tries to kill the main witness against him until he's executed in the nick of time (fortunately, and surprisingly, he doesn't come back as a ghost). "The Wrong Turn" (18) has a young couple on the road winding up in a halfway house between life and death. Unable to accept that they were killed in an accident, they escape—or so they think, but they learn that no one can outrun Death. The series wrapped up its run after nineteen issues. Other artists for the comic included Steve Ditko and Pete Morisi, aka PAM. *Ghost Manor* returned with a second volume in the bronze age.

Ten

Dell and Gold Key

DELL

Dell comics generally published magazines based on licensed characters and cartoons. In the silver age, they made an effort to expand their line with different types of material, including horror/supernatural comics. First they came out with *Dracula* in 1962. The first issue was a one-shot, "The Vampire's Curse," about physician Sir Basil Shawcross, who tells his friend, Professor Janos Tesla, that he has just received word that his son, Bruce, has died while in Transylvania. Tesla, who studies folklore and believes in vampires, is afraid that there is no hope for Bruce, who according to his letters became engaged to a beautiful woman he met in a cemetery and who found him "red-blooded." Tesla accompanies Shawcross to Transylvania, where they not only discover Bruce has indeed become one of the undead, but are taken to Castle Dracula for a confrontation with the count. They manage to survive the encounter, although a frustrated Dracula spits out oaths of vengeance. The beautiful painted cover depicts a handsome Dracula carrying a woman from her bed in moonlight, but the scene does not appear in the story until the very end. The inside art is merely serviceable. Had Dell chosen to do sequels they might have come up with a series as good as Marvel's *Tomb of Dracula* ten years later, but instead *Dracula*'s second issue did not appear until 1966, and by this time Dracula had been turned into a costumed hero.

In this revisioning, a modern-day descendant and scientist wants to save the family reputation by helping mankind, but the formula he develops enables him to turn into a bat and command other normal bats as well. Apparently the rumors about the Draculas being vampires are unfounded. The New Dracula battles such foes as a man who wants to control the weather via specially outfitted blimps. A woman he meets named B. B. Beebe discovers his secret, drinks his formula, and becomes his partner, Fleeta (short for *fledermaus* or bat). Obviously the series was geared for younger readers and completely eliminated the horror elements of the character. *Dracula* in his new guise only lasted three issues. Ten years later Dell reissued these issues, but the series still didn't catch on, probably because even kids realized it was terrible. Dell's Frankenstein character, also a super-hero, appeared briefly in the final story.

Dell came out with the one-shot 80 page *Tales from the Tomb* in 1962. This is a bizarre hodge-podge of edgy horror stories, black comedies, and EC-type tales without the graphic gore. "Mr. Green Must Be Fed" is a weird one about a sweet old landlady of a rooming house who feeds guests to a horrible green creature that comes out of a rug. In "Still Life" a young artist shows a lady friend a picture he drew of a stunted tree with a supposed curse on it, asking her to pose for him so he can add her to the picture. When she shows up at the appointed hour, she looks at the painting and sees a drawing of the young artist hanging from the tree—then looks up and sees him dead and hanging from the rafters. "Oh, How We Danced" has a lonely young man named Les meeting a beautiful woman named Sharon at a dance. They hit it off, and have a great time, but she tells him she has a boyfriend and has to leave. Les follows her in his car—and discovers she came from an automobile wreck that occurred in the woods two years before.

The odd but amusing "Two for the Price of One" concerns Walter, who wants to divorce his wife Paula and marry an actress named Vera. When he sees a midget who looks exactly like him, he cooks up a wild way of getting Paula to agree to a divorce and a juicy settlement. Telling Paula, who has a phobia about short men, that he wants to try to save their marriage, he takes her for a drive and goes out to an old house that is supposed to be haunted, suggesting it would be fun to explore. An elderly midget—a friend of the first little person—answers the door and shows them around. After awhile Walter goes up into the attic, but sends his tiny lookalike down in his stead. The elderly midget cries out "That's what happened to *me*!" Thinking the little man is her husband and that he's shrunk in size, a horrified Paula runs off, yelling at Walter that she's divorcing him and will give him millions to get rid of him. Once Paula has left, the two midgets shout out to Walter that it's safe to come down out of the attic. "I'm down," Walter says, but unfortunately he has somehow become a comically squashed-looking troll of a man who is even shorter than the midgets!

"The Mudman" is a beautifully drawn story (George Evans) about a boy and his dog encountering the swamp creature who murdered the boy's father years before. The one-page "Goblin's Ball" is a five-panel story about two parents who are talking about their little boy, George Jr,. and his imaginary goblin pals. Before leaving to go play, George tells his mother that his friends want to play ball using George's head for the ball. "Go ahead, it's your head," his mother tells him, laughing at how silly it all is. Later the phone rings and it's the police telling them of how Mrs. Jones' window is broken and their son is somehow involved. "Did she have to call the *police*?" asks the mother. Sick, holding his stomach, the father bends over and says, "Yes—she *had* to—call police." It's hard to tell if this parody of parents learning that their child is dead and dismembered, while too ridiculous to take seriously, is meant to be funny or not, but it isn't.

Dell brought out *The Wolfman* in 1963. Although Universal Pictures retained the copyright, the story was entirely different from their Wolfman movie with Claude Rains and Lon Chaney, Jr. In the comic, a young man named Milo Zac returns to the small European village of Kavlek where he was raised by his aunt and uncle, intending to marry his fiancee Lyana and set up a medical practice. Unfortunately, the peasants are so superstitious that they believe more in witchcraft and gypsy cures than they do in modern medicine. Another problem is an evil man named Vorcla, who demands money from farmers to protect them, their livestock and families from his wolf packs. Milo is convinced that Vorcla is a faker with no supernatural powers and brings about his arrest. Vorcla is ordered to leave town, but he returns to get revenge upon those who testified against him, attacking them with his wolves or setting fire to their houses. The townspeople are more furious with Milo than they are with Vorcla, for the former nearly convinced them that Vorcla was harmless. Vorcla puts a demonic spell on Milo which sort of turns him into a Mr. Hyde. Milo's friend and fellow doctor, Albert La Forge, comes to Kavlek at Lyana's urging, and manages to dispatch the evil Vorcla with his silver cane, freeing Milo from his influence. Universal presumably disallowed the use of the wolfman image except on the cover, but it seems strange that Dell would bother with a wolfman comic that had no wolfman—or even a werewolf—in it. Dell's *Werewolf* series, which lasted three issues in 1966, was a super-hero spy comic.

Ghost Stories

Dell debuted *Ghost Stories* in 1963. The first issue contained two stories that not only were *not* ghost stories but which were probably responsible for more kids having nightmares in the early sixties than any other horror comic of that era. "The Werewolf Wasp" had young Bobby bringing an unusual wasp to his friend, the kindly entomologist Professor Larvay. When the professor doesn't answer his door, Bobby is afraid he might be ill and enters the house through a cellar door, only to discover large cocoons, inside which are terrified, groaning little boys. The professor appears without his usual gloves and head net, so for the first time Bobby can see his hideous face and spider-like body with its multiple arms. As Larvay rushes forward to make Bobby his latest victim—and meal—the wasp breaks out of its jar and attacks and kills him, while Bobby rushes to get help for the boys.

Even scarier than "Werewolf Wasp" was the classic "Monster of Dread End." In this dark and disturbing story, parents in the busy, happy neighborhood of Hawthorn Place awaken to discover their children missing. Then milkmen and others begin finding desiccated, shriveled little corpses which turn out tragically and horribly to be the missing youngsters. Frantic parents do their best to protect their little ones from whatever is snatching them in the night and killing them—to no avail. In one heart-rending sequence, a couple board up the windows in their twin sons' bedroom, only to enter the next morning to find the boards smashed and the little boys vanished. Eventually everyone moves away, the streets are cordoned off, and the shunned neighborhood becomes known as "Dread End." Into this place of horror comes fifteen-year-old Jimmy White, whose sister was the first victim eight years earlier. Still hoping to find whoever killed her, he moves about the streets and excites the interest of some*thing* that lives below. Suddenly he sees a gigantic, scaly hand creeping up out of a manhole; the arm it is attached to is many yards long and climbs up and over the nearby buildings in search of prey. The next few pages show the cat and mouse game that results as the hand senses Jimmy and tries to grab him in its loathsome paw, until police show up to riddle the obscene thing with bullets. The origin of the creature (nor what the rest of it looks like) is never divulged, only that it crushes its victims and feeds via osmosis through pores in its palm. Details weren't necessary as the story achieves its goal of brilliantly evoking a sense of the terrors of both childhood and adulthood. Writer John Stanley was presumably merely crafting an entertaining horror story but he managed to strike deeper chords than he realized.

While "Dread End" disturbed the sleep of many a young reader, it is arguably even more disturbing to grown-ups, as the horror isn't just what happens to the innocent children but the terrible effect it will have on their parents for the rest of their lives. It's ironic that the

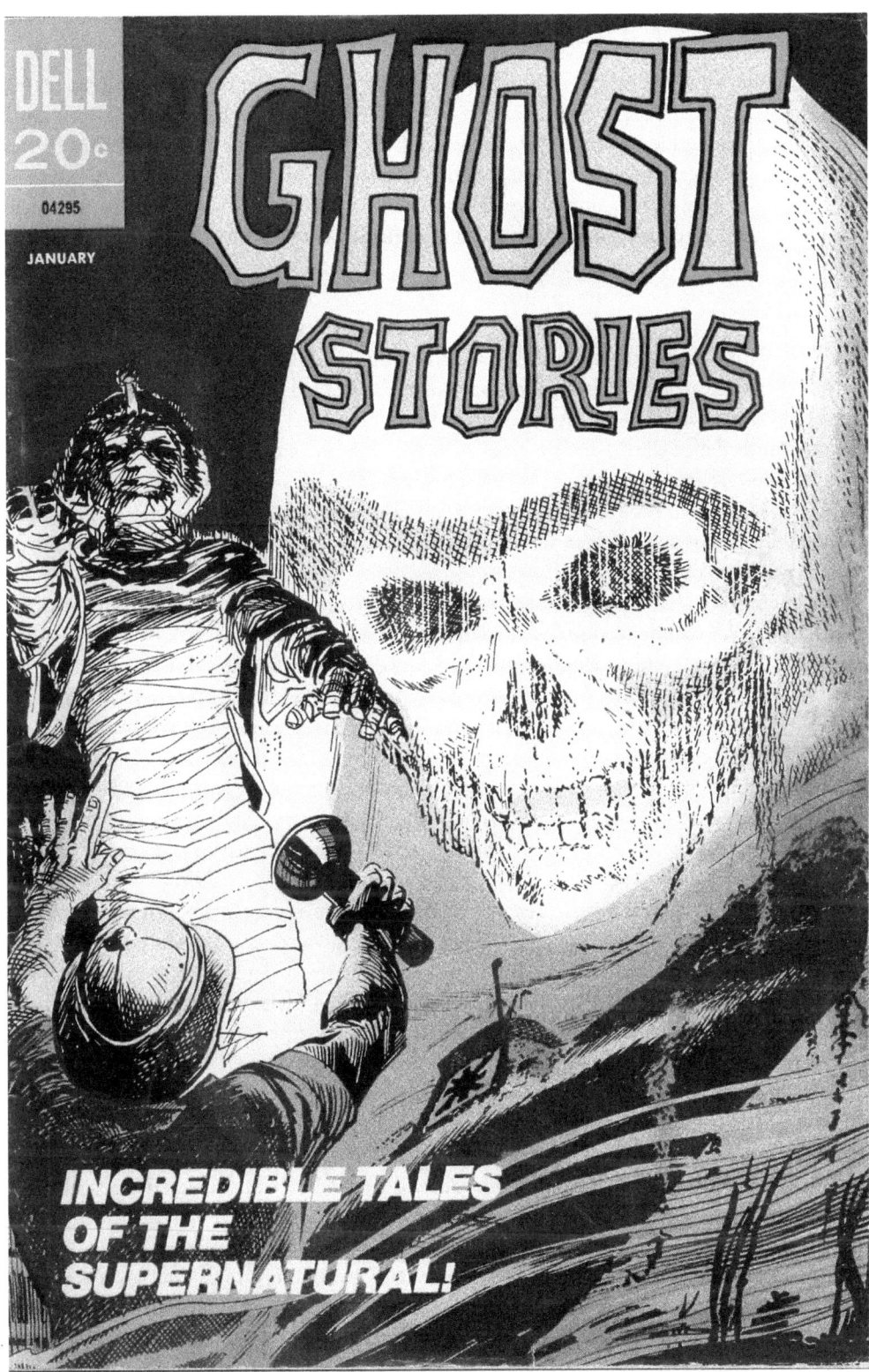

Dell's *Ghost Stories* snuck in some gruesome horror stories in what was supposed to be a mild ghost comic.

story was published by Dell, as during the controversy over horror comics during the fifties, Dell always maintained that their comics were always in the best of taste. True, "Dread End" shows no dripping blood or gore, the corpses of the children are not shown, there are no hacked-off limbs or adulterous spouses taking axes to one another, but the story is just as repellent in its own way as anything published by EC. It is the one story that many readers remember with a genuine shudder decades after having first read it. The superlative art by Ed Robbins is another factor in its favor.

Frankly, *Ghost Stories*, while an entertaining comic, never again presented a story as memorable or as dark as "Dread End." There were, of course, lots of stories about travelers being aided by people on lonely roads and in isolated houses who turned out to have died years before, or people turning up at desperate moments to offer aid and succor who had also either disappeared or expired. Sergeants would lead their shell-shocked injured men to safety, only the sergeant had died the day before. And so on. In one of the more memorable of these stories in *GS* 17 people are prevented from committing suicide by a mustachioed, compassionate bobby who, as usual, is dead. It turns out that he killed himself after his wife and children were among dozens of passengers incinerated in a fiery train crash. Only his wife and children were never on the train ...

But there were also tales about bodies buried in greenhouses that turn into malevolent plants, a woman rushing to save her daughter from a train crash she dreams about only to die in a car accident—as her daughter dreamed; and dead cats who show up as giant phantoms to terrorize greedy landlords. Some stories were nonsensical, illogically plotted, with intriguing ideas that went nowhere or had flat wind-ups. "Appointment with Sam Mara" (*GS* 4), in which the same man is always seen at the scene of horrendous disasters, is another variation of Ray Bradbury's classic tale "The Crowd" with a creepily amusing final twist. "Escape Act" (*GS* 6) is a suspenseful tale in which a woman and her lover try to kill her escape-artist husband—they replace a key he uses to get out of an underwater trunk with a fake one— but even dead he manages to get even with them.

Occasionally there was a more original premise, such as a story in *GS* 7 in which an odd man with a rare blood type miraculously shows up to give transfusions to men who were severely injured while committing crimes, but each time the bad guy ultimately dies and the weird man disappears. There was the lion tamer in *GS* 13 who tries to kill a hated lion, rumored to be reincarnated from a maniac, but when the dust settles the dead lion is wearing the man's clothing and the man has a strangely feline countenance.

Not all of the stories in the later issues featured ghosts. "The Thing in the Swamp" (*GS* 12) is an effective chiller about a group of men encountering and killing a very large scorpion in a swampy area of an isolated valley. Legend has it that unless special care is taken, the scorpion will keep returning to life, getting larger and larger each time, which it does until the final panel shows its gigantic shadow hovering over the horrified and much tinier men below. Another eerie moment occurs in "In the Pool" (*GS* 13), in which a nasty man has a Roman palazzo refurbished and uses stone blocks from an old wall to fashion an elegant swimming pool. When his guests complain about something weird and evil in the water, he dives in and sees horrible, grimacing faces on the blocks of stone and drowns, unaware that the wall from which he built the pool consists of ancient gravestones.

Beginning with the twenty-first issue *Ghost Stories* became a reprint title until the 35th issue, which contains an interesting story entitled "The Second Crew." In this the commander of an American destroyer during World War II fires upon a Japanese sub and sinks it, only to learn that the war had actually ended some minutes before. Although no one could ever blame him (and it's never revealed if the Japanese sub knew the war was over or if they would have torpedoed the ship), Commander Carlson is wracked with guilt. Having no family, he travels to post-war Japan, learns which sub he destroyed, and "adopts" the families of the dead men, bonding with and helping the wives and children. After his death, Carlson's ghost travels to the crew of the submarine, and tells the spirits of the dead sailors that he is taking them home. The sub rises to the surface with Carlson's hat inexplicably hanging from a valve. It would be all too easy to deconstruct the story, but it still manages to be strangely touching and humane.

In the same issue "Do Unto Others" has four self-absorbed and callous individuals watching a sixty-five-year-old man, Horace Spector, being mugged and murdered as they do nothing to help him or even call the police. Horace's ghost rises from his grave, appearing each time one of these people is in danger, bringing rescue for them and then disappearing. At the end these four people have Spector's body dug up from potter's field and re-committed in hallowed ground with a headstone saying "Gone, but Not Forgotten." The story is sentimental and perhaps unrealistically upbeat, but effective. The next two issues also contained reprints and then the series was gone. Frank Springer was the main artist for the series.

Dell's *Frankenstein* debuted in 1964. The story starts out as an adaptation of the 1930s movie (with the monster modeled on the famous Boris Karloff portrayal) then goes in its own direction, as Victor Frankenstein, his assistant Fritz, and the Monster make their way across the ocean to the United States. Only when they arrive in New York City is it made clear that the story is taking place in modern times. Victor storms into a scientific conference and demands to speak, whereupon he tells how he's created life, even as his idiot assistant inadvertently awakens the Monster from its trance. Ultimately the monster bursts into the conference and attacks everyone; he is supposedly burned to death on a fiery ship at the conclusion. Two years later the second issue of *Frankenstein* came out and had no connection with the first issue aside from the name. Now the Monster calls himself Frank Stone and wears a red jumpsuit and flesh-colored mask that make him look normal. Saving a rich old man in a car accident with his super-human strength, he becomes the millionaire's sole heir when he dies. He then embarks on a double-life as a rich playboy and super-hero. The idea was not as bad as it sounds, and *Frankenstein* was fun for younger readers, but the stories and villains were a little *too* childish and the series only lasted four issues.

GOLD KEY

A comic book based on *The Twilight Zone* debuted from Gold Key in 1962. The first issue has a compelling, if predictable, story entitled "Voyage to Nowhere," in which two men, Roy and Dan, spot a woman struggling in a small boat to reach land during a storm. Unfortunately she's lost amidst the waves and presumably dies. But back on land the men learn that the woman, Carlotta, actually died fifty years ago. Roy is especially fascinated by Carlotta and makes up his mind to save her the next time her boat appears in the mist. Dan tries to convince Roy that it is all just an illusion and that the woman's sad fate cannot be changed. Roy swims toward her boat and is soon lost in the mist. Dan is suspected of murdering Roy, and his case isn't helped when the authorities find fifty-year-old fragments of

Carlotta's boat on shore. But when they, too, see Carlotta's boat in the mist—with both Carlotta and Roy on board this time—they finally believe Dan's story.

In *Twilight Zone* 5 nearly every story is a winner. "The Legacy of Hans Burkel" has to do with a jinx on a U-boat. "Poor Little Sylvester" is an amusing story about a precocious child who outwits his greedy and unloving guardians. In "The Fortune Hunters" two twentieth century men print modern confederate money and sell it as genuine Civil War currency, but get their comeuppance when they wind up back in the nineteenth century. Two of the stories in *TZ* 7 were especially compelling. In "The Shield of the Medusa" a man uncovers the shield that Perseus used to kill the Medusa by tricking her into looking at her own image in its mirrored surface. Her face has become imprinted on the shield, and it alone is capable of turning people to stone. A jealous associate steals the shield and runs amok with it until the protagonist is able to defeat him. (There was a very exciting sequel to this story in *TZ* 24 in which the protagonists again attempt to get rid of the shield, but also have to deal with sailors intent on stealing it, as well as an angry giant squid.) "The Man Who Haunted Himself" has an intriguing premise. A greedy and heartless land owner dies for a time when his heart stops. He is successfully revived by doctors, but discovers that his ghost was created during the time he was dead, and is now haunting *him* and becoming his conscience.

In *Twilight Zone* 9 the fascinating "Creatures on Canvas" has a painter entering his own paintings and interacting with the people there to find out who stole one of his most treasured masterpieces and murdered a night watchman. In "The Man Who Could Read the Future" in *TZ* 13 an injury gives a man the ability to solve crimes by touching objects that were used in, or affected by, those crimes. His power expands so that he is alerted when a crime is being committed, and can foresee disasters as well. But this ability eventually brings about his own ironic death. In the whimsical "The Joiner" (*TZ* 26) a timid, hen-pecked man named Alvah Petty with a shrewish wife and obnoxious son finds escape by joining every group he can find. His son makes up a phony "intergalactic" group and sends his father out to a non-existent address to teach him a lesson. But Alvah does find the intergalactic group at this address and at the end of the story is taking off in a spaceship to explore the universe. For him the trip will take five hours but for everyone back on earth two hundred years will pass. "My gracious! How will I ever explain that to my wife?" says Alvah—with a smile.

Twilight Zone's editor seemed to delight in running stories of "losers" (as they were referred to by narrator Rod Serling) who try to make a better life for themselves but wind up in far worse situations—even when they are not evil people. "Trapped Between Lives" (*TZ* 29) is the story of Bernie Madsen, a homely peanut vendor at ball games who hates his looks and his life and sees an ad for people who want to change their lives. He goes to the address and winds up with a handsome new body which belonged to another man who wanted to make life changes. Then he learns that the cost will be $500 a month. He is convinced that will be no problem with his new appearance, but without references or employment and education history no one will hire him. He resorts to crime to avoid the beatings he receives when he doesn't pay the money, but one day an elderly robbery victim drops dead of a heart attack. Horrified and guilt-ridden, Bernie demands his old body back, but learns it was taken by someone who wanted to simplify *his* life. Running from the police, Bernie winds up at the baseball stadium and literally bumps into "himself" selling peanuts. The police are able to capture him, the new Bernie Madsen is hailed as a hero, and the old one—more miserable than ever—is taken off for a lengthy stretch in prison. An even more terrible fate awaits the unhappy protagonist of "A Matter of Time (*TZ* 41), who builds a watch that can slow down time for everyone but him. When he accidentally kills his boss he runs from the police using the watch but winds up trapped in a blurry non-existence when the watch breaks down.

On occasion there were monsters on the loose. "Something New in Town" (*TZ* 47) is about man-eating creatures, possibly a type of giant alien insect, who resemble simple light poles but can come alive to grab up humans and devour them, leaving behind only pieces of torn clothing. The protagonist, who becomes another meal, comes across an empty town and realizes that everyone in it has been eaten. Unfortunately, the too-tasteful story didn't have enough grisly atmosphere or gruesome touches to make it really come alive.

In "The Medallion" (57) a middle-aged antique dealer, Edgar, who takes care of his mother, hopes a magical medallion can literally take him out of his unhappy life but his mother gets to it first; the story expertly etches both the love and resentment Edgar feels over having to constantly look after his aged parent and the characterizations are very good. "Portrait of an Artist" (58) has a bit of EC flavor in its tale of a haughty artist who is hired to do a painting of a room in the home of a wealthy couple. As he does his work he discovers that the room is beginning to resemble his more abstract painting of it and that there is no longer an exit. He decides to paint himself into the artwork so he can leave the room, but as human figures never interested him and his knowledge of anatomy is weak, what finally emerges from the room is a grotesque travesty of the handsome man he used to be.

In the seventies *TZ* published an unfortunate number of very badly plotted stories that seemed cobbled together just to fill up pages. "Makeover" (*TZ* 84), about a cosmetics queen who stays eternally young, is a bland rip-off of *The Picture of Dorian Gray* with no real plot or pay-off. An untitled story in *TZ* 90, in which the young callous owner of a badly run nursing home becomes old and winds up in the place's abusive care, is a vastly inferior version of a golden age horror story. However, one of the worst stories was published back in *TZ* 3 in the sixties; it centered on a dyspeptic boss who hated pigeons and forbade anyone to feed them. When he finds his middle-aged secretary doing just that, he gives her two week's notice. But it turns out that she is a representative of the pigeon world, and at the end of the story both she and her boss—who has not just converted to a pigeon-fancier but a *pigeon*—fly out the window, leaving their spectacles behind. Because, as the narrator says, who ever saw pigeons wearing glasses? The story was definitely for the birds.

Twilight Zone became double-sized with the eighty-third issue (half of the stories were reprints) and got a more futuristic-type logo with the following issue. The double-size was gone the next issue, but the new logo and reprints remained. *Twilight Zone* lasted ninety-two issues and many years longer than the television program. Other notable stories include: "All's Quiet on the Eastern Front" (36)—a World War I soldier gets his wish for the war with its noise and bloodshed to end but not in the way he expected; "The General's Statue" (38)—when the arm of a statue keeps falling off it proves disastrous for the sculptor and prescient for the general who posed for him; "Long Laugh the King" (41)—a jester uses special make up to resemble his king, only to be betrayed by him, but has the last laugh; "The Haunted Taxi" (42)—a cab driver has to drive around the ghost of a man who was murdered in the taxi's back seat until he picks up his killer; "The Man Who Kidnapped Death" (43)—a man entraps the death-imp who has come to claim him and begins a life of death-defying adventure knowing he can't be killed, but death always has the last word; "A Call for Mr. Travers" (45)—a man receives phone calls giving prophecies of deaths and disasters; "The

Experiment" (45)—the earth turns out to be a mere bit of contamination in an experiment to create stars in a laboratory in a universe of giants; "Nightmare in Miniature" (48)—two men come upon a city of tiny prehistoric men and dinosaurs; "The Supreme Penalty" (49)—suicides go to a special dimension which is run like a police state and are sentenced to go back to the lives they hated if they conspire against the government; "Forget Me Not" (55)—a black comedy about an absent-minded man who brings the wrong wife back from the dead; "The Stand-In" (59)—a wealthy, fatuous man who is bored by the parties he must host and the people who attend, has a robot built to take his place, then discovers that all of his equally bored guests have already done the same thing.

Twilight Zone, like most Gold Key comics, had (uncredited) painted covers. One of the most striking (TZ 43) depicts a bellboy beginning a terrifying plunge out of a highrise hotel window (he manages to save himself in the story inside). Also notable are the covers for *TZ 63* (a man trapped in an elevator with shadowy claws hovering above him) and for *TZ 64* (a man falling in front of a subway train).

Boris Karloff Tales of Mystery

Boris Karloff Thriller, based on the TV show hosted by the famous actor, debuted in 1962. It combined fictional stories with short accounts of true weird happenings around the world. The first issue had two stand-out stories":The Hand in the Wall," about a man who tries to drive his cousin crazy so that he can get his money; and "The Plague of Gornau," in which an immoral witch-finder gets his well-deserved comeuppance. In *Thriller* 2 "The Island" is an excellent and highly ironic tale of a mousy bank employee who steals $30,000 and plans to live on a South Seas island, unaware that there have been some changes there since it was mentioned in his guidebook.

By the third issue the title was changed to *Boris Karloff Tales of Mystery*, and there were many more memorable stories. "The Five Casks of Greed" (13) concerns a man who discovers five ancient casks full of treasure, but none of the casks can be opened until an act of evil is performed. The first evil acts are not so terrible, but eventually the man becomes a mass murderer. But he breaks the rule that he must wait ten years between opening each cask, and pays a frightful penalty for doing so. In "The Phone to the Past" (14) an ambitious man discovers that by dialing a special number on a certain phone in Grand Central Station he can speak to famous people from the past such as Machiavelli and Casanova, who help him at his job and with his wife. He is undone, however, when he asks Lucretia Borgia for an undetectable poison to murder his boss. The poison may have been undetectable back in Lucretia's day, but a modern-day autopsy clearly reveals traces of it and he's arrested.

In *TOM* 15's "Captives of the Camera" a honeymooning couple have their pictures snapped by a weird man and discover they've somehow been sucked into a strange world located right on the film strip inside the camera. Trying to escape, they make their way from one place to another, discovering varied locales—with more captives—that exist side by side, separated only by a mist. *TOM* 20 has two interesting tales: " The Death Bell" has a man struggling to keep a bell from ringing that would signal the death of his beloved, while "The Sleeping Dragon" is a lively tale of a young couple trying to stay out of the clutches and long, red, snarling tongue of a reawakened dragon.

TOM began temporarily running reprints combined with new stories with the 21st issue. In *TOM* 24 one story ends with narrator Karloff saying that it had occurred in "a weird corner of the *Twilight Zone*," an error that no one noticed before the issue went to press. When *TOM* began running all-new material again, the focus was squarely on aliens and, especially, monsters, like in DC's sci fi comics. As the silver age drew to a close there were stories about swamp beasts, walking petrified trees, a blob that devours everything in its path, and a "monster mountain" that turns out to be a huge living creature. Most of these were pure schlock, unfortunately.

The TV show had long since been canceled but as the years went by the comic carried on with efficient if unspectacular artwork and some interesting stories. "The Eyes of the Monster" in *TOM* 32 is an unusual jungle horror story in which a hideous creature kills only those who look upon it. Closing your eyes so you don't actually see the beast saves your life—even if the monster can see you—but the protagonist has seen the creature and is pursued by it even while surrounded by dozens of natives who stand about with their eyes tightly shut. "The Mystic Clay," used to fashion an animal or person, can bring its subject to life once it is finished, and is used by an angry, neglected artist to gain vengeance upon his critics.

And the monsters kept coming: a skeleton of a stegosaurus that comes to life in a museum when the very last bone is fitted in; an insectoid god creature that pulls itself out of a strip of film even as it's being projected; a Venus fly-trap that grows to huge proportions and engulfs the botanist who made it; a formula that not only replicates a frog and a man but turns them into savage giants; another giant who causes havoc in an elevator shaft; huge oysters that send out sticky pearls with membranes attached to pull down swimmers and trap them in their shells; a chameleon creature that can assume the form of any inanimate object it chooses (and winds up a huge boulder that may or may not be dead); gigantic caterpillars driven above ground by hunger; and a sorcerer's seeds that can grow into hungry monsters.

These creature tales were all entertaining if minor but now and then they were of more interest than usual. "What Crowded Skies" (*TOM* 39) took its cue from the fifties creature feature *The Giant Claw* in its tale of something that is obliterating airliners and leaving not a trace behind but which doesn't show up on radar. More sophisticated radar equipment reveals a huge winged creature zeroing in on the latest doomed plane, and the panel, drawn by Win Mortimer, depicting this reptilian creature crunching its gigantic jaws down and destroying an airliner filled with terrified passengers is horrifically effective. The story ends too abruptly however. ("The Speed of Fright" in *TOM* 55 also has an interesting flying monster that could only be seen by pilots going at super-sonic speed.) "Live Bait" (*TOM* 50) almost has an EC-like flavor in its tale of two men who discover a gigantic man-eating lizard called a pachako on a tiny South American island whose surrounding waters are filled with piranha. The natives in their party have fled, taking the only boat. Since none of their ammunition will pierce the monster's hide, Hopkins suggests that he and O'Neill flip a coin to see who will fill his pockets with knock-out powder and allow the creature to consume him, killing the beast and sparing the other man. O'Neill is chosen to be the live bait, but discovers too late that the coin had two heads. Before the pachako can devour him, however, the beast drops dead. Apparently Hopkins climbed a tree for safety and a good view, unaware that the beast could also climb trees, so he was eaten along with the rest of the knock-out powder, saving O'Neill in the nick of time. (It is never explained how O'Neill will manage to get off the island.)

Other memorable monster stories include "The Carved Head" (*TOM* 51), a flavorful, well-drawn tale in which a group of pirates come afoul of a sea monster; "Off the Beaten Path" (51), in which a couple try to save their son from a huge, hulking monster that crawls out of a burial ground; and "The Ant Monster" (54), in which two exterminators on vacation are bedeviled by an uncanny giant ant that turns out to be a projection from one little hateful insect. "Guest of Honor" (61) tells the true story behind an expedition to capture a legendary mountain creature even as the leader of the expedition tells lies to make himself look good, but gets his comeuppance in a most unusual way. "Like Father—Like Son" (73) tells of a father who fought a dragon to ensure a future for his son, but whose son turns out to be much more special than anyone realized. In "Who Was That Monster …?" (76) an old magician's much younger wife outwits herself when she tries to bring a monster into the act.

Occasionally there was a more unusual storyline, such as "Monster On My Back" (*TOM* 39), in which a shipwrecked man finds an injured elderly fellow on a deserted island, and follows his instructions to carry him to the other side of the island where there supposedly is a trading post. But during the journey, the old man keeps getting heavier and heavier, until the protagonist sees a reflection in the water and realizes his "passenger" has turned into a grotesque ape-like monster (well depicted on the cover). It turns out he is a 200-year-old sorcerer who paid a price for discovering a formula for immortality: he turned into this creature that can absorb the life forces of others and is now doing so to the unfortunate man who is carrying him. He was imprisoned on the island for mankind's safety by a more powerful wizard. The shipwrecked man is able to outwit the sorcerer, however, and he sinks into a bog without a trace. In "One of You Died Last Night" (76) a scientist who specializes in cloning informs his guests on an isolated island that during the night one of them passed away and has been replaced by a clone, causing paranoia and suspicion; the idea was better than the execution. Another notable non-monster tale was "Food for the Gods" (*TOM* 63), about sacrifices made to a giant idol.

In the seventies *Tales of Mystery* briefly expanded its page count, running half new material and half reprints. Then it alternated regular-sized issues of all-new material with issues that contained only reprints from the sixties. The comic's lengthy run ended with the 97th issue in 1980. Like other Gold Key comics, *Tales of Mystery* had painted covers, among the more memorable of which are on *TOM* 64, which shows a man being lifted out of the water under a bridge by a huge, scaly claw; *TOM* 71, which has a red dragon-like dinosaur hovering over men standing atop an oil derrick; *TOM* 79, upon which a sultan is lifted off his feet by two huge, hairy paws; and *TOM* 95, in which a horrible, cackling face emerges from the smoke coming out of several flasks as an equally cackling man nearby delights in the treasure he's discovered.

Dark Shadows

Dark Shadows was a Gothic after-school soap opera that debuted on ABC television in the sixties. The ratings picked up enormously after the show introduced a vampire named Barnabas Collins, leading the way to all manner of supernatural creatures and storylines. A comic series based on the show was a natural and came out from Gold Key in 1968. Just as the character of Barnabas Collins took over the TV show, so did Barnabas dominate the comic book series, appearing in every story and on every cover. Along for the ride were

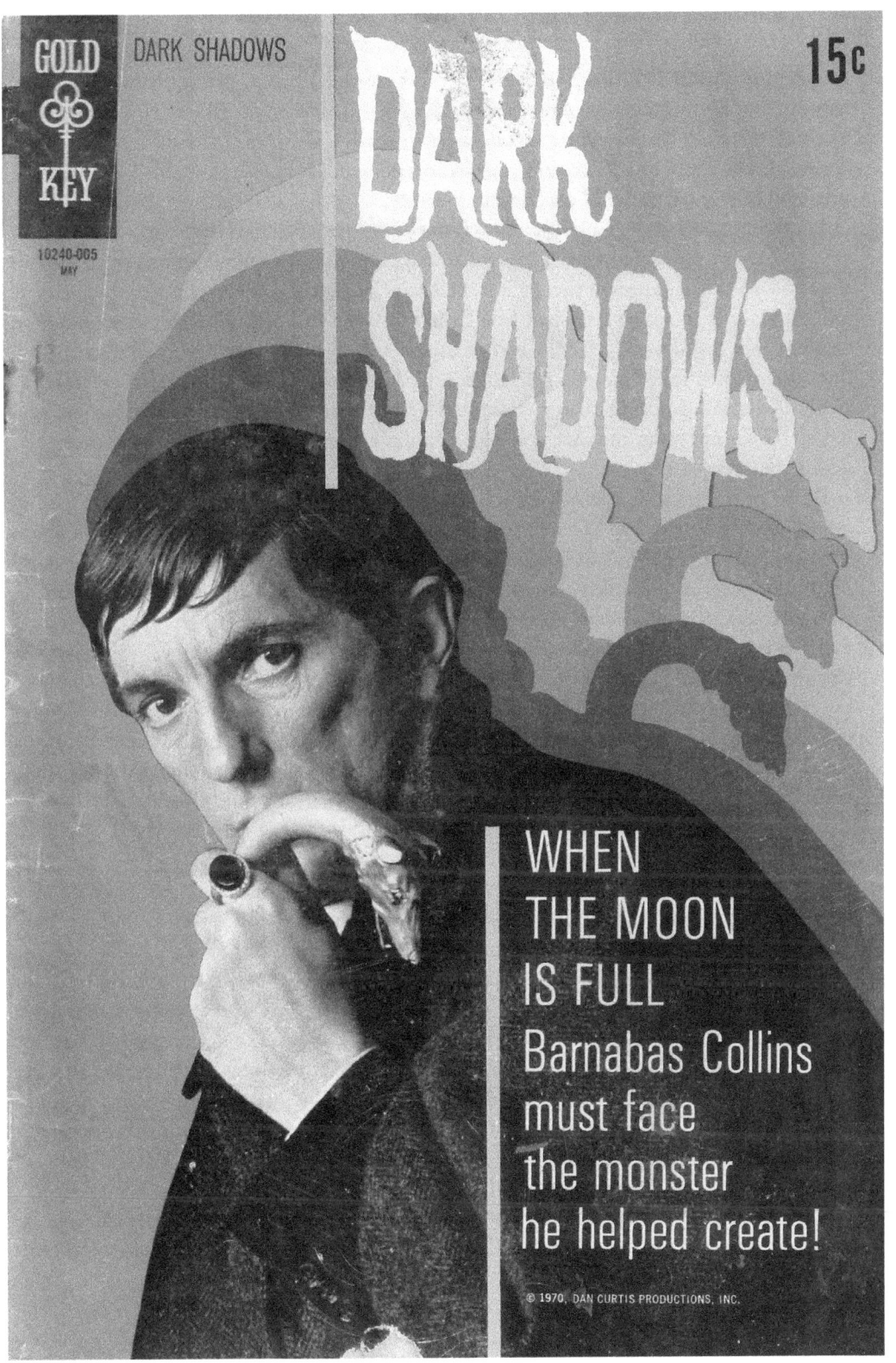

Gold Key snatched up the rights to the popular afternoon Gothic soap opera *Dark Shadows*.

Angelique the witch, who had originally put the curse on Barnabas; Willie Loomis, Barnabas' servant; the bloodsucker's helpmate, Dr. Hoffman; Elizabeth Collins, who lives in the haunted mansion Collinwood; and many of the other denizens of Collinsport, Maine. Although the comic used the same characters and similar situations as the TV series, the stories were original and on occasion interesting.

In *Dark Shadows* 3 the Collins family comes under attack from the 200-year-old spirit of a Native American named Charley Setauket. Barnabas uses his special powers to go back in time and learn what angered the man. It seems one of Barnabas' ancestors, Jeb Collins, was a thief; his furious father banished him from his home and ordered Jeb's two brothers to build a cabin for him to spend the rest of his days in. Instead, Jeb ran off and the brothers put the aforementioned unwilling Setauket into the cabin prison in his place, where he eventually died of starvation. Barnabas tracks down Jeb in the past and, discovering that the man is dying of consumption and wants to make amends, helps him exchange places with Setauket, lifting the curse.

By the fourth issue Barnabas was for a time no longer under his vampire curse (following events on the TV series) so new menaces were concocted. *DS* 5 had a centuries-old wolfman, William Starbuck, arriving in Collinsport to get revenge on Barnabas because he unfairly holds him responsible for his son's death and his own lycanthropic curse. In the following issue Barnabas fears his relative Quentin Collins has again become a werewolf but several murders in Collinsport actually turn out to be the work of a living mummy. Barnabas was a vampire again by *DS* 8, an interesting story in which the tormented bloodsucker is alarmed by an occultist who's come to Collinwood for the stated purpose of tracking down a supernatural being. Barnabas wonders if it's himself or Quentin that the man is after, but it turns out that the occultist hopes to be bitten by a vampire so that he can attain immortality. He doesn't quite get his wish.

In subsequent issues Barnabas battles 300-year-old pirates only he can see; living dolls that want to drive a stake through his heart; an 80-year-old immortal warlock who switches bodies with him as he had with many others before him; and an overzealous tour guide who hopes to thrill his group by killing a real live vampire. In *DS* 18 a gangster from New York comes to Collinwood to hide out, discovers Barnabas' secret, and tries to get him to put the bite on his rival, who's come looking for him.

Quentin Collins, the werewolf, was given a much larger role in the comic than before, such as in a story in *DS* 20 when Julia Hoffman creates a serum to help Barnabas with his vampirism. Quentin hopes the serum will help him, too, but it only turns him into another type of vampire. In a wild story in *DS* 23, Barnabas and Quentin wind up in a village populated entirely by vampires and where a gigantic monster Hell Hound suddenly appears to tear apart the entire town. In *DS* 27 Quentin discovers an old alchemist's formula that prevents him from turning into a werewolf, but when he learns that a strange side effect fills him with a hatred of Barnabas and might make him responsible for his destruction, he destroys the formula out of friendship. Quentin was the second most popular character both on the show and in the comic book.

In *Dark Shadows* 24 Barnabas is forced to give an emergency transfusion to a very wealthy man named Markovian who is near death after a car accident. Dr. Hoffman tells Barnabas that they have to take a chance because without blood he will certainly die. As he feared, Markovian turns into a vampire, which delights him, because now he knows he can survive the frequent attempts made on his life. Markovian has become dictator of his country Romanique, where the oppressed citizenry fervently wish for his death. Hoping to find a way to destroy the man, Barnabas lives with him in the palace where all the windows are painted black. With the aid of rebels and Markovian's own sister, Barnabas is able to defeat Markovian for good.

In the 35th and final issue of the series (1976), which kept publishing even after the TV show went off the air, Elizabeth Collins hopes to interest a publisher in the book that Barnabas has supposedly been writing when he's locked away during the daylight hours. The whole business is due to the manipulations of evil witch Angelique, who is behind the scenes in many of the stories. Of course there's no book, until Barnabas travels through time to acquire the diary of a woman named Sarah Collins. The comic series ended with Barnabas feeling safe that his cover story is still secure, but as tormented by his everlasting life of a vampire as ever.

The art for the series was a bit on the cartoonish side at times but not unattractive. The vampires and werewolves of *Dark Shadows* undoubtedly influenced to some extent later comic series such as Marvel's *Werewolf by Night*.

Part III

The Bronze Age, 1970–1983

Eleven

Dracula, Frankenstein and Werewolf by Night

With the coming of the seventies and comics' bronze age, there were many changes in the comics industry, especially in regards to horror comics and the depictions of horror. This coincided with a general public re-interest in the horror genre itself, including films, TV shows, fiction, and comic books. There was also a relaxation in the comics code, so that comic books could once again feature vampires and werewolves (which had crept back into some silver age series, as noted) and zombies, and there was a corresponding lessening of the restraint against gore. The seventies offered an amazing horror boom which included the incredibly popular works of Stephen King and dozens of other horror authors, mad slasher films, TV shows with horror themes, and of course, comic books. Marvel, DC and Charlton went after the horror readership with a vengeance, with the first, in particular, offering dozens of new series with a macabre slant and even putting out anthology comics consisting solely of golden and silver age reprints. Dell and Gold Key also got into the act, as well as the short-lived and new Atlas comics.

Marvel's most successful horror title, *Tomb of Dracula,* debuted in 1971 and takes place in modern times. Frank Drake comes to Transylvania with his fiancee Jean, and her ex-boyfriend, Frank's alleged friend Clifton Graves, who's still bitter over his break-up with Jean. Frank, whose family name was originally Dracula, is a descendant of the famous count, who may or may not have been a vampire. Frank's late father had amassed a fortune, which Frank ran through in three years, losing most of his friends along with his money. When Clifton learns that Frank's only asset is an ancestral castle in Transylvania that his father could never get rid of, he suggests they make money by turning it into a tourist attraction.

Unfortunately, inside the castle Clifton falls through a weakened patch of flooring and stumbles across Dracula's tomb. Not believing in vampires, he removes the stake from the skeleton inside the coffin and Dracula comes back to life. By the end of the first issue Clifton has been thrown into a deep pit, the castle has been set afire by villagers, and Jean has been transformed into a vampire by Dracula's bite. Gerry Conway scripted and Gene Colan provided the art, which was somewhat crude at first. When Tom Palmer took over the inking with the third issue, there was a marked improvement. Archie Goodwin temporarily took over the scripting with the third issue as well.

In *Tomb of Dracula* 2, the action moves to London, where Dracula and Jean pursue Frank and a now-rescued Clifton after the men have taken Dracula's coffin from the ruins of the castle. Frank is able to repel his unliving cousin, but is also forced to kill the woman he loves as she tries to put the bite on Clifton. Frank attempts suicide in the following issue but is rescued by Rachel Van Helsing—great grand-daughter of the man who drove a stake through Dracula's heart—and her hulking mute Indian associate Taj, who convinces Frank that his new purpose in life can be assisting them in hunting down the creatures of the night who made all of their lives so miserable and corrupted their loved ones.

Frank has sold the castle to an aging ex-model named Ilsa Strangway, who has turned to the occult in hopes of regaining her youth and beauty. Dracula, who's turned Clifton into his living slave, wants the castle back and turns Ilsa into a vampire so she can grow young again. But he's cruelly tricked the woman—Ilsa is unaware that even after feasting a vampire can grow no younger than he was when he first joined the ranks of the undead; Dracula is eternally thirty. Ilsa is appalled by the acts of blood-drinking she commits, especially when she learns that her monstrous acts against innocents won't make her young again. She begs Rachel to destroy her, and she complies (*TOD* 4). Gardner Fox scripted *TOD* 5–6, which has the Lord of the Undead escaping his pursuers by going through a mystic mirror and winding up back in the days just after Van Helsing "killed" him, but he fails to gain vengeance on his original opponent. He then travels back to the twentieth century wherein he imprisons Rachel and Frank in an oubliette, a literal black pit and medieval torture chamber, where they are rescued by a "Moors monster" who is actually the disfigured, very hirsute son of a wealthy lord in the area. Frank and Rachel have declared their love for one another, but Frank—who was taunted by Dracula that his blood also runs in *his*, Frank's, veins—is afraid he could turn into a vampire (unlikely unless he's bitten) and determines to give her up.

Marv Wolfman became the new writer of the series with its seventh issue, introducing additional vampire-hunters Quincy Harker and his daughter Edith, who use more technological methods to trap the undead. They debuted in a wild tale wherein Dracula sends hypnotized children, against whom they can't fight back, to kill Frank, Rachel and the others even as the count conspires with a vampire-doctor to use a special projector to create an army of the undead. However the undead doctor has a conscience and a daughter who doesn't know of his status, and in giant bat form he battles it out with Dracula in the skies above the selected cemetery. The good doctor loses the fight, but the count loses his army as the projector is smashed on the hallowed ground.

Wolfman tried to add dimension to the character of the count, but on this he was not always on the mark. In *TOD* 8 Dracula is befriended by a young man named David who is anxious to escape from the isolated town of Littlepool that few other residents, including his girlfriend, Andrea, have any desire to leave. David has no idea that Dracula is Lord of the Undead until the latter saves his and Andrea's lives from an attack by two other vampires. When the rest of the town gets wind of the fact that Dracula is in their midst, they form a posse, but David and Andrea protect the count, probably out of gratitude (and presumably unaware that the vampires who attacked them were harmless Littlepool residents that Dracula himself turned into the undead shortly before). Dracula expresses not only gratitude toward David but even a certain affection, which is completely out of character for the creature who sees humans as less than cattle. "You have the protection and friendship of Dracula," says the count, "who will not long forget you." Dracula even avoids feasting on Andrea because she is David's girlfriend. Compare this to the utter contempt with which he treats Clifton Graves, who brought him back to life, however inadvertently.

Much later it made a little more sense for Dracula to develop some feeling for the pathetic Sheila Whittier, who lives in a castle he wishes to inhabit, and who claims she is being preyed upon by a ghost. It turns out that her own father wants to sacrifice her to the devil. She comes to see Dracula as her savior until she realizes how truly evil he is. Dracula only keeps Sheila alive because he needs a living human to serve him as Clifford Graves once did, but in spite of himself he comes to care for her, possibly because she loves him and looks up to him instead of being horrified and repulsed. Things do not go well as far as their relationship is concerned, however. On the other hand, it's hard to know what to make of a sequence in *TOD* 30 in which Dracula comes across a little blind girl whose parents are having an argument. Her father accidentally kills his wife, after which a furious Dracula kills the father. The King of Vampires then expects the little girl, around ten-years-old, to thank him for getting revenge for her and is amazed when she gets hysterical instead. Of course it's hard to imagine Dracula even bothering to involve himself in this domestic dispute in the first place.

TOD 10 introduced a character who was to have a life far beyond this comic book series: Blade. Blade was a hip, arrogant, slick black dude who hunted vampires with a passion, his only weapons a series of wooden knives. Blade was cut from the same cloth as many of the African American anti-heroes appearing in "blaxploitation" movies of the period. In his first appearance he killed three of Dracula's lieutenants and then crossed swords with him on a yacht peopled by the rich, famous and powerful that the count wished to master and influence. Blade hated all vampires because one of them had murdered his mother even as she was giving birth to him. Generally a loner, Blade teamed up with Frank, Rachel and Quincy after Dracula turned Edith into a vampire and her father was forced to kill her (*TOD* 12). Blade actually managed to kill Dracula in *TOD* 13 but the count's mind-slaves spirited off his body before his head could be severed. But it is none of these minions who revive Dracula by removing Blade's, uh, blade, but rather a revivalist who exhibits the count's corpse to attract the faithful into his tent. Told of his mistake by the vampire-hunters, the man tries to rectify it to no avail. "You summoned death to *me*, mortal, and so *you* died, as is only befitting," sneers Dracula. "Where you looked to others for guidance, Dracula seeks only himself!"

As for Blade, he seemed to meet his end at the hands of Dracula in *TOD* 17. Not every reader approved of the character, either because of his personality or his race. In TOD 17 the editor printed an otherwise positive letter in which the writer referred to Blade as a "jungle bunny" and urged them to get rid of him before he "ruined" the mag. The editor responded: "We always wondered if receiving congratulatory mail could be depressing. Now we know." (Blade eventually proved so popular that he starred in no less than three motion pictures.) Blade turned out to be alive in *TOD* 19, just before Quincy Harker, who thought he'd become a blood-sucker, could drive a stake through his heart; apparently he was immune to a vampire's bite and remained not only alive but human. In an excellent story in *TOD* 58 in which Dracula did not even appear, Blade helps an old friend whose wife is possessed during daylight hours by the mind of a sleeping vampire.

Although early issues of the comic implied that Dracula had been dead in his crypt since the nineteenth century, this was revised in *TOD* 15 when it was revealed that Dracula had actually been active throughout Europe, building an army of sorts, until only three years before Clifton Graves stumbled across him in the basement of Castle Dracula. The count had been killed by a furious Scotsman who was hurled to his death in a pit even as Dracula breathed his last (temporarily).

Rachel Van Helsing always attacked Dracula with her not-so-trusty crossbow, but as he would always evade the shaft by reverting to mist it made both him and the readers question the lady's intelligence. Rachel and Dracula are thrown together in *TOD* 19 when Rachel tries to escape from Dracula with a book containing spells that are dangerous to vampires. Dracula climbs aboard her helicopter, throws the pilot to his death, and the odd couple wind up crashing together in snow-bound mountains. Dracula keeps an injured Rachel alive as a potential food supply while she plots his death. In a highly illogical turn of events, Rachel kills a hungry animal that is about to tear out Dracula's throat, which (even given her "humanity") makes little sense, as only a page or two before she was attempting to slay him.

For months a sub-plot had been brewing in the comic concerning a certain Dr. Sun, who has an interest in vampires and goes so far as to kidnap one for experimentation. In *TOD* 20–21 Dracula and company at last encounter the doctor, who turns out to be a disembodied brain (very much reminiscent of the Brain in DC's super-hero comic *Doom Patrol*; Dr. Sun also wants to rule the world). Dr. Sun needs a constant supply of blood to stay alive, and also must have a vampire to go out and bring him victims. A man named Brand had been turned into a vampire by Dracula some time before and is now working for Sun, who hopes to make him (and then himself) the Lord of the Undead instead of the willful Dracula. But Brand turns out to be just as willful, and after seemingly defeating Dracula turns against his bodiless master, who teleports out of his grasp. Rachel, Frank and Dracula all survive the explosion of Sun's HQ.

Dracula's daughter Lilith made her debut in *Giant-Size Chillers* (soon to be retitled *Giant-Size Dracula*) 1. She is the unloved daughter of Dracula's hated first wife, who committed suicide after being thrown out by her husband and turning her baby girl over to a gypsy. Another gypsy turned Dracula into a vampire, so he attacked any gypsy he could find, including the son of the old gypsy woman raising Lilith. In retaliation the woman cursed the child, turning her into a vampire who could walk about in daylight and who could be reborn in the body of any young woman who wanted to kill her own father. For instance, a recently married young lady who watches her father kill her husband is transformed and completely possessed by the spirit of Lilith. Lilith despises her father and only wants to make his un-life utterly miserable.

TOD 25 introduced a hard-boiled private eye named Hannibal King who helps a grieving widow discover why her husband of one day was murdered by a vampire: seems he had inadvertently learned the location of some of Dracula's coffins. King was basically a stereotype and the story a parody, evidenced by the scene in which the babe—the grieving widow—improbably gives him a smooch on the lips. However, the last panel reveals Hannibal's secret: he, too, is a vampire. King encountered Blade in *TOD* 45, rapidly explaining that he never attacked people or turned anyone into a vampire before Blade could have a chance to kill him. Together the two of them managed to kill the vampire who'd attacked Blade's mother.

Marv Wolfman's writing could occasionally be a trifle purple, overdone, and pretentious, but he could also turn out some powerful and intriguing scripts. His words, and the artwork by Colan and Palmer, laid the atmosphere on thick. (*TOD* 31, in which Dracula stalks the family of Lord Singleton of Parliament, and then Singleton himself, has the flavor of Sax Rohmer at his best.) The series really began to kick in to high gear in its third year. Stories went beyond the usual formula of vampire hunters trying to trap Dracula and vice versa, and there was more of a focus on characterization. *TOD* 26–29 feature a fascinating story arc in which Dracula enlists the aforementioned Sheila Whittier to help him gather the parts of a mystic relic called the chimera. The last possessor of the chimera, Prof. Eschol, was murdered by an unknown person, and his son, David, now has only a piece of the relic. After Dracula manipulates the heavens and creates conflagration with that one piece, Sheila renounces Dracula, destroys the chimera, and runs off with David, incurring Dracula's supreme wrath, although he seems genuinely stricken when she commits suicide after he shows up at her door with David's corpse.

As this was going on we learned that Rachel's fellow vampire hunter Taj has a wife and son back in India, all of whom had been attacked by vampires. The wife's legs were crushed by a wagon as she attempted to escape, Taj lost his voice after Dracula's teeth tore his neck, and their infant son was drained of blood, turning him into a vampire. Although the boy has never attacked anyone, the townspeople now deem him a danger and want to kill him, leading Taj to return to India at his wife's urgent request. Neither is aware that it was Dracula who ignited the fears of the townspeople behind the scenes, just as he arranged to have Frank Drake go off to "find himself" on a job in South America. Rachel is held captive by vampire women, and Quincy Harker is left all alone. In *TOD* 32–33 Dracula and Harker at last confront each other in the latter's mansion, equipped with elaborate doom traps for the Lord of the Undead. But as Dracula succumbs to these weapons he tells Harker that Rachel is his prisoner, and if he dies, so, too, will she. Wolfman's script for this issue was especially well-crafted, especially when it came to the dialogue between the two old foes, one human, one not. "I'll miss you, Harker," says Dracula. "It will be a very long time before someone of your caliber challenges me with more of these amusing charades."

Wolfman continued to come up with intriguing situations and devilishly interesting characters to surround the demonic protagonist. For instance, in *TOD* 34–35 the count meets misanthropic fashion house owner Daphne Von Wilkinson, who agrees to get him some needed information if he murders four of her enemies. This he does, but after Daphne gives him the intell, he brings everyone on the woman's hit list—now turned into blood-lusting vampires—into her office to "thank" her. On the other hand, Wolfman—and he has to take full responsibility for this as by now he was editor as well as author of the comic—made a major miscalculation in adding the nebbish writer Harold H. Harold (a Woody Allen clone) and his crush, the intellectually challenged secretary Aurora Rabinowitz, as supporting characters. It was one thing to have Dracula's trick on Daphne illustrate his wicked, sadistic sense of humor, but Harold and Aurora were strictly dumb comedy relief in a series that didn't need any. Worse, they tagged along during a story arc in which Dr. Sun managed to kill the count, only to have Harker and the others bring their long-time hated enemy back to life because only he could stop Sun, whom they deemed a worse menace than the count. (*TOD* 37–38) What happened to Daphne was humorous, but Harold and Aurora introduced a note of low comedy that severely decreased the tension and excitement of these stories. The moronic Aurora, who had a crush on Dracula, was particularly irritating. Listening to the vampire hunters discuss times when they could have killed Dracula and didn't for one reason or another, she suggests to Quincy Harker that it was because the count was "so dreamy." This to a man whose wife and daughter had been killed by the count, and whom Harker had to kill in turn to prevent their being reborn as vampires. *TOD* 56 completely departed from the main storyline of the comic to present an illustrated look at Harold's mediocre vampire novel; it was as forgettable and ill-advised as Harold's book.

As sales of the book were decreasing, possibly because of the glut of horror titles that Marvel and other companies were releasing, it was decided to bring the Lord of the Undead into the regular Marvel universe. First there were mentions of Morbius, the vampire who was one of Spider-Man's foes. Then Dracula battled Marvel's Sorcerer Supreme, Dr. Strange, in *TOD* 44, and the Silver Surfer in *TOD* 50. As the good doctor often fought on the supernatural plane, this at least was not as disastrous as it could have been, and the Surfer appearance attracted new fans to the book, although after awhile Dracula was also intermingling with the likes of Spider-Man (actually an excellent story by Len Wein, with Ross Andru and Don Heck art in *Giant-Size Spider-Man* 1 in which the two characters, working at cross-purposes, barely bumped into each other) and putting the bite on members of Marvel's famous mutants, the X-Men, in their respective series. Fortunately, super-heroes were generally kept out of the main series.

Instead there began a story arc in which Dracula appears at a ceremony of Satanists headed by one Anton Lupeski, and is mistaken by most of the unholy congregation for the Devil himself. The beautiful Domini, who'd been raised in a convent, becomes the Bride of Dracula, and gives birth to his son, the golden-hued Janus. Wolfman credibly relates the circumstances, background and emotions which pushed Domini to become a bride of Satan. In a bizarre, even ludicrous turn of events, Dracula fights a "demon" who turns out to be an angel and messenger of Jesus Christ (*TOD* 52). And all the while Dracula, who'd been a nobleman, thirsts to become emperor of the world through Lupeski's—now Dracula's—church. Trying to kill Dracula with the aid of Frank, Rachel and the rest, Lupeski accidentally kills little Janus, and is savagely murdered by Dracula in return. But Domini manages to bring Janus back from the dead, not as a vampire, but as the aforementioned heavenly messenger, whose sacred mission is to kill his "father," Dracula. If all this sounds a trifle confusing, it was.

Seeking fertile story ideas, Wolfman strayed a bit too much into the religious and metaphysical and there were times when the scripting seemed improvised. We all knew the folklore that vampires were creatures of Satan, but in *TOD* 63–64 Wolfman has Dracula confront no less than the Devil himself, who—to put it simply—wants to destroy the count to preserve the balance that would be lost if Janus did not slay his father and go on to other matters. Admittedly, the conversations between Lucifer and the ever-arrogant Dracula are interesting, even if much of the story and dialogue is just so much goobledygook. However, there was a truly inspired result from this: Satan does the worst thing he could possibly do to Dracula—he makes him human again.

Only in the early days did Dracula hate being a vampire. Now he revels in his undead status, and he is horrified to discover that he has lost all of his supernatural powers, even if he can walk around in sunlight and no longer fear a crucifix. He seeks his daughter, Lilith, in the hopes she will turn him into a vampire again. Unfortunately Lilith still hates him and during a stage show of a Dracula play in Greenwich Village tries to kill him, first as a bat and then via her command of rats and mongrel dogs (*TOD* 67). Even the presence of Harold J. Harold, in some ways now more of a pathetic figure than a comic one, didn't ruin this frenetic and exciting issue.

In disguise Satan gets Dracula to renounce the Devil, leaving him literally betwixt heaven and hell—and once again a vampire. In *TOD* 69 Dracula risks his life by wielding a crucifix to not only hold off a horde of vampires who want him savaged at the bequest of a new Lord of the Undead, but to save the lives of some children who have allowed him sanctuary. In the seventieth and final issue of the series, Dracula challenges Torgo, the new Leader of the Vampires, to a fight to the death, which Dracula wins. However, looking over the crowd of bloodsuckers who had eagerly thrown him over for Torgo once he turned human for a spell, he is disgusted by his subjects and wonders what possible glory there can be in being leader of such worthless creatures. A dying Quincy Harker kills Dracula, and blows up himself, the count and even the castle. In the moving finale, Rachel reads a posthumous letter from Quincy in which he begs her not to let her awful life experiences make her so bitter that she will be forever closed off from love. Rachel realizes that perhaps she has a real future with Frank. Harker also theorizes that Dracula was just as tired of their eternal struggle as he was.

Dracula had been a hero in his own country in his lifetime, admittedly a cruel man in a more barbaric age, and after his death became in essence a sadistic and conscienceless serial killer—albeit one driven by an awful curse and hunger. *Tomb of Dracula* lasted the longest of all the serial horror comics, and despite some awkward writing, obtuse moments, and Harold J. Harold, with its interesting plots, atmospheric art, well-drawn characters, and a highly dynamic, occasionally contradictory protagonist, it became one of the most memorable comic series ever published.

Some excellent stand-alone stories were published in the sister publication *Giant-Size Dracula*, such as a Chris Claremont tale (illustrated by Don Heck) in *GSD* 3 in which a woman, Elianne, who has gained immortality via human sacrifice, pursues Dracula down through the centuries and finally has a last stand against him in modern times. Dedicating her entire existence to destroying the man who turned her father into the undead (her father, in turn, wiped out the other members of Elianne's family before she killed him), she has become as ruthless as any terrorist. After kidnapping Quincy Harker from a party, she orders her men to slaughter every man, woman and child remaining in the room. The ending contrasts the happy woman she had been before Dracula entered her life with the immoral, savage harpy of vengeance she has become. In *GSD* 5 David Kraft's "The Art of Dying" (illustrated by V. Redondo and Dan Adkins) tells parallel stories that come crashing together in the climax. A paranoid man driven crazy by dreams forces a zeppelin to proceed into the heart of a storm, risking the lives of everyone aboard. Meanwhile a young soldier who has come afoul of Dracula desperately tries to outrace him as he is pursued by the vampire from town to town and finally into the Alps. There is truly no one who can help the man avoid his horrible fate. Dracula catches up with him just as the zeppelin arrives, and the final act is played out on board. *GSD* 4 has a creepy tale (David Kraft; Don Heck/Frank Springer) entitled "Let It Bleed" wherein Dracula comes to a small town to seek out a powerful force that radiates from a mountain called the Devil's Heart. This force influences many of the residences into performing terrible acts. Inside the mountain Dracula finds a literal giant heart beating inside its catacomb, as well as tragedy for the supporting players—or victims—of the drama.

Werewolf by Night

"Werewolf by Night" first appeared in the second issue of *Marvel Spotlight*, a try-out mag, in 1972. The original title had been *I, Werewolf*, but although it was changed it was decided to retain the device of having all the stories narrated by the main character. Jack Russell lives with his mother, stepfather Phil, sister Lissa, and a nasty chauffeur named Max Grant (in subsequent flashbacks the name was changed to Garth). At his eighteenth birthday party something comes over Jack and he runs off into the night, mutating into a werewolf (actually a wolf-man). Searching for him in her car, his mother has an accident and is hospitalized. Before she dies, Jack arrives at the hospital in his human form and is told by his mother that he inherited the curse of lycanthropy from his biological father, her first husband, a European baron and warlock killed by a silver bullet while out on the prowl. Now his son Jack, of age, will turn into a werewolf every time there is a full moon. Jack swears to his mother that he will never do anything to harm his stepfather, but he becomes convinced that the brutish Grant had something to do with his wealthy mother's accident and may have even been hired by Phil to do the deed. The werewolf kills Grant but leaves his stepfather alone—for the time being. Gerry Conway did the engaging and interesting script, while Mike Ploog delivered some effective if not especially elegant artwork.

The following issue introduced husband and wife Nathan and Andrea Timly, who kidnap Jack and hold him prisoner until he tells them the location of a mystical book of secrets, the Darkhold, that had belonged to his father. Trouble is, Jack has never heard of this book, and only escapes from the crazy duo after becoming a werewolf. Writer Buck Cowan, who also hopes to find the Darkhold, shows up in *Marvel Spotlight* 4, wherein he tells Jack that his mother's old castle has been sold by her stepfather to a man named Miles Blackgar, who had it transported stone by stone to an island off the west coast. The mad Miles' daughter, Marlene, turns out to be a gorgon who freezes the werewolf into a stone statue, but in the next issue—the first issue of the new *Werewolf by Night* title—Jack reverts to normal flesh and blood as he returns to his human form. Both Miles and Marlene are turned into statues when the latter inadvertently uses her power in a mirror. Buck and Jack manage to find the Darkhold, which is in Latin, and give it to a Father Joquez to translate.

Unfortunately, in *Werewolf by Night* 3, Joquez is possessed by Aelfric, the mad monk, a Satanist who was burned at the stake many centuries before. Aelfric reveals how Jack Russell's father took some scrolls which had originally belonged to him and bound them together to form the Darkhold. Aelfric creates a mist that snakes across the valley turning anyone it touches into a skeleton. Jack and his sister just manage to escape this menace when they encounter Joshua Kane, a macho hunter who holds Lissa prisoner so he can track the ultimate game: a werewolf. Joshua is undone by his own terror, however, and his more flamboyant brother Luthor enters the picture (*WBN* 5). Luthor tells Jack that he has a formula that can prevent Lissa from also turning into a werewolf and will give it to him if he kills the man who allegedly drove him into bankruptcy, the billionaire recluse, Judson Hemp. But when the werewolf discovers that Hemp is a senile elderly man after getting past his security, he can't go through with the murder. Killing Luthor's bodyguard and companion in self-defense—"I will miss him," says Luthor—Jack watches as Luthor commits suicide. Len Wein temporarily took over the scripting with this issue, and Ploog began to ink his own pencils, giving the art a decided lift, but the next few issues had different inkers and soon Ploog temporarily left the series. Tom Sutton, Gil Kane, and Werner Roth filled in until he returned.

An alarming number of people seemed to know Jack Russell's hairy secret, and he is kidnapped by those seeking to use him for one purpose or another on a regular basis. In *WBN* 6–7 he's hauled off to a carnival of freaks by Swami Rihva, who works with a nasty diminutive lion tamer named Mige, and a kindly circus strong man named Elmo, among others. Hypnotized by the swami, Jack is exhibited as the Wild Man of Borneo. This was a more or less reasonable supernatural-based story but when Gerry Conway returned to scripting he came up with an outlandish plot (*WBN* 9–10) wherein a secret group called the Committee, who also know Russell's secret—and whose goal is to improve the economy!—decide to use him and other weird beings to sow terror among the citizens of Century City. How this is supposed to improve the economy is never made clear. The committee employs a masked former sound man named Sarnak to transform the homeless into a legion of dread. The atrocious story was more of a super-hero kind of tale than anything else.

The aptly named Marv Wolfman of *Tomb of Dracula* took over the scripting chores beginning with *WBN* 11. He inherited the Committee but also introduced a psychotic vigilante named the Hangman who went about punishing evildoers and locking up their female victims for sake-keeping. Next came the sorcerer Taboo, who also wants to get his hands on the Darkhold, and his ward and "familiar," the beautiful Topaz. Taboo has been manipulating the members of the Committee, as well as Topaz, who has strange powers of her own, ostensibly in the hopes of ultimately bringing his son Algon out of his twenty-year coma. But what he really wants are the usual dreams of power. Phil Russell, who had been kidnapped by the Committee and is now in the hands of Taboo, winds up being temporarily mind-switched into the body of Algon and ordered to go after the werewolf. But when Taboo is crushed beneath a statue, Algon dies, Phil's mind winds up back where it belongs, and Topaz is free of her evil guardian.

Jack had believed his stepfather to be responsible for his mother's death but in *WBN* 14 he discovers that she was actually killed by blackmailers who threatened to reveal everything about Jack's biological father's weird history. In a bizarre twist, Phil reveals for the first time that he is actually Jack's *uncle*, and that Gregory Russoff, Jack's father, was his brother. Apparently Phil knew all about the curse, although it did not affect him. It makes little sense that Jack and Lissa wouldn't have been told long before that their stepfather was already related to them.

Beginning in *Tomb of Dracula* 18 and continuing in *Werewolf by Night*, Marvel acceded to readers' demands and brought together its two chief horror stars. Jack travels with lovely Topaz to Transylvania to explore his father's old manor and try to learn if there's a way to remove the curse. Dracula attacks Topaz, completely unconcerned that she happens to have a werewolf by her side (Jack had transformed at that point); but something about the woman makes him forget about going for an easy kill. Drac and the werewolf fight it out in the former's castle and environs, with no clear victor. Rachel and Frank show up and pursue the vampire into *TOD* 19. Jack has learned that his grandfather, after driving a stake through Dracula's heart, was bitten by a female werewolf that Dracula kept prisoner in his castle, but he doesn't learn why the Prince of Darkness had a lycanthrope for a captive. Later stories seemed to forget all of this, simply blaming everything on the curse of the Darkhold.

Mike Freidrich briefly took over the writing of the script and unfortunately brought back the Committee and its new leader, a bulky, strong super-villain reject named Baron Thunder. Even worse was Ma Mayhem, an old hag with supernatural powers. The latter kidnaps Lissa because she is nearing her eighteenth birthday and will hopefully turn into a werewolf like her brother. A more interesting development has Jack's testy Jamaican neighbor Raymond Coker turn out to be a werewolf, and the two of them discovering that the only way to end the curse of lycanthropism is for a werewolf to kill another werewolf in the light of the full moon. Doug Moench then took over the scripting chores, turned Ma Mayhem into a young beauty who'd been in elderly disguise, and has Jack rescue his sister from her clutches. Coker lost his curse when he inadvertently killed a shifty cop who turns into a werewolf due to a mystical ring he wears (*WBN* 21). Mike Ploog was replaced on the art by the team of Don Perlin and Vince Colletta. Neither Ploog's nor Perlin's art could ever be described as pretty, but Ploog had a certain quirkiness to it that many felt suited a supernatural strip. Perlin was good at layouts, with a certain cinematic style.

Moench was said to be more experienced with the supernatural, but his stories still seemed to smack of super-hero stuff. His opponents for the werewolf included Atlas, an embittered and disfigured sword and sandal actor who is trying to kill off his old colleagues (including Jack's friend, Buck, who'd been a screenwriter); Winston Redditch, who develops a Jekyll/Hyde formula that turns him into the depraved "Deprayve," and the Hangman, back at his job of murdering evildoers such as Jack—and Deprayve. The worst of these was probably Dr. Glitternight, a lower case, evil Dr. Strange who messes with Topaz's soul when she seeks his help in boosting her fading powers. His appearances were enlivened by the fact that they were played out with the more interesting storyline of Jack's sister Lissa turning eighteen and becoming a werewolf herself. In *WBN* 29 she converts to a grotesque were*demon* due to the interference of Glitternight, and she and her brother have a battle royal in their family's old castle. Through convoluted and unconvincing means she is allegedly cured of her curse, leaving Jack the soul *loup garou* in the family.

A major event for the series almost occurred in *WBN* 31. Jack had once wondered why Buck hangs with him and helps him out all the time despite all the werewolf baggage—and a twenty-year age difference—and some readers might have wondered if Buck were gay, but in this story the older man shows up with a date, a recent widow named Elaine, and her little girl, Buttons. When the child wanders off in a blizzard, Buck rushes to find her, also aware that Jack as the werewolf is out in that blizzard. Jack had hoped he wouldn't encounter any people in the blizzard, but he runs into Buttons, and Buck sacrifices his own life to save her. Instead of attacking the child, the werewolf attacks, slashes, and apparently kills Jack's best friend.

However in the following issue we learn that Buck is still alive, but after a major operation is now in a coma. A more significant event is the introduction of a character named Moon Knight, who is hired (as well as given his name and costume) by the Committee—yes, they are still around—to capture Jack Russell, the werewolf. Moon Knight, a mercenary and anti-hero but essentially a good guy and super-hero, eventually got his own series. He succeeds in capturing Jack, but when he learns that he's just an ordinary young man with a curse, and that the Committee wants to use the werewolf to commit murders with impunity, he lets him go to wreak havoc on all of the members (*WWN* 33).

Arguably the best story arc in the series occurred in *WBN* 34–37, a creepy, suspenseful tale which may have been influenced by Richard Matheson's *Hell House* and other haunted house stories. Jack, Lissa, Topaz and Elaine travel to the home of the late spiritualist Belarac Marcosa in the hopes of finding a way to save Buck's life, as the man mentioned the house during a brief time when he temporarily came out of his coma. The evil influences of the house affect everyone, and cause traumatic and violent hallucinations. Topaz appears to have been murdered at one point, and Buck seemingly shows up from the hospital. Everyone has trouble distinguishing reality from illusion. At one point the characters, trapped inside the house, hear police sirens and think they've been rescued. They manage to get the front door open and see a host of cop cars—from which emerge desiccated corpses wearing uniforms! The spirit of Marcosa appears, becloaked, with red rubies on his two front teeth like blood drops. Freeing the spirits of Marcosa's many victims enables Jack and the others to escape and to destroy Marcosa for good. One of the spirits enters Buck's body and brings him back to life. This was supposed to be the end of the series, as sales had been steadily dipping, but there was a brief reprieve when sales improved.

Considering the stories that followed it's no wonder that *WBN* only lasted a few more issues. Moench introduced some weird cosmic characters named the Three Who Are One (then the Three Who Are All) who keep telling Jack that big changes are coming (just as the editors of the comic promised a new direction). Jack winds up in Haiti with guest star Jericho Drumm (AKA Brother Voodoo, more on whom later) and Topaz, attempting to rescue Raymond Coker from the clutches of Dr. Glitternight. It turns out that the Three Who Are One (or All) were once the Five Who Are One, and Glitternight was once their fourth member. The fifth, a super-hero type called Fire-Eyes, put in a brief appearance before rapidly expiring.

The big change was that Jack could now control his transformations as well as remain dominant even after he converts to a beast. A bigger change was that *WBN* essentially turned into a super-hero comic —but not for long. *WBN* 42–43 had Jack taking after crooks à la Spider-Man and winding up first in a battle with the Armored Avenger, Iron Man (due to a misunderstanding), and then tackling the Masked Marauder and his Tri-Animan. *WBN* 43 was the final issue. Perlin was not an untalented artist but the best word one could come up with for his overall work on the series was mediocre.

After his series ended Jack Russell and his werewolf alter ego disappeared for a couple of years, then the story of Jack's search to find a cure for his curse continued in other Marvel comics such as *Spider-Woman, Ghost Rider* and *Dr. Strange*. Jack guest-starred in *Moon Knight* 29–30 in 1983 (the one-shot character had by now become a minor star in his own right) in which is on the run from the minions of a man named Schuyler Belial, the "Morning Star," who claims to be Satan's representative on earth. He has promised his followers that he will produce the Beast, and wants to capture Jack to exhibit him as same. Jack can still control his transformations but during a full moon he still becomes all-werewolf. He runs to Moon Knight for his help. The two wipe out the Satanists in a climax that takes place in a penthouse at 666 Fifth Avenue. Bill Sienkiewicz's dynamic art brought the werewolf to life in highly dramatic fashion; for once the man-beast actually looked scary. The stories were written by the usual werewolf scribe, Doug Moench.

For better or worse, Jack Russell had become part of the Marvel superhero universe. In 1998 he was given a six part mini-series, and continued to appear from time to time among Marvel's super-heroes.

Frankenstein

The Monster of Frankenstein (AKA *Frankenstein*) made its debut in 1973. In the very effective first issue written by Gary Friedrich and drawn by Mike Ploog, Robert Walton IV (great-grandson of the last man to see the monster) takes an unsavory crew in 1898 on a search for the frozen body of Frankenstein's monster, which they find. Walton manages to quell a mutiny, and tells the cabin boy the story of Victor Frankenstein and his creature (as described in Mary Shelley's novel). Before he can finish, however, the ship is engulfed by a sudden storm, and in the hold below a fire begins to melt the ice encasing the monster, who starts to stir.

In the next two issues the rest of Shelley's story is related in flashbacks as the Monster revives, kills most of the sailors, but spares the lives of Walton and the cabin boy, Sean. After the ship sinks, the three seek shelter in an abandoned cabin on shore, but Sean dies. In *MOF* 4 the creature thinks back to what happened after his final encounter with Victor Frankenstein: the monster encountered a tribe of deformed outcasts and was accepted by them, until they were all slaughtered by an invading horde. Falling into frigid waters, the Monster remained in suspended animation for 100 years until his fateful encounter with Walton. Now Walton, dying of exposure, tells him where he can find a descendant of Victor's who might help him. Gary Freidrich's script was a highly skillful blend of action and pathos. In the following issue the Monster saves a beautiful blond from an angry, supposedly bewitched mob, falls in love with her (and it is inferred has sex with her as well), then discovers that she's actually a werewolf and the townspeople had very good reasons for wanting her dead.

With the sixth issue the title (at least on the cover) was changed to *The Frankenstein Monster*. Although the Monster was supposed to have sought the help of his creator's descendant, now he was determined to kill him—but when he arrives at his castle finds not a Frankenstein heir but a mad colonel who has somehow grown a giant spider, whose bite turns men into mindless slaves. In *FM* 8–9, with John Buscema now handling the art chores, the Monster encounters Dracula after an old gypsy vampire maneuvers "Franky" into helping her revive the Lord of the Undead. The Monster is the definite victor of this famous meeting of classic creatures. The Monster is forced to kill a beautiful gypsy that he had cared for after Dracula turns her into a bloodsucker. Her bite temporarily strips the Monster of his ability to speak. Buscema's work was always professional, but it lacked that special quirkiness and atmosphere generated by Ploog, who'd gone on to other strips.

The Monster finally catches up with the sole living Frankenstein—or vice versa—great grand-nephew Vincent Frankenstein and the latter's grotesque hunchbacked helpmate Ivan, in *FM* 10–11. Friedrich's scripts for these issues, in which Vincent proves as obsessed and nutty as his ancestor, seem like a riot of Universal studio horror clichés with "Franky" and Ivan coming to blows, then developing a friendship, then hating each other again even as Vincent plans on switching their brains into each other's bodies. Vincent is finally shot to death by the housekeeper, who hates him for his neglect of his dying wife. The dead wife leaves behind yet another little Frankenstein but the Monster is mercifully unaware of this. Bob Brown and Vince Colletta did the art, which was solid if unspectacular.

Doug Moench took over as scripter with the twelfth issue, with Val Mayerick, assisted by a variety of inkers, on the pencils. Marvel's editor-in-chief and chief spokesperson Stan Lee often joked about Marvel's mistakes in continuity and the like, but *FM* 12 had a doozy. In the last issue the Monster, shot by Vincent and bleeding profusely, staggers out of the latter's modest home in London, but at the opening of *FM* 12 is now lurching out of (the formerly abandoned) *Castle Frankenstein* a continent away "oblivious to the squalling" of the aforementioned infant (and no wonder)! The strip now took a major change in direction, with

Opposite: It had to happen: Dracula meets Frankenstein in *The Frankenstein Monster* 9 (Marvel).

the Monster falling off an icy cliff and winding up in suspended animation for several more decades, waking up in our modern era.

In this way the color comic was brought into alignment with the series "Frankenstein–1974" (Friedrich/Buscema) which appeared in the black and white magazine *Monsters Unleashed* (issues 2 and 4–10). In this an unscrupulous man named Derek McDowell discovers that the Frankenstein monster, still in suspended animation, is on exhibit in a sideshow, where everyone assumes it is a clever fake. McDowell's colleague, Dr. Owen Wallach, dying of cancer, helps him bring the monster to life but without a mind of its own, under their control. McDowell tries to find a young body to put Wallach's brain in, but then hits upon the idea of switching the doctor's brain with the Monster's. Upon awakening in his hideous new form, a furious Wallach strangles McDowell. Wallach then uses a machine to switch brains with a handsome acrobat, but a mouse gets into the works and—yes, Frankenstein winds up with the mind of a mouse, the rodent rather pleased that it's now larger than everyone it used to be afraid of. Fortunately, this situation is corrected through convoluted means and the Monster's brain winds up back where it belongs. Unable to speak due to injuries from a fire, he wanders about seeking love, beauty, and an end to his loneliness. Doug Moench and Val Mayerick then also took over the black and white series. "The 11:10 to Murder" in *MU* 10 had the monster encountering a sympathetic young woman on a train whereupon assassins are trying to kill the President; it shouldn't have worked at all but it was surprisingly effective.

Meanwhile, in the color comic Moench kept the monster busy but the series never recovered from the switch in time periods, which was hoped might improve sales and didn't. The monster gained a sidekick in the person of teen Ralph Ciccone, whose parents were murdered by a horrible clone-creature cobbled together by Ralph's weird father. Then "Franky" and Ralph are caught in a tug of war between two factions who both want the monster: members of a sinister group called ICON, who want to make a horde of monster-soldiers; and Veronica Frankenstein, a descendant of Victor's, who wants to befriend and help the monster and indeed operates on his vocal cords so that he can speak. In the eighteenth and final issue the Monster meets the Baroness *Victoria* von Frankenstein but with the cancellation of the series we never learned what her plans for her ancestor's creation might have been. Val Mayerick's work on the strip was merely serviceable.

Ghost Rider

Ghost Rider made his debut in *Marvel Spotlight* 5 in 1972. Although the character went on to success in both comics and films, at first it seemed as if there could hardly be a worse idea for a comic book series. Johnny Blaze is orphaned after his stunt cyclist father is killed in an accident, and raised by an associate, Crash Simpson, and his family. On her deathbed, Crash's wife, who has been like a mother to Johnny, begs him not to enter the arena as a stunt rider and he agrees to honor her wish. Although Crash and his daughter, Roxanne, who loves Johnny, eventually find out about the death bed promise, they still excoriate him as a coward for not riding. There is nothing to prevent Johnny from riding for his own pleasure, however, which he does, developing great skill. When Crash reveals just before a big show at Madison Square Garden that he is dying of an unspecified disease, Johnny—although he had previously betrayed no interest in the occult—makes a pact with the devil: Satan can have his soul if Crash does not die. Unfortunately, attempting the riskiest stunt of his career, Crash is killed in the show—Satan reminds Johnny that the agreement was for Simpson to not die of his *disease*, and he didn't. Johnny must still honor his commitment. Due to the intervention of Roxanne, Satan is denied Johnny's soul, but he still must pay a price: he turns into the Ghost Rider, his handsome face replaced by a blazing skull, as he rides in black leather on his motorcycle each night. The concept and script were by Gary Friedrich, and the art by Mike Ploog.

In the next issue Crash, who apparently went to Hell, is back on Earth in disguise as Curly, the leader of a gang of motorcycle hoods. Satan has promised him his life back if he can snare Johnny's soul. Crash seems quite willing to sacrifice both his daughter and the boy he raised until he realizes that the eternal life he craves will be spent in Hell as a slave of Satan's. He helps Johnny, and drops dead for the second time. Although Satan was wisely kept off stage for most of the time in *Tomb of Dracula* and *Werewolf by Night*, he practically became a supporting character in *Ghost Rider,* stripping the series of a certain mystery and making it more cartoonish than Marvel's other horror comics (although there was worse to come). Satan assured Blaze that he would always protect him from mortal harm, as his dying at others' hands would prevent him from capturing his soul.

In *Marvel Spotlight* 8–11 Blaze comes afoul of the Apache Snake Dancer, who tries to use supernatural means to get vengeance for his people (although he's more interested in acquiring power). Worse still is his daughter, Linda Littletrees, who turns out to be a pawn of Satan known as Witch-Woman. The stories purported to delve into the injustices faced by Native Americans, a popular theme in fiction in the seventies, but as usual this was just a framework for the action. At one point Snake Dancer turns into a gigantic serpent that slithers after Johnny in an effective sequence. It also develops that Bart Slade, Johnny's manager, has a bitter jealousy of his employer, but when he eventually attempts a Herculean jump himself he smashes into a canyon wall. Tom Sutton did the pencils for these stories.

As Ghost Rider was given his own title, Satan himself jumps into Witch-Woman's body and continues to seek Johnny's soul. The first issue also introduces Daimon Hellstrom, an exorcist called in by Linda Littletrees' boyfriend in an effort to save *her* soul. (Hellstrom turned out to be the Son of Satan, and was given his own series in *Marvel Spotlight*.) Then Johnny battles a demon in the guise of a Las Vegas mobster, and receives a pardon for past criminal acts by the Attorney General. Linda decides to try to steal Johnny away from Roxanne. The writer-artist combo of Tony Isabella and Jim Mooney took over the strip with *GH* 6, which also brought our hero more in alignment with the regular Marvel universe. He battled members of the Zodiac, a super-team that bedeviled the Avengers (or more accurately a man who could change into whichever member of the group he wished) and teamed-up with the Stunt-Man, who had first battled, then befriended, Daredevil. Daredevil's former girlfriend, Karen Page, became a member of Ghost Rider's supporting cast when he went to work for a movie studio.

However Satan was back cursing and plotting in *GR* 9–10. Taking Roxanne down to Hell, he convinced her that her father would relive the death of his wife over and over for eternity unless she renounces her protection of Johnny Blaze, who could, he argued, protect himself. Roxanne does so, only to learn that the Devil had tricked her and her father wasn't even his prisoner. Johnny manages to beat off Satan's emissary, Inferno, and gets out of his clutches with the divine interference of a *deus ex machina* in the form of a bearded, long-haired Christ figure who is apparently meant to actually be Jesus Christ! (He nearly became as ubiquitous in the strip as Satan had been.) Satan would no longer make ostentatious appearances or overt efforts to gain Johnny's soul, but he still hopes to claim it in the future, and sends Inferno, in a new guise, to monitor Blaze's every movement. Roxanne, who is shattered that she had been tricked so easily, goes off to find herself. Although Johnny has lost many of his powers, he can still revert each night to the Ghost Rider (Later the change would only occur when there was danger, regardless of the time of day). As if to make it clear that he was now, more or less, a reluctant super-hero, *GR* 11 guest-starred Marvel mainstay the Hulk. Johnny even became a member of the new super-team *The Champions*.

Still, there were occasional supernatural stories, such as in *GR* 12, when Johnny tries to save an elderly German flier from the ghost of the man he killed during WW1, the Phantom Eagle. Johnny teamed up again with the Son of Satan in *GR* 17–19. In *GR* 19 he discovers that for some unexplained reason he is completely free of Satan's curse, although he retains his powers. Satan is no longer after his soul, and would guest-star no more. Marvel had gotten flack about the appearance of Satan in their comics—not to mention Jesus—but sales figures also dictated a change to a more standard super-hero series. Johnny teamed with Daredevil for one issue, and then the "new" Ghost Rider debuted in *GR* 21. From now on Blaze would face not Satan but a variety of super-villains. The series lasted for 81 issues, and years later engendered two fairly awful feature films starring a much-too-old Nicolas Cage as Johnny Blaze.

The Son of Satan

Daimon Hellstrom first appeared, as noted, in the first issue of *Ghost Rider*, then hopped into his own series, "The Son of Satan," beginning with *Marvel Spotlight* 12. By day Hellstrom was a God-fearing good guy and exorcist of assorted demons. By night, if he lost control, he reverted to the Son of Satan, complete with colorful outfit, a trident, and a chariot drawn by flying Hell horses. In either guise he hated his father, who disowned him after he rescued the Ghost Rider from Hell. Hellstrom's trident was one weapon that Satan had no defense against. Gary Friedrich wrote the script, with Herb Trimpe on art.

Marvel Spotlight 13 revealed that Satan had come to Earth in mortal guise because he wanted a male heir in the unlikely event he was destroyed. Daimon's sister was the first to learn who her father really was, and she was delighted by the knowledge. When Satan revealed himself to the girl's mother, however, the horrified woman had to be institutionalized. Her children were taken away, her "husband" disappeared, and she eventually died. When Damon returned to the family mansion years later after studying for the priesthood (!), he discovered his mother's diary and after learning the truth felt nothing but hatred for his father. He braved Hell itself for a showdown but in their first battle there was no clear victor.

A new creative team—Steve Gerber as writer, Jim Mooney and Sal Trapani on art—took over with *MS* 14. Satan affected a change in his rebellious offspring: Daimon would always remain a *combination* of the would-be priest and the Son of Satan. Henceforth there would be no more transformations and his dual natures would always be at war with one another. This, of course, insured that Hellstrom would spend most of his time in his spiffy super-hero type outfit. Daimon relocated to St. Louis after he was contacted by a parapsychologist named Dr. Katherine Reynolds to come exorcise demons from a building in the university. Divinity student Byron Hyatt also joined the supporting cast.

In *MS* 16–17 a battle between Daimon and his father in St. Louis brought forth a fiery demonic serpent named Kometes whose mere presence initiated cataclysmic activities around the globe in a beginning of a realignment of the oceans and continents. The last time Kometes appeared in the skies above Earth the continent of Atlantis sank into the ocean. Daimon, Katherine and Byron take a time trip back to Atlantis just before the disaster to seek the aid of a sorceress whose knowledge will help save the planet in the future. In MS 18–19 Daimon helps to exorcise the she-demon Allatou from the body of a young woman, although Allatou made his task more difficult by continually jumping into the body of the original victim's mother and father, not to mention a skeptical reporter who comes along with Katherine. Gene Colan of *Tomb of Dracula* did the art for these two issues.

Sal Buscema then took over the art for the remainder of the series. Daimon had his hands full with an old gyspy seeress named Swabada, who brought Tarot cards to life on her mission of vengeance, and Father Darklyte, who led the Legion of Nihilists, but used his misguided followers for his own purposes. Katherine is killed by the attack of a griffin in MS 23, but appears to come back to life via Darklyte's magic lantern. Mike Freidrich co-wrote this story with Steve Gerber, and Chris Claremont took over the scripting chores of Hellstrom's final appearance in *Marvel Spotlight* 24. Coming to the aid of an old friend, Daimon discovers that a young woman has been possessed by another she-demon who wants dominion of the earth. Daimon's evil sister, Satana, appears, and Daimon tries his mighty best to kill her. She survives his attack and wipes out the she-demon before she can kill Hellstrom, but she warns her brother that she'll kill him and take his soul if he ever crosses her again. And with that Daimon got his own series, *Son of Satan*.

In *Son of Satan* 1–3 Daimon is bedeviled by a three-headed opponent known as the Possessor, who was really a former carnival man with psychic powers named Rafael. When two demons attempted to possess him, he turned the tables on them and absorbed them into his mind and body, their heads winding up attached to his shoulders. The Possessor managed to defeat Daimon and add Hellstrom's head to his collection, using his hell-spawned power to take on the very Devil in his dominion. Daimon is able to defeat the Possessor from within, inadvertently siding with his father, but this does nothing to patch up their relationship. Satan seals off all the entrances to Hell, but vows that he will eventually destroy his hated offspring when he least expects it. (In this way the series meant to say farewell to Satan just as he had been excised from the pages of *Ghost Rider*.)

The next story arc was a convoluted and forgettable business in which Daimon joined the faculty of a Georgetown University but found himself victim of the machinations of Mindwash, who was actually a crippled elderly man in the service of an other-dimensional god called Annubis. A witch named Seripha Thames briefly joined the supporting cast. Daimon Hellstrom wanted to get further in touch with his human side by interacting with other people, but he remained a one-dimensional character and the potential of the series went untapped. John Warner scripted all but the final issue, and artists included Jim Mooney, Craig Russell, and Sonny Trinidad, who did especially nice work on issue seven.

The eighth and final issue of *SOS*, scripted by Bill Mantlo, was meant to be a fill-in, but it proved to be the best Son of Satan story ever published. Daimon winds up in Hell, where he learns that a revolution is brewing during Christmas Eve, the one night of the year when

Satan slumbers. But the beautiful woman who is importuning him to help Hell's legions is actually a hideous old hag and it's all just a plot to ensnare his soul. Satan claims that Daimon's mother was also evil and that Hellstrom's dual nature is a fabrication; his son is completely corrupt. This, too, proves to be a lie and the final twist is that the entire story is a dream dreamt by, of all people, Satan. Russ Heath's artwork made Hell and its denizens truly frightening, with grotesque, macabre and just plain scary demons, and a host of lost souls tortured in all variety of disturbing manners. There was a surprise in virtually every shuddery panel.

When his comic was canceled, Daimon Hellstrom disappeared except for some guest appearances in Marvel's super-hero mags such as *The Defenders*. As for his sister, the succubus Satana (who could suck away men's souls with a kiss, leaving them withered husks), she appeared in her own brief and forgettable series in the magazine *Vampire Tales* 2–3, but had better luck in another brief series in the black and white magazine *Haunt of Horror* 2 and 4–5. In these stories she is sent on a mission by her father, whom she has always loved and followed, unlike Daimon, but when she returns discovers that four demons who wish to take over Hell are out to destroy her. She is aided by an ex-priest named Michael Heron, who engages her human emotions, and an old demon friend, Zannarth, who is killed. The demons turn out to be a manifestation of a man named Miles Gorney, who demands that she renounce Satan and acknowledge him as the new ruler of Hell. She refuses, engages in a battle with Miles' minions, then discovers that Miles is really her father in disguise; the whole business was merely to test her loyalty. Not only does this infuriate the succubus, but she in turn enrages her father when she refuses to take the dying Heron's soul, allowing him to die with his soul untainted. Satan banishes her from Hell. Chris Claremont did the script for the final installment.

Satana next appeared in a color try-out comic, *Marvel Premiere* 27. In another interesting Claremont story, Satana learns that her old tutor, Dansker, who resents her father and wants to escape his slavery, has possessed a young woman, leading her to be accused of witchcraft. (Dansker's gruff bearded head on the top of the woman's voluptuous body certainly makes for a bizarre apparition.) Dansker is determined to be free of Hell and take over the world for his own purposes, but Satana manages to stop him—although she is unable to save the woman's soul. Satana, while still an edgy character (she saves a little boy after murdering his father), has developed super-powers of a sort and seems to be veering somewhat away from her dark side. The character had possibilities, but a new series for her never developed.

Twelve

Man-Thing, Morbius and More

Man-Thing

In 1972 two color comic derivatives of the golden age Heap series in *Airboy* made their debut: DC's *Swamp Thing* and Marvel's Man-Thing, who got his own strip in *Adventure into Fear*. Man-Thing first appeared in 1971 in the magazine *Savage Tales* in a story by writer Gerry Conway and artist Gray Morrow. Professor Ted Sallis is one of several scientists working on the "ultimate soldier formula" at a research base located in the Everglades. A woman named Ellen is secretly a spy for the evil organization AIM (Advanced Idea Mechanics) and she tries to steal the formula. When AIM agents pursue Sallis he injects the only sample of the formula into his own bloodstream in hopes of saving his life, but instead his body combines with elements of the swamp to metamorphose into a hulking, mossy creature with black eyes and a kind of narrow elephant's trunk hanging down between them. Whenever this "Man-Thing" touches anyone who is full of fear, a chemical reaction makes their skin burn, which is what happens to Ellen when the creature touches her face. (The story was reprinted in the magazine *Monsters Unleashed* 3. *Monsters Unleashed* 5 had a new story in which Ellen, her face repaired, goes to the bayou to kill Man-Thing, but realizes who he is, her anger transmuting into guilt. This was very well-written by Tony Isabella with effective art by Vicente Alcazar.)

A second story was written (Len Wein) and drawn (Neal Adams) featuring the character, but when *Savage Tales* was discontinued it was decided to use it as part of a story in the jungle hero Ka-zar's strip in *Astonishing Tales* 12–13. In this Ka-zar and his sabretooth tiger go to the Everglades to search for Ted Sallis at the request of Dr. Barbara Morse and her fiance Dr. Paul Allen. The new framing pages were written and drawn by Roy Thomas, John Buscema and Rich Buckler. Neal Adams' art on the pages originally drawn for *Savage Tales* were especially striking as they retold the character's origin and showed an encounter between Man-Thing and the elderly Dr. Calvin, the only person who senses there is a strong connection between the monster and the missing Sallis. Ka-zar both helps and battles Man-Thing, then rescues Dr. Calvin from the forces of AIM. Allen is revealed to be another member of that group and is killed by Man-Thing. Ironically, Len Wein, who wrote the installment originally intended for *Savage Tales*, had already written a one-shot Swamp Thing story for *House of Secrets* and later became the writer for the *Swamp Thing* series. Both Man-Thing and Swamp Thing had alarmingly similar origins—both were equally influenced by the Heap—but each strip was to go in its own direction. One big difference was that Swamp Thing could think and knew who he was, while Man-Thing forgot most of his life as Ted Sallis and was more instinctual than intellectual. In that he resembled the Heap. Man-Thing was attracted by strong emotions, especially fear, and was a kind of empathic creature.

Man-Thing's series began with *Adventure into Fear* 10, in which the "monster" rescues a baby thrown off of a bridge by a hateful, uncaring father. The memorable cover shows Man-Thing walking off with an adorable baby boy cradled in his hand as misunderstanding farmers shoot at him from the background. The inside story and art were by Gerry Conway, Gray Morrow and Howard Chaykin, but they were replaced for the next issue by Steve Gerber and Rich Buckler. They had an inauspicious debut, a forgettable story about a brother and sister conjuring up a demon that Man-Thing battles and defeats. However, the story in *Adventure into Fear* 12 was an interesting character study of two opposites, a white racist cop and the black man he pursues, neither of whom are of especially sterling character, and the way their lives change for the worse after they encounter M-T. For the first time Gerber uses the expression "whatever knows fear, burns at the Man-Thing's touch!" (Normally the article was not used in conjunction with Man-Thing. It was Man-Thing, not *the* Man-Thing.)

Unfortunately Gerber followed this up with a trilogy bringing back the brother and sister (Jennifer and Andy Kale) and throwing Man-Thing into an absurd supernatural (and worse, a sword and sorcery) storyline wherein demonic influence is causing crazy things to happen all across the globe. Man-Thing and his young friends travel into exotic dimensions and at one point M-T has to fight a gladiator named Mongu in an arena while Jennifer winds up outfitted like a warrior princess. It was all Marvel Seventies Schlock and some fans rightly complained that the scientific-based Man-Thing did not fit neatly into such types of fantasy storylines. Val Mayerick's artwork similarly did not impress.

Worse still—and unfathomable—was a story in which Man-Thing met a character named Wundarr who was clearly based on Superman, having been shot off a dying planet by his scientist father. This was followed by a human interest story in which assorted types—a drunk driver who causes a deadly bus accident, a soldier, a hippie, a young woman and a kid, all survivors of said accident—encounter Man-Thing as they try to emerge from the swamp. Gerber, like other comic writers of the period, often looked to the headlines and the social unrest and upheaval of the seventies for inspiration, but the scripting for this was obvious and awkward. Man-Thing's final appearance in *Fear* before getting his own series brought back Jennifer Kale and the sword and sorcery elements in a blithering mess that one can only hope was meant to be a parody. The only notable thing about the issue was the introduction of an alien fowl who later became known as Howard the Duck and got his own satirical series as he traversed the land of "hairless apes." (Howard also got two amusing horror parody back-ups in *Giant-Size Man-Thing* 4 and 5 in which he battled Gorko, the Man-Frog—a man turned into a giant frog—and "Hellcow," a not-so-contented cow that had become a vampire.)

The story continued in *Man-Thing* 1 wherein Howard was (temporarily) killed off and Mayerick's art was more rushed and unattractive than ever. It seems incredible that when

Opposite: A horrifically charming cover for *Fear* 10 starring Man-Thing (Marvel).

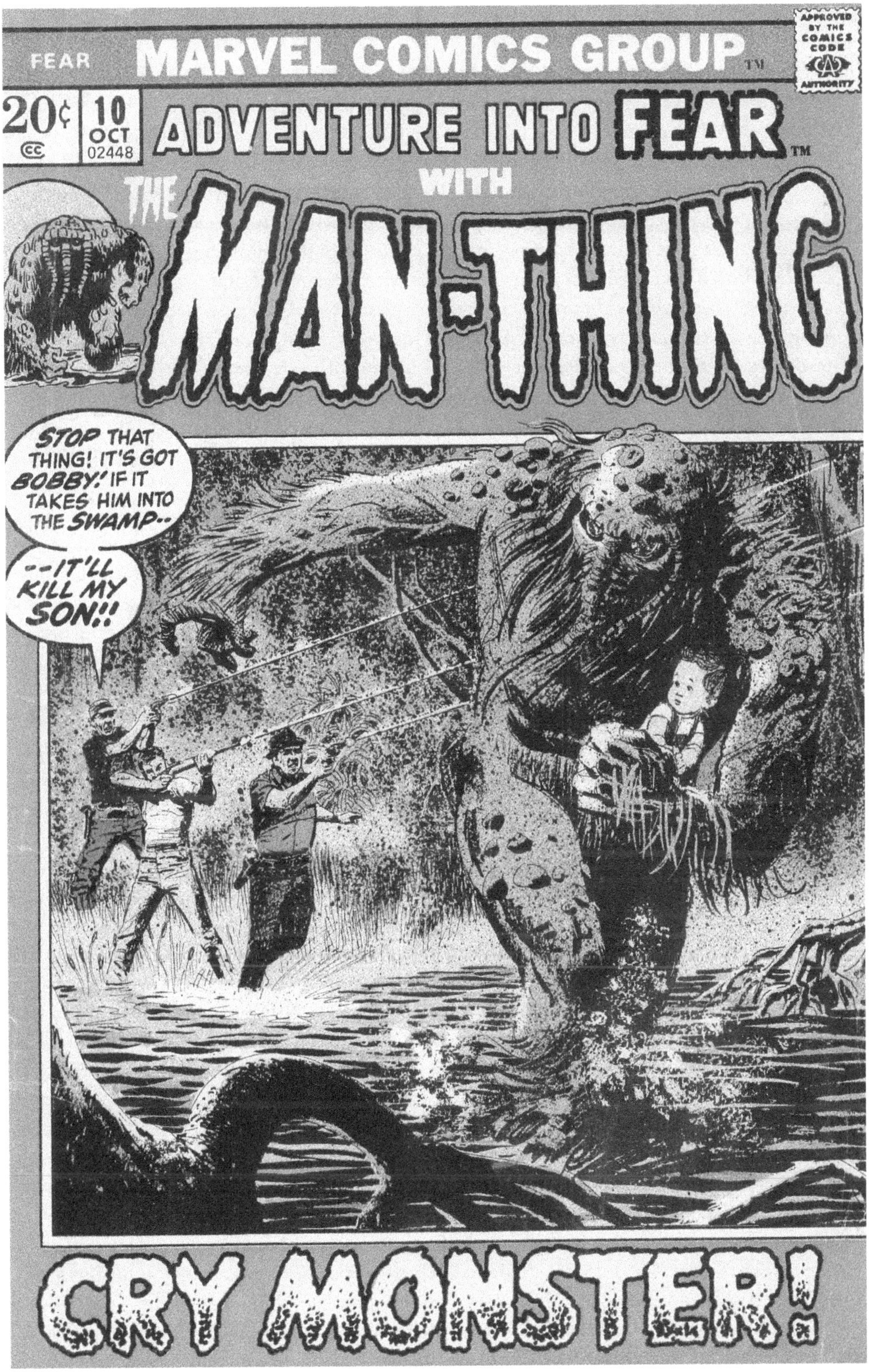

many good, well-drawn and intelligently written series were biting the dust, that the sales of *Fear* would have been good enough to warrant Man-Thing getting his own title, but such was the case. Fortunately, things began improving with the third issue, which introduced the bizarre costumed Fool Killer, and in which Mayerick's pencils were inked by Jack Abel, giving the strip a bold new look, highlighted by a two-page spread in which Man-Thing saves a group of people coming out of a downed helicopter from an advancing array of hungry alligators. The Fool Killer, whose origin was recounted in the following issue, was a religious fanatic who'd been raised by a phony evangelist whose touch had supposedly healed his paralyzed legs. Discovering that his mentor didn't practice what he preached drove the young man over the edge, so he set out of kill off all fools—everyone from protestors to criminals to drug users to the insufficiently pious—using a ray of purity that quickly burns them to cinders. Unfortunately the Fool Killer was himself killed off at the end of *Man-Thing* 4.

The Mayerick-Abel team was replaced by Mike Ploog and Frank Chiaramonte. Ploog's work was always quirky and atmospheric and suitable for the strip. His best work on the series—and one of Gerber's best stories (which Ploog co-plotted) appeared in *Man-Thing* 9–10. In this the Man-Thing becomes embroiled in the lives of old married couple Maybelle and Ezekiel, who live alone in the isolated swamp with their equally superannuated hound dog named "Dawg." Maybelle initially wanted to shun society and the big cities as her husband did, but now the two have grown apart and she watches with jealousy as Ezekiel neglects her and spends most of his time with Dawg. When the woman suffers a heart attack and briefly dies, the essence of her hatred coalesces into a living being that takes over trees, gators and other bayou dwellers in an attempt to kill both man and hound dog. Revived, Maybelle realizes with horror what has happened and tries to stop it by killing herself, but Dawg attacks and destroys her demonic force and is killed. Maybelle and Ezekiel become close again as the former realizes how wrong she was to hate her husband's sweet-natured and beloved pet. Sentimental, of course, but very effective, and Ploog's rich, well-detailed art turned Dawg into just as important a character as the old couple and Man-Thing, who repeatedly saves the lives of the man and dog as Maybelle's demonic spirit attacks. It could be argued that Ploog was more of a cartoonist than an illustrator, and his work wasn't for every taste, but when the subject matter was right his work was very impressive.

Gerber's follow-up in *M-T* 11 was a well-intentioned but muddled story of a disfigured vet and friends kidnapping the vet's own sister to help publicize the plight of men who return from Viet Nam with shattered faces and who then can't get jobs because of their appearance. Unfortunately, the "relevance" angle seemed merely tacked on to the story. Equally muddled was an otherwise interesting two-parter in *M-T* 13–14 in which Man-Thing enters the Bermuda triangle and is embroiled in an ages-old conflict between an ancient, wizened satyr and a bold female pirate. At the end of the story this fiercely independent, strong and beautiful woman decides to meekly stay with the hideous aged satyr so he can regain his lost youth and prowess. Even Gerber and the editors admitted the story was ridiculously chauvinistic and a big mistake. *M-T* 15 revealed some of the background of Ted Sallis as a woman he wanted to marry has nightmares in which she remembers meeting the scientist years ago in Greenwich Village. By this time Ploog had left the series to be replaced by John Buscema; Alfredo Alcala and Rico Rival also worked on the series.

John Buscema's first major art job for the character appeared in *Giant-Size Man-Thing 2*. Buscema was a more traditional artist, and his work also had a slickness and storytelling dynamism that the strip had previously been lacking. Buscema's nearly sublime work in *GSMT* 2 bolstered an already excellent story in which Man-Thing is captured and put on exhibit in New York's Museum of Natural History due to the machinations of a wealthy widow who thinks he murdered her husband, F. A. Schist, who had appeared in several earlier stories. Of course M-T breaks out to wreak havoc à la King Kong. As good as this story was in a pure action sense (with good characterization to boot), "The Kid's Night Out" in *GSMT* 4 was a certified masterpiece.

"The Kid's Night Out" begins with a funeral for a 17-year-old boy who was essentially murdered by a macho, insensitive gym coach who sadistically forces the overweight, unathletic Edmond Winshed to run around and around the track until his heart gives out. His only friend, Alice Rimes, is appalled at the dishonesty in the priest's eulogy, which makes it sound as if Edmond was happy and beloved by his family and classmates, which is anything but the truth. She is determined to see that his diary is published so everyone can see how they contributed to his misery—"The world can be a very happy place if you ignore everything going on around you," he writes—but Edmond's chief tormentors don't want the truth to see print. Through the main story and the prose passages of the diary the reader develops such a loathing for the innocent boy's various enemies that the ending—when Man-Thing, instrument of revenge, enters the high school and assaults the guilty, maiming some of them and killing the coach—acts as pure catharsis; in real life these people would have gotten away scot free. The story of callous, stupid "educators," cruel students, and their persecution of anyone who is different, packed a wallop when it was first published and in these days where bullying has become a national problem—and pastime—resonates just as strongly. Ed Hannigan, Ron Wilson and Frank Springer did the effective artwork.

Jim Mooney became the new artist beginning with *M-T* 17, the beginning of a manic two-parter teaming a maddened macho man in a Viking outfit (who first showed up the previous issue) who wants to kill anyone who has lowered the standards of masculinity (such as glittery rock stars) with outraged mother Olivia Selby, who founded a decency brigade in Citrusville when she discovered the school's text books were supposedly promoting communism, filthy sex, and godlessness. Absurd and as unsubtle as anything written by Gerber, it nevertheless encapsulated the tensions occurring in the country over various social and artistic movements during this period.

The final four issues of *Man-Thing* were typically weird. Thrown into a sewage treatment facility in Citrusville and temporarily dissolved, Man-Thing reconstitutes himself and becomes a "self-contained eco system" which no longer has to stay near the swamp to survive. In *M-T* 19 he gets into the back seat of a car driven by self-described born loser Richard Rory, a reporter who had appeared sporadically throughout the series, along with fellow passenger Carol Selby, daughter of the aforementioned Olivia Selby, who wants to escape the book-burning and other madness of Citrusville, and they all wind up in Atlanta. Unfortunately Carol is only seventeen, which means Richard, a born loser indeed, is technically guilty of kidnapping, for which he is arrested and sent back with Carol to wretched Citrusville and seen no more.

Man-Thing 19 also introduced the most interesting villain since the Fool Killer. The Scavenger is a man born without a sense of touch, who can't even feel a kiss or any sensation but numbness. He attacks women who are dissatisfied with their marriages and their lot in life, his passionate smooch sucking away their energy and fleshly substance and reducing them to skeletons; in return for this he is awarded human sensations. One can only imagine what those who objected to Gerber's pirate story thought of what this story said about women, but Gerber chose to wrap up the series when it was canceled with the twenty-second issue with a return to the sword and sorcery silliness with which it had begun. Gerber himself appears in the final issue to relate how a wizard told him the *true* stories of Man-Thing and he only served as typist. The series ended as inauspiciously as it debuted, but despite these forgettable lapses, it was an unusual and noteworthy comic that managed to last a bit longer (when you count the *Fear* issues) than *Swamp Thing* and was decidedly more memorable. Man-Thing met Spider-Man in *Giant-Size Spider-Man* 5 in which he got caught in the middle of a fight between the web-slinger and his monstrous half-human foe, the Lizard. It was very entertaining, with a terrific art job by Andru and Esposito.

Man-Thing Redux

But this was not the end of Man-Thing, who returned in a new series of the same name in 1979. Jim Mooney was again tapped to be the artist (with Bob Wiacek on inks), while the initial writer was Michael Fleisher. A scientist, Dr. Oheimer, is overtaken in his car by government agents who want him to help them recover Ted Sallis' formula from the mind of Man-Thing. He agrees to do so not so much for the formula, but to bring back Sallis' formidable mentality. Man-Thing is captured and injected with Oheimer's own formula, which begins rejuvenating his normal human mind. Oheimer is unaware that the people he is working with are actually enemy agents. He has managed to bring Man-Thing's mind to a childlike level, hoping to eventually make him physically human as well, when U.S. Agents attack and he is killed as they fire on Man-Thing. Man-Thing picks up the doctor's broken body and escapes.

Due to an experimental teleportation device Man-Thing winds up in the Himalayas where he encounters three people—married couple Russell and Elaine and their "friend" Roger—searching for the legendary Abominable Snowman (*M-T* V2, 2–3). Roger covets Elaine for himself and brings about Russell's death, and confuses Man-Thing with the Snowman. Roger wants to capture Man-Thing for exhibition, but he is so stupid that when a race of actual Yeti are discovered, his only response is to order his men to shoot them! The action in these well-written issues came fast and furious and the series was off to a good start.

Despite that, Fleisher and Mooney were replaced by Christopher Claremont and Don Perlin for the fourth issue, which was really a carry-over from the *Dr. Strange* series and was wrapped up in that magazine. *Man-Thing* 5, on the other hand, has an excellent story that combines Steve Gerber–like character delineation with plenty of action, as a young woman, Barbie Bannister, whose parents were murdered by her drug-dealing "boyfriend," is chased by him and his associates through the swamp, with the ever-empathetic Man-Thing intervening in his usual vague but definitive way. She and sheriff John Daltry, who helps her, became part of the comic's supporting cast; both are on hand for a two-part story in *M-T* 7–8 which is a sequel to Steve Gerber's controversial pirate story in *M-T* 13–14, volume 1.

In this a literally airborne Flying Dutchman ship of piratical spirits emerges from the mist in the air above the everglades and bombards an airliner with cannonballs, the ghost pirates boarding the ship to loot her, kidnapping the women, and then letting the plane collapse from its stasis field to crash into the swamp. Claremont insightfully describes the torrent of emotions experienced by rescue workers who find not a single survivor, only bodies. Unfortunately the second half, which details Sheriff Daltry and Barbie's battle against the pirate leader, Captain Fate, on board his ghost ship, is less successful, although parts are quite harrowing.

Claremont kept recycling old Steve Gerber ideas, including such characters as Jennifer and Andy Dale, who appear in a story in which a man who is the personification of death inexplicably shows up in Citrusville. As Gerber had before him, Claremont put himself and other Marvel staffers in the final issue (*M-T* 11) as he tried to wrap up some of the loose ends. Much better than these particular issues is *M-T* 9, which has an excellent fill-in story by Dickie Mackenzie and Larry Hama detailing Man-Thing's ironic encounter with the grandparents of a baby whose young mother and father died from drinking stagnant, poisoned water. However talented Claremont may be—and a couple of his Man-Thing stories were quite good—one suspects that if Fleisher had continued writing the series it may have lasted more than 11 issues. It also would have been interesting to see what might have happened had the initial concept been followed, with Man-Thing regaining all or part of Ted Sallis' mind and memory. Or would he simply have become another Swamp Thing?

By all rights, the mindless, mute Mind-Thing should not have been such an interesting character, but one not only never knew what kind of story he would appear in, what part he would play, but whether he would prove to be "hero"or menace. Although most of the fearful people whose flesh burned at his touch were bad guys, occasionally good, understandably frightened people were victims, or were at least endangered. This aspect was often played up to good advantage.

Marvel's Other Vampire

Michael Morbius, who had first appeared in *Amazing Spider-Man*, was a Nobel-prize winning scientist who is dying of a rare blood disease. Trying to find a cure, he instead turns into a living vampire who needs human blood to survive. Morbius appeared in several of Marvel's super-hero comics as a bloodsucking costumed villain, although in the daylight he was tormented by thoughts of the people he had murdered for sustenance. In 1973 he was given a series in the black and white magazine *Vampire Tales*, and also became the headliner of the color comic *Adventure into Fear* beginning with the twentieth issue. Morbius was different from Dracula, not only because he was not "undead," but because he had a conscience, the fact of which never helped him overcome his manic desire to drink blood and commit murder.

In *Fear* Morbius becomes a pawn in a war between a demon-priest named Deamond and a weird group called the Caretakers that wants to create a super-race to supposedly save mankind. Morbius' fiancee Martine, for whom he had been searching, is now in thrall to Deamond and hates her former beloved. Morbius winds up being taken to a dimension of cat-beings who have such a problem of over-population that their leader wants to use Morbius to thin their ranks, a prospect he finds morally repugnant. Aside from a brief battle with the vampire-hunter Blade from *Tomb of Dracula* in *Fear* 23, the stories were absurd fantasies that go in all the wrong directions. There was even a little girl who could turn into her future self, a whip-wielding warrior woman. What this had to do with Michael Morbius is debatable; the stories were pretty awful. Both writer Steve Gerber and artist Craig Russell would do more memorable work elsewhere.

Doug Moench and Frank Robbins took over the strip with the twenty-fifth issue. They quickly dispensed with the Caretakers and Deamond and settled on a more intriguing storyline. Morbius is pursued by Simon Stroud, a private detective, who thinks he is responsible for a rash of vampire murders, in which the victims also come back as vampires. He shoots Morbius, who manages to get away from him, but arrests Martine for harboring a killer. However, the true vampire killer, a female, is exposed, as Martine explains that Morbius can not infect anyone with vampirism like a true vampire. Although Robbins' work was quite cartoonish, it was also rather effective at times.

Unfortunately, this storyline was put on hold while Morbius and Stroud battle a demon from another dimension who wants to take over the earth. Hellseyes is a giant who has eyes all over his body, lives in a dimension where crabs sing about the Wizard of Oz, and wears out his welcome very quickly. Fortunately *Fear* 30 has an excellent tale by Bill Mantlo and George Evans in which Morbius and Stroud face off against a whole horde of vampires in a sinister mansion. Stroud is troubled that these "real" vampires still cast a reflection and don't instantly dissolve in sunlight. In the next and final issue Morbius discovers that it was his bites that created these new "atomic" vampires who have radioactivity in their blood. Martine becomes a bloodsucker after being attacked by one of them but is cured by Morbius' serum. Although Stroud urges Morbius to seek help and plead insanity, the latter flees into the night. As often happens, the series only began to reach its potential with the final issues.

The Morbius strip in *Vampire Tales* was somewhat more intense. Morbius rescues a young woman named Amanda Knight from a demonic sect, then takes her to Malevolence, Maine to find her parents, after which they wind up in a ghost town. Their battle with Demonfire lasts for several installments. The verbosity of Don McGregor's scripts pretty much strip the stories of their entertainment value. However, writer Doug Moench and artist Sonny Trinidad's "Feast of Blood" in *Vampire Tales* 10 is a big improvement. In this story Morbius decides that he will go "cold turkey" and not harm another soul no matter how much he craves blood, but things don't work out as planned. This story, more than any other, illustrates the extreme torture of Morbius "addiction" and makes him more sympathetic than usual, despite the high body count, as Morbius takes revenge on a group of miners responsible for the death of his caring landlady. *VT* 11, the magazine's final issue, has an even better story, also by Moench and Trinidad, in which Morbius and a beautiful woman named Morgana decide to crush a conspiracy of powerful, well-connected vampires in London called the Brotherhood of Judas. As Dracula often employed British higher ups as slaves, it was hoped that this story might finally bring Marvel's two chief and very different vampire characters together but it was not to be. As with the color series in *Fear*, the last two Morbius stories in *VT* finally realized the character's potential—and then he was gone.

An interesting aspect of Morbius' character is that he was a scientist who absolutely did not believe in the existence of supernatural vampires such as Dracula (at least until the aforementioned tale in *VT* 11). Less interesting over time was his alleged remorse over his many victims. As the bodies piled up one had to wonder if a truly decent person would allow themselves continued existence knowing it would always be at the expense of innocents.

The Living Mummy

With comics inspired by Frankenstein, Dracula, and the Wolfman, it was no surprise when Marvel introduced "The Living Mummy" in the fifth issue of their *Supernatural Thrillers* series (1972). Pharoah Aram-Set uses African slaves to build a massive temple to his ego, and plans to murder them all once the job is done. Their leader, a strong and tall king named N'katu leads a revolt, murders the pharoah, and tries to slay Nephrus, the high priest and wizard. Instead Nephrus consigns him to certain hell: he paralyzes the slave-king with a potion that keeps him conscious, wraps him in mummy dressings, and entombs him for centuries. 3000 years later fresh air revives N'katu, who stumbles about as a "living mummy" causing havoc due to his increased strength, frightening appearance, and essential insanity after being unable to move or speak for so many years. He is subdued and taken into custody, as it were, by archeologist Dr. Skarab (!), who is a descendant of the nasty Nephrus. Steve Gerber did the interesting script, with Rich Buckler and Frank Chiaramonte on the art.

The Living Mummy was given a continuing series beginning with *Supernatural Thrillers* 7 with Tony Isabella and Val Mayerick as the creative team. Although Dr. Skarab had thought the mummy dead, it turns out he was only unconscious; the bolt of electricity that felled him in his previous appearance has cleared the cobwebs from his mind and made him sane again. He wakes up in, and escapes from, a museum in New York, scares off some nefarious dudes attacking a woman in Central Park, and is fired on by the police. Deciding to remove his wrappings so he won't look so scary, he sees the withered, brittle flesh of his hand and realizes his entire body must look that way—and how long he was buried in the Egyptian sand—and feels utter despondency. He is then spirited away to Cairo by a group of extra-dimensional Elementals who want him to steal an ancient artifact which they tell him can return him to his human form. But when N'kantu realizes that they hope to enslave the world, he refuses to do their bidding (*ST* 8).

The Living Mummy had great potential, but co-plotters Isabella and Mayerick then spent the next few issues doing everything they could to convince the reader that it was no mere silly horror series—and succeeded with a gullible few even while making a shambles of the strip. The situations and writing became so overly intense, especially during sequences that occurred during a civil war in Cairo with the Elementals and their supporters on one side, and the resistance on the other, that they even tried to wring unlikely pathos out of the death of a hungry mouse trying to snatch a crumb amidst the carnage! The result was depressing in more ways than one—and not a lot of fun. The trouble was that the "serious" tone of the strip never jelled with the intrusion of the Elementals, who never came off as anything other than a particularly mediocre set of super-villain rejects. The cast of supporting characters—the four Elementals, Dr. Skarab, anthropologist Ron McAllister, his girlfriend Janice, and two con men named the Asp and Oldden who may or may not have had a repressed homosexual relationship—expanded to such a degree that the Mummy himself was sort of crowded out of his own comic. Writer John Warner and artist Tom Sutton wrapped up the book's run—it ended in the final and fifteenth issue of *Supernatural Thrillers*—but by then it was too late to do anything with the utter, tedious mess that The Living Mummy had become. The ambition of the creative team unfortunately exceeded their abilities. N'kantu would reappear sporadically in various Marvel comics up to the modern age, still hoping to either die or become human once again.

Brother Voodoo and the Golem

The origin of Brother Voodoo was told in *Strange Tales* 169–170 in 1973. Jericho Drumm, a black "author, scholar, noted psychologist," returns to Haiti, where he was born, when his aunt tells him that his identical twin brother, Daniel, the island's Houngan (or spirit master) is seriously ill. Daniel challenged the evil Damballah, an alleged Serpent God in human form, who put a voodoo curse on him. Jericho has never believed in the supernatural, but when Daniel dies he honors his last wish and carries his corpse deep into the jungle to the home of Papa Jambo, who teaches him what he will need to know to defeat Damballah and become the "greatest Houngan on the face of the Earth." Drumm does a dance over the bones of his brother, collapses, and wakes to discover that his brother's spirit is now and forever a part of him and can be called upon when required; he can possess others and force them to do Jericho's bidding, for instance. Papa Jambo conveniently dies, while the new Brother Voodoo challenges Damballah and his army of snakes and defeats him. The latter's servant, Bambu, switches allegiances to the new top houngan in town, no fool he. Whenever Brother Voodoo appears or disappears in a plume of smoke, the vivid sound of drums can be heard.

Brother Voodoo, with its nutty voodoo flavorings and Hollywood-style Haiti shouldn't have worked at all, but it was entertaining and well done by writer Len Wein and artists Gene Colan and Dan Adkins. The strip only lasted for three more issues of *Strange Tales*, however. Frank Giacoia and Dick Giordano inked the final three installments of the series and the results were splendid. *ST* 171 introduced Baron Samedi, Lord of the Undead, and his pack of "zuvembies." (Zuvembi was the Marvel Comics word for "zombie." When the Comics Code Authority allowed comic books to use vampires and werewolves, it did so because famous literary works had been written about such creatures. Zombies, however, had never had a classic like *Frankenstein* or *Dracula* to champion them and hence were still taboo. Nobody was fooled by the soulless, undead "zuvembies," but Marvel wasn't allowed to call them zombies!) Another cop-out: The "zuvembies"—at least in this story—turn out simply to be living men whose minds are being controlled, not ghouls at all, and the Baron is in the payroll of a sinister secret group named AIM that plagued many Marvel super-heroes.

The action switched from Haiti to Drumm's home in New Orleans for *ST* 172–173. A number of women have been found dead and mutilated after receiving strange gifts of black roosters. Loralee Tate, the daughter of a police inspector, is the latest to receive one, and is rescued by Brother Voodoo as she attempts to flee robed characters who want to bring her to the Dark Lord. She is then taken from Drumm's home and BV asks the aged priestess, Mama Limbo, for her help in finding her. The trail leads to the home of Desmond Drew, who is annoyed by BV's abrupt intrusion but nevertheless answers his questions. As Brother Voodoo disappears in his usual cloud of mist and those drums that accompany his exit begin to sound, Drumm tells Drew to sleep well. "Sleep well?" asks Drew. "With all that racket you're making?" Drew doesn't like Brother Voodoo but he admits "he knows how to make an exit." And with this issue, Brother Voodoo made an exit from *Strange Tales*.

The Dark Lord story was finished in the black and white magazine *Tales of the Zombie* 6, wherein we discover that the Dark Lord's agent, the Black Talon, is Desmond Drew in disguise, and that his mother—who turns out to be Mama Limbo—was not only behind the cult but was killing virgins in the hopes that bathing in their blood would make her young again, like a latter-day Elizabeth Bathory. Brother Voodoo made one more appearance in

Tales of the Zombie 10, the final issue, in an excellent Doug Moench story wherein he is called back to Haiti when a power-mad man resuscitates the corpses of old friends' of Jericho, and tries to sacrifice the young daughter of one of them. The exciting story was complemented by striking art by Tony DeZuniga.

Strange Tales 174 introduced a new feature, the Golem, which was inspired by the Jewish legend of the clay statue that comes to life in Prague and helps the Jews against their oppressors. In modern times elderly archaeologist Abraham Adamson and his companions dig in the desert in a spot where he's sure the Golem has been buried for years and are rewarded by finding the hulking statue. Adamson and his crew, including some of his relatives, are celebrating their find when a group of Arab Army deserters enter their camp. Adamson is shot and Omar, the leader of the deserters, decides to take the others with him deep into the desert so they can't report the murder. But before he dies Adamson reads words from an ancient parchment, his tear drops onto the statue, and suddenly the old man's spirit brings the Golem to life to save his kidnapped relatives. Abraham's niece notices that the Golem seems to have the same twinkle in his eye that her late uncle had. Len Wein contributed a nice, compact origin tale, while the fine art was by John Buscema and Jim Mooney.

After a reprint issue of *Strange Tales*, the Golem was back in *ST* 176–177, with striking art by Tony De Zuniga/Steve Austin and a story by Mike Friedrich. As Adamson's relatives try to take the Golem back to the dead man's university, they are beset by demons conjured by a weirdo named Kaballa the Unclean. He is hoping to use the Golem for his own purposes, but the rock man is able to fight off the demons with relative ease. It is theorized that the Golem is not possessed by Abraham Adamson's spirit, but that the archeologist's life force only helped bring the creature back to life. Whatever the case, this was the last appearance of the Golem. On the letters page the editors explained that they goofed with the Golem, and never could get the correct handle on the direction the series should take.

Man-Wolf, Scarecrow and It

Man-Wolf was the name of a werewolf character who, like the vampire Morbius, had first appeared in *Spider-Man*. He was actually John Jameson, the hero astronaut son of Spider-Man's nemesis, newspaper publisher J. Jonah Jameson. Both characters had been around since the very early days of the series, but young Jameson didn't become a wolfman until *Amazing Spider-Man* 124–125 in 1973. Jameson had picked up a red rock from the moon and had it turned into a pendant. Unfortunately, the pendant becomes grafted to his skin, and turns him into a werewolf whenever the moon comes out. Spider-Man rips the pendant off of Jameson's chest, but the living vampire Morbius grafts it back on for his own purposes (*Giant-Size Super-Heroes* 1). Man-Wolf was given his own series beginning with *Creatures on the Loose* 30, largely because of the success of *Werewolf by Night*. Jameson is unable to control his transformations, and as Man-Wolf, seems determined to kill those he loves the most: his father, and his fiancee, Kristine Saunders. Meanwhile the FBI is after him because they think he went AWOL. P.I. Simon Stroud, who would later hunt Morbius, is assigned the job of tracking Jameson.

There was the usual change in creative teams from Doug Moench and Tony Isabella on stories to George Tuska and Vince Colletta on art until David Kraft and George Perez settled in to round off the series. Man-Wolf developed more as a sort of twisted super-hero series with little true emphasis on horror or even science fiction. Kraven the Hunter tries to hunt down Man-Wolf for an associate whose identity is still undisclosed as of the final issue. Man-Wolf and Nick Fury battle Marvel villain and ten-time loser Hatemonger, and in the final issues Jameson goes on a mission to a moon base that has been taken over by weird aliens searching for a "weirdstone." The series came to an abrupt end with *Creatures* 37, none of the loose ends being resolved, and not enough readers giving a damn. However some time later Marvel finally published the last two installments of the series in *Marvel Premiere* 45–46, which featured some exciting George Perez pencils. After becoming a "god" to beings from another dimension, John Jameson returns to Earth, reunites with Kristine, and is apparently once more wholly human.

The sinister Scarecrow first appeared in *Dead of Night* 11 in 1975, then made a second appearance some months later in *Marvel Spotlight* 26. The scarecrow was a vengeful being sans origin who came out of a painting that is a gateway between our world and a dimension of an evil god, whose acolytes try to steal the painting and are painfully murdered by its silent guardian. Although there were some human characters in the stories—a painter, his girlfriend, and his writer brother—the Scarecrow had no personality and its hard to see how he or it could have sustained a successful series. The most interesting thing about the second story was the bizarre inclusion of a gigantic captive fish being exhibited before the public at a venue that becomes the latest battleground for the Scarecrow and the demon cultists. It's entirely possible that the whole thing was meant to be a joke. Or a fish story.

Inspired by a story that appeared in one of Marvel's old monster mags, "It" appeared in *Astonishing Tales* 21–24 (1973). Special effects man Bob O'Bryan had saved the earth by using his skills to defeat aliens who controlled a 100-foot-tall flying, colossal stone man named "It." However, his studio is unable to use the now dormant creature in a new sci fi TV series because of its ungainly size. O'Bryan comes up with a way of recreating It's actions with FX, but Grant Marshall, the star of the show, resents the publicity build-up Bob will get and causes an accident that leaves the man paralyzed. But when the mad Dr. Vault tries to steal It—Vault is dying and needs a new body— Bob discovers that he can transfer his consciousness into the creature and make it come alive. Trying to reduce the size of the colossus to a more manageable eight feet, Vault can only manage to get it down to thirty feet. Meantime Bob pretends he wants nothing more to do with his fiancee, Diane Cummings, the female lead of the TV show, because he doesn't want her to get stuck with a "cripple," a hoary cliché if ever there were one.

In the next three issues Bob/It becomes embroiled in a fight between two factions of gargoyles from another galaxy. The evil leader of one faction, Granitor, is also a giant. Dr. Vault teleports Marvel's classic monster Fin Fang Foom from China, and the big dragon helps the good gargoyles win the war before Vault takes control of Fin and forces him to attack It. The dragon eventually resists Vault's control and the battle is over. .. and so was the series. At times the strip, written by Tony Isabella, came off like an extremely bad Japanese monster movie, but it did have its charms. The art had an old-fashioned look to it, with Dick Ayers drawing the series so that the new panels would match the reprint panels used from the old monster stories of the fifties and sixties.

Godzilla

After trying to wrest the rights from Japan's Toho studios for years, Marvel comics finally was able to come out with *Godzilla* in 1977. There were several differences from the film series: Godzilla was treated seriously and not like a camp object; the big lizard now romped in North America instead of in Japan; and he was placed squarely in the Marvel universe when Nick Fury of SHIELD showed up to supervise attempts to contain the creature in *Godzilla* 1. (In *Godzilla* 3 the Champions super-team took on the monster.) Of course there had always been monsters and dinosaurs in the Marvel super-hero Universe. The X-men had explored the prehistoric savage land years before, and Iron Man was to have a protracted battle with the dragon Fin Fang Foom.

Members of *Godzilla*'s supporting cast included Dr. Yukio Tagakuchi, who had been there in the fifties when underwater atomic blasts revived and irradiated the monster, despite his protests; his 12-year-old grandson Robert, who thinks of Godzilla as a misunderstood hero; Tagakuchi's assistant, Tamara Hashiaka; and agent Jimmy Woo, who'd actually been introduced in another series years before. The debut issue, well written by Doug Moench, was a smash. Herb Trimpe, whose pencils for super-hero strips always seemed a bit lackluster, did some of the finest work of his career as he brought the big lizard's ferocious and destructive rampages to life. Moench wrote every issue and did superlative work, while Trimpe penciled all but a couple of issues. Fred Kido and Dan Green were the main inkers on the series.

In *Godzilla* 4–5 Godzilla encounters a series of grotesque giant monsters created by a crazed geneticist who calls himself Dr. Demonicus. Although others argue that Godzilla is more intelligent than he appears and is not out to harm anyone (which begs the question as to why he smashes through cities with their tiny inhabitants in the first place), the dyspeptic "Dum Dum" Dugan of SHIELD is not convinced of Godzilla's alleged benevolence even after the monster saves him from one of Demonicus's creatures. Dugan's colleague Gabe Jones is sympathetic to Godzilla and there is some clumsy inference that he somehow identifies with the animal, especially when it's shackled, because Jones is black. Like *Gorgo* and *Konga* of the silver age, the series downplayed any innocent deaths that surely must have occurred due to Godzilla's stomping amidst skyscrapers and bridges in such places as Seattle and San Francisco. Godzilla may not have been "evil," but his sheer size— a casual swipe of his tail could knock over a building—makes him a terrible danger to humanity. At times the danger was provided by humans, such as when Godzilla is held captive on a base with armed nuclear missiles that he nearly activates when he escapes.

Godzilla 7–8 introduced a gigantic robot built by Dr. Takaguchi and christened Red Ronin by his grandson, who becomes the only person able to pilot the robot. Initially Godzilla thinks Red Ronin is attacking him, leading to a battle, until the child inside is able to make the lizard understand that he is his friend. *Godzilla* 9 has the big guy invading Las Vegas— "The King of Monsters Goes for Broke!" reads a caption on the cover—in a human interest story that not only follows the monster but also a man in a casino betting his last dime so he can get money for an operation for his mother. The man wins a bundle but Godzilla's smashing entrance wipes it all away. Which is just as well as it turns out the disturbed man's mother has been dead for three years.

The comic series was generally not as idiotic as the movie series—and Godzilla certainly looked better— but it was influenced by the films to a certain extent. For instance, *Godzilla*

12–14 has a three parter in which Godzilla saves earth from an attack by three weird outer space monsters, which helps soften Dugan's heart toward the giant creature. Much more interesting are more unique stories such as in *G* 15–16 with the monster interacting with some ranchers and cattle rustlers—one startling scene has a cowboy lassoing Godzilla's tail, while another man throws a lasso around one of the big guy's front teeth—and a story arc in which Godzilla is shrunk in size to 12 inches (*G* 17–20). Taken to New York he escapes into the sewers and defeats a nasty voracious rat that wants to snack on him, then grows to man-size on the docks. At twenty feet in height he battles the famous Fantastic Four in *G* 20–21. Mr. Fantastic, the leader of the group, uses arch-foe Dr. Doom's time machine to send Godzilla back to the prehistoric past. However, the Big G winds up in a Jack Kirby-created alternate past from the comic *Devil Dinosaur*, and winds up first fighting the big red tyrannosaur of that name and then teaming up with him (*G* 21–22). Unfortunately it turns out that Godzilla's irradiated body doesn't react well with the time stream, and he's snapped back to our reality at his full height and smack in the middle of Times Square!

G 23–24 has both the Fantastic Four and the Avengers struggling to contain Godzilla's destruction as he tries to knock over the Empire State Building and is prevented from this by the muscular sinews of the Mighty Thor. Rob convinces Godzilla to calm down and retreat, and the big green lizard wades into the ocean and is heard from no more, at least in Marvel's *Godzilla* series, as this was the final issue. Years later an American film would bring the Japanese monster into Manhattan, and like the comic not have a single person smushed or eaten. Although there had been talk of bringing Godzilla and the Hulk together, this never happened; neither did Godzilla meet an even more obvious adversary, Fin Fang Foom. *Godzilla* was very reminiscent in some ways of Charlton's monster movie comics, *Gorgo*, *Reptisaurus* and *Konga*, with their hulking, dangerous but sympathetic monsters.

Marvel Anthologies

Marvel also published a number of anthology horror titles in the late sixties and seventies. Some, such as *Where Monsters Dwell*, did only reprints of fifties horror stories while others, such as *Chamber of Darkness*, which debuted in 1969, presented mostly all-new material. Like DC's horror comics, *Chamber* used creepy hosts—"Headstone P. Gravely" and "Digger"—to introduce the stories while a romanticized version of Stan Lee himself introduced adaptations of classic horror tales. When it was suggested that Marvel was imitating DC, the editor reminded the readers that EC used hosts in its comics years earlier than DC, but in later issues some stories were introduced by the artists who drew them. There were also reprints, most of them the work of artist Steve Ditko.

Most of the stories weren't memorable but there were some exceptions. "Always Leave 'em Laughing" in *Chamber* 1 seems a little mean-spirited because the poor schnook protagonist who only wants respect but winds up a court jester, doesn't seem to deserve his fate, but his character isn't developed very well, which was the case with most of the stories. "Face of Fear" in *Chamber* 2 is forgettable but for the excellent artwork by Syd Shores. "Day of the Red Death" in the same issue was an interesting variation on, and updating of, Poe's "Masque of the Red Death" with the world's survivors in a kind of bunker with the latest scientific safeguards. There was another acceptable Poe adaptation, "The Tell-Tale Heart," in *Chamber*

3, as well as a moody adaptation of H.P. Lovecraft's "The Music of Erich Zann" in the fifth issue. Artists for the series, which lasted only eight issues, included Jack Kirby, Sal Buscema, and former EC Artist Johnny Craig; writers included Len Wein and Denny O'Neill.

Tower of Shadows also debuted in 1969 with "Digger" as the initial host, although the artists and now writers of some of the stories then introduced their own work. In the third issue writer Len Wein and artist Gene Colan offered "The Moving Finger Writhes" [*sic*] in which an unsuccessful, hen-pecked husband discovers a dusty tome that contains his life story in a old book store. Turning the pages—although he fears looking at the end—he discovers how he'll make a fortune at the race track and then dispose of his greedy wife, until he realizes all the rest of the pages are blank ... because he's crushed to death at a construction site. This story was the best of a decidedly weak field when it came to original tales in *Tower*.

Tower was a schizoid comic and dumping ground of work that wouldn't fit anywhere else, such as a series of acceptable if minor sword and sorcery tales written and drawn by comics veteran Wally Wood. (An interesting touch in one story has the protagonist noticing eyes suddenly appearing in the earth beneath his feet, which is then full of mud-like creatures pulling themselves out of the ground.) Artists included everyone from Jim Steranko to Barry Smith, John Buscema to Neal Adams. Apparently the reprint title *Where Monsters Dwell* was outselling *Tower* (and its companion mag *Chamber*) because *Tower* began sneaking in reprints with the sixth issue, and even featured a reprint monster story on the cover of *Tower* 7. It was nothing but reprints and Wally Wood fantasy until the ninth and last issue, wherein there was an excellent adaptation (Roy Thomas/Tom Palmer) of "Pickman's Model" by H. P. Lovecraft, which was, of course, head and shoulders above the original stories in Marvel's and most other horror comics. After that the title of the comic was changed to the aforementioned *Creatures on the Loose*, which ran reprints for several issues and then original series.

In 1972 Marvel also debuted *Supernatural Thrillers*, which ran adaptations of famous horror, science fiction, and fantasy stories before becoming the host of the aforementioned "The Living Mummy." *ST* 1 featured an excellent adaptation of Theodore Sturgeon's short story "It" (the genesis of the Heap and other muck monsters) by Roy Thomas, with art by Marie Severin and Frank Giacoia. The second issue featured an acceptable adaptation of H. G. Wells' "The Invisible Man" by Ron Goulart and Val Mayerick, while *ST* 3 adapted Robert E. Howard's monster story "The Valley of the Worm," which featured not only a giant snake but an even bigger slithering horror of worm-like mien. This was well brought to life by artists Gil Kane and Ernie Chau, even if the climactic battle was disappointingly brief. The following issue contained a fair-to-middling version of Stevenson's classic "Dr. Jekyll and Mr. Hyde." And with that the adaptations were gone.

Another anthology comic, *Chamber of Chills*, debuted in 1972. It was a combination of original stories, adaptations of such writers as Robert E. Howard, and reprints. "Thirst" (*COC* 2), written by Steve Gerber, and with art by Craig Russell and Dan Adkins (who also plotted) was a nifty piece about a vampire stowaway on a starship in 2180 A.D who decimates the crew, who discover there are no modern methods for dealing with the undead and not a bit of wood on board to be used for a stake. John Jakes' "The Opener of the Crypt" (*COC* 4), with art by Frank Brunner, is an excellent sequel to Poe's "The Cask of Amontillado," in which a young man, convinced the story is true, hunts down the very house it took place in and discovers the tomb of the unfortunate Fortunato in the dank, rat-infested basement, with dire results. In "Pawn of the Devoured" (Skeates/Pike/Monte) in the same issue a starving ship-wrecked man is astonished to see groups of ants forming the words "Eat Us," which he does. In this way the devoured ants are able to not only gain control of the man's mind but begin the metamorphosis of his body, so by the time a group of soldiers land on the island they are confronted with the hideous, rather repulsive spectacle of a giant ant with a human head. Rounding out the stories in *COC* 4 is "The Demon from Beyond," an exciting tale by Gardner Fox, stylishly drawn by Howard Chaykin and Joe Sinnott, in which a man heroically comes to the rescue of a maiden in distress and saves her and many others from an other-dimensional demon who demands a sacrifice. "Prey for Keeps" (Moench/Wilson/Abel) in *COC* 7 is a well-done variation of "The Most Dangerous Game" in which the unarmed man that two hunters are pursuing turns out be very dangerous indeed—he's a werewolf. *Chamber of Chills* ran occasional reprints of golden and silver age horror stories until it became an all-reprint comic beginning with the ninth issue. While not every story was a winner, *Chamber of Chills* was not a bad comic and deserved a longer run of original stories.

Giant-Size Chillers came out in 1975. It was originally to have been a normal-sized book entitled *Chilling Tales*, which was still on the masthead inside. The first issue had a brief framing story about an ice house with a history of horror and violence and whose custodians are killed every five years, which would have made a good full-length piece. Instead there were stories of sea monsters, little people with gold treasure, aliens, etc., all of which were mediocre, as well as some equally unmemorable golden age reprints. In the second issue the reprints outnumbered the original stories, two of which dealt with dying old men and greedy relatives. The third and final issue ran reprints from recent Marvel horror comics such as *Chamber of Darkness, Tower of Shadows*, and *Monsters on the Prowl*, series that had briefly run original stories before turning into reprint titles; none were memorable. The she-cat super-heroine Tigra, the were-woman, then took over the comic. *Marvel Chillers*, which replaced *Giant-Size Chillers*, presented sword and sorcery and super-hero stories.

The second volume of *Journey Into Mystery* debuted in 1972, the first issue adapting Robert E. Howard's "Dig Me No Grave," but it was one of the two new stories in the book that took the honors. "House" by Steve Englehart was a creepy tale wherein a man stops for rest in a deserted house and discovers during his stay that the domicile is literally devouring him, a nice horror piece (with very effective art by Ralph Reese) marred only by a dumb gag (no pun intended) at the very end. The second issue presented a creditable adaptation of Robert Bloch's 1943 *Weird Tales* story "Yours Truly, Jack the Ripper" by Ron Goulart and Gil Kane, as well as a not-bad new story by George Alec Effinger in which a school's top athletes are turned into zombies by an energy vampire. Subsequent issues offered an excellent adaptation of Bloch's "The Shambler from the Stars" (Goulart/Starlin/Palmer), in which two men summon up a servant-demon whom they cannot control; an equally good version of Lovecraft's chilling "The Haunter of the Dark" (Goulart/Colin/Adkins); and a new story, Steve Gerber's "The Price is Flight" (4), in which a carnival magician levitates a crude young heckler who challenges his ability and by doing so suffers a heart attack, dooming the man to keep floating up, upward, until he disappears into the atmosphere. The comic had a brief run of five issues, and while most of the material was new, it also ran a couple of reprint stories.

Thirteen

DC's Horror Anthologies

When it came to horror, DC Comics specialized in anthology comics, some of which began life in the golden age, but they also published some continuing series with supernatural themes, such as *Swamp Thing*. *House of Mystery* was their main horror title, while *House of Secrets* switched primarily to science fiction stories and super-heroes. DC added the long-running *Ghosts* and many other series over the years.

An all-new, revamped *House of Mystery* debuted at the very end of the silver age in 1968 with the one hundred seventy-fourth issue, asking readers, "Do You Dare Enter the House of Mystery?" as the cover portrayed a skeletal hand, with sinister eyes in the shadows above, beckoning from the door of a Gothic structure to three frightened children on the steps outside. (Subsequent covers would feature these same youngsters in macabre situations, often unrelated to the stories inside. They appeared on every cover up until the bronze age when they appeared intermittently.) The inside contents, however, were quite disappointing, as they consisted of a quartet of mediocre "weird" sci fi/fantasy tales, including one starring investigator Mark Merlin. In other words, the new *House of Mystery* at first wasn't much different from the old one. The following issue, however, introduced Cain, the bearded, elf-eared caretaker, who introduced each issue and narrated/appeared in some of the stories. The second issue had two fair-to-middling horror stories about a diamond with a curse on it and statues of gargoyles that come to life.

House of Mystery 184, the first bronze age issue, features "The Eyes of the Basilisk," in which a gigantic snake emits such poison that it can kill with a mere glance like a slithering gorgon. The wizard Canthos, who turns out to be Cain, suggests to the king that he offer the princess's hand in marriage to whomever can kill the monster. One arrogant man after another goes after the beast only to go down in defeat, as the creature keeps busy gorging itself on cattle and downed knights, strewing about empty armor "cracked open by the great serpent as a squirrel cracks open a nut to get at the nutmeat within." Finally one man defeats the basilisk by holding a mirror up to it; he is saved from seeing the creature's death glance because he is blind. The tale was written by E. Nelson Bridwell and drawn by Gil Kane.

The following issue boasts "The Beautiful Beast," a weird jungle story about an escaped convict who encounters a sensual, fierce priestess who can transform into a snake; the story isn't much but it is exquisitely illustrated by Al Williamson. The issue after that has another fantasy tale, Jack Oleck's "Nightmare," about a lonely girl who is befriended by a statue of Pan come to life, and who at one point winds up in a strange forest full of frightening, half-seen creatures. This is beautifully illustrated by Neal Adams; there is an especially striking panel in which the child lies on a pathway as shadowy beings with lighted mouths and eyes slowly advance upon her. It is one of many stories in horror comics that explored the link between childhood and a belief in the supernatural and fantastic, a belief that often ends when the child becomes an adult. The other story in this issue is an amusing business about an Egyptian princess who has been transformed into a cat by a man who is obsessed with her and refuses to let her go even after centuries. But she uses his potions to not only return to human form but to transform him into a mouse—with her cat friends waiting anxiously for a meal.

House of Mystery 200 presented "Francis X. Bushmaster's" "A Breath of Black Death," illustrated by Tony DeZuniga. Teron is a cruel pharoah who loves only one person, his boy Tatuk, whom he sees as his whole life and future. Teron's wife, who is not the child's mother, is jealous of Tatuk and poisons him. Teron is given the opportunity to travel into the underworld to bring his son back to life, but when he gets there he discovers that if the boy is to live again, *he* will have to stay behind; they can't both return to the land of the living. Teron chooses to save himself, leaving his son behind, proving which of the two is the true object of his adoration. But when Teron returns to Earth, he promptly expires, or so it seems, but he is entombed forever in a kind of living death which the Gods have decreed is a fitting punishment for his selfishness.

A slash of blood on a victim in a story in *HOM* 194 convinced one reader that the comics code was unbending a bit when it came to depictions of gore. And an EC flavor did manage to sneak its way into several stories in the comic. One story in *House of Mystery* 218 ends with a man being hung up by killer vines outside his home, and displayed for wretching tourists to see, one vine poking its way out of his mouth. The other story in the issue has another villain caught in an ice freezing machine and found in two blocks of ice. Of course in an EC comic the man caught by vines would have looked a lot worse, and the dead ice man would have been scattered about in grisly ice *cubes*. "Cake" (233) features a gal who jumps out of cakes for horny men at parties. She and her boyfriend rob the home of a rich dowager, whom the boyfriend murders when the old woman comes home too soon. The boyfriend merely gets shot by police, but the woman, inside another cake, winds up in the wrong suite where a new cake-cutting device is being demonstrated, winding up in literal pieces. What makes it different from an EC story is that we aren't shown the pieces; we can only imagine what happens to her inside the cake when it's sectioned. What makes it similar to an EC story is not just the grisliness of the ending, but the fact that the more horrible death is reserved for the nicer of the two perpetrators, as the woman was reluctant to help with the robbery and is appalled by the murder.

There were stories "borrowed" from golden and silver age comics and TV programs, such as the exterminator who falls for a woman who's really a giant black widow spider, and the one about the nephew who manages to convince his wealthy old aunt to kill herself but she decides to take him along with her by poisoning him, too. And what by now was the old chestnut about the man who becomes immortal, boasts that he can't die, then winds up paralyzed and in a hospital bed for the next hundred years or so. Occasionally there was something original, such as Cary Bates' "Manslaughter" (*HOM* 240), in which a detective investigates a series of murders in which the victims are sort of "prepared" the way you would prepare meat—smoked, tenderized, etc.—and at each murder scene a cut of beef has been stolen. The killer turns out to be a deranged farmer trying to piece together his favorite bull, Mortimer, who was accidentally taken to the slaughterhouse, by using the stolen cuts of meat.

Arguably the best story to appear in the comic was Joe Orlando and John Albano's "The Demon Within" in *House of Mystery* 201. In this a little boy with an impish sense of humor is able to transform himself into a hideous gnome and takes childish delight in scaring the bejesus out of his sister, classmates and others. Horrified by his ability and what people might think about their family because of it, the boy's conservative and uptight parents take him to an institution for treatment, then ultimately have him lobotomized when nothing works. The final panel shows neighbors marveling at how well-behaved the boy is as he sits blankly, devoid of all fun and personality, on the beautifully trimmed front lawn of his home.

Artists Jack Sparling and Mike Sekowsky did some fine work for the series. *House of Mystery* also presented the darkly comic (sometimes so dark that they were frequently unfunny or merely silly) scribblings of Sergio Aragones.

House of Mystery became a 100-page super-spectacular beginning with issue two hundred twenty-four, although there were only a couple of new stories amid a lot of reprints. This format only lasted for six issues. With issue two hundred fifty-one it was turned into an 80-page "Dollar Comic" with all-new material, which unfortunately included idiotic unfunny "stories" with brothers Cain and Abel arguing with horror hosts Destiny or one of the witches. This format lasted nearly a year. The first three issues seemed to consist mostly of hastily scribbled "C" material cobbled together to fill the book, but *House of Mystery* 254 was a big improvement, with several memorable stories. In Michael Fleischer's and Jess Jodloman's "The Night Job," a man who pulls the switch to electrocute men on death row is told to fake one man's death or his own wife will be executed; it has a good final twist. In Lois Maiwald's and E. R. Cruz's "The Curse of the Sea Monkey," a captain cruelly exploits an intelligent sea creature that he puts on exhibit but discovers that he should have left well enough alone when he falls overboard while returning its corpse to the sea and undergoes a hideous transformation. Jack Oleck and Abe Ocampo's "Skin Game" features a mink rancher who constructs a new thingamajig that will skin the cute and trusting little animals *alive*, but the angry beasties make him go through the process first *himself*. Arnold Drake and Marshall Rogers' "The Devil's Plague," presents a small-town doctor who ministers to especially ignorant townspeople. When he hires an excellent female assistant over their objections, he eventually comes to attribute a plague of madness among his patients to her, but the truth is even more bizarre.

Jack Oleck and E. R. Cruz's "Wake Up the Dead" (258) combines several different elements to good effect: a man who can call up the spirits of the dead to do his bidding; a brain transplantation; a man who kills his wife's apparent lover and becomes victim of her revenge; as well as a couple of extra twists. "Father to the Beast" (257) is a fairly standard werewolf tale but it does boast a striking full page panel by Arthur Suydam depicting the werewolf smashing through a wooden door, grabbing a man in his arms, and sinking his teeth into his bare chest, leaving the door and the victim's shirt both in shreds. The comic then returned to a normal format. "The Husker" (261) was nothing special but for a scene in which the devil peels a piece of corn and there are the faces of dozens of souls captured on each kernel.

Paul Levitz had taken over from Joe Orlando as editor of *House of Mystery* some time before and he turned the reigns over to Jack C. Harris beginning with issue two hundred seventy-six. The contents were abysmal and the comic seemed to get worse during his six-month tenure, although he probably had to use a lot of material that had already been commissioned. Len Wein took over with *HOM* 282. The comic introduced a new continuing series, "I, Vampire" in issue two hundred ninety in 1981. Lord Andrew Bennett was a favorite in Queen Elizabeth's court in 1591, a cheerful man who could be heroic but preferred poetry to warfare. His lover was gentle Mary Seward, one of Elizabeth's handmaidens. When Andrew is bitten by a vampire whom he destroys, he hides away and drinks animal's blood. Mary discovers his dread secret, and wanting to spend eternity with him, begs him to bite her, and he complies. But Mary becomes a vampire in the classic tradition, not only evil but desirous of controlling all humanity. Horrified by this change in personality, Andrew rejects her and she vows revenge. Centuries later in modern times Mary is the leader of a sinister secret agency called the Blood Red Moon, and Andrew is out to stop her once and for all, with the aid of a young woman named Deborah Dancer and an old Russian man named Dmitri Mishkin. Deborah is in love with Andrew, but oddly his heart still belongs to Mary.

The Blood Red Moon has its fingers in many pies, including a racist group that wants "impure" groups thrown out of America. Mishkin is shocked to see that a young woman who assists this group is his own mother (293), although she appears to be much younger than he is. Mishkin actually met Andrew when the former was just a little boy, just after Mary murdered his father and took his mother as her slave (or possibly lover). Andrew vowed to help him free his mother from Mary's influence, but obviously this hasn't worked as the young boy is now an old man. The creator of the series and the writer for the first few mediocre installments was J. M. DeMatteis; the art by Tom Sutton. Bruce Jones took over writing the strip in *HOM* 299 and gave it a new direction. Andrew almost succumbs to his blood lust when he is trapped with Mishkin and Deborah, and decides he no longer wishes to put either of them in danger, either from the Blood Red Moon or himself, so he leaves them a note and takes off by himself. As Andrew is hitching a ride with a man named Matt Kittner, Mary's agents attack, and Kittner is killed, his chest impaled and face burned beyond recognition, causing Andrew to decide to take his identity.

However, in *HOM* 302—"I, Vampire" now appeared in every issue, running 12 pages—Andrew winds up at the home of Kittner's widow, and is still using his own name. Blood Red agents follow him and not only kill the widow, but her young son, who had looked up to Andrew as a surrogate father. Adding to his worries is that he is finding it more difficult to repress his blood hunger, and has no supply left of the blood he had taken with him on his journey. He feels guilt over attacking animals, and is afraid he'll one day assault an innocent person. He finally catches up with Mary and her cohorts at a carnival and interferes with her plot to kidnap a wealthy man's child. Ernie Colon was guest artist for *HOM* 304–305 and he gave the strip a sleek, dramatic visual power that it never had with Sutton's pencils; finally the potential of the series was revealed. Colon's art gave the already suspenseful story an added tension and immediacy. Bruce Jones' scripts were also becoming more ingenious.

In *HOM* 305 a vaccine for cancer is distributed but it has the effect of making humans' blood poisonous to vampires. (It later developed that the cancer cure was a hoax.) Mary pretends she still loves Andrew and tricks him into going back in time with her via magic rings, ostensibly so that they can live together as ordinary humans again, but they actually wind up in London during the time of the Jack the Ripper murders. Mary hopes to kill off the

British mother of the scientist who created the cancer vaccine, preventing both him and it from ever existing. Her plan is to make it look like a ripper murder but the real Jack the Ripper gets in the way. (A few issues later it develops that the scientist himself was a vampire.) Then Mary drags Andrew into another time period where she nearly succeeds in murdering a young girl who turns out to be Deborah Dancer. Finally Mary and Andrew wind up in the time period when they were still human, and are able to interact with their past selves, with disastrous results (*HOM* 309).

Dan Mishkin and Gary Cohn took over the writing chores with *HOM* 310, with, variously, Adrian Gonzales, Paris Cullins, Don Day and Tom Sutton on the art. They introduced mutant spider-like creatures in the subways that were somehow tied in to the cancer cure (*HOM* 312–313), as well as an embittered vampire who wrongly blames Bennett for his undead state and wants revenge in an excellent story in *HOM* 314. Mishkin encounters his vampire mother Dunya, who turned him into one of the undead, before he is forced to kill her as he himself is dying. Bennett learns that the Russians had developed a powder that could supposedly remove all the negative traits of vampirism—blood-thirst, being allergic to sunlight—while retaining immortality (*HOM* 317). When Andrew consumes the powder he is delighted with the results, but it has the side effect of making him paralyzed even as Mary, whom he has tracked to Paris, comes upon him this state. It turns out that the powder was meant to be consumed by normal humans, who would then be turned into vampires who could live forever without turning into bloodsucking monsters. As Andrew lies in a state of rigor mortis, Mary puts the bite on Deborah, unaware that the latter has eaten some of the powder. Therefore, instead of becoming Mary's slave, she is able to drag her out into the sunlight to her destruction. As Deborah tries to embrace her beloved Andrew, he collapses into ashes, finally at peace after 400 years (*HOM* 319).

This was the poignant wrap up for a highly interesting series that would have rivaled *Tomb of Dracula* had it lasted longer and had more consistent artwork. Meanwhile, one of the best "I, Vampire" stories actually appeared in *The Brave and the Bold* 195 when Andrew Bennett teamed up with no less than The Batman to take on the Blood Red Moon, a tale sharply told by Mike Barr and beautifully illustrated by Jim Aparo. (Previously Batman had teamed with the "House of Mystery" in *Brave and the Bold* 93 when Cain narrates a Denny O'Neill tale, with excellent Neal Adams artwork, in which Bruce Wayne saves a boy's life on a ship and then becomes embroiled in a mystery on an island, with supernatural elements aiding and abetting him all the way through.)

By this time DC had canceled virtually all of its horror comics, and even the longest-running, *House of Mystery,* had only two more issues to go, disappearing with issue three hundred twenty-one. There were some notable stories appearing concurrently with the run of "I, Vampire," however, such as: "Old Haunts" by Bruce Jones, which presents a man who's convinced that a woman who haunts an old house is actually alive. He discovers the hidden room where she hides away by day out of guilt, feeling she's indirectly responsible for the death of her husband. The man convinces her to give up her penance, go out in the sunlight and embrace life again. She does just that—and the man disappears. Of course *he* was a ghost (*HOM* 294). Gerry Conway's "The Idol of Millions" presents a rock singer who has lived for many decades under different names, always as a successful singer of one type of another. He stays virtually immortal by sucking away people's life force as he sings to them. When he's in a car accident he desperately needs more life energy and makes his way toward a building which turns out to be a Home for the Deaf, dooming him (apparently he didn't consider that some of the staff may have been able to hear). The story has admirable art by Denys Cowan and Tony DeZuniga.

Jones and Campbell's "Heaven's Above" (*HOM* 300) is similar to the type of stories that Alfred Hitchcock used to present on his television show. Gnome-like Harry Brown is jealous of his tall handsome self-absorbed business partner, John, especially when he thinks that he's seeing Harry's wife behind his back. He arranges for his partner's death by accident—this involves an ax blade dropping from the ceiling at just the right moment—but things go horribly awry. Joey Cavalieri and Trever Von Eeden's "New Generation" is an ironic tale of mankind trying to wipe out a deadly animal but only managing to make matters worse, and Bruce Jones and Tom Yeates' "The Scoop" is an ingenious story of a man, who needs money for his wife's operation, making a bargain with an alien reporter who wants a photo of Earth's most fearsome animal (*HOM* 301). Bruce Jones and Dan Spiegle's "Benny's Friend" is a touching Christmas story about two brothers and a pile of money that goes missing (*HOM* 302). The remarkably downbeat "As I Grow Pale and Thin" by Todd Klein and Ric Estrada concerns a young boy who discovers a lonely playmate in the attic of his new home with tragic results (*HOM* 304). Bruce Jones' "Buried Treasure," about a gangster who fakes his death and hides out underground in a secret vault, is an apocalypse drama with a lot of over-familiar and derivative elements, but Dan Speigle's artwork brings the claustrophobic nightmare vividly to life (*HOM* 307).

Other notable stories include: "What's the Youth" (*HOM* 178)—a man asks an ugly old witch for a potion to make him young so he can court a beautiful lady, unaware that the witch also partakes of the same potion; "Voodoo Vengeance" (193)—a man who lords it over Haitian natives and tries to outwit them is undone by the occult machinations of his little houseboy; "Last Ritual, Last Rites" (207)—a man fears that his much older wife's Hindu servant is keeping her alive with magical spells even as he's trying to poison her, but discovers too late that the servant has an entirely different purpose; "They Hunt Butterflies, Don't They?" (220)—a man who guides a collector into a jungle in search of a rare and valuable species of butterfly discovers there's a very good reason why no one has ever captured one; "The Hunter" (220)—a bored hunter who's snagged vampires, werewolves and even Frankenstein's monster decides with the aid of an occultist to travel to Hell itself to hunt down Satan.

Also: "Night of the Teddy Bear" (222)—during a spree of killings by a maniac who wears a teddy bear mask, nervous Caspar Twinge steps outside his door to bravely answer a call for help and meets a sad and ironic fate; "Demon from the Deep" (223)—a scarred man tells a handsome young sailor of his desperate battle against the many-tentacled and infectious kraken; "Upon Reflection" (223)—a Dorian Gray derivative in which the devil plays a clever, mean trick on a vain young man who adores his image in his mirror; "The Man Who Died Twice" (225)—the devil plays an even more evil trick on a man who desperately wishes to become an aristocrat; "The Perfect Host" (265)—a man who breeds giant spiders for purposes of revenge discovers that the largest of his pets has special plans for him; "The Mouse of History" (267)—whatever a man writes in a special book comes true, but when his pet mouse nibbles on the page to make a nest for its babies, the words that are left add up to doom; "Black Mass" (270)—a fire and brimstone preacher thinks he sees the Devil in a pretty parishioner he's attracted to, but winds up literally tolling the church bell for an eternity; "Deadly Peril at 20,000" (284)—a stewardess takes extreme, some might say murderous, measures to get a corpse riddled with deadly plague off of an airliner along with the grieving and hysterical wife who won't let anyone near her dead husband's body.

Writers for the series included Howard Post, Jack Oleck, and Bob Kanigher, while artists included Bill Draut, Neal Adams, Joe Orlando, Gil Kane, Wally Wood, Jerry Grandenetti, Alfredo Alcala, and Jim Aparo.

House of Secrets

House of Secrets ("There's no escape from the ... House of Secrets") was also revamped as a horror comic at the very end of the silver age, beginning with the eighty-first issue in 1969; Joe Orlando was again the editor. The stories in the first issue actually had to do with a haunted house full of secrets, and starred pudgy, gap-toothed Abel, the brother of Cain, the host of *House of Mystery*. Abel, who has a somewhat competitive and uneasy relationship with his more sinister brother, becomes caretaker of this strange house, and relates one story about a blackmailing photographer who has disappeared inside its chambers. The lead story explains how a new owner tried to move the house over state lines but the Gothic structure broke free of the tractor that was transporting it and nearly ran the owner over before he ran right off the edge of a cliff in terror. Abel became an irritating presence in many of the stories. Eventually the silly two or three page prologues starring Abel were dropped, and his appearances were limited to a brief intro at the start of each story.

House of Secrets 83, the last silver age issue, had an effective cover showing a sinister elderly woman climbing a winding stairs in a tower as two young girls cringe and hide in the shadows. The grim story inside, "The House of Endless Years," written by Gerry Conway and drawn by Bill Draut, tells of a house which automatically ages anyone who steps inside it; three innocent children who venture within become old and are unable to ever leave. Just as this story deals with a terror of aging in a somewhat callous way (true, the children thoughtlessly refer to the old woman who lives in the house as an old hag, but they are after all, just children), another tale, about an old widow who gets love letters in the mail from a monster, turns her loneliness into nothing more than a sick joke. But then, being old and lonely were alien concepts to most of the comic's generally younger readers. *House of Secrets* tried various cover strategies in the bronze age. Frightened children overlooking mysterious scenes were used frequently, as well as some Gothic covers. There were science fiction and fantasy stories to go with the horror. The comic wasn't very memorable until around 1973, when there was some improvement in the book.

The stories in *House of Secrets* 105 and subsequent issues occasionally illustrated that a sense of EC-style cynicism—or realism—had crept back into some horror comics; editor Joe Orlando had done work for EC in the golden age after all. In "Vampire" (105/Fabe; Talaoc) a father insists his little boy, a former child star, start acting like a normal, adventurous boy and follow him into a famous silver mine in Nevada. An old prospector warns the group that the mine is inhabited by vampires but the father only scoffs, even as the other men in the party disappear one by one. The prospector insists the boy has become a vampire after being bitten by a bat, but the man assures his son that there are no such things as vampires. He should know, since it was he who killed the other men, just so he would have no witnesses to his murder of the boy. The man is not the man's natural father, and wants to get his hands on his two million dollar trust fund. There is no last-minute reprieve for the terrified child, who is thrown to his death only moments before a real vampire—the prospector, of course—arrives to feast on the boy's murderer.

In Jack Olek's "Skin Deep" (*HOS* 107) an ugly man uses a magical mask to make himself handsome and murders his rival, only to discover that his beloved is also wearing a mask and is far more hideous than he is. In Steve Skeates' "Winner Take All" (107) a man murders a hobo after the two find money in a house within which they take refuge during a flood, only to get trapped and fall prey to ravenous rodents. John Albano's "And in Death There is No Escape" (109) features a sociopath who murders wives and others, gains immortality, and winds up being turned into a twisted, charred thing that will live in agony forever, another variation on a popular golden age premise. Michael Fleisher's "Night Game" (114), in which a hockey player, who blew up his teammates' plane after they discovered he was throwing games, winds up fricasseed by their ghosts and turned into a skeleton is sort of a PG version of EC's famous "Foul Play." All of these stories were simply new versions of golden age classics.

House of Secrets almost had a change of direction with issue one hundred forty, which began a series starring the Frankenstein-like Patchwork Man (who'd first appeared in a story in *Swamp Thing* 2-3) with a full-length story written by Gerry Conway and drawn by Nestor Redondo. Gregori Arcane had stepped on a landmine and been pieced back together—not very well—by his brother. Now a near-mindless but sensitive creature he is under the "care" of Dr. Chomes and his team, which consists of Christian, Darlene Greer and Andrew Harty. The story was to be continued in the following issue, with a ten page installment each issue thereafter, but *HOS* 141 didn't appear until nearly six months later; there had been a temporary cancellation. When the comic returned there was no sign of the Patchwork Man.

The one hundred fiftieth issue of *House of Secrets* featured a special full-length story written by Gerry Conway and drawn by Gerry Taloac, "A God By Any Other Name," which guest-stars the Phantom Stranger and Dr. Terrance Thirteen in a tale that spans centuries. Both in the distant past and modern times the evil Moloch influences a human being, Robert Korman, to do evil, such as designing computer technology inside a futuristic building to cause people and machines to run amok. As usual, the Stranger and Dr. Thirteen disagree on the aspects of the supernatural in the case, coming together in the "House of Secrets" where Abel is caretaker. *House of Secrets* was eventually incorporated into the giant-size *Unexpected*.

Other notable stories include: "Rest in Peace" (100/Oleck; Alcala)—a chef is turned into a veritable mind-slave by a piggish, voodoo-practicing landowner in 1740 Haiti, but his victim gets revenge after his tormentor dies; "The Sacrifice" (101)—a warlock gets a surprise when he plans to sacrifice his loving and willing wife so that he can regain his lost youth once again; "Make a Wish" (102/Oleck; Cruz)—a small boy who can enter a magical land of leprechauns and endless frolic is forced to turn his back on the mysteries and delights of childhood due to well-meaning elders (Oleck also wrote a similar story, "Make Believe" for HOS 124); "A Lonely Monstrosity" (102/Albano; Redondo)—a young couple's plans to rob their disfigured building superintendent of his life savings backfires with grotesque results; "Like Father, Like Son" (116/Oleck; Redondo)—a man plans to substitute his own son for himself when Satan, who made him rich, comes to claim his soul, but Satan knows something that the poor fool doesn't.

Other memorable stories: "All Dolled Up" (130)—an evil stepmother gets her comeuppance when whatever happens to her stepdaughter's doll also happens to her; "The Island of Crawling Flesh" (131)— a scientist thinks he's discovered the cause of a grotesque and frightful plague that is ravaging the native population but keeps it to himself so he can continue to study the disease's awful effects; "The Contortionist" (132)—when a man steals a special formula to become the world's most famous contortionist he discovers that there's a down side to using it; "Last Voyage of the Lady Luck" (136)—an orphaned boy uses a magic ship to increase the coffers of his aunt and uncle but the price for the poor lad is too high; "Who Goes There?" (142)—a woman's obsession with finding the ghost who haunts her dreams leads to tragedy; "The Shark Man Cometh" (145)—the obese owner of a shark attraction kills his stunt diver and hires a replacement, whose command of sharks is quite uncanny; "Snake's Alive" (146)—a slithering chain of islands turns out to cover an enormous hungry serpent; "A Gift of Evil" (147)—a well-meaning man exchanges his soul for gold given to him by aliens he mistakes for demons, but discovers too late that the gold isn't all that it seems to be.

Witching Hour

Witching Hour, edited by Dick Giordano, was another DC horror comic that debuted at the very end of the silver age, early 1969. The hostesses were witches Mildred, Modred, and Cynthia, the last of whom was young, attractive, and up-to-date; she insisted the two older ladies' stories were old-fashioned but that hers were hip. Her story was actually the worst in the issue, and the others weren't much better, although a tale of a tormented dwarf who takes refuge in a tower had definite possibilities.

"A Face in the Crowd" (*WH* 6) is a remarkably stupid story about a Jewish man, Arnie, who quite understandably is hoping to find and murder the Nazi concentration camp commandant, Bulgart, who ordered the deaths of all of the inmates, even though the war was over. His rabbi—incredibly—urges him to forgive and forget. Arnie goes berserk when he thinks he sees the man he hates, but it turns out to be an illusion. He walks down the street thinking that perhaps the rabbi is right and he should forget, almost bumping into the very man he is seeking. "A Face in the Crowd" is typical of careless fiction that feeds off of the Holocaust without betraying any knowledge or understanding of its special horrors or the emotional effect on its victims. When narrator Cynthia says that "perhaps it was all for the best, Bulgart *was* such a nice guy—a man after my own heart" it's as if she's tastelessly saying that she was a Nazi!

Witching Hour occasionally recycled ideas with some minor changes. There were at least two sad stories in which little boys realized they had died; and two in which men who dream of being eaten by insects turn out to be bugs themselves. There was also a lot of recycling of ideas from the EC era. Frequent writer George Kashdan came up with some ironic and clever stories which now and then had original elements, such as "What Gruesome Grave Awaits Me?" (*WH* 53). In this a man whose hobby is visiting cemeteries has a unique experience when he discovers a graveyard in which the tombstones are decorated with tasteless sculptures that depict the horrible deaths of the people in the graves below.

"A Piece of Death" (77) concerns a puzzle that depicts the death of the person working on it; they put in the last piece and their death occurs. Carl Wessler was another frequent contributor, one of his most memorable tales being "The Thing in the Teakwood Chest."

Witching Hour was another popular DC horror anthology comic.

(*WH* 63). In this a thief has a devil of a time getting rid of a chest that he steals because he thinks it must contain something valuable. Instead he discovers that inside the box is a gruesome and hideous severed head. Each time he throws the box away it keeps magically reappearing. Finally he runs onto the subway tracks to escape the police, trips, and is run over by a train. His severed head turns out to be the very one he imagined he saw in the box.

In its own way *Witching Hour* could be as gruesome as the old EC comics, but rarely as sadistic. The artwork was less intense, and while there was gore, it was not played up as much. Also the years between the fifties and seventies had seen more graphic approaches to horror in films (even in films that were not horror per se) so that nothing in the horror comics of the bronze period could be considered quite *that* shocking. The comic was popular enough to be bumped up from bi-monthly status to eight times a year and then became a monthly with the seventy-fifth issue. After ten more issues it was incorporated into the giant-size *The Unexpected* along with *House of Mystery* and *Doorway to Nightmare*. *Witching Hour* was one of the better latter-day horror comics. While it wasn't always terribly original, and the three witch hostesses could be tiresome, the comic was always entertaining and frequently quite good to look at. Artists included such stalwarts as Gil Kane, Wally Wood and Mike Sekowsky. Gray Morrow offered some striking portraits of men lost in alternate dimensions or nightmare universes. And there was some exemplary work from Al Williamson, Stanley Pitt; Rubeny; E. R. Cruz; Ernesto Patricio, Rico Rivel, Fred Carrillo, Frank Redondo, Buddy Gernale, and Abe Ocampo. As the series drew to a close there was also work from old stalwarts Curt Swan and Dick Ayers.

Other notable stories in the series included: "The Haunted House in Space" (*WH* 14), which presents the odd sight of a crumbling Gothic mansion sitting atop a futuristic craggy asteroid; and "The Mournful Bells of Santa Morte" (21), in which two soldiers who discover a treasure go back to get it after the war's end but fall victim to their own greed. Also: "Laugh, Clown—Die, Clown" (21)—a woman discovers why a clown who cares for her never takes off his make up; "Another Candidate for the Morgue" (24)—a series of strangulations in post-war Germany; "When the Scorpion Strikes" (24)—the protagonist discovers the horrific reason why he keeps dreaming of being attacked by a scorpion that is as big as he is (a similar story appeared in *WH* 54); "Trapped" (30)—a little boy is pursued by ghosts who have a poignant purpose behind their actions (a similar story appeared in 47); "Name Your Poison" (32)—an old man and a drifter enter into an unholy alliance; "Who Must I Kill Tonight?" (47)—a loving family man is unaware that his night job has him acting as a hypnotized hit man for a mysterious employer; "The Corpse Held a Winning Hand" (54)—a card player poisoned by the other players can't elude death but he gets a diabolical revenge on them afterward; "Stand-in for a Corpse" (55)—a man takes a dead man's place for money but discovers that the price he has to pay is way too high; "Played to Order" (83)—a witch doctor who uses voodoo dolls to get rid of his president's enemies, decides to get rid of the president, which proves not to be as easy as it sounds.

The Unexpected

In early 1968 DC changed the title of its sci fi series *Tales of the Unexpected* to *The Unexpected* with issue one hundred five, but the content remained more or less the same, with numerous reprints. A big change didn't come until issue one hundred eighteen in 1970 when the logo read "Have You the Nerve to Face the ... Unexpected?" It became a slick, entertaining horror-suspense comic that made full use of many concepts that had been published before. Mercifully the comic had no inane host, although a fellow called Judge Gallows narrated an occasional story. Gallows always claimed that he had been forced off the bench by colleagues who thought his judgments were the result of senility, and his stories explained the circumstances that may have caused him to lose his mind. For instance, George Kashdan's "Know No Evil" is a bizarre concoction in which a plant-like sentient organism can sort of absorb evil so that a person can commit crimes right in front of everyone but no one will interpret his actions as criminal—and it gets weirder after that. There were some interesting if ill-formed ideas in it but the story was pretty much a mess.

Although Carl Wessler's "Man in the Attic" (*Unexpected* 123) has a highly unoriginal title, its tale of a landlady who rents an attic room to a man—whom another elderly female boarder is convinced is a notorious strangler—has a neat twist at the end. George Kashdan's "Till Death Do Us Unite" (127) is a fairly standard tale of a man haunted by his murdered wife and/or his own guilt but it boasts superb, moody art by Jim Aparo. "There's More than One Way to Get Framed" (128) adds some amusing wrinkles to the old tale of a painting that can be entered by its owner, this time under the glow of a certain candle. "Farewell to a Fading Star" (129) takes the familiar tale of an actress who can't face the fact that she's aging and makes the lead character even more manic and desperate than usual.

Although it's basic idea was not a new one, Carl Wessler also scored with his tale "How to Get Rid of a Corpse" in *Unexpected* 139. Jacques and Eddie mug a drunk after leaving a bar, but when the latter objects to the way Jacques wants to split the booty, Jacques shoots him. After that he has a hell of a time finding somewhere to dump the body, preferably where it will never be found. Pretending Eddie is only dead drunk, Jacques tries to leave his corpse in an empty car, the river, even the sewer, but each time somebody interferes. Finally he decides to take Eddie back to the rooms they shared in a ruined tenement, and decides to make it look as if his dead pal committed suicide, pressing the gun into his outstretched hand. But as Jacques congratulates himself and sips brandy, rigor mortis makes the corpse's fingers tighten on the gun, firing a bullet that kills his killer, even as an overturned candle ignites the brandy and incinerates both bodies. Jerry Grandenetti's flavorful and atmospheric artwork was an added plus.

Bill Dennehy's "Blind as the Night," in which a rich blind man buys an eye from an impoverished youth but still can't see anything because of a black out, is a blatant borrowing of the story "Eyes" presented on the *Night Gallery* telefilm three years before, the only differences being that this monstrous millionaire buys only one eye instead of both and is male instead of female. On the other hand, Dennehy's "A Madman's Loose Among Us" (141) is a quirky and unpredictable story, very well drawn by Lee Elias, about a strange couple who take in a starving, homeless young man then fear that he's an escaped lunatic and take steps to stop him. Dennehy also scripted "What Evil Lurks in the Night" (143) an intriguing tale of a cemetery caretaker who discovers his double robbing the graves, with a fine art job by Jack Sparling.

Bob Donnelly's "Color the Snow: Red" (150) is a tragic tale of a half-witted young man, Norman, who lives with a kind family, bunking in their garage. Norman is horrified when the neighborhood's grumpiest old man, Mr. Fletcher, torments him by telling him that he'll be put away in a nuthouse, simply because he finds the lad playing hide and seek on his property. In addition, Norman is witness to Fletcher's dismaying treatment of the youngsters, his buddies, in the area and takes it too literally when they wish the awful old man were dead. Days go by and Fletcher is not seen, until Norman drags a snowman into his benefactors' living room and they watch in horror as the snow melts away to reveal Fletcher's battered corpse. By killing the old man, Norman has brought about the very fate that so terrified him, being put away in an institution, separated from anyone who might care for him. If there was any weakness to the story it was that the villain/victim of the piece, Mr. Fletcher, is one-dimensional, and the premise of the sad half-wit who kills is a bit of a cliche. Still the story is effective, bolstered by evocative art by Alfredo Alcala.

The Unexpected became a giant 100-page comic with issue one hundred fifty-seven. At first only about a third of the comic was new, but when it became apparent that the comic would go back to normal size, the last couple of 100-page issues were packed with new material that there might not be room for later. Only one stood out, George Kashdan and Alex Nino's "When Is It My Turn to Die?" in *Unexpected* 162. In this clever and unusual mystery a number of people mysteriously killed and found with the imprint of a cloven hoof on their foreheads are said to be victims of Satan, until the murderer's true motive and method are uncovered by a female police detective.

Although the last line of every story read "and it was so *unexpected*" or "he had an *unexpected* surprise" and so on, the endings were often just what you expected. There were more stories in which people having nightmares about sharks or cats turned out to be sharks or cats dreaming about humans, more old chestnuts in fancy dress, and a lot of stories that began well and had flat and predictable wind-ups. With issue one hundred eighty-nine *The Unexpected* became a dollar comic like *House of Mystery*. DC was bringing out a number of new comics, and decided to combine *The Unexpected* with *House of Secrets* and *The Witching Hour*, all of which had respectable sales, into one giant comic to make room for many new titles. *The Witching Hour* section would appear every other issue, alternating with 25-page stories already commissioned for the defunct *Doorway to Nightmare* (see Chapter Fourteen). A lot of inventory stories were trotted out, including science fiction tales that were an odd fit with the comic's basic slant.

The dollar format lasted only eight issues and produced little of lasting merit, but there were a couple of interesting pieces. Carl Wessler and Nestor Malgapo's "The Harpies are Coming" (191) deals with a embittered worker who develops psychic power after an accident involving a computer. He decides to make money off of his gift by telling people that he can prevent their upcoming deaths for a small fortune. In one chilling scene he tells a wealthy man he can save his life for $25,000, and when the man agrees, tells him he already saved him by preventing him from getting onto an elevator which moments later crashes killing all aboard. "You could have saved those people!" screams the horrified if living millionaire. The miserable protagonist meets his end in the form of flying harpies who have the faces of people whose lives he could have saved but didn't, mostly because they were too poor to ante up. Oleck, Tanghal and Workman's "The Beautiful and the Damned" (193) presents a beautiful woman who nags her unloved scientist husband to continue experiments that will prevent her growing older; instead an injection she takes too hastily turns all of her bones to jelly and she collapses into a grotesque puddle of flesh on the floor.

Unexpected returned to normal size with issue one hundred ninety-six, although *Witching*

Hour, *House of Secrets* and their respective hosts remained part of it for a time. (The comic also ran leftover stories from the short-lived sci fi comic *Time Warp*.) As for the comic's contents, there wasn't much to celebrate. Michael Uslan's "Hopping Down the Bunny Trail" (*Unexpected* 202) generated a great cover for the issue featuring a giant bunny rabbit with nasty incisors that was scarier than anything in the monster rabbit movie *Night of the Lepus*, but the story, in which cute little children are lured to an old house and set upon by a mutated rabbit who dumps them in chocolate so he can bite their heads off (the way they do to chocolate bunnies) was as sick as it was stupid. Ironically, it generated more letters of comment than any story ever published in the comic, much of it favorable, although one published letter took the editor to task. One imagines that the perversity of killing cute kids in a grotesque manner and by an almost comical monster made it appealing, and even disturbing, to certain readers. The same issue had an unoriginal but genuinely creepy tale of animals attacking people at a campgrounds, with a lot of suspense being generated over who or what was responsible for a number of savage deaths. It was actually the better of the two stories.

The last few issues of *The Unexpected* were edited by Dave Manak and degenerated into a dumping ground of inventory stories, mostly science fiction, often written and drawn in amateurish fashion. (Ironically, when the comic began life as *Tales of the Unexpected* it was primarily a science fiction comic.) The various horror hosts were nowhere to be seen, which made sense as there were no more horror stories and only a couple of suspense or supernatural items. Joe Kubert did a series of surprisingly unremarkable covers for the final issues, the last of which was 222 in 1982. Whatever its flaws, on a whole *The Unexpected* was generally entertaining.

Other notable stories included: "Marry Me in My Grave" (146), in which a man who pretends to be the long-lost suitor of a wealthy old woman gets several unpleasant surprises; "Good Night, Sweet Nightmares" (155), wherein a man tries to find a family that he persistently sees dying in a burning house in his dreams, leading to a surprising resolution; and "My Son, the Mortician" (179), in which a young man can't seem to get the hang of his father's undertaking business until a dramatic development lessens his tension.

Finally 1969s *DC Special* 4 promised 13 tales with shock endings, but inside were some framing pages with children asking Cain from *House of Mystery* and the witches from *Witching Hour* to tell them some stories, most of which were silver age reprints with very little shock value.

Fourteen

More Sinister Houses

The Dark Mansion of Forbidden Love appeared in 1971, possibly in reaction to the success of TV's Gothic soap opera *Dark Shadows*. It had mostly full-length romantic mysteries in a double-sized format, with the emphasis on Gothic atmosphere. Like the heroine of the TV show, the heroine in the first issue of the comic comes from an orphanage and goes to work for a wealthy woman in a dark manor. Laura believes her friend Bettina was murdered in the house, and although she faints a lot, manages to uncover the truth, despite the efforts of a very nasty old lady. The art by Tony DeZuniga is highly effective. In *DMFL* 2 "The Honeymoon of Horror" presents a young woman, Ellen Drew, whose husband dies in a car accident. Ellen is taken to an inn to recover, but when she awakens she's in a strange house with people she's never seen before, who tell her that her name is Mary and that she's engaged to a completely different fellow. She is told that "Ellen Drew" and the accident were just a childhood fantasy of hers and her high fever has affected her memory. In this genuinely suspenseful story Ellen/Mary bounces back and forth from believing she really is Mary to being convinced she's still Ellen Drew until she finally learns the truth. "Kiss of Death" in the third issue concerns a young nurse in 1910 who travels to Hungary to care for an aging count, falls for her doctor, and fears she's falling under a vampire curse. "The Gray Lady of Coburn Manor" in *DMFL* 4 by Dorothy Manning is probably the best of the early lot, an excellent murder mystery set in a small British town where a couple have come to an allegedly haunted house to prepare it for its conversion to a hotel. Ernie Chau did the art.

The title was changed for the fifth issue to *Forbidden Tales of Dark Mansion*, removing the romantic element from the title if not from the inside pages; apparently the comic had been purchased more by horror fans than romance enthusiasts. The revised comic did not have an auspicious debut. The first story, "They All Came to Die" took place on an island where several people had been invited by an unseen host they'd never met. Each of the guests had at one time been accused of murder. Anyone familiar with famous mystery fiction will recognize that as the plot of Agatha Christie's "Ten Little Indians" of which Jack Oleck's script was a blatant rip-off: it was not just the killer-stalks-people on-an-island premise, there were also significant similarities between points of the plot, the characters, and the motives of the killer, as well as his identity. All Oleck did was change the names. If the editors of the series—Dorothy Woolfolk and Ethan Mordden—couldn't recognize the storyline of one of the most famous mystery novels of all time, one that by the seventies had even been filmed several times (both as *Ten Little Indians* and *And Then There Were None*) they clearly had no business editing a mystery comic. They were quickly replaced by Joe Orlando.

FTDM 6, a regular-sized comic, revealed a new direction. The stories were "true" tales of psychic phenomena and horror. The first story, illustrated in super-star artist Jack Kirby's usual dynamic style, deals with a psychic who works with the police. The second, scripted by Mike Friedrich and drawn by Jose Delbo, is an intriguing tale of a woman, saddled with an ill, boorish husband, who is courted by a wealthy gentleman. The question is: what should she do about the inconvenient husband? It was allegedly based on the diary the woman left behind. Future issues dropped the "true story" business and presented bizarre horror-fantasy tales introduced and narrated by an unnamed hostess. Denny O'Neill took over as editor and made the comic more like DC's other horror titles, adding silly dark humor and flippant answers on the letters page; the hostess became more like Cain and Abel. O'Neill had planned to run a number of adaptations of classic macabre stories but only one materialized: an adaptation of Nathaniel Hawthorne's "Feathertop," in which a witch brings a scarecrow to life and sends him out to romance a wealthy man's daughter. But when he catches sight of his true self in a mirror... (*FTDM* 15).

There were still a few memorable stories in the series: A man encounters a giant spider and a beautiful woman and discovers the surprising (if rather improbable) relationship between the two (*FTDM* 7). An ugly and nasty woman who wants to be beautiful helps a witch doctor wipe out a rival tribe, then in return is transformed into a beauty—but only by the standards of the natives. When the transformation is complete her face looks just like a shrunken head, complete with thread though her lips so she can't speak, perched pitifully, like a large onion, atop her normal shoulders (*FTDM* 9). "The Man Who Waxed and Waned" is a gruesomely amusing tale of a hit man on the run who meets his match in an old witch who makes wax effigies of people (*FTDM* 13). The fifteenth issue was the final one.

Debuting at the same time as *Dark Mansion* was a similar title, *The Sinister House of Secret Love*. "The Curse of the MacIntyres" in the first issue is a weird mish mash of curses, deformities, a deranged giantess, a nasty dwarf, a search for a secret formula and the usual beautiful heroine in a big old house with a handsome man and an assortment of strange people. "To Wed the Devil" in *SHSL* 2 has an assertive but unlikable heroine who discovers she must renounce her fiance and marry a baron who can save her father's bank from going under. The story was no great shakes but it was well-scripted by Len Wein and beautifully illustrated by Tony DeZuniga. "Bride of the Falcon" in *SHSL* 3 by Frank Robbins is a bizarre tale of a deaf woman who travels to Greece to answer a personal ad from a handsome man with wicked scars and a paralyzed "mother"; Alex Toth and Frank Giacoia did the art. "Kiss of the Serpent" in *SHSL* 4 takes place in India where a young governess is bedeviled by her handsome employer's nasty twin and a curse involving a cobra.

Like *Dark Mansion*, *Sinister House* underwent a name change with its fifth issue to *Secrets of Sinister House*, similarly downplaying the love stuff, although there was still some romance on the inside pages. "Death at Castle Dunbar" by Lynn Marron and Michael Fleisher (with art by Mike Sekowsky and Dick Giordano) is an excellent and suspenseful full-on Gothic tale about a woman investigating her sister's disappearance in a Scottish castle where she is torn between the warm, welcoming Laird who'd been the woman's husband and his much less friendly brother. The story is a riot of ghosts in wedding gowns, secret passageways, heaving bosoms, old crones with secret knowledge, mysterious locked rooms, and handsome guys with testy dispositions. The format completely changed with the sixth issue, which has an ugly witch named Eve as a cackling, unfunny hostess and a variety of macabre short stories which often had a lighter tone to them.

For instance, the zany "Young Man Who Cried Werewolf" features a young man who tells police that his date has been bitten by a werewolf-vampire and now is one herself, leading one cop to contact a specialist to protect him from his possibly bitten partner (*SSH* 8). M. Fabe's "Paying with Fire" presents a young boy who is bullied by his building's super and pretty much treated miserably by his parents and other adults until he gets a pet lizard with amazing abilities (*SSH* 8). In Shelley Mayer's "Rub a Witch the Wrong Way" a woman complains about the odor coming from an upstairs neighbor's apartment, but is unaware the woman is a witch. The witch casts a spell that has the complainant reliving the same dreadful day over and over again. Although it is a light, unremarkable story, its creepiness comes from the notion of someone utterly controlling your life and future without your even being aware of it (*SSH* 9). "Bedlam" is an ironic tale of a woman who chooses a simple-minded ox-like man from the famous seventeenth century asylum to help her hunt for her murdered husband's treasure (*SSH* 11). The otherwise mediocre "Deadly Muffins" is enlivened by the appearance of rats the size of elephants on an isolated island (*SSH* 13).

SSH 15 has two especially notable stories, however. In "The Claws of the Harpy" (Fleischer/Carly/Sparling) a mousy man finds himself advancing in his career when his rivals meet their deaths at the claws of a huge bird of prey, that just happens to be a pet of his wife's. But she seems *surprised* that her bird might be responsible ... the gruesomely macabre wind-up shows that birds can make their nests in the strangest of objects. In John Albano's "Mr. Reilly, the Derelict," Reilly is an aging ex-fireman who was disfigured saving somebody's life, and hasn't been able to work or get a job—and is shunned by people—because of his ghastly appearance. When he develops the temporary ability to make his most fervent wish come true, he gives up the chance to look normal in order save the life of a small boy about to plunge to his death at that self-same moment. Full of abject despair over the missed opportunity that might have changed his whole life, Reilly returns to his room in the home of his son and unsympathetic daughter-in-law. "He's got a roof over his head," she says, "and us to look after him—what more could an old derelict like him wish for?" With evocative art by Jess Jodloman, this was the type of sensitive and affecting story that you rarely found anymore in mainstream horror comics. Murray Boltinoff took over as editor with issue sixteen and did away with Eve and the silly tone, but at least half the stories were old reprints. *SHS* 18 was the final issue.

"If you don't believe in ... GHOSTS, we challenge you to read true tales of the weird and supernatural" was emblazoned across the top of DC's new horror title. *Ghosts* hit the newsstands in 1971. The lead tale of the first issue, "Death's Bridegroom," written by Geoff Brown and drawn by Jim Aparo, concerns a gigolo, Ron, who romances a wealthy woman, Sharon, who was left at the altar years ago (à la Dickens' Miss Haversham) and gets her to agree to marry him. His friend Cy thinks something strange is going on but Ron is too greedy to listen. On the day of the wedding the guests arrive in cars from an earlier era, and attack Cy when he tries to stop Ron from going inside the mansion. Cy goes to get the police, but when they return all they find is a crumbling and empty old mansion, no Sharon, no guests—and no Ron. In subsequent issues most of the stories weren't even that good, although there was some improvement with the eighth issue: "The Cadaver in the Clock" concerns an old woman whose mummified remains are placed inside a grandfather's clock and whose spirit comes forth periodically when her dying wishes aren't met; and "To Kill a Tyrant" posited the theory that Joseph Stalin was killed by the evil subconscious stare of a loyal servant who, blind in childhood, had been the recipient of the dead Rasputin's eyes.

The twelfth issue of *Ghosts* added some EC flavor in its tales of a miserable landowner who chains prisoners up until they die of starvation, and whose ghosts claim the life of his ancestor, and especially a story in which a young man with a hateful, always-complaining, and persnickety employer kills him and puts a perpetual motion machine, constantly ticking the time away, inside his chest; this story doesn't even have a ghost, although it is suggested that the murderer dies via supernatural means when a large clock falls on top of him. The lead story has to do with mummies that come to life, and an archeologist who runs one of them through with his sword, only to discover that the same fate has overtaken his wife, who has somehow been wrapped in mummy dressings as well. "Have Tomb, Will Travel" in the following issue concerns a gangster who puts his latest victim into a car in a junk yard and laughs as the vehicle and the body inside are squashed to nothing. In a development that mirrors more than one EC horror story, the remains of the car (and victim) become part of a new automobile that the killer, naturally, winds up driving, with predictable results.

As the series progressed, it got harder to accept the comic's not very serious claim that the stories were "true," although they sometimes incorporated real-life events. "The Dark Dream of Death" (*Ghosts* 14) has a series of disparate individuals enduring disturbing dreams in which children are trapped and desperately crying out for help. It turns out these are psychic forecastings of an actual tragedy that occurred in Aberfan Wales in 1966 when a flood of coal sludge slammed into the village and destroyed the school and half of the children attending classes at the time. One could argue that using such a horrible event, especially one in which so many very young children were crushed or suffocated, as mediocre comic book fodder, is of questionable taste.

"The Hell Beast of Berkeley Square" (*Ghosts* 10) deals with a mysterious, terrifying creature that haunts one particular bedroom in an old British house and whose appearance literally frightens stout men to death. "The Bride Wore a Shroud" (14) concerns a cursed wedding dress that brings disaster to any woman who wears it on her wedding day. "Death Weaves a Web" (14) presents a nasty uncle of a young boy who collects spiders; when he steps on a black widow he imagines it growing to giant-size and entrapping him as he dies slowly of a bite from the arachnid's *ghost*. "The Ghost in the Devil's Chair" (21) presents an adventurer who hopes to make money off of a mystical place where Satan-worshipers used to gather to pay homage to "the mighty one," but who winds up in an electric chair instead. "The Winged Spectre" (80) concerns a man whose testimony sends a murderer to his grave, and is bedeviled by a moth that contains the dead man's vengeful spirit. In "Phantoms of the Deep" (82), a shark attacks the man who hunted it, not realizing that he is the ghost of the man he bit in half, and that it, the shark itself, is also a ghost after dying at the man's spear.

Ghosts 95 reintroduced the character of Dr. Terry Thirteen, a disbeliever in the spirit world who has given up ghost-breaking to write a book and go on the talk show and lecture circuit. He is tempted out of "retirement" to investigate a supposedly haunted theater in Rutland, Vermont, where an alleged ghost has already caused the death of one stagehand. Thirteen reveals that the true culprit is an actress who wanted to be let out of her contract in the worst way. At the end of the story, however, Thirteen learns that the person who approached him at the opening has the same name and appearance of the long-dead actor who was supposed to be haunting the theater.

Dr. Thirteen met the ghostly super-being The Spectre (also known as Lt. Corrigan of the police department) in *Ghosts* 97 when he and several others are held hostage by terrorists. The Spectre uses his supernatural powers to destroy the gun men instead of simply capturing them, infuriating Thirteen, who vows to track him down to not only expose his hocus pocus—as he also did with the Phantom Stranger years before—but bring him to justice. In the next issue Thirteen discovers that his father died not in an accident as he'd always believed, but due to the machinations of his crooked business partner; the Spectre shows up to impersonate the ghost of Thirteen senior and send the partner to an early grave sans trial. In *Ghosts* 99 Thirteen not only encounters Spectre during a bank robbery, but is taken by him to the spectral plain as he hovers near death from a bullet wound. Thirteen meets his father in the after-life, but decides even before waking that none of it is real, and vows to return to ghost-breaking with a vengeance. In the next issue he uncovers a plot by a voodoo priestess to blame accidents in a hospital on ghosts and acquires an assistant in the form of "Mad Dog," a former Army medic who works in the hospital. And then Dr. Thirteen was gone, along with editor Jack C. Harris.

The next few issues had a merry-go-round of editors—finally Dave Manak took the reins until the final issue—and a host called Squire Shade was introduced; all you could see of him was his old-fashioned clothing, including a top hat. Robert Kanigher's "Honeymoon in Hell" (*Ghosts* 105) details the comeuppance of a heartless French mercenary, Armand, in the 1700s who seduces and abandons a poor, beautiful woman, Serafina, driving her to suicide. When Serafina's brother confronts the soldier on the day he's to marry a wealthy woman, Armand kills him. Then there is an earthquake, during which Armand winds up literally kissing the skeletal corpse of Serafina before the earth opens up and buries them both. The story was distinguished by very effective art by Fred Carrillo, who did some fine work for the series.

Ghosts lasted for over ten years and for 112 issues and it went out on a high note: Stan Timmons' "A Little Knowledge," the last story in the final issue. Detective-Lt. Michael Flynn comes into possession of a list of names with the date, time and manner of their deaths, including his own, written next to them. Flynn decides to cash in on the list by contacting many of the names—he tells people he's a psychic and that he knows how they are supposed to die; they can avoid their unpleasant fates if they pay him for the info. He only tells people who have the money to pay up, and accumulates quite a fortune. One day he refuses a poor man's begging entreaties to tell him how his little girl is supposed to die, and a wrath-like cloaked figure appears at his door: Death, who tells Flynn that his finding the list after Death lost it has caused no end of trouble. Death has been unable to bring peace to those dying in agony, and people who were supposed to depart this life have cheated fate. Flynn agrees to give Death the list—he has memorized many of the names and plans to get even more money—on the condition that Death permanently strike him from the list, making Flynn immortal. Death agrees to the terms, and Flynn winds up buried along with his wealth in a deep grave from which there is no escape, eternally unable to die no matter how desperately he might wish to, the fate of many other horror comic protagonists before him.

Other memorable *Ghosts* stories include: "The Haunted Catacombs" (47)—a desperate wife searches Rome's catacombs for her missing husband and uncovers a tragedy; "The Burning Bride" (63)—the ghost of a jilted woman fashions a deadly wedding gown for the rival who stole away her fiance; "The Haunted Gondola" (69)—a man is warned too late not to take photos of a funeral gondola in Venice, and becomes its next occupant; "Harem in Hell" (88)—a man tells his new bride that the ghosts of his three former murdered wives will be residing with them but wife number four learns a trick or two from her husband. "Dread of the Deadly Domestic" (*Ghosts* 96) features a housekeeper who pretends to be the ghost of her dead sister, the head of the household's first wife, whom she believes he murdered, but two real ghosts stop her in her tracks. In "Spectral Witness" (101) a man who murdered his partner is brought to justice by the ghosts of cult members who seek shelter inside a haunted cavern. "Plant You Now, Dig You Later" (105) is the old chestnut of a wanted man feigning death with a potion but has a different and grisly final twist.

In "Fingered" (109) an unhappy, hen-pecked middle-aged man infatuated with a beautiful young women he sees in a bar concocts an ingenious plan to eliminate both his wife and the young lady's boyfriend, but makes a fatal error. "Network of Vengeance" (110) by Bill Kelly is a bizarre tale of a group of men who kill off dozens of television critics, whom they blame for the suicide of the network president, in creative accidents, using their corpses as the first audience for the premiere of *From Beyond the Grave,* in which famous dead people are interviewed; Angel Trinidad, Jr. contributed the attractive artwork. *Ghosts* 70 had some unusual spirits in that they were the ghosts of killer bees that had been sprayed to death by the protagonist after a harrowing battle with them.

Weird War Tales

Weird War Tales, edited by Joe Kubert, debuted in 1971. In 1944 a young soldier gets separated from his platoon in war-torn Europe, and winds up at an old house where a wizened stranger bids him rest as he tells him some eerie stories of the war. Kubert drew the framing pages for each issue—along the same lines as in the first issue—which consists of reprinted war stories with a supernatural slant and some new material. *WWT* 4 presents "Time Warp," in which sailors attempting to get an important new bomb sight are menaced by all manner of prehistoric beasts; it was clearly a homage to "The War That Time Forgot" stories that ran in *Star Spangled War Stories* in the silver age (see chapter nine).

Joe Orlando took over as editor with *Weird War Tales* 8, the first issue to have all-new material written by such comics veterans as Robert Kanigher and Arnold Drake. The latter's "Ace King Just Flew in from Hell" (*WWT* 15) is an excellent tale wherein a small boy who idolizes his grandfather, a war hero, is taken on a flight by his spirit, wherein he can see the horrible deaths of war close up and realizes that combat is nothing to be romanticized or glorified: "The men who fight wars are rarely the war lovers." Eventually Paul Levitz did the actual editing.

Drake certainly lived up to the "weird" aspect of the comic with his "More Dead Than Alive," drawn by Alfredo Alcala, in the following issue. A soldier keeps getting seriously injured, but shows up as good as new after each incident. His arm is supposedly blown off, yet he comes back from the hospital with both arms in good working order—but, strangely, one of them bears a dead soldier's tattoo. When he loses one of his eyes in combat, he miraculously shows up with two perfectly good eyes—only one is brown and one is blue. And so on. A mysterious lady doctor is keeping him alive with spare body parts, but after his latest misadventure his lungs are damaged and the woman doesn't have a spare set. The soldier attacks her in a rage, paralyzing her, and forcing her associate to shoot the soldier dead. At the end of the story we see the utterly bizarre spectacle of the woman doctor's head transplanted on the dead soldier's burly body, with her healthy lungs now inside his hairy chest!

Weird War Tales concentrated, like most war comics, on World War II, but there were also tales of Vietnam, alien invasions, the Vikings, the Civil War, World War I, the Seminole wars, prehistoric man, and every type of battle imaginable. There were supernatural ghost stories and science fiction tales. Many of these were inventory stories from the war and horror boom that had been gathering dust for years. There was a series called "Day After Doomsday" which featured ironic vignettes of people left alive after an apocalypse: a man goes into a bank, finds millions of dollars, and realizes there's absolutely nothing to spend it on, and so on. These shorts generally weren't worth the paper they were printed on. A couple of unpublished back-ups from Jack Kirby's *Kamandi* entitled "Tales of the Great Disaster" also wound up in *Weird*. Although he was never as intrusive as other horror hosts, each issue was introduced by Death, depicted as a skeletal man wearing different military outfits.

Occasionally the comic published full-length stories, such as George Kashdan's "Isle of Forgotten Warriors" (*WWT* 28) in which U.S. and Japanese forces battle for supremacy on a South Seas island, only to discover that the natives have the magical capacity to shrink people, and they all wind up tiny captives on an island no bigger than a small sand bar. "The Dead Draftees of Regiment Six" (*WWT* 41) looks at the civil war draft riots of 1863, in which innocent blacks and abolitionists were hanged, and which were started by draft laws which primarily affected those too poor to pay their way out of the Army or hire a substitute to take their place. In this story, written by Michael Fleisher and Russell Carley and with art by (Jose) Garcia Lopez, the riots are begun by the avenging spirits of drafted soldiers in an ill-fated regiment foolishly sent against, and cut down by, superior rebel forces.

Len Wein took over as editor with issue ninety-three in 1980 and introduced the "Creature Commandos" by J. M. DeMatteis. A startling new Army project labeled "M" for monster is unveiled on a midwestern base in 1942. The subjects include 4-F Warren Griffith, a farm boy afflicted with a type of lycanthropy in which he imagines he's a wolf, who can now turn into a literal wolf thanks to the work of Army scientists, although he has the unfortunate habit of inadvertently changing back to human at inopportune moments. Then there's Sgt. Vincent Velcro, who has been turned into a vampire via fluid from vampire bats, and a marine named "Lucky" Taylor who is put back together as a kind of mute and sensitive Frankenstein's monster after stepping on a mine. Griffith was as anxious to be changed as he was to serve his country, Velcro faced jail for attacking a superior officer so complied with the scientists, but Taylor simply woke up in an operating room to discover that the same men who'd saved his life had turned him into a monstrosity—and they weren't Nazis!

Meeting these grotesque misfits, under the command of gruff, tough Lt. Shrieve, for the first time, an appalled general spits: "They are a terrible, reprehensible assortment of human dregs—and I hope I never set eyes on them again!" However, the same general adds that he thinks they may make one hell of a secret weapon and wants them sicked against the Nazis as soon as possible. In their first adventure they destroy a stronghold where the Germans are making androids with which they hope to replace Allied leaders.

The series could have been schlocky and idiotic but creator J.M. DeMatteis turned in scripts that focused as much on the humanity of the characters as on their monstrousness. In *Weird War Tales* 97 the Creature Commandos return to rescue a French lady doctor from her Nazi captors, only she turns out to be a Nazi impersonator meant to lead them into a trap. They face an impersonator of Hitler in *WWT* 102 as part of a cruel plan to use innocent, brainwashed and drugged schoolchildren as unstoppable soldiers with baby faces, then take care of a nest of Nazi sympathizers with headquarters in a bucolic American town (105). In 108 they invade a concentration camp and allow themselves to be captured so they can *kill* the same lady doctor from *WWT* 97 before she can create a incredibly deadly nerve gas (the Nazis have threatened her family), an act which leads Taylor to attempt suicide. (However, it is never explained why they couldn't have broken the woman out instead of killing her.)

Robert Kanigher took over the series with a two-parter in *Weird War Tales* 109–110, in which the boys must blow up a damn in order to wipe out murderous panzer divisions. His scripting was taut and the characterizations good (if handled with less subtlety), but unfortunately, he made the mistake of introducing a ludicrous female member of the group, Dr. Medusa. During the mission Lt. Shrieve's face is so badly banged up that he requires plastic surgery, the operation done by a beautiful lady doctor, Myrna Rhodes. The commandos are sort of hoping that the obnoxious man, who has taunted them continuously, will get a face to match theirs, but when the bandages come off he's as good as new. Angered, they rampage through the hospital, inadvertently unleashing fumes from experimental chemicals, which affects the doctor, inexplicably giving her ... a head full of snakes like a Medusa! Aside from her strange appearance, Dr. Medusa has no special powers and can't turn people into stone, she just looks weird and can fire a gun; the snakes don't do much, either, although eventually they did bite people's faces. There is no internal logic to chemicals giving a woman a scalp full of living snakes.

Eventually the Creature Commandos took over the covers as well as the magazine itself. Lt. Shrieve was made especially hateful, supposedly as a cover up for his real feelings, but this was carried too far, making it a wonder that none of the commandos ever killed him, until he finally shows some emotion when he wrongly believes that Lucky has been killed. The group go to Lourdes hoping to be cured, but wind up battling Nazis instead, then rescue another lady scientist who has constructed a time machine. Shunned and feared even by people whose lives they fight for, the disheartened bunch volunteer to be the first to test the machine, hoping to find a world where they can be accepted. Instead they wind up on a post-nuclear Earth where (borrowing an idea from an old *Twilight Zone* episode) everyone is beautiful and looks exactly alike but have also grown into giants. Fascism proves to be alive and well, however, when these future people decide to put the commandos to death because they are "different" (*WWT* 119). They escape for one last adventure.

Creature Commandos is an entertaining series, but it would probably have had more resonance had DeMatteis remained as scripter. Kanigher's silver age sensibility (he was the creator of Metal Men, among others) gave the strip more of a silly streak than it needed. However, the art could rarely be faulted. Dan Spiegle did some fine work for the series, as did Fred Carrillo, who turned in an especially splendid art job for a full-length Commandos story in *Weird War Tales* 115.

Wein's second innovation for *Weird War Tales* was to present new installments of "The War That Time Forgot," as noted a series combining soldiers and dinosaurs that originally appeared in *Star-Spangled War Stories* in the silver age. The first of these, "The Eye of Hell" (*WWT* 94), deposits several Army men in 1943 on a Pacific atoll where they try to rescue a beautiful female about to be sacrificed to a hungry tyrannosaurus rex in a lost prehistoric society. The simple plot was bolstered by Robert Kanigher's harrowing script and Franc Reyes adept illustrations. There were five more segments. *WWT* 99 had soldiers rescuing downed fliers while dealing with pterodactyls. In *WWT* 100 the Creature Commandos enter the War That Time Forgot by engaging not only with monsters but with Japanese forces that hope to employ the dinosaurs as weapons. In *WWT* 103 an allosaurus picks up a sub carrying many injured men and nurses and carries it to the top of an active volcano, but when the volcano blows its top the dinosaur carries the sub back to the sea where the beast dies from an assault by a flock of pterodactyls. Three frogmen, one of whom keeps having visions of beautiful women, wind up in a cavern full of prehistoric beasts in *WWT* 106. The strange story in *WWT* 109 presents a World War II Circe-type who is able to turn soldiers into dinosaurs, although it is not suggested that this is how all those prehistoric beasts survived into modern times. The final installment of "The War That Time Forgot" in *WWT* 120, features a female King Kong–type and dinosaurs getting in the way as a rescue is attempted of a platoon of marines trapped in a cave. Fred Carillo's artwork made it one of the best drawn of the G.I. vs. dinosaur segments. Other artists for the series included Dave Cockrum, Bob Hall, and Joe Staton, but even with smooth inks by Jerry Ordway the latter two pencillers were especially not right for the strip.

Mike W. Barr became editor with issue 104 and E. Nelson Bridwell edited the last few issues of the series. In the one hundred twenty-fourth and final issue of the comic a tongue-in-cheek one-page story showed the Creature Commandos being shot in a missile toward Germany, their very last mission, only the missile goes awry and takes off into outer space. *Weird War Tales* had a more than respectable run—its success enjoined *G. I. Combat* to run "Bizarre Battle Stories"—and was the more unusual of the horror-type comics of the Bronze age. Some other notable stories included: "Death Camp" (*WWT* 72)—a compassionate German soldier assigned to guard duty in a concentration camp with a particularly evil commandant bonds with an old Jewish man who comes to love him; "Through the Past Darkly" (94)—a man who is believed to have been a Nazi is sent back to the death camp as a Jew in a reenactment that tragically backfires; "Dog Tag Lottery" (102)—a young soldier who can foretell which of his buddies will meet the grim reaper next makes a tragic sacrifice for a friend; "Stolen Skin" (105)—a commandant of a concentration camp tries to escape retribution by putting his mind in the body of an old Jewish man, but winds up the victim of Nazis. The comic also had its share of monster stories: *WWT* 68 featured a Godzilla-like monster named "Rotirra" sent against U.S. Forces by the Japanese.

Weird Mystery Tales

Weird Mystery Tales, with a be-cloaked, skeleton-like figure named Destiny as host, debuted in 1972. The first issue has an odd, rambling lead story by writer/artist Jack Kirby about an apparition that warns people of future events (originally intended for the magazine *Spirit World*), and a creditable second story, "The Brothers Beaumont," about two men—Robert and Roberto—who are unrelated, but who look alike. Whatever happens to Roberto, who becomes a crook, affects the more solid citizen Robert; if Roberto has a bad fall, Robert gets a bum leg despite the lack of a break. Roberto is not all bad and once the two realize the bizarre co-reality of their existence, he is concerned that the innocent Robert will die when he, Roberto, is fried in the electric chair for murder. Things work out for Robert, who doesn't die when Roberto does, although as a final twist some of Roberto's "bad boy" consciousness makes its way into Robert's head.

Another story by Jack Kirby intended for *Spirit World* was the lead story in *WMT* 3: "The Burners" is an excellent and creepy look at horrifying cases of so-called "spontaneous combustion" (not referred to as such in the story, however) with the theory that the victims, who burn to ashes in minutes when nothing else is ever touched, are lonely, old, depressed people who somehow, subconsciously, will themselves to die. The splash panel, showing a woman in a chair, alive and well one minute and just ashes (with smoke coming out of her empty shoes) is as chilling as it is somewhat comical.

Joe Orlando took over as editor with the fourth issue. Unfortunately, he didn't recognize the lead story, Jack Oleck's "The Devil to Pay," as an old chest nut about a group of monks keeping the Devil a prisoner in their monastery. The following issue has decent stories, however, such as Sheldon Mayer's "Will You Listen?" about the spirit of an executed strangler who takes over people's bodies, and Jack Oleck's "Legacy of the Damned," in which a woman and her lover try to kill off the husband, who's trying to raise a demon—but only after they get him to change his will.

Eventually the witch Eve shared hosting duties with Destiny but the comic remained a mixed bag. Michael Fleischer's "The Sunken Pearls of Captain 'Hatch'" (10) is a not-bad story about a search for a fortune in jewels in the wreck of an old sailor's ship, but the main selling point is Jess Jodloman's stylish and adept artwork. There was Jack Oleck's EC derivative "Island of the Damned" (11), in which a beautiful gypsy lady pretends to love a deformed millionaire, Count Phillipe, who has turned his island home into a retreat for those who are shunned due to their deformities. The gypsy and her lover think they have killed the count, but it turns out he has two heads—he disguised the second head as a hump— only one of which is dead while the other lives for revenge. A character having two heads as a shock ending was quite popular during the golden age. John Russell's short story "The Price of the Head," in which a native keeps a white man alive through a long ocean voyage only because he can get good money for his head, was somewhat awkwardly adapted by E. Nelson Bridwell for *Weird Mystery Tales* 14; as noted the plot had been borrowed for more than one golden age horror tale.

Tex Blasidell took over as editor and there was decided improvement in the fifteenth issue. In Michael Fleischer's "Doom on Vampire Mountain," a mousy but loving husband sacrifices his life to keep a horde of vampires, who have taken the form of large, voracious bats, away from his greedy wife, who hopes to find money in the mansion where the bloodsuckers have taken residence. The story was okay, but again its main interest was Jess Jodloman's beautifully crafted artwork, especially a half-page panel depicting a giant bat knocking the husband off a cliff's edge as it gorges itself on blood from his neck. The second story, Paul Levitz's "Drive-In Death" is an amusing tale of a husband, who is driven mad by his wife's insistence on eating at the same hamburger joint every night until he gives in and gets her a cook. He poisons the wife but winds up out-witting himself and going to prison where he gets—what else?—hamburger for dinner. The final story, David Michelinie's "Blood Moon," about an oil driller who encounters a family of Native American werewolves, also benefited from excellent art by Rubeny.

In David Michelinie's "The Curse of the Fool Moon" (16) a homely and lonely high school student uses a spell to turn into a werewolf in order to scare his tormentors, but he's unable to control his blood lust enough to keep from slaughtering them, and is unable to reverse the awful curse when his harridan mother throws out the book of spells. Frank Robbins' artwork, while far from conventionally pretty, is perfect for this story, helping to create a very sympathetic monster. Paul Levitz's "The Return of the Serpent" (18) deals with a sea captain, told his ship will be turned into a dry-docked casino, who calls upon an ancient serpent-god to help him, but winds up feeding almost everyone on board to the creature's hungry maw. The cover for the issue rather graphically depicted this huge beast stuffing screaming people into its mouth and clutching them in its claws. Robert Kanigher's "Baker's Dozen" (20), very well drawn by Fred Carrillo, is more of a suspense story than a horror tale but it is an effective enough piece about a jolly fat baker who stuffs counterfeit money in his rolls and takes deadly action against the associates who short-change him.,

Weird Mystery Tales lasted 24 issues and featured the work of such talented artists as Alfredo Alcala, E. R. Cruz, Ruben Yandoc, and Abe Ocampo. Some of its covers were memorable as well, especially *WMT* 23, which has a man dangling from the straw of a witch's broom as she flies across the night sky, and *WMT* 17, which depicts an alligator clad in torn human clothing walking down a staircase. *WMT* 12 shows an old woman protesting to a concerned friend that she isn't alone in the background, while the molding, cobweb-covered corpse of her husband reposes in the foreground. The cover of *WMT* 22 depicts a man, taking the place of the mechanical rabbit, being chased by particularly ravenous dogs at a dog track.

Secrets of Haunted House, Tales of Ghost Castle and *Doorway to Nightmare*

Secrets of Haunted House debuted in 1975. This was hosted by the tiresome quartet of Cain, Abel, Eve and Destiny. The lead story in the first issue, "Dead Heat," concerns two ambulance drivers who bet on how many of their pick-ups on a dangerous stretch of road called "The Twist" will survive, and who get a surprise when they answer a call and discover their own dead and twisted bodies, a familiar premise but still effective. "Pathway to Purgatory" (*SHH* 3) is the torturous tale of a miserable crippled duke who commits fiendish crimes in order to get healthy legs but winds up with something he didn't bargain for. After four issues the comic went on a brief hiatus and was back in 1977, with the hosts being given the opening pages to foolishly bicker and bore most readers. *SHH* 12, edited by Paul Levitz, is notable for the especially gruesome "Yorick's Skull" by Bob Toomey. Tom McKinny is understudy to egotistical and obnoxious actor Roland Squire, who berates him for dropping the prop skull of Yorick used in *Hamlet,* then insists he dress in drag as Ophelia during a rehearsal. When McKinny can take no more insults from Squire, he impulsively beheads him with an ax. Later he boils the head and uses the skull in place of the prop skull he broke, but during the performance Squire's skull hops around as if it's alive, causing McKinney to fall into the orchestra pit. As he falls his head is sliced off by the sharp edge of a music stand, plopping

DC's *Secrets of Haunted House* had a relatively short run compared to other DC horror titles.

down directly in front of Roland Squire's grinning skull. Frank Redondo's art got it across without making it all too nauseating. "Life Sentence" in the same issue, written by Stuart Hopen and Catharine [sic] B. Andrews, also had an EC flavor in its tale of a judge and a professor who conspire to have their elderly brains placed in their infant clones, only to watch in horror as their baby faces grow instantly old and wizened on their newborn bodies.

After the pretty awful double-sized fourteenth issue, *Secrets of Haunted House* went on another hiatus for about a year, returning with Jack C. Harris as editor and shrouded Destiny as the main host, sometimes appearing in stories known as "Tales of Destiny." *SHH* 31 presented the first installment of a regular series starring the blind and apparently psychic sleuth "Mr. E," who was created by Bob Rozakis, with art by Dan Spiegle. The first story also introduced the young Irish immigrant, Kelly O'Toole, who goes to work as housekeeper for Judge Kobold, the "twice-cursed man," who turns out to not only be a vampire responsible for several murders but a wolfman as well, and a recurring antagonist for Mr. E. Kelly can't figure out how Mr. E's clients find him when she can never uncover the advertisements for his services that they always refer to. Mr. E took on a lady Frankenstein, a malevolent leprechaun, the witch-hounds of Salem, and solved the secret of a curse where all the water in town turned to blood. His best adventure was in *SHH* 38 in which Kobold returned as one of four men in a sinister consortium, and Speigel's artwork was better than ever. In the long run, Mr. E was too similar to the Phantom Stranger and other mystic, enigmatic heroes.

Still, he was the best thing about the comic. There were only a few other passably interesting stories. George Kashdan's "To Bug You to Death" (*SHH* 19) undoubtedly gave more than a few viewers the willies in its tale of a strange bug that flies up a man's nose while he's camping and eats away part of his brain, although it was undoubtedly inspired by/borrowed from a similar story that appeared on *Rod Serling's Night Gallery* four years before. Kashdan's "Die from Laughter" (30) presents a clown who is cursed so that his face paint will never come off and who can only die at the hands of another man. This man winds up tattooed with the same face paint after his murder of the clown, as do the members of a crowd who unwittingly cause the second man's death. When cartoonist Dave Manak took over as editor Destiny was removed along with Mr. E and a few pages were given over to the idiotic antics of chubby horror host Abel. The comic mostly became a dumping ground for amateurish, unoriginal stories written and drawn by people who had little flair for the horror genre; indeed the bad fantasy, sci fi and comic tales crowded out the horror. The forty-sixth issue was the final one.

Tales of Ghost Castle debuted in 1975 and lasted for three issues. Stories were narrated by geeky Lucien, the librarian of the musty archives of the castle. At first there seemed to be an attempt to create some kind of EC flavor to the comic. Paul Levitz's "A Child's Garden of Graves," the lead story in the first issue, concerns an adopted child who murders her parents' two natural children, and is somewhat at odds with the humorous opening pages with Lucien. In David Michelinie's "The Mushroom Man," a ne'er-do-well nephew murders his uncle and buries him in the older man's mushroom bed. When the cook inadvertently serves him some sauteed mushrooms, he gets terrible stomach pains. The next morning she finds him dead in his bed, large mushrooms and other fungi grossly sprouting from his corpse. "Snake Eyes," in the second issue, is a bizarre tale of a woman who keeps surreptitiously tormenting and poking at the snakes she hates. When one of them escapes and bites her, she desperately chugs an experimental toxin—and turns into a snake, whereupon she is thrown into their communal cage where they are waiting to have their way with her. The best story in the very short-lived series is Jack Olek's "The Demon's Here to Stay" in the final issue, which concerns a heartbroken couple who come to the conclusion that their half-witted but good-natured son has been possessed by a deadly demonic force. They are importuned to turn him in to the police, and he is burnt at the stake as a witch—only for his parents to discover as they themselves lay dying that it was not their son but his dog who was the demon.

Doorway to Nightmare debuted in 1978 and lasted five issues. The series centers around a mysterious woman named Madame Xanadu—possibly the only really attractive female host in a horror comic—who runs a fortune-telling emporium in a back street of New York's East Village. The first issue concerns an actress, Cindy, who falls for a playwright, David, only to have him fall under the spell of a set designer named Erika. Erika is dying and has turned to the supernatural for help, and with David's permission is siphoning off some of his life energy to save herself; when she's through she assures David he will be fine. Only it turns out that Erika is thousands of years old and has no intention of leaving David any drop of the energy she requires. Cindy and Madame Xanudu interfere in Erika's ritual, David is saved, and Erika reverts to an ancient crone and collapses into sludge. The mediocre story was written by David Michelinie and drawn by Val Mayerick. There was no explanation as to how Cindy knew of Xanudu's existence, nor why she would come to her with her tale of the lovelorn, as she had no knowledge of the supernatural aspects of the case until after speaking to the madame.

Subsequent issues dealt with a woman scientist who opens a dimensional doorway to Hell and is possessed by a demon; a young Chinese-American woman who is possessed by an ancient princess after falling in love with a NYC detective; and another woman who fights to save the soul of her boyfriend, a reluctant gang member taken over by an evil force. Although *Doorway to Nightmare* wasn't really a Gothic or romance-horror comic there was nevertheless a romantic element to every story. Another difference is that the stories in every issue are full-length. Arguably the best tale is "Blood Red Tear" (*DTN* 3) a decided love story between a human female and a mysterious if romantic man who turns out to be a vampire and who makes a final sacrifice for love. This was written by Bill Kunkle and Roger McKenzie and drawn by Ric Estrada and Romeo Taghal.

When *The Unexpected* became a large-size dollar comic, *Doorway to Nightmare* was incorporated as one of the back-up features. These were generally forgettable, although *Unexpected* 194 had an interesting tale of a man who hates and hunts werewolves because one supposedly killed the woman he loved, and whose current girlfriend is dismayed by his violent actions and his obsession with his dead lover. Madame Xanudu enters and exits the action in her usual strange way, and the story is nearly undone by awkward scripting. This is not true of the following issue's tale, "Deadly Homecoming," by Dennis O'Neil and artist Johnny Craig (who did much work for EC comics back in the day). Soldier Johnny is home from Vietnam with his buddy Pete, but his girlfriend Vanessa is horrified to realize that every time an angry Johnny wishes someone would kill themselves, including her own father, his victims comply in gruesome ways. But it all has to do with a demon that entered Pete after he murdered a Vietnamese woman who resisted his advances; now Johnny is under Pete's control. Madame Xanadu advises Vanessa and gives her an amulet that reveals the truth, which eventually forces Pete to commit suicide himself with a grenade. "He wasn't a bad guy," says a now-normal Johnny, who obviously has a high boiling point.

Fifteen

Phantom Strangers and Swamp Things

The Phantom Stranger

In 1969 at the very end of the silver age DC decided to revive two characters from the 1950s, The Phantom Stranger, and Dr. Thirteen, the Ghost Breaker. They were both re-introduced in *Showcase* 80 (1969), which consisted mostly of reprint material with new framing pages that turned the two heroes into uneasy allies. Dr. Thirteen is still convinced that every weird occurrence has a natural explanation and doesn't believe the Stranger is the ghost or supernatural being that he pretends to be. This was carried over to *Phantom Stranger* 1 (second volume), which also consisted primarily of reprints. A new story had both men investigating a series of explosions in Chinatown heralded by the sight of a shadowy dragon. Dr. Thirteen proved that there was a human agent involved and vowed to expose the Stranger as a hoax any way he could.

In *Phantom Stranger* 2 the framing story has to do with a man who supposedly has nine lives and keeps cheating death. Both the Stranger and Thirteen narrate reprint tales from *Phantom Stranger* vol. 1 and *Star Spangled Comics*. In the new story the Stranger exhibits unusual sensitivity when he tells a little boy, who's apparently just seen his father die in a fiery car explosion, "they won't find more of the driver than a few charred bones." Dr. 13 proves that the whole thing is a hoax done with hypnotism and trickery, but the little boy still wonders about the Stranger and how he can disappear so fast (although Batman could do the same thing). *PS* 3 contained another reconstructed tale combining reprint material with new pages as Dr. Thirteen and the Stranger re-investigate a haunted amusement park that first appeared in the Stranger's 1952 series.

With the fourth issue, *Phantom Stranger* began presenting all-new stories that shifted more firmly into the supernatural. A beautiful and evil witch or she-demon named Tala is introduced, but Dr. Thirteen remains convinced that both she and the Stranger are faking their mystical powers, and he is more determined than ever to prove his unlikely colleague a phony. There was the unfortunate addition of a foursome of painfully hip teens with weird names. At least the fourth issue has some fine art by Neal Adams. Mike Sekowsky then took over both the art and scripting and while the former is fine, the stories are silly and unmemorable. The fifth issue depicts a battle between the Stranger and Tala for the soul of a dead Lothario who treated his women like dirt. The sixth issue has the Stranger and Thirteen narrating stories again, but these are all-new material by Sekowsky and Robert Kanigher, not reprints.

The formula was for the two men to investigate strange new occurrences while one or the other—or both—would narrate (new) tales from the past that related to the current situation. But there was also experimentation with full-length tales with no flashbacks, as well as two separate stories for the Stranger and Thirteen. Bill Draut did some art for the series, followed by Jim Aparo. Denny O'Neill also worked on scripts.

In *Phantom Stranger* 8 it seemed that Dr. Thirteen would have to admit to the reality of weird, supernatural beings when he and his wife come across some humungous Arctic giants who have arisen from their icy tomb. The Phantom Stranger convinces the giants that they have no place in the modern world, but simply stands by as they take Maria Thirteen off to be entombed by them as per their law. Fortunately, it turns out that Tala has masqueraded as Maria to play a joke on the giants. Dr. Thirteen is convinced the whole thing is a delusion, but Maria is not so sure. One wonders if secretly the Stranger had been anticipating the anguish experienced by his hostile, disbelieving rival had Maria really been gone for good. The Arctic giants returned in *PS* 19 in one of the best stories of the series.

There was some hoopla on the letters page when 18-year-old Gerry Conway was installed as scripter beginning with the tenth issue. Conway created a supernatural adversary for the Stranger named Tannarak. In the next issue, set against tensions in the mid-east, Tannarak is the main villain, although there are also evil aliens working behind the scenes. Although Conway was capable of some great stories, these were not among them, and his tenure on *The Phantom Stranger* only lasted two issues. Meanwhile, Tannarak returned in *PS* 17 and eventually became an ally of the Stranger's when they developed a common foe.

Although Dr. Thirteen was convinced the Stranger was a phony, the stories continued to paint him as a supernatural being, especially *PS* 14, written by new scripter Len Wein, in which a wealthy man named Broderick Rune has the Stranger's heart transplanted into his own dying body. But he is haunted by the Stranger wherever he goes—in his mirror, on the grounds of his estate, even when he tries to escape the visions by going overseas, the Stranger continually intoning that he wants back what belongs to him. At the end of the story they find Rune's body lying on the beach—without a heart. It is clear that the Stranger, while he may or may not have been human, has undefined extra-special powers and is some kind of extraordinary creature.

Under Len Wein's tutelage the Stranger becomes a globe-hopping righter of wrongs who pops in and out of dangerous situations, saving lives, suddenly appearing and disappearing without rhyme or reason. For a time his chief adversaries became a group of mystic assassins known as the Dark Circle. He stops the murder of an infant destined to be the New Lama (*PS* 20) and prevents the assassination of a mid-eastern spiritual leader at the hands of a criminal who is resurrected after having a date with an electric chair (21). Although Tannarak was originally employed by the circle, he teams up with the Stranger when the evil group feel he has outlived his usefulness. Another member of the cast is the blind psychic Cassandra Craft, who first appeared in *PS* 17 and later briefly becomes the Stranger's girlfriend. In *PS* 24 the uninteresting villainess Tala returns and turns out to be leader of the Dark Circle, but she and Tannarak are apparently destroyed during a battle. The Stranger lets his blind girlfriend think he has been destroyed, too, apparently because he thinks she'd be better off, or at least safer, without him. Throughout it all, Jim Aparo's art is nearly sublime, beautifully composed, with fluid figures and a style that is elegant and distinct.

Writer Arnold Drake and artist Gerry Taloac became the new creative team beginning with *Phantom Stranger* 27. Their work was not appreciated by the fans, and in truth, it was mediocre. Taloac was temporarily replaced by the more suitable Bill Draut in *PS* 32, which also featured a better than average Drake script in which the Stranger comes to the aid of an old woman accused of being a witch. In the next issue Drake briefly brought his creation Deadman/Boston Brand—a spirit who can inhabit people's bodies and is searching for his murderer—into the fold and set him off on a collision path with the Stranger in an entertaining team-up, with nice art by Mike Grell. Drake introduced a sort of running antagonist for the Stranger in the person of Dr. Zord, who uses chemicals and spells to put powerful people under this thumb. Drake's stories bringing the Stranger into conflict with mobsters were off the mark, and he was replaced by David Michelinie as writer. He contributed an interesting tale in *PS* 36 in which a put-upon secretary gets even with her nasty boss against the Stranger's advice and pays the ultimate penalty. Readers had complained that Drake made the Stranger a mere narrator in his own book, but in this story he only showed up now and then to admonish the protagonist. Michelinie was then replaced by Paul Levitz. In the meantime Taloac's art became much more eye-appealing.

In Paul Levitz's first story, taken from a plot outline by Arnold Drake, the Stranger seems like a pious Mary Worth preaching at people and against sin, and a bit batty besides. In the next issue, the Stranger is more of a man of action, like the Shadow. In *PS* 39–40 there is a three-part story guest-starring Deadman, Cassandra Craft, and the villainous Nathan Seine, who blames the Stranger for his wife's death, with art by Fred Carrillo. The addition of Deadman did not boost sales as hoped, so the magazine was canceled with the forty-first issue. The main trouble with the series is that the Stranger is completely one-dimensional, with no true identity or origin. (Deadman wondered if the Stranger might also be a ghost, simply because he was able to see his disembodied form.) On top of that, *The Phantom Stranger* was simply not a very memorable comic book. The character reappeared time and again, even joining the Justice League at one point, although he was never a typical "super-hero."

Spawn of Frankenstein

Len Wein and others scripted mostly forgettable Dr. Thirteen back-ups in *Phantom Stranger* drawn by Tony DeZuniga. A major, unheralded change occurred for Dr. Thirteen in *PS* 18 in a story by Steve Skeates that betrayed no understanding of the character at all. Thirteen attends a séance, and scoffs at the thought of anyone calling up an actual ghost. Instead what appears in the ether is an honest-to-goodness alien. Instead of trying to prove that the alien is a fake, which Dr. Thirteen would have done, he immediately accepts that it is a *real* alien while poo poohing the notion that the medium called up a ghost! The Dr. Thirteen character that had been established for years would have no more believed in aliens than he would have in spirits. However, Skeates' next story, in which Thirteen uncovers the secret behind the ghostly voice of a dead father accusing his son of murdering him, was more on the mark. And his atypical Thirteen story in *PS* 22 is an excellent study of how a greedy man manipulates his fellow townspeople into hating another fellow, whose only crime is to be a weird loner, simply because he wants to buy his soon-to-be-valuable property.

In *Phantom Stranger* 23 the Dr. Thirteen strip metamorphosed into "(The Spawn of) Frankenstein." In the first installment a man named Victor Adams removes a block of ice from the Arctic and brings it back to his university. Inside is the perfectly preserved Frankenstein monster, whom Victor wants to revive, to the university board's dismay and utter disapproval. An obsessed Victor decides to go ahead with his plans in his own home, but his concerned wife, Rachel, gets in touch with a friend, Dr. Thirteen. Thirteen and Maria show up at Victor's home just as the monster begins to awaken. Something goes wrong with the electrical equipment employed in the resuscitation process, Victor is killed, and Maria put into a coma. Dr. Thirteen mistakenly believes that this is all the monster's fault, although the creature tried to save everyone when the ceiling collapsed, and vows to hunt him down and destroy him. The creative team was Marv Wolfman on scripts and Mike Kaluta on art; the two did a lot of work on Marvel's horror comics as well. The truly scary, cadaverous and hideous monster was much more in the lines of what Mary Shelley described in her novel than what you usually saw in movies.

The Monster steals Victor's corpse and plans to resurrect it so Victor can feel the same pain he did, but he is sidetracked by demons who enter his mind and cause him to battle the Phantom Stranger in a forgettable full-length story in *PS* 26. Steve Skeates took over the scripting with the following issue with Bernard Bailey on art. They contributed a continuing story, with Frankenstein involved with a snake god, that was so poor it sank the series completely; it was discontinued with the 30th issue. Marvel Comics did a much better job with the monster. As for Dr. Thirteen, he returned for a minor back-up in *PS* 34 with his wife out of her coma and no thoughts of vengeance on Frankenstein's monster. He also appeared in a back up story in *Adventure* 428 in which he discovered why a pair of spectacles could induce madness in the wearer. After that he turned up in *Batman* 341–342 where he investigates an alleged haunting of Wayne Manor and stumbles upon the batcave, and again in *Batman* 354 wherein he proves a "ghost" is just a hologram.

Swamp Thing

Two new series derived from the old Heap strip in *Airboy* comics of the golden age—itself derived from Theodore Sturgeon's story "It" (see Chapter Seven)—debuted at the same time in late 1972. Man-Thing appeared in Marvel's *Adventures into Fear*, and *Swamp Thing* had actually started out as one-shot short story in *House of Secrets* 92 the previous year. In *HOS* "Swamp Thing" deals with a scientist named Alex who is murdered via a manufactured explosion by his best friend, Damian, who covets his wife, Linda, whom Damian later marries. Damian had dragged Alex's still living body out into the swamps where, like the Heap decades before, it merges with the vegetation and transforms into a grotesque monster. Alex hangs around the house observing things through the window even as Damian realizes that Linda is slowly growing suspicious. As Damian now tries to murder Linda, the Swamp Thing breaks in and kills him, but his vocal cords have atrophied and he cannot speak to his beloved and goes away.

The story—words by Len Wein and art by Berni Wrightson—wasn't all that memorable (arguably the best story in *HOS* 92 had to do with a man's obsession with what the dying see just before their deaths) but it got a very favorable fan reaction. A year later *Swamp Thing* debuted with the same creative team. Wein and Wrightson worked in the Marvel style instead of the usual DC method. They would discuss the basic storyline, then Wrightson would begin the art chores before the script was written, becoming co-plotter as Jack Kirby was with Stan Lee. Alex and Linda now became the scientific team of Alec and Linda Holland working on a chemical to "create gardens out of deserts." Their bio-restorative research is coveted by governments and other interested parties, and they are assigned a liaison in Lt. Matt Cable and put in a supposedly secure house in the middle of the bayou. When Alec refuses to sell out to representatives of the corpulent Mr. E of the Conclave, a bomb is exploded in his lab. Burning, in anguish, Alec rushes out into the swamp where he merges with moss and mud and other things and emerges the grotesque Swamp Thing. What features you can see of his face are rather skeletal. He can still think clearly but is unable to speak with ease. When Linda is also murdered, ST kills the ones responsible. Completely unaware of the monster's origins, Cable transfers to Interpol and is determined to hunt down Swamp Thing, thinking it also killed the Hollands.

In the second issue ST is kidnapped by an aged madman named Arcane, who uses supernatural means to take on the form of Swamp Thing, even as Alec gets his own human body back. At first Alec is delighted, until he discovers that Arcane only wants to use the Swamp Thing's strong, invulnerable physique to get a terrible vengeance on the villagers far below his castle who shunned him throughout his life. Alec makes the heroic sacrifice of taking back the Swamp Thing's form, and Arcane and his horde of freakish manufactured "un-men" fall to their deaths. In the third issue Cable and Arcane's nubile niece Abigail hook up after a battle with the Patchwork Man, Arcane's brother, but they and the Swamp Thing wind up in the Scottish moors for the absorbing fourth issue. In this the parents of a werewolf deliberately cause plane crashes so they can find a healthy man into which to transfuse their son's blood, making him normal while dooming the other. Unfortunately, there have been no survivors of the crashes until Cable comes along, but Swamp Thing comes to the rescue. A full page dramatic panel of the werewolf confronting his parents is a stunner.

In *ST* 6 the creature winds up in the recreation of a Swiss village in Vermont, where an elderly clockmaker has filled the town with robot duplicates of the deceased, including Alec and Linda Holland. (In the letters column for that issue speculative author Harlan Ellison compared *Swamp Thing* to the likes of Nureyev, Van Gogh, Chaplin and Mark Twain, an almost laughable overstatement if ever there were one, which might have been what he intended.) Swamp Thing at last caught up with "Mr. E"—actually Nathan Ellery—of the Conclave, the man ultimately responsible for his condition and the death of his wife, in *ST* 7, which guest-starred Batman, who was also on the trail of Ellery, who falls to his death at the end. Swamp Thing then fights a demon in the town of Perdition, and befriends an alien whose spaceship has crashed in the same swamp in which he was spawned, before encountering the resurrected Arcane in a new, hideous body along with some of his Un-Men; the diminutive "living brain," who is merely a misshapen head atop a gnarled hand, is the most inspired of these creations.

Nestor Redondo took over the art with the eleventh issue, in which Swamp Thing helps destroy the remnants of an ancient race of giant, man-eating, intelligent worms. Two issues later Swamp Thing is captured by Cable and his associates and finally manages to tell Cable the truth of his identity. Cable, whose life the Swamp Thing has saved on several occasions, arranges for the "monster" he had formerly been hunting to escape. David Michelinie became new scripter with issue 14. During his tenure Michelinie introduced Father Bliss, who put a demon inside Swamp Thing (that resembled another reddish demonic type that battled Marvel's Man-Thing on more than one occasion); a princess who uses the living dead to fight a revolution; and an outcast alien named Solus who adds Swamp Thing to his kidnapped intergalactic menagerie. Michelinie also briefly resurrected Nathan Ellery, who is still determined to take over the world and remained a mediocre opponent. Nestor Redondo turned in some solid art jobs.

Michelinie wrote two memorable installments of the series. *Swamp Thing* 18 takes place in Serenity Village, a "geriatric Disneyland" in which the key to treatment is helping residents find their inner child. In truth the elderly inhabitants, sick of the condescension accorded older people in our society, have turned to casting spells to suck away the energy of younger people in order to regain their own lost youth. "Have you ever tried living in a world where wrinkles are treated like plague?' asks the now-youthful leader of the Seniors. "Where at the magic age of 65 one's worth is turned off like a light switch?" His middle-aged son, who now looks older than his father, later says: "He couldn't understand that the old has to make way for the new, whether in seasons, ideas ... or people."

Michelinie's best issue—and the best of the series—was "The Solomon Plague" in *Swamp Thing* 22. In this our shambling friend almost finds a home amongst the survivors of underground bomb testing, during which radiation leaked out from the caverns to irradiate the inhabitants of a small desert town nearby. They have all mutated into pale apparitions whose faces are somewhat skeletal like Swamp Things; they assume he is just a more extreme mutation. Conflict occurs when some of the understandably bitter residents of the medical bunker want to escape and tell the world about what happened, but they have also developed a deadly illness that could infect and conceivably destroy the world's entire population. The head scientist, who built the bomb, has to shoot his own son in the back to keep him from escaping and spreading the plague.

Gerry Conway alternated with Michelinie as scripter. In an interesting two-part story in *ST* 19–20 it develops that one of Swamp Thing's arms, which was severed back in the third issue and quickly regenerated, has taken on a life of its own and grown into a whole new Swamp Thing. However, this duplicate is fairly mindless and in that way resembles Marvel's Man-Thing. Alec Holland contemplates suicide, but instead winds up in a lengthy battle with his double. When the double is killed, Cable and Abigail assume that Alec is dead and are seen no more in the series.

Swamp Thing 18 had unveiled the series' potential, but even before it was published sales figures necessitated some radical changes to the comic, making it more of a super-hero title. In the final two issues Gerry Conway brought in a new evil group named Colossus (even though some readers wondered whatever happened to the Conclave) and its costumed operatives Sabre and Thrudvang, the earthmaster. It was essential for Colossus' plans to secure Hollands bio-restorative formula, so it was incredibly witless that they would use two such idiotic employees, one of whom was psychotic and the other a nearly mindless simpleton, for such an important task.

In the meantime Swamp Thing hooks up with his hitherto unmentioned brother Edward, also a chemist, who manages to recreate the same situation that brought the Swamp Thing into being and reverts his brother back to normal. The final, twenty-fourth issue brought an entirely new creative team: writer David Anthony Kraft still working from Conway's plot; and artists Ernie Chua and Fred Carrillo. In this a now-normal Alec Holland tries to protect himself and Edward's assistant, Ruth, who's falling for him, from the attack of Thrudvang, who seems to have forgotten that the whole point is not to kill Holland but find out about his formula. It was cheesy super-hero stuff but not without some appeal.

The next issue blurb announced Hawkman as guest-star but this never materialized. The readers never learned what would happen now that Ruth's interest in Alec had aroused his brother's jealousy, or about the strange sensations the supposedly cured Holland kept feeling and what they might signify. Swamp Thing would have several more series with differing concepts in the decades to come, but those questions would never be satisfactorily answered.

The Demon

Jack Kirby's *The Demon* debuted in 1972. Etrigan the Demon is in the employ of Merlin the Magician, hated foe of Morgaine Le Fay. In the final days of Camelot, Merlin casts a spell on the demon that turns him into a human being, then goes into hiding. Centuries pass, and in the modern world we meet Jason Blood, a handsome red-haired demonologist with a white streak in his hair, Etrigan's other half. Le Fay is still alive, aged nearly to the point of mummification, and she still wants to find Merlin so she can use his spell of immortality to make herself young and vital once more. The first two issues detail her efforts in this regard, bring out the demon in Jason Blood, set the two adversaries against each other, and introduce a supporting cast consisting of psychic U.N. delegate Randu Singh; Harry Matthews, who is Jason's best friend; and Glenda Mark, a woman whom Randu has introduced to Jason. (Kirby drew her hairline so high that she often looked as if she were going bald.) When the Demon emerges from Jason it is the former who is in control, and the Demon has a penchant for running amok even as he manages to get the job done. The demon can be called or submerged with the use of a certain spell. Etrigan's look—red eyes, horns, scaly ears, yellow skin—was influenced by a mask that Hal Fosters' Prince Valiant wore before going into battle in one of his adventures.

Demon 3 features the menace of a cult of "reincarnators," who worship an idol in the shape of an eye and can cause anyone to suddenly revert to a past life, using them to kill off their enemies. *Demon* 4–5 brought Merlin, the Demon's master, into the picture, and pits the magician and Etrigan against the Iron Duke and his henchwoman, the witch known as Ugly Meg. The witch employs a horrible creature that can transform into anything a person fears the most, frightening them to death, than back into its more benign form, a small creature that resembles a monkey. The Iron Duke wants to exchange minds with Merlin to gain his power and knowledge, and enlists Meg's help to this end, but Meg has her own plans. It develops that Meg is the true power of the pair because she is tapping into the magical mind of a tentacled dream-creature hidden in the cellar of the duke's castle. Merlin and Etrigan triumph over the duo and send the dream-creature back to its own mystic realm.

Demon 6 brought the Howler, an anthropologist named Eric Schiller, who has become the host of a being known as the Primal Entity. This entity transforms Schiller into a shaggy, destructive monster whose howling chills the blood of the inhabitants of Transylvania. The

Demon thinks he's defeated the beast with his ability to shoot flames from his hands, but Schiller turns up on a plane and tells Jason Blood that he was the monster the Demon battled the night before. Jason tries to do an exorcism on Schiller, but he is interrupted by Glenda, and things go awry, with the result that Schiller falls from a window and dies. A man in the crowd apparently becomes the new host of the Primal Entity, and there's a howling in the city that night.

Demon 7 brought the Witch boy, Klarion, who with his cat Teekl, simply shows up and tells Jason he is his nephew, even though Jason has no relatives, certainly none as weird, if engaging, as Klarion. Klarion seeks refuge from the elders of his coven, who are after him because he tried to seize control of the group. Klarion's mistake is that in trying to take over the mind of the demon, he is challenging mighty Merlin himself, so he winds up summarily banished. However, Klarion does not take kindly to this and in a few issues would make his way back to Jason and cause all manner of mischief.

While Jason seemed to be fully aware that he had lived many lifetimes—his apartment has paintings of him done in different eras—his exact relationship to, and knowledge of Etrigan, isn't made quite clear until *Demon* 8. After Etrigan battles a masked "phantom" who tries to steal Merlin's sword, Jason wakes up in a sewer with no knowledge of how he got there. He now realizes that his human form is simply meant to hide the demon, but Blood has no intention of letting Etrigan completely take over his life. Jason has a vast collection of occult artifacts, and uses the philosopher's stone to create an all-consuming frost that will not only drive Etrigan out of his body but destroy him. He feels peace when this is accomplished, but is afraid that feeling will vanish if he has to deal with enemies, such as the Phantom, who may prove too challenging to a mere human, however immortal.

This comes about in the following issue when the Phantom, clearly inspired by *The Phantom of the Opera* (and who, unmasked, even resembles Lon Chaney in the classic silent film), kidnaps Glenda, and Jason and his friends pursue them into the sewers. Jason uses the philosopher's stone to bathe himself in fire in the hopes it will resuscitate any spark of Etrigan that remains, and it works—the demon lives. The Phantom of the Sewers is revealed as Farley Fairfax, an actor of long ago whose face was destroyed by the Soul-Snatcher, a demonic being summoned by his co-star, a jealous actress—and practicing witch—named Galatea. Etrigan causes dead Galatea's spirit to temporarily inhabit Glenda's body, she brings back the Snatcher to restore Farley's face, but the man dies even as his good looks dissolve into his true aged appearance (*Demon* 10).

Kirby continued his stories inspired by horror films—as well as an unfortunate tendency toward parody—with a three-parter in *Demon* 11–13. Etrigan's adversary is Baron von Rakenstein, a mad scientist not so affectionately known as Baron Evilstein, and who has a nasty little assistant, naturally known as Igor. The Demon uses his ever-handy philosopher's stone—taken from his alter-ego no doubt—and turns the two of them into vultures. Things were back on track in *Demon* 14–15, which brings back the devilish witch boy Klarion, who is so angry at being summarily exiled by Jason that he enacts a plan to utterly destroy the demonologist. First Klarion makes Jason dream of a bizarre creature called Gargora, who has a huge head from which sprout tentacles and whose tapering ends bear the faces of the souls she's captured. Then Klarion summons a spirit and gives it form—Jason's form—and Jason/Etrigan finds himself becoming less and less visible as the doppelganger takes on more and more substance, and goes about trying to murder Jason's friends. After a battle between real demon and faux demon, Etrigan is triumphant and banishes the nasty little fiend once more. A great panel shows Klarion smiling wickedly as he contemplates the evil he's done while his cat Teekl wears the exact same expression. Teekl later transforms into a human form.

Morgaine Le Fey was finally brought back for the sixteenth and final issue of *The Demon*. She nearly succeeds in turning Etrigan into one of her personal slaves, but she is stymied by an angry Glenda, who has finally found out about the link between Jason and the Demon, and Warley, one of Le Fey's acolytes, who gets his mistress the philosopher's stone, but decides to keep it for himself after turning Morgaine into an Egyptian mummy. Warley himself then falls victim to evil forces. And so ends the story of the Demon, although the character would appear again from time to time.

The Demon was very well drawn in Kirby's usual dynamic fashion (with an inking assist from Mike Royer), but he both wrote and edited the book and Kirby the editor hadn't enough influence on Kirby the writer. Although there were continued stories, the series never had an internal momentum; characters would just show up and disappear as needed without becoming much more than stick figures, including Jason Blood. Demons are supposed to be Satanic creatures, but this aspect was never addressed in any definitive fashion. Kirby never seemed to have a clear idea of what he wanted to do with the character.

Kirby deliberately did the book in a golden age fashion, dividing each story into chapters with separate titles and employing a dramatic narration whose style was old-fashioned (if effective on that level). Unfortunately the 70s was a period of increased maturity and growth in the comic industry, and nostalgia was not what most readers wanted. It's not surprising that *The Demon*, whatever its strengths and charms, didn't last very long. The character had an appearance with Batman in *The Brave and the Bold* 109 while *The Demon* was still being published. This was a memorable story with excellent Jim Aparo art that had the two characters teaming up to stop a monstrous mutated sailor from murdering other seamen. The two re-teamed for a more absurd story in *Brave and the Bold* 137 in 1977 wherein the two had trouble taking care of a powerful Chinese sorcerer. This was another Bob Haney tale with art by John Calnan and Bob McLeod. A creepy sequence has the sorcerer turning Etrican into a fly and we can see the demon's normal form trapped and superimposed over the insect's wings.

The Night Force

The Night Force was first introduced in a preview/prologue in *New Teen Titans* 21 in 1982. In the first issue, alcoholic tabloid reporter Jack Gold goes on assignment to interview the mystical Baron Winters at the sprawling Wintersgate Manor. The mystical-looking, bearded Winters appears to be in his forties but is rumored to be much older. Gold doesn't put much stock in Winters' alleged abilities, but when he opens a back door he swears that he's looking out into a scene from 1800s Paris. In the meantime, Vanessa Van Helsing, a resident of a padded cell at Potomac Psychiatric Hospital who seems to draw unhealthy energy to herself, is undergoing another attack, after which, as usual, she is drenched in blood but hasn't a single wound. Vanessa's seizures correspond to demonic manifestations throughout Georgetown. Her physician, Dr. Rabin, asks for her guardian, Baron Winters', help, but he refers her to Dr. Donovan Caine, a parapsychologist and psychic researcher at Georgetown College.

Caine is doing work for the military—they want him to "tap into the energy we call evil"—but is unaware that his two liaisons have been murdered and replaced by doubles. Vanessa is released into Caine's care, as he thinks she's a virtual gateway to Hell. Behind the scenes there is an unseen man who seems to be plotting against everyone else. This is the intriguing beginning of the series co-created by Marv Wolfman and Gene Colan of *Tomb of Dracula* fame.

In the following issues Caine, using Vanessa, manages to raise the devil, or rather an evil force that has always been called Satan, "not Satan by any means," as the Baron puts it, "but merely a case of life imitating art." Whatever it is, it kills Caine's wife, while the fake agents, who work for Russia, take off with Vanessa to London. Baron Winters gets Jack fired from his paper so that he can come to work for him; apparently, like the Shadow, he uses several agents for various supernatural cases that come his way. Vanessa is then spirited off to Science City in Siberia for experimentation and it is there that the series unfortunately turns into *Carrie* or *The Fury* as Vanessa's full evil power is totally unleashed, causing massive death and destruction, and obliterating the psychic research center. Jack is able to calm her down by telling her that he loves her, which he doesn't, then worries about spending a lifetime with a woman he not only doesn't love but who could turn him and thousands of others into toast if she ever learns the truth. Unfortunately, Jack doesn't realize that Vanessa has been completely cured, which Baron Winters, seeing how happy Vanessa is with him, doesn't ever intend to tell him. Why the Baron would want his ward to spend her life with a unsavory fellow who doesn't like her remains unexplained, as does how Vanessa can live with all the deaths that are on her hands, evil force or no evil force. Another problem is that not a single character in the comic, including the baron, is sympathetic or especially likable.

A new storyline begins in *Night Force* 8 which has a great cover showing a barely seen tentacled monstrosity at the top of a staircase dropping down two skeletons it has apparently picked clean. A brownstone in Manhattan has become host to a horror that kills several tenants. Rather than risking one of his usual operatives on what will probably become a suicide mission, Winters takes a sociopathic killer named Brooks and places him in the brownstone to investigate and hopefully kill off the creature. Brooks is a hardened killer, but even he is freaked out by what he discovers. An alien entity has moved into the building, provides the tenants with everything they could possibly need from food to computers, but simply will not let them leave. If they try to escape the building, it turns on them, and it always feeds on anyone who dies. Watching the creature devour one dead man, even Brooks has to toss his supper. He is appalled that most of the tenants have simply accepted the situation, but he definitely wants out. Even when an escape is provided, some of the traumatized tenants are too scared to go outside, preferring to stay with the devil they know. Brooks improbably sacrifices his life to destroy the alien.

The third story arc begins in *Night Force* 11, when the baron is called in by a couple who have bought an old stone manor that is haunted by the ghosts of certain American businessmen; they backed Hitler financially only to be murdered by him. Baron Winters takes Vanessa through one of his back door time portals to Hollywood of 1933 to see what he can do before their deaths occurred, but he is driven off by a gargantuan six-headed beast with crowns atop its manes. Winters calls in his ex-wife Katina and their son Gowon, who despise him for the way he treated Katina, to save Vanessa and Jack from the same ghosts when they visit the manor (Baron Winters can only leave his house through his various time portals; he cannot walk out his front door into the twentieth century). In the fourteenth and final issue of the series a demonic creature named Alphus Omega, who is apparently behind the machinations of the aforementioned businessmen, is destroyed by the combined efforts of Winters, Katina and Gowon working from the past and present. A secretary is inadvertently brought back from 1933 and stays to work for the baron. Although the cover of the thirteenth issue declared that the baron's origin would be told inside, in truth the series ended leaving more questions than answers about the weird Baron Winters.

There were plans to do a four-issue *Night Force* mini-series every year, but one didn't materialize until 2012. In between there was a new ongoing series in 1996 with Wolfman as scripter and Brent Anderson doing the art, which lasted 12 issues.

Sixteen

Charlton, Gold Key and Atlas

Ghostly Haunts began life as volume one of *Ghost Manor* in the silver age. Beginning with the twentieth issue in 1971 the title was changed and the hostess, Winnie the Witch, as intrusive as ever, was retained, making one wonder why Charlton bothered to change the title in the first place, especially when they brought out a second volume of *Ghost Manor* the very same year (this time hosted by a "Mr. Bones"). Although much of the material in the comic was third-rate and amateurish, there were some good and interesting stories now and then (and Winnie receded more into the background). For instance:

Nick Cuti's "No Way Out" (28) features a man who imagines that all of the doors leading out of his Gothic house have disappeared and there is no way he could go outside—for 27 years. The zesty "Sewer Patrol" (31), written by Nick Cuti and with excellent art by Jack Abel, deals with the myth of alligators in the sewers of New York City, and for good measure throws in giant squids, mutated by radioactive waste, and even a horde of piranha. The cover story to *GH* 41, "A Lovely Night in Paris," written by Joe Gill and illustrated by Tom Sutton, takes place in the sewers of Paris where a gendarme pursues a pretty tourist underground and discovers a frightful world full of hideous, large-domed mutants, voracious rodents, and a giant rat-monster awaiting a sacrifice.

Joe Gill's "A Nice Place to Die" (39) is about a nice old couple with aches and pains who suck away the life force of their much younger, and not nearly as nice, domestics, becoming younger and healthier as the servants get more and more decrepit. Tom Peterson's "The Possessed" (44) deals with a homely witch who casts a spell on a man to make her appear beautiful; everyone else sees her true ugly self and wonders what he sees in her. After her death, her ghost continues to bedevil him by making him appear hideous to any woman who is attracted to him. But she finally wins him over by transforming herself permanently into a ravishing beauty. Since "Beauty and the Beast" (52) eight issues later had the exact same premise (with a much flatter ending) it is possible that editor George Wildman sometimes gave more than one writer the same idea to develop and either chose the best script, or, in this case, used both of them issues apart. There were other very similar stories in the comic as well.

Steve Morisi's "Executioner" (45) presents a daring highwayman whose criminal parents were hung years before, and whose dreams are continually haunted by the specter of a noose. An old gypsy fortune teller assures him more than once that "although your life is one of

Ghostly Haunts was only one of many horror titles published by Charlton in the bronze age.

evil ... no noose will ever claim you." When he's arrested for murder, he wonders in his cell what will happen to prevent his death by hanging. Although the ending may not be a big surprise, it is still satisfying to see the look on his face as he's marched out to the courtyard to become the area's first victim of the new "la guillotine." Pellowski's "The Deepest Cut of All" (46) is a Jack the Ripper story with some clever, if unlikely, variations. Joe Gill's "The Trapper" (47) is a standard tale of an illegal fur trapper who kills the game warden trying to catch him in the act, is bit by a rabid fox, and suffers such hallucinations that he winds up caught in one of his own painful traps, but it boasts moody and skillful artwork by Jose Recreo Ferrer.

One of the best stories published in *Ghostly Haunts* or indeed any horror comic is Nicola Cuti's "The Man Who Hunted Satan" in *GH* 42. Amos Burr tells three clergymen that if they can each gather two million dollars he can literally deliver the Devil to them to do with as they wish. They accompany him to Turkey, where they are attacked by a Satan-worshiping cult known as the Baaloites, who kill one of their number. Amos' wife Clara confronts him as to why he insisted she come along, and figures out she was meant to be a lure for the devil, although Amos assures her that she would have been safe. In the basement of the main temple of the Holy City of Ephasus the group finally confront the fallen angel, Lucifer, who is blond, handsome and actually quite "angelic." He explains that artistic representations of him were "all constructed by artists who used their own hideous souls for models." Furthermore, he explains, he is not responsible for all the evil on earth, as mankind itself is responsible for "wars, murders, and crimes against their fellow creature." He is a mere scapegoat. The story notes that the Devil is a notorious liar, but implies that this is, indeed, the truth about Satan. The story was much more intelligent that most of the stuff being published in horror comics of the period.

"Long, Long Revenge" in *Ghostly Haunts* 53 also has an excellent premise. Walking home with money desperately needed for his family, a man is killed by a robber, but his consciousness remains aware as he is reborn into a newborn baby whose father is—the man who killed him. As the baby grows into a child, he determines to make his "father" pay for his actions and tries to murder him on one occasion. Later he visits the home where he lived with his wife and daughter, and finds his father waiting for him in the shadows; he has finally figured out who he really is and why his own son hates him so. Just as the boy prepares to be murdered for a second time, his father reveals that decades have gone by since the original killing and it was actually his grandfather who did the deed and was executed for it. While it's hard to believe the boy couldn't have done the math in the first place, the story is still compelling if perhaps a bit slick.

The series lasted for 58 issues, the last two of which consisted of reprints.

Ghost Manor and *Ghostly Tales*

The second volume of *Ghost Manor* debuted in 1971. The host is the butler of the manor, Mr. Bones, who has a ghoulish grin, jagged teeth, an impish if sinister appearance, and a very high forehead. The first story tells how Ghost Manor got its name: the owner of the house, an immoral monster named Farnham Farr, disappeared on his wedding day, imprisoned in a secret soundproof room by the ghost of the builder, whom he murdered. On rare occasions

Bones is a participant in a story; generally he functions as narrator. The nadir of the series is Nicola Cuti's "Doomship" (33), which is nothing more than Richard Matheson's excellent short story "Death Ship" (which was turned into a memorable hour-long *Twilight Zone* episode) transplanted from a space ship on an alien planet to a nineteenth century cargo ship sailing to China, one of the most blatant and meretricious "borrowings" in all of horror comicdom, especially ironic as Cuti was capable of turning out perfectly good stories of his own.

Among the more memorable tales are: "The Wolf Howls for You" (12)—Safe in his castle with selected guests Count Dimitri gorges himself on food, but allows desperate peasants to starve or fall prey to the wolves that roam outside until he encounters one beast he cannot control; "I'll Love you Forever ... and Ever" (20)—a dying woman arranges for her lover to become a vampire so that he can give her the cursed kiss of immortality (the very next issue had a story with a very similar title and was also about a couple with a vampiric bent); "Guest of Honor" (32)—a patriarch figures out which of his family members is a werewolf ravaging the area and arranges for his disposal, but the werewolf poisons him and everyone else before they can kill him, although they get even with him a century later.

Ghost Manor started reprints with its thirty-fourth issue in 1977 but lasted for another 43 issues before closing up shop with issue seventy-seven in 1984.

Ghostly Tales 91, the first bronze age issue of the comic, was a special issue with a full-length story, "Bloody Mermaid," written and drawn by Sanho Kim, whose work was amateurish but undeniably compelling and promising. The story told of a man who thinks a woman is being victimized, until he learns she was turned into a mermaid by a curse two hundred years ago, and has nothing but hatred for the human race, which she preys upon like a vampire. Editor George Wildman obviously thought highly of the Korean artist; his name was put on the cover of the next issue to present one of his tales, which was "The Promise" in *GT* 101—even such veterans as Steve Ditko, who did work for the series, didn't get their names on the cover. In his second story for the comic, Kim did a variation on a Korean ghost story, which often has a man encountering and marrying a woman with a strange or horrible secret. "The Promise" takes place in 1958 and concerns a Korean soldier trying to escape from pursuing Japanese. A pretty Korean woman agrees to let him hide out and protect him from the soldiers if he agrees to marry her sister, which he does. The two sisters are excellent swordswomen, and cut down the Japanese who come to the house with surprising ease. Later, the man's bride is ashamed to show her full face to him because it turns out one side of her face is horribly disfigured. She was burned when the Japanese set fire to her house and killed her family, including her sister, who is a ghost. She begs her husband to leave her with child before he leaves, but as he is disgusted by her appearance he refuses. As he passes the grave of the dead sister outside, an arm protrudes and grabs him until he is spotted and killed by Japanese soldiers. Kim's art had a decided skill and attractiveness, though it cried out for a talented inker to smooth over the rough spots and give it a more polished appearance. Kim's work was definitely less inspired when he was illustrating another person's story.

Ghostly Tales 106 has an especially good cover showing a gigantic tentacled monstrosity rising from a lake behind two fishermen. The octopus in Nick Cuti's story "Those Tentacles" isn't nearly as big as the one on the cover but it is of sufficient size to carry off one of the fishermen, Hal. Although Hal begs for his buddy Jake to use the spear gun on the octopus, Jake lets the creature carry off his friend, busy spewing curses, because he covets his wife, with whom he's been having an affair. But it turns out the faithless wife has yet another lover, and worse, Jake sees tentacles coming out of every manhole, pipe and sink that he comes across. A psychiatrist convinces Jake that the tentacles aren't real, although artist Tom Sutton creates the illusion of them being *everywhere* in the shadows. Finally the tentacles get Jake, who can't see them but can certainly feel them crushing the life out of him.

Other notable tales: "A Thing of Beauty" (*Ghostly Tales* 81)—a hideous witch uses a special brew to convince a man that she's beautiful and that he's a genius, but even when he learns the truth he prefers his deluded life to the one he had before; "The Work of Genius" (83)—a painter who is nearly starved to death by a man who takes credit for his work gets even with him from beyond the grave by making a special painting of the king; "Cave of the Octopus" (88)—two divers discover a gigantic octopus guarding a ship wreck, but his intentions for them may not be what they assume; "Answer the Phone, Dottie" (95)—a nasty teenage girl makes threatening anonymous phone calls to a woman who asked her to get off the hood of her car, but doesn't realize who she's messing with; "Ghost Artist" (101)—a jealous artist murders the successful cartoonist he works for but discovers that a demonic force has virtually chained him to his drawing board.

Ghostly Tales began publishing nothing but reprints with issue one hundred forty-four, and finally closed up shop twenty-five issues later in 1984.

Haunted

Haunted debuted in 1971. The host is an unnamed, tiny and transparent sprite, imp or ghost with a hood who flies through the pages as it narrates the stories. *Haunted* 7 has an interesting cover depicting a spider in the foreground and a man and a woman looking at it with some alarm from the background; it's impossible to tell if it's a giant spider about to spring on them or if the perspective makes a normal-sized spider look larger. In the story "Along Came a Spider and ..." the arachnid is of normal proportions, but artist Steve Ditko draws the bug in such a way that it always seems to be hovering menacingly and gigantically over the characters, especially a dissolute boarder who gets a room in a middle-aged woman's home, and plans on romancing her for her money. The landlady insists that the boarder never disturb the spider in its web, and he agrees, much to his regret. Although the story has a lot of suspense—personified by the spider—its conclusion is only mildly satisfying.

Haunted 20 was a special issue with a full-length story entitled "Mountain of Fear" with clear Lovecraftian overtones. Written and drawn by Tom Sutton, whose work was crude yet quite effective in spots, it deals with a man who has made a pact with elder gods, a subterranean world of monsters and dinosaurs, and has a creepy ending in which the heroine comes across her own crypt, realizes she's been dead for quite a while, and crumbles into a dusty skeleton in front of the hero. The main artists for the series were Steve Ditko, whose work was always well laid out and composed if not always representing him at his best, and an artist who used the pen name PAM, moonlighting police officer Pete Morisi. PAM's art was attractive and also well-composed, if not quite moody or atmospheric enough for a horror comic. For every gifted professional like Wayne Howard, *Haunted*—and the other Charlton horror comics—hired half a dozen amateurs who were still learning anatomy and the basic rudiments of illustration. Since Charlton paid lower rates than DC or Marvel, they had to get by with newcomers or with old pros who could work very fast and for little money. As for writers, Joe Gill turned in a number of tales, and Nicola Cuti wrote several stories with imaginative premises.

Haunted got a new look and host with the twenty-first issue, in which the title was changed (on the cover only) to *Baron Weirwulf's Haunted Library*. The Baron was a shaggy, bearded fellow who narrated stories from his haunted castle. The stories remained much the same. *Haunted* was already publishing reprints by its thirty-third issue but it continued in this fashion until the seventy-fifth and final issue in 1984. *Haunted* will not go down as one of the more memorable horror titles, but occasionally there was a memorable story, for instance:

"Like Father, Like Son" (*Haunted* 10)—a man comes across a town in which there are no children because the adults breed by dividing into two people and so on like unicellular animals; "A Handsome Devil" (11)—the devil forces a plastic surgeon to change his ugly face into a handsome one with very unexpected results; "A Budding Evil" (17)—a horrible doctor feeds mangled remains of people to his man-eating plants; "The Survivor" (18)—an astronaut murders his companion in a space capsule because there's only enough air supply for one, but his victim has the final gasp; "Film Freak"—a woman sick of her movie-loving husband builds equipment that places him in his favorite movie wherein he will die at the tentacles of a hideous alien monster; "The Reuger Formula" (24)—a lab assistant smitten with her boss accidentally creates an economy-sized Komodo Dragon that nearly eats him; "Uncle Stanley Isn't Dead" (27)—a couple who murder an old man for his money must live in his mechanized house and raise his little niece, who insists the man is alive and living in the basement, where he has control of everything; "Bones of the Ancients" (32)—an Indian brave discovers a gigantic and voracious snake god deep in caverns below his village.

Midnight Tales and *Haunted Love*

Midnight Tales, which debuted in 1972, was the brainchild of African American artist Wayne Howard, who had worked under Wally Wood. The magazine, which gave Howard unprecedented credit as creator on each cover, presented stories (generally written by Nick Cuti) that were narrated by the strange Cyrus Coffin (aka "The Midnight Philosopher") and his niece Arachne. Cyrus and his brother, Elias, Arachne's father, are on an archeological dig in Greece when they discover the real goddess Arachne in her sleeping, giant spider form. Elias hopes to use the spider to kill off a man who unfairly wants to share credit for the brothers' discoveries, but it backfires and Elias himself is killed; Cyrus then raises his orphaned little girl. Each issue of *Midnight Tales* has a different theme, with three stories narrated by Coffin or Arachne or other characters they encounter. One issue would feature tales of the future (foretold in a seer's crystal ball) or stories involving children, or fairy tales and so on. The second issue has Coffin lecturing at Xavier University and telling stories to the strangely subdued and spooky high school seniors of the incoming class of '76 only to discover that the class of '76 had been killed in a bus accident the year before. The issue ends with Coffin and Arachne learning that the students have turned into skeletons. Despite the light tone, there is something disturbing about the deaths of so many bright young people, especially as the tragedy is treated mostly as a macabre joke.

The third issue, with speculative tales of the future, features two memorable stories. In the first, intelligent animals now outnumber humans and rule the earth. Human skins are especially valuable—as fur pieces were in the past—and a young couple are pursued by poachers. Instead of being skinned they wind up as stuffed corpses in an exhibit of "Adam and Eve." In "Lost in Transit," teleporting from place to place via machine has become so commonplace that houses don't even have doors. A short circuit in the machinery results in an accident which displaces a lost little boy in time and space so he retains his consciousness but becomes disembodied, to his parents' horror but his delight. The fifth issue's theme was Satan and features a darkly amusing tale called "Honeymoon in Hell." An elderly couple tell how they importuned Satan to allow them to spend a week in Hell when they were newlyweds and were continually beset by irritating minor demons and the like, but the Devil refuses to let them leave early. At the end of the story it is revealed that the "elderly" couple returned from Hell just last week! The seventh issue deals with a primordial ooze called the Goo who falls in love with an alien computer and gets unfairly blamed for murders committed by a jealous professor.

There were other memorable stories in the series' short run. In Nick Cuti's clever "The Kilgore Monster" (*MT* 8) the fishermen of a small island off the coast of Scotland set sail to destroy a slithering sea beast that comes to the surface periodically. The legend has it that when the beast dies, so will Kilgore. They manage to destroy the serpentine monster after it smashes one of their ships, but discover that the animal is even larger than suspected—it carries the entire island of Kilgore on its body, and the town is indeed destroyed in the monster's death throes. The story reminds one of a tale from the Arabian Nights in which Sindbad's crew lands on an island that turns out to be a slumbering sea beast who's been asleep so long that vegetation has grown on its back. In "The Strange Mr. Milque" (*MT* 10) a kindhearted vampire finds that falling in love is his undoing; and in "The Bee" (13), well drawn by Joe Staton, the title creature, grown to giant size due to atomic testing, poses a threat on a Japanese island (13).

Arguably the best issue was *Midnight Tales* 17 which features a full-length story in which Cyrus Coffin is apparently killed by a vampire, who's put on trial with Arachne as the chief prosecution witness. Written and drawn by Wayne Howard, the excellent "Tomb of Hemon-Chirops" looks at Coffin's death from the pov of first Arachne, then the vampire, and finally from Coffin himself, who was actually bitten by a snake before the vampire sunk his fangs into him. The vampire inadvertently sucked out the snake venom and dies from it, while Coffin—who only appeared to be dead—is not only alive but remains fully human. With the next issue, *Midnight Tales* was gone.

The series deserves credit for being something different. Some of its funny covers and twist endings were real "groaners" but the series was done with some enthusiasm and inventiveness. As usual, George Wildman was the editor.

Haunted Love, a collection of Gothic mystery tales, debuted in 1973. Nicola Cuti and Joe Staton's "Richard" in *HL* 2 concerns a young woman, Terese, who goes to a medium and becomes smitten with a spirit named Richard who appears each time she's there. She demands that the medium have her next séance at her house; unfortunately Madame Toulrose is a fake. "Richard" is only the face of her handsome dead son, Michael, projected over a black mask worn by his homely, living brother, the real Richard. Richard has also fallen for the

Opposite: Charlton's *Midnight Tales* was the brainchild of writer-artist Wayne Howard.

beautiful Terese, and feels terrible at the way his mother is duping her. He agrees to plant the ghost projector at Terese's home, but tells his mother it will be his last séance—he is getting out. But something goes wrong and the ghostly "Richard" is revealed as a fake. Terese rushes after the mask-wearing Richard, telling him that she's glad he's real and that she loves him, but Richard is afraid she'll no longer feel that way when she sees his real face. But when the mask is removed, Richard now looks like his brother. "Thank you for your gift, Michael," thinks a teary Richard as he and Terese embrace. The story was a variation on an idea used more than once in the golden age.

Haunted Love lasted for eleven issues but "Richard" was arguably the first and last memorable story the series produced. Most of the scripts were cobbled together by Joe Gill with a variety of artists and either had poor ideas or were dismally executed. There were occasional glimmers of interest. "Mother's Day" in *HL* 5 features an evil, ages-old woman who continuously becomes her own grand-daughter by possessing the infant after her, the old woman's, death. Gill returned to this theme in the very next issue with "Sleep, My Love," in which another evil, dying old woman hopes to permanently enter the body of her beautiful young nurse and start life anew; this version is a bit more developed and interesting.

Monster Hunters

Charlton's *Monster Hunters*, also edited by George Wildman, debuted in 1975. The original premise has old Colonel Whiteshroud leading a group called the Monster Hunters, their prey consisting of both animals and humans. Sometimes the colonel would participate in the adventure; other times he was merely the narrator. As the first few issues came out, however, the whole interesting idea of the club was basically forgotten, and the colonel only narrated some of the tales. *Monster Hunters* basically became just another Charlton horror title, as some of the stories didn't even have monsters in them. (Including evil humans in the mix made just about anything or anyone capable of being labeled a "monster.") The first issue is a mild forgettable business that at least has one memorable panel depicting "Nessie" rising malevolently from Loch Ness to confound a man who had been convinced the monster was only a hoax.

"Kukulkaton," written and drawn by Tom Sutton, deals with a Mayan demon and three people who are searching for treasure in the catacombs of a submerged cavern (*MH* 2). The demon is said to rip out the still beating hearts of sacrificial offerings, and it does so to the fourth member of the party. They find the treasure—but also the writhing hideous mass of the demon, which has ten thousand beating and blood-red hearts affixed to it. In a bit of bad taste that has nothing to do with demons or monsters one of the characters—admittedly a bad guy—refers to the natives with a distasteful racist slur. "Thief's Gold" concerns an old wizard who inadvertently conjures up a hungry dragon when he only wants gold, and learns that he'll get the gold if he provides human flesh for the dragon, which he ultimately does—to his regret (*MH* 5). Although there is no monster in it, Joe Molloy's "A Fitting Wife" (*MH* 7) is an amusing story in which first the nasty, vicious commander of the sultan's troops, and then the corpulent sultan himself, come afoul of the beautiful Joumana, whom they both desire but who turns the former into a dog, and the latter into a pig.

The comic didn't ignore vampires and werewolves. "Blood Oath" (*MH* 7), written and drawn by Mike Zeck, is an exciting story about an elderly man whose daughter is the latest to be killed by a vampire preying on the townspeople, and who takes on the undead one himself in his musty castle when the other men in the village refuse to aid him out of fear. One of the best stories in the comic, and one of the most unique werewolf stories ever published, is "The Untouchable Killer" (*MH* 8) by Carl Wessler, with art by Larson and Boxell. In this a murdering werewolf is protected by the law, neither killed nor imprisoned, because he is a *Siamese twin* and the brother who is attached to him is completely innocent. In the end this decent brother, horrified by the other's actions and lack of remorse, goads a person into killing him—both of them, of course—and ending the curse forever.

The comic finally turned back to its original premise with the ninth issue, an excellent full-length tale entitled "The Hour of the Werewolf," in which Colonel Whiteshroud goes to a spooky estate to try to ferret out the identity of whichever person inside suffers from the curse of lycanthropy and is savagely attacking the others (Cuti/Zeck). Then *Monster Hunters* went on hiatus for nine months, returning to the stands in late 1977. *Monster Hunters* 10 has an interesting cover story about a tentacled man-eating Kraken from the deep, which examines its connection to a mysterious woman with webbed fingers who lives at a lighthouse located near the monster's attacks. "The Monsters Have Surrounded the House" (*MH* 11) has a kid finding a formula that seems to create giant-size dogs, spiders and other incredible monsters but the reality is that he, his parents and the entire house they live in has become so reduced in size that amoebas and other microscopic creatures seem like behemoths to them. A "Giant on the Beach" washed up from an undersea world protects a family from big deadly bugs that fly out of his hair and clothing (*MH* 11).

"The Montego Frame" is another story without a monster in sight, but it is an interesting piece about a woman who buys a new frame for her portrait but is unaware that she actually died years ago and that only the old magical frame is keeping her alive (*MH* 11). Colonel Whiteshroud disappeared from the comic and was replaced by a green-haired, bespectacled, unnamed hostess and even on occasion by Dr. Graves. The comic reprinted some stories from earlier Charlton horror comics, and the seventeenth issue was a complete reprint of an earlier issue of *Monster Hunters*. The book ended with its eighteenth issue, having become a clearing house for various Charlton horror tales. If *Monster Hunters* had stuck with its original premise, it probably would have had a much longer run. Writers for the series included Joe Gill, Nicola Cuti, and Tom Himes, with art by Steve Ditko, Enrique Nieto, Joe Staton, and others.

Creepy Things and the Rest

Creepy Things, edited by George Wildman, came out in 1975 and lasted only six issues. In addition to the usual vampires, there were giant mollusks guarding a treasure, a voodoo woman who shrinks a slumlord down to tiny size so he can experience the rats that infest his building first-hand, and other macabre stories and monsters. In the amusing "Mutant" (*CT* 4) a murderous lieutenant and his wife who have just robbed a payroll and killed a guard, come across giant wasps and rats, as well as a mad scientist who irradiates them and turns them into monsters before being eaten by another one of his slimy experiments. In "Bookworm" (4) a man buys an old blank journal in which to write his dull autobiography, and discovers that the book absorbs both body and soul of the user—in this case, himself—until the next one who purchases the book releases him. The man is only too happy to stay safe and warm inside the book, hopefully to be freed at some future time when there is a cure for old age, but instead to his horror realizes that the old journal has attracted the gnawing attention of voracious book worms. The cover of the final issue features a humongous spider crawling into a window beyond which a mother and child lay peacefully sleeping. "The Hairy One" inside deals with a witch doctor who transforms himself into a giant tarantula. The trouble with *Creepy Things* is that most of the stories were minor and forgettable, and even the better ones were poorly developed. A troll-like horror host named Mr. Dee Munn began appearing with the third issue and was no help at all. Writers for the series included Joe Gill, Mike Pellowski, Nick Cuti, and Tom Tuna, with artwork by Steve Ditko, Mike Vosburg, Tom Sutton, and others.

Beyond the Grave debuted in 1975 with a ghoulish and generic narrator named "Mort Tishin." At least one story has an interesting premise—"Nightmare Flight" (*BTG* 1) has the spirit of Jack the Ripper possessing a airliner passenger who uses a knife on more than one stewardess—but few were executed with any special flair. The comic lasted a mostly sorry six issues before coming back in 1983 as a reprint title with stories culled from many of Charlton's horror mags; in this format is lasted until the sixteenth issue. Writers and artists were the usual suspects.

Scary Tales debuted in 1975. The hostess was the red-haired and bosomy Countess R. H. Von Bludd, who is introduced in cutesy fashion in a prologue to the first issue. A longer, more serious story the following issue details how she was forced to marry a vampire count and eventually succumbed to the vampire curse— after first dispatching her nasty spouse with a wooden cross-bow. "The Card of Death" in the third issue reveals that she was a very reluctant and good-natured vampire who could not bring herself to slack her thirst with innocent blood. She travels abroad on vacation and manages to find a few decidedly evil people to make well-deserved victims of her peculiar appetite. In the eleventh issue (after being absent from the comic for several issues) she performs a hypnotic nightclub act with a whip, then bites every mesmerized man in the audience just enough for a taste of nourishing blood but not enough to kill them.

After a bunch of mostly forgettable stories—the usual ghosts, demons, deals with the devil and so on—*Scary Tales* was already doing reprints by its fourteenth issue. There was no new material until the thirty-seventh issue in 1983, and then it was science fiction. With the exception of the fortieth issue, which featured super-hero type sci-fi stories, the comic published nothing but reprints until it expired with the forty-sixth issue, taking Countess Von Bludd with it into the ether.

GOLD KEY

Gold Key's *Grimm's Ghost Stories* debuted in 1972, hosted by a witch named Hephzibah Grimm. "The Wand," the lead story in the second issue, is unremarkable in most respects but it does ensnare its main character in a situation that would throw anyone into abject despair. Arnold Tate takes a job as night watchman in a castle that has been turned into a

Opposite: Gold Key's entry in the bronze age horror anthology field was *Grimm's Ghost Stories*.

GRIMM'S GHOST STORIES

25¢

Only in death could he be with his ghostly love!

© WESTERN PUBLISHING COMPANY, INC.

museum. The disembodied spirit of a magician appears, and tells him he will make him rich if he takes a priceless medieval wand out of its glass case; the ghost can not touch it. Arnold does as he is importuned, but discovers that the wizard now has the power to put his consciousness into Arnold's body; the magician does so and goes off. Arnold is now a spirit and can only hope someone will come along whom he can similarly trick. Although the sorcerer tells Arnold that his own greed is at fault, Arnold doesn't seem like a bad fellow and during the whole interchange even wonders if it is all just a dream. Now he has lost his own young and handsome body, forever cutting him off from loved ones, and has to remain as he is or doom another to the same fate; even should he find a victim he might wind up walking around in the form of someone decades older, ugly, or with other unpleasant aspects.

"Childhood Ghost" (*GGS* 3) certainly presents an interesting situation. Ken and Paul take a trip to their home town with their wives, stopping off at an old "haunted" house that they last saw when they were twelve. At that time they saw a spectral form in an attic window, at which Ken lopped a baseball; when the window shattered the two ran off. Walking through the house as adults they come to the attic—and find a skeleton with a crack in its skull, the baseball lying beside it. Ken actually killed whoever was playing ghost in the attic. The only trouble with the story is that it's somewhat hard to believe that no one was ever reported missing all those years ago—unless the "ghost" was a playful transient.

The first few issues of the series plodded along with acceptable if unmemorable stories of murder victims seeking revenge as ghosts, haunted houses with malevolent spectral occupants, all very similar to DC's *Ghosts*. It was not a true horror comic, but more in the line of supernatural fantasy, with occasional tales of humorous or darker occurrences. With some exceptions the art was never anything to boast about, although there were some very well-drawn covers. Some of the stories, however minor and derivative, at least had a certain manic energy, a good case in point being the tales in *Grimm's Ghost Stories* 11. In "The Golden Eyes" a woman murders her husband, places his body inside his golden statue, then knocks out the eyes with a chisel when she senses them staring at her relentlessly; the dead man's ghost then maniacally pursues her until she falls off a cliff to her death. "Old Trees Never Die" presents a battle between the new owner of a house and a dead tree that he wants removed, despite the fact that it's the town's oldest landmark, with the tree resisting everything from chainsaws and explosives until finally it thrusts its branches up through the floor of the owner's bedroom and strangles him. "The Trouble with Emma" is a harrowing tale of an awful old woman's ghost doing the best it can to make her brother and his wife join her in the hereafter whether they want to go or not. In the issue's final tale, "On Canvas," an art forger who gets a visit from the ghost of the painter whose work he so successfully copies at first thinks the dead man wants to help him but gets caught in a trap from beyond. While neither the art nor the scripts made these tales classics, they did do an admirable job of pulling the reader along, which was not always the case in the comic.

Eventually *Grimm's Ghost Stories* published many stories that were more silly than grim, mild-mannered stuff such as tales of haunted supermarkets, dopey ghost pets, old grandmas who refused to leave their homes even after dying, and the like. On occasion there would be something with a bit more bite, however, such as Arnold Drake's "Funeral Pyre" in *GGG* 49. Visiting Khafir, Colonel Burwell is appalled by the practice of incinerating the living widows of dead men on the same funeral pyre. When Burwell learns that the Rajah's wife, Solange is much, much younger than he is, and should probably outlive him by many years,

Burwell reminds him of this terrible, long-held tradition. The Rajah secretly agrees with him, and leaves instructions in his will that Solange is not to die after his demise. The Rajah's son wants no stepmother to threaten his power, so he ignores the codicil and lies about the will after his father's passing, and the home office tells Burwell that he is forbidden to interfere. That night the Raja's ghost angrily implores Burwell to carry out his wishes and save the girl, which Burwell, initially stymied, manages to do with a little stealth and trickery.

Grimm's Ghost Stories lasted for sixty issues with an occasional reprint of an earlier issue thrown in and renumbered for good measure. The last few issues had both old and new material. Writers for the series included the prolific Arnold Drake, Donald F. Glut, "Freff," John Warner, and Paul S. Newman; artists included Jose Delbo, Luis Dominquez, Oscar Novelle, Frank Bolle, and Jack Sparling.

Some other memorable stories in *GGG*: "The Night Watchman" (*GGS* 14)—the ghost of a crippled, illiterate man who was miserably treated by everyone in life at lasts elicits tears from a compassionate child; "The Poisoner" (22)—a man trying to prove that a woman back in the nineteenth century was innocent of poisoning various people gets a chance to test his theory when he gets a visit from her ghost; "By the Bones of Shakespeare" (25)—a group of actors who defy a curse to dig up the immortal bard's remains wind up dying in manners à la Shakespeare; "The Glass Coffin" (52)—a nasty man insists that his transparent coffin not be buried and be placed standing up outside his house so that he can watch over his family—and they can watch him decompose.

Dr. Spektor

The Occult Files of Dr. Spektor debuted in 1973; Adam Spektor was Gold Key's answer to Charlton's Dr. Graves. Handsome, caped, and bearded, he lives in the Gothic style Spektor Manor in upstate New York, and has a beautiful Native American secretary named Lakota Rainflower (who was subjected to a lot of somewhat patronizing remarks about her ancestry by the doctor). The first issue has both of them traveling to Transylvania to deal with a vampire, Baron Tibur, who has been brought back from the dead. There are the usual quota of cliches—a coachman refuses to take them any closer to the vampire's castle, for instance, like in virtually every Dracula movie ever made—and some new notions, such as Spektor actually managing to cure the vampire with some chemicals and sending him on his merry way. Spektor did not take part in every story, although he was always the narrator, such as in an excellent tale in *OFDS* 2 about an artist who discovers that the mystical brushes he uses cause him to paint scenes of disasters during his sleep which always occur for real on the following day, as the brushes were formed from the skins and bones of a witch burned at the stake.

Spektor tussels with a mummy who takes possession of his body and makes passes at Lakota, who reveals her feelings for Spektor in the third issue. In the fifth issue Spektor is possessed by the ghost of Henry Jekyll, causing him to briefly transform into Mr. Hyde, and fears he may have committed a murder actually perpetrated by a descendant of Henry's, who also took the formula. In a very lively story in *OFDS* 6, which also features the doctor's black psychic friend, Elliott Kane, it develops that an ancestor of Henry Frankenstein has discovered the actual body of the not-so-mythical monster hidden inside the castle and brought it back to life. Now the monster wants a mate, and decides Lakota's brain will be useful until Spektor manages to save her from such a dire fate. In the eighth issue Spektor's opponent is no less than Count Dracula, who is casting spells to bring certain notorious vampires back to life and wants to bring the cured Baron Tibor (from the first issue) back into the fold, to no avail.

OFDS 7 introduces a villain named Ostellon, a sorcerer in the employ of the shadowy Dark Gods (a variation of Lovecraft's Old Gods) who twice tried to destroy mankind and failed. Each time it was an ancestor of Spektor's who foiled the wizard's plans (these ancestors were Dagar, a sword and sorcery hero, and Tragg, both of whom also had short-lived Gold Key comics) so the mere presence of Spektor in a tomb enables Ostellon to come back to life, whereupon he animates skeletons and does his best to destroy both the doctor and Lakota. Unfortunately for Ostellon he fails again, but the Dark Gods tell Spektor that other servants of theirs will soon come after him. In the very next issue the witch, Kareena, tries to enslave Spektor with a smooch, but when that doesn't work she materializes the mummy Ra-Ka Tep, Mr. Hyde, the Frankenstein Monster, and a bloodthirsty Baron Tibor and directs them all to attack Spektor, until he realizes they are only illusions. Kareena turns out to be an ancient, rather unlovely hag.

In *OFDS* 11 the doctor is bitten by a werewolf, becomes one himself, and attacks both Lakota and Elliott before being subdued and determining to find a cure before the next full moon. This issue was the first time that the series had a story that continued over several issues. In *OFDS* 12 Spektor, having failed to find a cure, leaves home and wanders aimlessly (and rather irresponsibly, considering his condition) until he comes across a hulking Oriental man named Dragon and his employer, a Fu Manchu wannabee named Dr. Tong. In his werewolf form Spektor attacks the two men but is captured by Dragon and put in a cage, whereupon Tong's lovely virginal daughter develops a crush on him. The storyline then turns even wilder than in previous issues as Spektor discovers that Tong has brought the body of the Frankenstein monster from the ruins of the castle in Germany, and plans to gain god-like powers by siphoning off energy from it and the werewolf at the same time. Unfortunately, Tong's horny daughter rebels, breaks the connection, and frees both monsters to have a battle like something out of the old Universal flick *Frankenstein Meets the Wolfman*. This issue marked the first time the comic had a full-length story, but our hero was still playing "Werewolf by Night" at the wind-up. In the next issue, however, Spektor is cured with the help of Simbar, the Lord of the Lions, a man who transforms into a half man-half-lion but keeps his human brain; he had been the subject of an back-up story in an earlier issue.

Kareena, once again young and beautiful, returned in an excellent story in *OFDS* 14, along with an unusual guest-star, Dr. Solar, Man of the Atom, a super-hero made up of energy who had appeared in his own series in the sixties. Kareena creates a double of Lakota, kidnaps the real woman, and casts a spell to make Solar nearly incinerate the double, after which Spektor is arrested for his secretary's murder. Together Solar and Spektor are not only able to rescue Lakota, but foil Kareena's plot to bring the Dark Gods back into our universe during a lunar eclipse. In another exciting story in the next issue, Baron Tibor returns to tell Spektor that he has developed an immunity to the doctor's formula and become a true vampire again; worse he is in love with Lakota and wants her for his undead bride. Adding to the insanity is the threat of Xorkon, an ancient sorcerer whose disembodied brain is kept alive inside a mystical globe and who wants Baron Tibor's body for his own. In the following issue Xorkon returns, this time wanting to put his brain inside the body of the seemingly unkillable Frankenstein Monster.

"Loch of the Leviathan" in *OFDS* 19 is one of the best issues of the series. In this Spektor, Lakota, and Spektor's cousin Ann travel to a Scottish castle and loch where there have been rumors of a monster. The Laird welcomes them into the castle but assures them he's never seen any monster, although the story's opening depicts a tentacled creature ensnaring a screaming couple and dragging them under the water. The Laird invites the two women to swim in a warm pool in an underground grotto beneath the castle, and they, too, are dragged under by the unknown animal. The octopus-like monster is the last survivor of a prehistoric species and over the centuries it has developed not only sentience but special powers, and it switches minds with the Laird. However, the Laird's consciousness has managed to reassert itself enough so that the monster whose body it inhabits no longer devours its victims, which include Lakota and Ann. Spektor helps to destroy the monster, and the Laird, reverting to his true age, crumbles into dust.

"A Lurker Stalks the Swamp" in the following issue features a benevolent monster who is modeled on the Heap and especially Marvel's Man-Thing, while *OFDS* 21 re-introduces a hooded hero known as the Owl, who comes out of retirement when he is blamed for the deaths and destruction caused by a winged demon. The demon was summoned by cousin Ann's despondent father, who is possessed by the creature until Spektor defeats it. The story is exciting, but at the end Ann and her father simply take off to resume their lives, apparently forgetting about all the bloody mayhem caused just as much by the father's irresponsible actions in summoning the demon as by the demon itself.

At the end of that story Lakota, who had never really shared Adam's interest in the occult and who indeed partially blames him for what happened with Ann's father, takes off for parts unknown to find herself. Spektor is despondent, but doesn't lack for female companionship for long, when Kareena, now reformed, returns the following issue, and Lu-Sai, the daughter of Dr. Tong, the issue after that. Kareena helps Spektor against the advances of an evil goddess desiring a mate, and Lu-Sai, whose father is still alive, is helped by Spektor as she tries to elude the pursuit of an dragon-demon who finally devours her father. The series ended with the twenty-fourth issue with Spektor and Lu-Sai comforting each other and perhaps embarking upon a new relationship. (The twenty-fifth and final issue was a reprint.)

The Occult Files of Dr. Spektor was one of Gold Key's best comics, with excellent, attractive and stylish art from Jesse Santos, and very enthusiastic scripts by Don Glut; it's a shame it didn't last as long as many other less interesting horror comics of the period. Dr. Spektor also served as the host of *Spine-Tingling Tales* for a four-issue run in 1975. One story recounts how the werewolf legend began in prehistoric times, while another presents a man who feeds off the energy of his wives and has lived for 400 years.

ATLAS

In 1975 a new company calling itself Atlas Comics came upon the scene, the brain-child of Martin Goodman, former publisher of Marvel, who hired Jeff Rovin and Larry Lieber, who was Stan Lee's brother, as editors. Although Rovin's expertise was with black and white magazines, he was hired to edit the color comics even as Lieber, whose experience was with color comics, was put in charge of the magazines. The company had ambitious plans and introduced a great many titles all at once, some of which were horror comics. Unfortunately, none of these lasted beyond two or three issues, primarily because Atlas went under only a few weeks after it made its debut.

Weird Suspense (1975) lasted for three issues and featured "The Curse of the Tarantula." During the dark ages a priestess of a strange cult preys upon the villagers of a middle European town with huge spiders that devour many of the people and capture others who are then turned into more giant spiders. The brave Count Lycosa wears the carcass of one of the spiders to find the priestess' hidden sanctuary, and then leads other villagers to the spot so they can slaughter the monsters and burn the witch at the stake. Before she dies she puts a curse on Lycosa that he and all his male heirs will become tarantulas, paralyzing and devouring their victims. Many years later a descendant of the count, who lives in seclusion, traps and feasts upon a pack of thugs who burst into his home after escaping from prison. This modern-day Count Lycosa doesn't actually turn into a giant eight-legged spider but a kind of arachnid-humanoid hybrid.

In the second issue of *Weird Suspense*, the original priestess returns from the dead via supernatural means and vows to track down and destroy the latest Lycosa, as well as ravage the Earth with her spider-monsters, but she's defeated by the actions of the Tarantula. The third and final issue of the series seemed to be an attempt to turn the Tarantula into a grotesque, dangerous anti-hero à la the Hulk as he reverts to his spider form and pays a call on the secretary who's in love with him (apparently Lycosa is an investment counselor). She had been hoping to have Lycosa over for dinner, but he's more interested in having *her* for supper! Instead he winds up battling—and ultimately eating—a man who can bring inanimate matter to life. Michael Fleisher created the series and wrote the first two issues—Gary Friedrich scripted the third—with Pat Boyette delivering some uneven but fairly attractive artwork. One has to believe that the many amusing and zany aspects of the definitely *weird* and awkwardly plotted series were at least partly intentional.

Tales of Evil debuted in 1975 and ran for three issues. The first issue has a trio of horror tales concerning a little girl who is possessed by a demon, a man who discovers that a formula he bought for restoring hair has turned him into a ravenous werewolf, and a man who kills a vampire, unaware he's really just an actor in a movie, as the real vampire stands by in amusement; none were memorable. The second issue of the series heralded "The Bog Beast" on the cover, making it seem as if it had turned into a try-out magazine for new series. The Bog Beast is an explorer from a world beneath the earth who encounters two radicals on the run, one of whom turns him into a circus sideshow for money while the other succeeds in freeing him. There was also a story about a downtrodden Puerto Rican youth who becomes a wolfman for purposes of revenge, and winds up getting run down like a dog when he reverts fully into a wolf, and one about a Boston subway train whose passengers are the newly deceased.

Tales of Evil 3 featured the Man-Monster on the cover. The Man-Monster—written and drawn by Gary Friedrich and Rich Buckler—is a playboy and former athlete who is exposed to some undersea bacteria and transforms into a red, hulking brute with great strength. A sinister costumed figure he apparently knows shows up and demands that he help him bankrupt a man neither of them can stand, the Man-Monster's wealthy father. The story was supposed to be continued in the first issue of *Man-Monster*, but this never materialized. In the same issue the Bog-Beast is given a fairly interesting back-up story in which he discovers mutilated corpses in an observatory and then encounters and defeats the ravenous wolfwoman who is responsible for the gruesome murders; in spite of this he is blamed for the crimes. This, too, was never continued. *Tales of Evil* had some interesting elements and decent artwork to it; Bog-Beast, in particular, might have been developed into something special with a little more time and luck. Other members of the creative team included Jack Sparling, Jerry Grandenetti, Tom Sutton, and John Albano.

The Brute ran for three issues in 1975. It tells the tale of a especially large caveman or missing link who has been in suspended animation inside a cavern in Montana for millions of years. He is discovered by three boys exploring the cave and brutally kills two of them. The boys' father, Carlson, wants the creature killed but wouldn't you know there's an anthropologist named Dr. Ann Turner who wants to keep it alive to study it. Carlson sets the beast free, illogically hoping it'll kill more people so everyone will see it's a menace, and Dr. Turner and Chief Frasier, who has a crush on the pretty scientist, argue over whether or not to destroy it. In the second issue the Brute is manipulated by a mad doctor into going after the man's enemies so he can turn them into amphibians. The third issue introduces a costumed cyborg named Deathstalker who manages to temporarily defeat the creature and there the series ended. The chief influence for *The Brute* seems to have been a Joan Crawford movie entitled *Trog*, which has a very similar premise and similar cliches, although the anthropologist in the comic seems positively demented. She refers to the beast-man as a "poor, helpless thing" after it's killed about a dozen or more people, and practically makes out with any guy who helps her in her pro-monster cause. On the cover of the first issue the Brute seems nearly twenty feet tall, but inside the comic he was more along the lines of eight feet. Michael Fleisher did the hackneyed scripts for the first two issues, while Gary Friedrich contributed the third, which showed a slight improvement. The series wasn't at all memorable but it did boast some very nice art by Mike Sekowsky and Pablo Marcos for the first two issues, and Alan Lee Weiss and Jack Abel for the third.

Morlock 2001

Morlock 2001 was another three-issue Atlas series that debuted in 1975. In the twenty-first century there is a totalitarian state where anyone who believes in free thought and independent thinking is considered a deviant, including a scientist named Kroschell, whose unusual plants are confiscated after his abrupt execution. Workers for the government are startled to learn that inside one of Kroschell's pods there is a humanoid male figure, whom they excise from the plant, christen Morlock, and turn into their executioner when it develops that his fingers can exude a green fungus that turns human beings into grotesque statues of foliage. Morlock almost manages to get a sympathetic girlfriend, but when it turns out that she was only a government spy trying to keep him in line, his rage makes him transform for the first time into a large, hideous tree monster with a maw and tentacles who picks the woman up—and promptly devours her! Morlock escapes, eventually reverting to human form, whereupon he learns that Korschell intended him as the first of an army of plant-human hybrids that would overthrow the government. There is only a little bit left of a serum that can prevent Morlock from turning into the primitive, man-eating plant form.

In *Morlock* 2 the plant-man is on the run—alternately eating or converting his pursuers into shrubbery, although he tries his best to avoid this—but he conveniently runs into a scientist named Bert Ling who has also been experimenting on human-plant combinations.

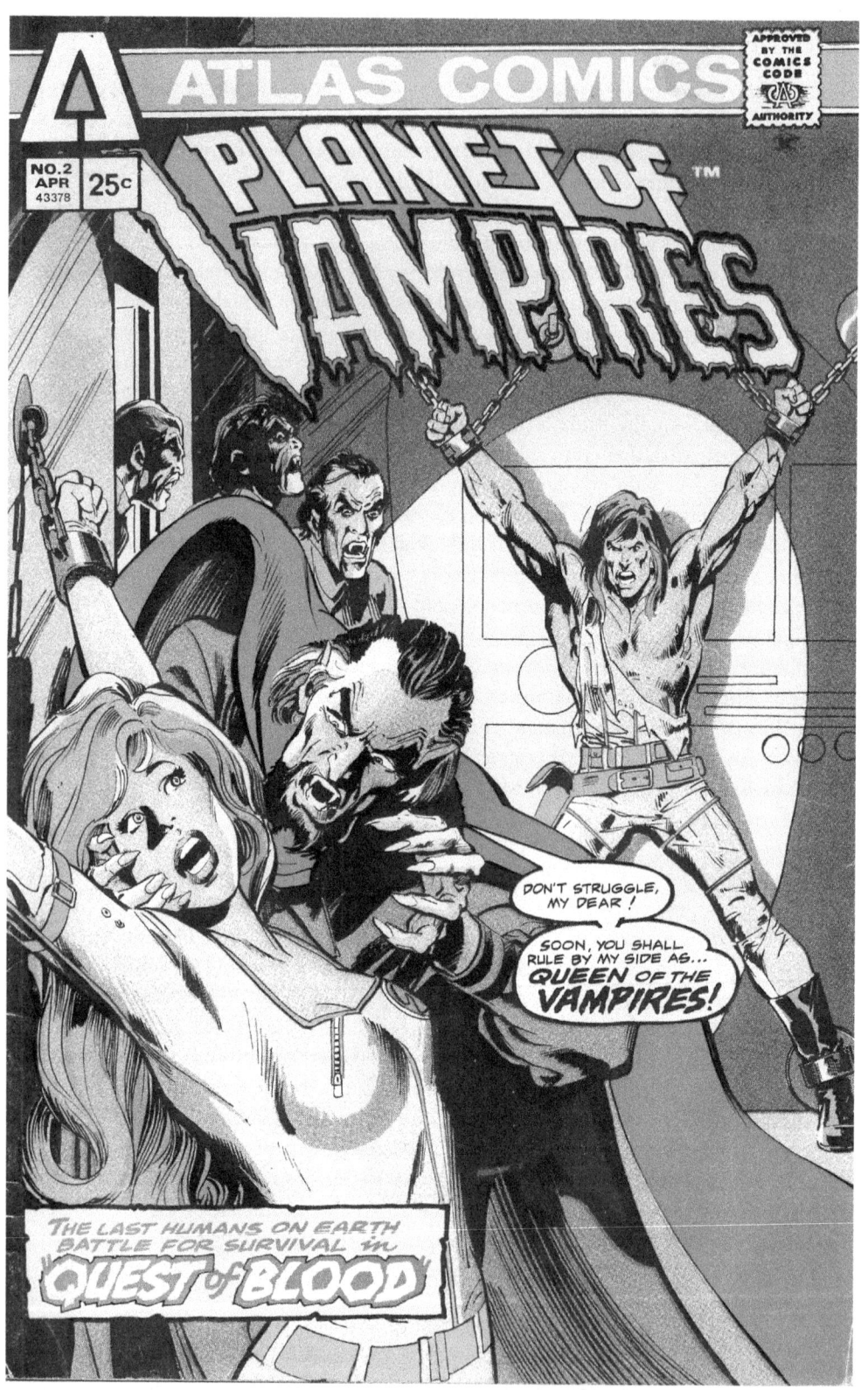

The short-lived Atlas Comics came up with an intriguing concept with its *Planet of Vampires*.

Ling's experiments so far have proved fruitless or dangerous, and Morlock has to rescue Ling's little blind daughter Karen from a couple of her father's grassy monstrosities. Learning that Morlock is wanted by the state, a guilt-wracked Ling decides to turn him in for the reward money, which may buy his daughter an operation. Unfortunately, little Karen tries to free Morlock from the shed into which her father has secured him. Unable to keep himself from changing into the tree monster, Morlock devours the child while Ling swears revenge. These first two issues had lively and loopy scripts by Michael Fleischer, and very nice art by Allen Milgrom and Jack Abel.

For the third and final issue the comic's logo read *Morlock 2001 and the Midnight Men*. The new creative team was writer Gary Friedrich and artist Steve Ditko. Morlock tries to save the life of Professor Whitlock, who has a huge, forbidden library, but the man is burned by the Thought Police. However, Whitlock survives and takes Morlock under his wing, whereupon the plant-man joins Whitlock's underground, which the latter rechristens the Midnight Men. Whitlock agrees to try to remove the tree monster curse from Morlock, hoping to steal the one other pod that was removed from Kroschell's laboratory for inspiration. Unfortunately, the Thought Police attack the Midnight Men's HQ just as Morlock begins to revert into his slobbering and voracious plant form. The last page of the final issue has Whitlock deciding to end Morlock's torment by shooting him and preparing to blow up his HQ, himself and his followers—along with the Thought Police—his finger poised on the very button. The next issue would have revealed if Morlock or anyone else survived, but it was not to be.

Morlock 2001 may sound quite insane and ridiculous, but it was an oddly compelling and entertaining—even edgy—strip while it lasted. It would have been a fun ride to see into what directions the writers might have taken the series and its highly unusual hero, but this was not to be.

Planet of Vampires

After *Morlock 2001*, Atlas' most ambitious series was *Planet of Vampires*, which also had a three-issue run in 1975. In 2010, Captain Chris Galland is the leader of a five-year expedition to Mars to catalog properties and life forms of the planet. Some years before this Galland had lost contact with Mission Control after news that a nuclear war had broken out. With some trepidation Galland and his crew, including wife Elissa, decide to return to Earth to see what's up. Landing near Manhattan, they discover a devastated world divided into savages and ostensibly more civilized people who live in a giant dome. Invited into the dome, Galland learns that the savages have become resistant to many of the virulent diseases that ravaged the planet after the war, while the "domies" have no such immunity; therefore they kidnap the men and women outside the dome and extract their bodily fluids to prepare a curative serum they ingest. The domies are especially interested in getting their hands on the blood of the astronauts who were off-planet during the holocaust. Galland and his crew escape from the dome, destroying their laboratory in the process.

In *Planet of Vampires* 2 Galland learns that the domies have become literal vampires, attacking the savages and sucking their blood, due to the destruction of their lab and fluid-extracting equipment. Galland importunes the varying bands of savages in the city to join

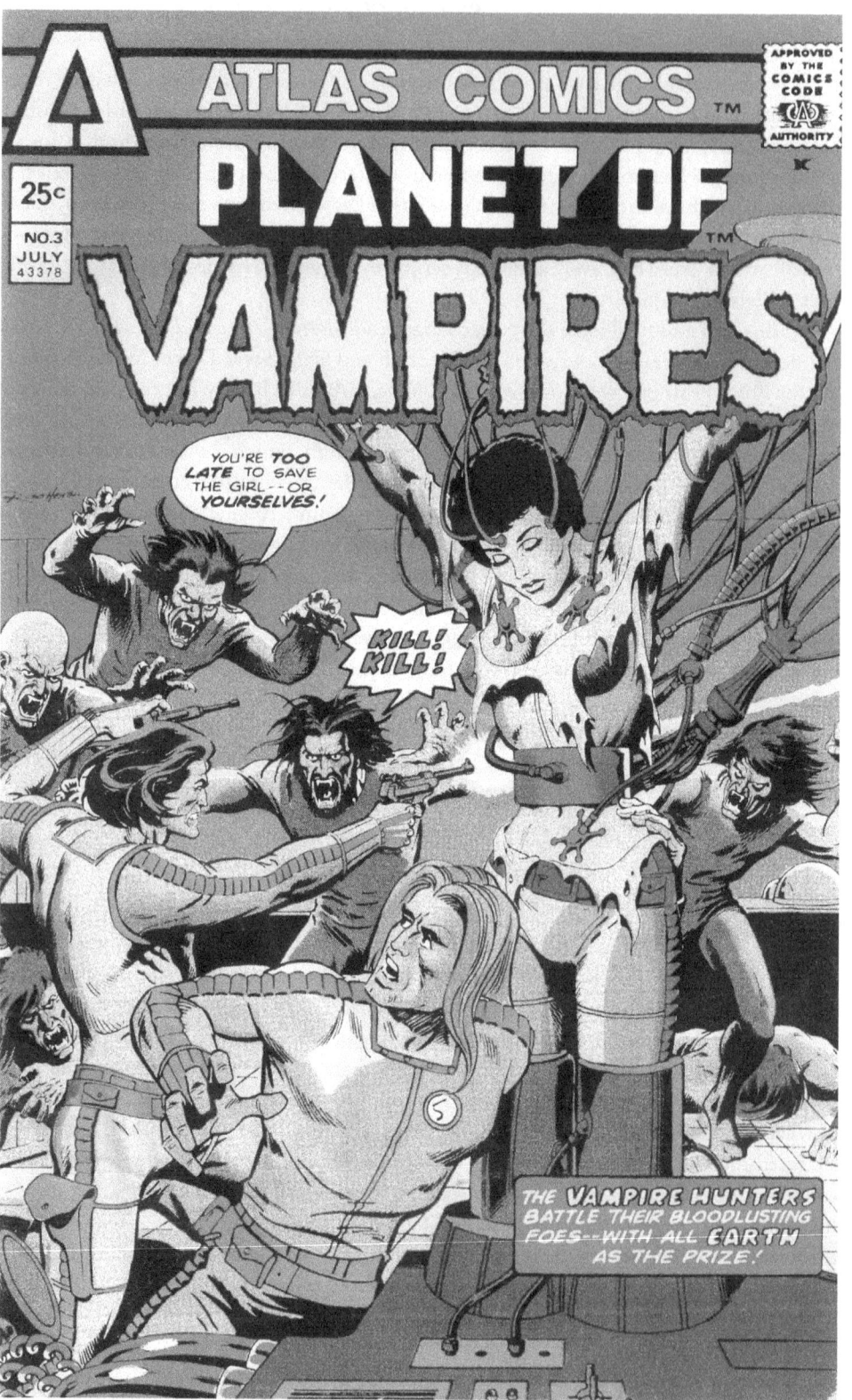

The third and final issue of *Planet of Vampires* left the readers hanging as well.

together against a common enemy, but before they can do so the domies attack with their vastly superior fire power and manage to make off with many women, including Galland's wife and the wife of another crew member, Craig. In the third issue Craig and Galland invade the dome to find their wives, but Craig's wife is already dead. The domies have somehow developed fangs in their mouths overnight. Galland finds Elissa and escapes, but as they fly across the country to escape New York, the find only dead cities. Instead of people they come across giant vampiric spiders and insects that nearly devour them.

Although imperfect in many ways and sometimes awkwardly scripted—seeing Craig, who is African American, one of the domies calls him "the black-skinned one" as if he'd never seen a black man before—*Planet of Vampires* is almost as entertaining as *Morlock* and had possibilities it was doomed never to realize. Larry Hama was the writer for the first issue, with John Albano scripting the last two issues. Pat Broderick and Frank McLaughlin handled the art chores for issues one and two, while Russ Heath drew the final issue.

Fright

The first and only issue of *Fright* (1975) from Atlas Comics featured the origin of the Son of Dracula. In this very interesting story by Gary Friedrich, Dracula rescues an alleged witch from superstitious townspeople and plans to feast upon her until he spots a birth mark which tells him that they are related. The woman, his cousin, tells him that she will bare him a son if he will promise not to turn her into a vampire. When the child is born, she tells him that she plans to go away with the baby and that Dracula will never see him again. Dracula is so outraged that he attacks her, but she remains human and flees the castle with the child. After giving the child to a woman who will raise him in America, she is again attacked by Dracula and turned into a full vampire, after which she commits suicide.

Dracula catches up with the child a few years later, but is repelled by his cross-wielding guardian. At this point the story becomes a little strange. The old woman who has raised the boy hides him in a wine cellar with the cross he always wears around his neck, kisses him goodbye, seals him inside, and then blows herself up to prevent Dracula from turning her into one of the undead. As the story then shifts to 1975, we can only surmise that the boy was in a state of suspended animation for many decades, until being discovered by a couple who raise him. Lying beside him is a book from his original guardian which tells him who he is and why he must always wear the crucifix. The Son of Dracula is now a grown man and a teacher known as Adam Lucard. His one dread is of succumbing to his father's curse.

Unfortunately, one of his students, a pretty blond co-ed who robs apartments to pay her tuition, enters his abode while Adam is sleeping and removes the cross from around his neck. She becomes the newly emerged Son of Dracula's first victim, and her brunette associate becomes his second. The story ends with Adam awakening from what seems like a drunken stupor and discovering the corpse of the student burglar. To save her from a vampiric fate he drives a stake through her heart. The story—and the saga of the Son of Dracula—ends with Lucard wondering if he should commit suicide or stay alive and try to triumph over this curse of blood. With excellent art by Frank Thorne and a fairly good script, Son of Dracula had distinct possibilities that, as with the rest of the Atlas line, were never to be realized.

Bibliography

Books

Alexander, Mark. *Lee & Kirby: The Wonder Years*. Raleigh: TwoMorrows, 2012.
Barr, Mike W. *Silver Age Sci-Fi Companion*. Raleigh: TwoMorrows, 2007.
Comtois, Pierre. *Marvel Comics in the 1960s*. Raleigh: TwoMorrows, 2009.
Diehl, Digby. *Tales from the Crypt: The Official Archives*. New York: St. Martin's, 1996.
Geissman, Grant, and Fred von Bernewitz. *Tales of Terror: The EC Companion*. Seattle: Fantagraphics/Gemstone, 2000.
Goulart, Ron. *Ron Goulart's Great History of Comic Books*. Chicago: Contemporary, 1986.
Sadowski, Greg. *Four Color Fear: Forgotten Horror Comics of the 1950s*. Seattle: Fantagraphics, 2010.
Schoell, William. *Comic Book Heroes of the Screen*. New York: Carol, 1990.
___. *The Silver Age of Comics*. Duncan, OK: BearManor, 2011.
Schumer, Arlen. *The Silver Age of Comic Book Art*. Portland, OR: Collector's, 2003.
Shutt, Craig. *Baby Boomer Comics*. Iola, WI: Krause, 2003.
Trombetta, Jim. *The Horror! The Horror! Comic Books the Government Didn't Want You to Read*. New York: Abrams, 2010.

Websites

Comic Book +. www.comicbookplus.com.
The Digital Comic Museum. www.digitalcomicmuseum.com.
Grand Comics DataBase. www.comics.org.

Index

Numbers in ***bold italics*** indicate pages with photographs.

Abel, Jack 196, 248
Adams, Neal 193, 210, 213, 237
Adkins, Dan 202, 207
Adventure into Fear 193–194, ***195***, 196, 199
Adventure Into Mystery 144–145
Adventures into Darkness 108–109
Adventures Into Terror 57–59
Adventures into the Unknown 5, 6–9, ***10***, 11–13
Adventures into Weird Worlds 61–62
afterlife *see* hereafter
age discrimination 25, 72, 88, 139–140, 165, 242
Air Fighters 113–114
Airboy 114
"Airboy vs. the Rats" 117
Albano, John 211, 216, 225, 269
Alcala, Alfredo 221, 228
Alcazar, Vincente 193
Alfred Hitchcock Hour 56, 63, 157
Alfred Hitchcock Presents 24, 31
"Ali Barber and the Forty Thieves" 85
Amazing Adventures 143
Andru, Ross 180
Aparo, Jim ***155***, 156, 213, 220, 225, 238, 239
Aragones, Sergio 211
Astonishing 56–57
Astonishing Tales 193, 204
Attack of the Crab Monsters 87, 105
Austin, Steve 203
Ayers, Dick 142, 143, 144, 204, 219

Bache, Ernie 152
backlash against horror comics *see* censorship
"The Bad Seed" 33, 102
Baffling Mysteries 93–95
Bailey, Bernard 76, 240
Barr, Mike 213, 231
Bates, Cary 210
The Batman 213, 240, 241, 245
The Beast from 20,000 Fathoms 122, 132
Beck, Dick 94
Bell, Johnny 112, 113
Beware 132–133
Beware! Terror Tales 77–78
The Beyond 95–96, ***97***, 98
Beyond the Grave 258
"The Black Cat" (Poe) 73
Black Cat Mystery 81–82, ***83***, 84
Black Magic 48–49, ***50***
Black Scorpion 141
Blade 177, 178, 199
blobs 25, 30, 34, 72, 75, 84, 94–95, 167
Bloch, Robert 208
Blue Bolt Weird Tales 130
Boris Karloff Tales of Mystery 166–168
Boris Karloff Thriller 166
Boyette, Pat 264
Bradbury, Ray 24, 31, 32, 54, 132, 162
The Brave and the Bold 213, 245
Bridwell, E. Nelson 209, 231, 232
Briefer, Dick 46
Brother Voodoo 185, 202
The Brute 265
Buckler, Rich 201, 264
buried alive 35, 38, 49, 55–56, 61, 86, 87, 107, 121, 227

Buscema, John 186, 196, 203
Buscema, Sal 191
Bushmaster, Francis X. 210

Cain, James M. 129
Campbell, John W. 7
cannibalism 21, 30, 41, 81, 99, 107–108, 119, 125, 127, 134
Carrillo, Fred 227, 230, 231, 233, 239, 243
"The Castle of Otranto" 5
censorship 11, 38, 104
Challenge of the Unknown 101
Chamber of Chills (Harvey) 86–89
Chamber of Chills (Marvel) 207–208
Chamber of Darkness 206–207
Chau, Ernie 207, 223, 243
Chaykin, Howard 208
Chiaramonte, Frank 196, 201
"Chicken Heart" 144
child hatred 24
Chilling Tales 133
"The Choir Master" 88
Claremont, Christopher 181, 191, 192, 198, 199
Classics Illustrated 42
The Clutching Hand 18
Colan, Gene 175, 178, 191, 202, 207, 246
Cole, Jack 122
"collector's Item" 24
Colletta, Vince 203
Colon, Ernie 212
"Color the Snow: Red" 220
"Conjure Wife" (Lieber) 144
Conway, Gerry 175, 182, 193, 194, 213, 215, 216, 238, 242, 243

274 Index

"Corker" 35
Craig, Johnny 31, 236
"Crawling Death" 87
Creature Commandos 229–230
Creatures on the Loose 203–204
Creepy Things 257–258
Crime Mysteries 133
Crime SuspenStories 31–34
"The Crowd" (Bradbury) 162
Crypt of Terror 19, 21
Cuti, Nicola 248, 250, 251, 253, 254, 257

Dahl, Roald 24
Daimon Hellstrom 189, 190
Dark Mansion of Forbidden Love 223–224
Dark Mysteries (master) 134
Dark Mysteries (story) 127, **128**
Dark Shadows (comic) 168, **169**, 170
Davis, Jack 29
"The Dead Lover Returns" 75
Dead of Night 204
"The Dead Sleep Lightly" 87
Deadman 239
death (as character) 12, 17, 64, 68, 77, 78, 92, 94, 109, 134, 157, 227, 229
DeMatteis, J.M. 212, 229–230
The Demon 243–245
Dennehy, Bill 220
DeZuniga, Tony 203, 210, 214, 223, 224, 239
The Devil *see* Satan
dinosaurs 9, 14, 145–148, 149, 150
Disbrow, Jay 130
dismemberment 39, 133
Ditko, Steve 74, 81, 125, 140, 142, 148, 150, 156, 206, 251, 252, 267
Do You Believe in Nightmares? 125
Dr. Death 72
Dr. Graves 153, 156, 257
Dr. Haunt 74
"Dr. Jekyll and Mr. Hyde" 81, 130, 207, 261
Dr. Strange 156, 180, 185, 198
Dr. Thirteen *see* Terry Thirteen
Donnelly, Bob 20
"Donovan's Brain" 125
"Don't Count Your Chickens" 63
Doom Patrol 178
"Doomsday" 82
Doorway to Nightmare 236
Dracula (character) 106, 158, 175–181, 183, 186, 262, 269
Dracula (Dell) 158
Dracula (novel) 106
dragons 9, 166, 168, 256
Drake, Arnold 211, 228, 239, 260
Draut, Bill 215, 238

EC Quickies 32
Eerie (Avon) 105–106
Eerie Adventures 134
"Eerie Glen" 108
Effinger, George Alec 208
Elias, Lee 89
Englehart, Steve 208
Evans, George 73, 76, 117, 159, 200
Everett, Bill 53
evil children 24, 33, 132

"Facts in the Case of M. Valdemar" 24
Fantastic Fears 103
Fantastic Voyage (film) 61, 87
Fate (as character) 92
Fear *see* Adventure into Fear
Feldstein, Al 37, 40
Ferrer, Jose Recreo 250
Fight Against Crime 127, 129
Fin Fang Foom 141–142, 204, 205, 206
Final Destination 68
"Final Escape" 56, 157
"Fingers of Fear" 71
"The Fixer" 33
Fleischer, Michael 198, 199, 211, 216, 224, 229, 232, 264, 265, 267
"The Foghorn" (Bradbury) 132
Forbidden Tales of Dark Mansion see Dark Mansion of Forbidden Love
Forbidden Worlds 13–16
Forgione, Bob 80
"Foul Play" 37, 126, 216
Fox, Gardner 176, 208
Frankenstein (Dell) 183
Frankenstein (Mary Shelley) 30, 42, 240
Frankenstein (Prize Comics) 42, **43**
Frankenstein monster (character) 55, 240, 261–262
The Frankenstein Monster (Marvel) *see The Monster of Frankenstein*
"Frankenstein-1974" 188
French revolution 25
Friedrich, Gary 185, 186, 189, 190, 264, 265, 267, 269
Friedrich, Mike 191, 203, 224
Fright 269
"From the Graves They Crept" 96, 98

genies 15
Gerber, Steve 190, 191, 194, 197–198, 199, 200, 201, 207, 208
Ghost Comics 112–113
Ghost Manor 156, 250–251
Ghost Rider 188–190
Ghost Stories 160, **161**, 162–163
Ghostly Haunts 248, **249**, 250

Ghostly Tales (from the Haunted House) 153, **154**, **155**, 156, 251–252
Ghostly Weird Stories 130, **131**
ghosts 13–14, 112–113, 139
Ghosts 225–228
ghouls 27, 34, 38, 80, 103
Giacoia, Frank 201, 224
The Giant Claw 141, 167
The Giant Gila Monster 105
giant insects 14, 15, 82, 84, 107, 121, 141, 142, 147, 156, 167, 168, 208, 257
Giant-Size Chillers (V1/1974) *see Giant-Size Dracula*
Giant-Size Chillers (V2/1975) 208
Giant-Size Dracula 178, 181
Giant-Size Man-Thing 194, 196–197
Giant-Size Spider-Man 180, 198
Giant-Size Super-Heroes 203
giants 17, 92, 117, 122, 124, 132, 140, 149, 167, 257
Gill, Joe 148, 157, 248, 250, 253, 256
Giordano, Dick 202, 217, 224
Glut, Don 263
Godzilla (comic) 205–206
The Golem 203
"Goodbye George" 63, 86
Goodman, Martin 263
Goodwin, Archie 175
gore 21, 22, 27, 29, 32, 34, 36, 39, 80, 81, 82, 85, 87, 88, 89, 94, 99, 102, 103, 125, 126, 127, 129, 136, 210, 219
Gorgo (comic) 148–150
Gorgo (film) 148
The Gorgon *see* Medusa
Goulart, Ron 208
Grandenetti, Jerry 112, 220
"Graveyard Rats" (Kuttner) 110, 122
"The Greatest Horror of Them All" 48
Green, Dan 205
"A Grim Fairy Tale" 27
"Grim Fairy Tales" 36
Grimm's Ghost Stories 258, **259**, 260–262
Grudko, Sy 96

Hama, Larry 199
The Hand of Fate 8, 92–93
Hannigan, Ed 197
Harris, Jack C. 212, 227, 235
The Haunt of Fear 34–38
Haunt of Horror 192
Haunted 252–253
Haunted Love 254, 256
Haunted Thrills 101–102
Hawthorne, Nathaniel 224
"Head of the Family" 48, **50**

The Heap 114–117, 193, 194, 240
Heath, Russ 64, 147, 148, 192, 269
Heck, Don 110, 180, 181
the hereafter 8–9
"The High Cost of Dying" 35–36
"The Hitchhiker" (Fletcher) 95
"Hop-Frog" (Poe) 125
Horrific 110, *111*
"Horror at the Lighthouse" 77–78
Horror from the Tomb 135
House of Mystery 67–70, 209–215
House of Secrets 215–217, 240–241
Howard, Robert E. 207, 208
Howard, Wayne 252, 253, 254
Howard the Duck 194

"I, Vampire" 212–213
Iger Studio 101
"In Gratitude" 40
The Incredible Shrinking Man 74
"The Invisible Man" (Wells) 207
Isabella, Tony 189, 193, 201, 203, 204
It (Marvel character) 204
"It" (Sturgeon) 114, 207
It Came from Beneath the Sea 143

Jakes, John 207
Jodloman, Jess 211, 225, 232
Jones, Bruce 212, 213, 214
Journey into Fear 136
Journey into Mystery (V1) 60–61, 139–141
Journey into Mystery (V2) 208

Kaluta, Mike 240
Kane, Gil 207, 208, 209, 219
Kanigher, Robert 146, 227, 228, 230, 231, 233, 238
Kashdan, George 217, 220, 221, 229, 235
Ka-Zar 193
Kida, Fred 205
"The Kid's Night Out" 197
Kim, Sanho 157, 251
King, Stephen 64, 144
Kirby, Jack 47–51, 140, 142, 143, 144, 206, 224, 229, 231, 232, 243–245
Konga (comic) 150–151
Konga (film) 150–151
Kraft, David (Anthony) 181, 203
Kubert, Joe 124, 148, 222, 228

L. Dedd 153
Landau, Kenneth 17
Lazarus, Harry 11, 12, 106
Lee, Stan 64, 66, 186, 206, 263
"Leinigen vs. the Aunts" 63, 119
Levitz, Paul 211, 228, 232, 233, 235, 239
Lieber, Larry 263
Lights Out! (radio show) 144

Lilith (Dracula's daughter) 178, 180
"The Little Monster" 63–64
The Little Shop of Horrors 46, 94, 133
"Live Bait" 167
The Living Mummy 201
"Lost Horizon" (Hilton) 109, 153
Lovecraft, H.P. 30, 80, 93, 109, 207, 252, 262

MacKenzie, Dickie 199
Malevo, the Living Ghost 5
Man-Thing (character) 193–194, *195*, 196–199
Man-Thing (comic) 196–199
"The Man Who Died Laughing" 11
"The Man Who Haunted Satan" 250
Man-Wolf 203–204
Manak, Dave 227, 235
Maneely, Joe 57, 58
Mantlo, Bill 191, 200
The Many Ghosts of Dr. Graves 156
"Map of Doom" 124
Marie Celeste 9
Marvel Premiere 192, 204
Marvel Spotlight 181, 190, 191, 204
Marvel Tales 54–55
"The Mask of Fu Manchu" (novel) 106
Matheson, Richard 74, 184, 251
Mayer, Sheldon 225, 232
Mayerick Val 186, 188, 194, 201, 236
McGregor, Don 200
Medusa 8, 113, 164, 182, 230
Menace 64–66
Men's Adventures 54
Michelinie, David 232, 233, 235, 236, 239, 242
Midnight Tales 253–254, *255*
misogyny 8, 40, 126, 196
"The Mist" 64
Mr. Bones 250–251
Mr. E 235
Mister Mystery 119
"Mr. Reilly, the Derelict" 225
Mr. Zero 129
Moench, Doug 184, 185, 186, 188, 200, 203, 205
Moldoff, Sheldon 75
"The Monkey's Paw" 36, 38
The Monster 113
Monster Hunters 256–257
"Monster of Dread End" 160, 162
The Monster of Frankenstein 185–186, *187*, 188
Monsters Unleashed 188, 193

Montes, Bill 152
Moon Knight 184
Mooney, Jim 189, 190, 197, 198, 203
Morbius 180, 199–200
Moreira, Ruben 69
Morisi, Pete 157, 252
Morlock 2001 265, 267
Morrow, Gray 193
Mortimer, Win 167
"The Most Dangerous Game" 30, 95, 208
"Mother's Day" 33
mummies 15, 80, 136, 201, 226, 261
Mysteries (Weird and Strange) 136
Mysterious Adventures 125–127
Mysterious Stories 134–135
Mystery Tales 63–64
Mystic 56
Mystical Tales 144

The Night Force 245–247
Night Gallery (TV show) 220, 235
Night of the Lepus 222
Nightmare (St. John's) 124–125
Nightmare (Ziff-Davis) 133–134
Nostrand, Howard 88

The Occult Files of Dr. Spektor 261–263
"Occurrence at Owl Creek Bridge" 135
Olek, Jack 210, 211, 216, 223, 232, 236
O'Neill, Denny 213, 224, 236, 238
Orlando, Joe 211, 215, 224, 228, 232
"Out of the Grave" 101
Out of the Night 16–17
Out of the Shadows 107

Palais, Rudy 110
Palmer, Tom 175, 178, 207
PAM (artist) *see* Morisi, Pete
Patchwork Man 216, 241
Perez, George 203, 204
Perlin, Don 184, 185, 198
The Phantom of the Opera 244
The Phantom Stranger 71, 152, 216, 237–240
"Pickman's Model" (Lovecraft) 109, 207
"The Picture of Dorian Gray" 98, 156, 165, 214
"The Pit and the Pendulum" (Poe) 134
Planet of Vampires **266**, 267, **268**, 269
Ploog, Mike 182, 185, 188, 196
Poe, Edgar Allan 24, 80, 125, 133, 134, 206–207

Index

Powell, Bob 73, 76
premature burial *see* buried alive
"The Price of the Head" 30, 103, 232
Prize Comics 42–44
the Purple Claw 132

"Queen of Spades" (Pushkin) 98

Rangers Comics 110, 112–113
Redondo, Nestor 216, 241–242
Reese, Ralph 208
Reinman, Paul 61
Reptilicus (comic) 151
Reptilicus (film) 151
Reptisaurus 151
"Revenge" (Samuel Blas) 31, 86, 132
Rice, Ken 95
Robbins, Ed 162
Robbins, Frank 200, 224, 233
Robinson, Jerry 62
Rohmer, Sax 106, 178
Roussos, George 108
Rovin, Jeff 263
Rubeny 233
Russell, Craig 200, 207

Santos, Jesse 263
Satan 9, 13, 14, 16, 17, 82, 84, 87, 95, 112, 130, 133, 135, 144, 180, 185, 188–189, 190, 191, 192, 214, 216, 232, 250, 253, 254
Satana 191
Savage Tales 193
the Scarecrow 204
Scary Tales 258
"The Screaming Woman" 32
sea monsters 9, 150
"The Secret Files of Dr. Drew" 112
Secrets of Haunted House 233, **234**, 235
Secrets of Sinister House see *Sinister House of Secret Love*
Sekowsky, Mike 211, 219, 224, 237–238, 265
Sensation Mystery 71
Shakespeare, William 59
Shock SuspenStories 38–41
Shores, Syd 206
shrewish wives 8, 12, 100, 105–106, 114, 119, 127, 142, 164
shrunken heads 105, 123, 125
"The Shrunken Skull" 86–87
Siamese twins 30, 57, 68, 257
Sienkiewicz, Bill 185
"The Silver Scream" 82
Silver Surfer 180
Simon, Joe 47–51
The Sinister House of Secret Love 224–225
Skeates, Steve 216, 239, 240
Skeleton Hand 17–18

Sky Wolf 113
social relevance 40, 64–65, 194, 196, 197
Son of Satan 190–192
Sparling, Jack 211, 220
Spawn of Frankenstein 240
The Spectre 227
Spellbound 59–60
Spider-Man 180, 198, 203
spiders 9, 15, 22, 23, 58, 63, 84, 94, 95, 96, 100, 132, 141, 148, 186, 210, 214, 224, 226, 252, 253, 258, 264
Spiegle, Dan 214, 230, 235
Spine-Tingling Tales 263
"The Spirit of Frankenstein" 5, 7
Spook (Star) 130
Spook Comics (Bailey) 135
Springer, Frank 163, 181, 197
Stanley, John 160
Star-Spangled Comics 720–71
Star Spangled War Stories 145–148
Startling Terror Tales 130
Stoker, Bram 106
Strange Fantasy 102
Strange Mysteries 135–136
Strange Stories from Another World 78
Strange Suspense Stories 75–77
Strange Tales 54–56, 141, 202, 203
Strange Terrors 123
The Strange World of Your Dreams 49, 51
Sturgeon, Theodore 114
"The Suicide Squad" 146–147
Supernatural Thrillers 201, 207
Suspense Comics 129–130
Suspense Detective 78–79
Sutton, Tom 189, 201, 212, 248, 252, 256
Suydam, Arthur 211
"Swamp Horror" 136
Swamp Thing 194, 216, 240–243
"The Switch" 25

Tales from the Crypt 19, **20**, 21–25
Tales from the Tomb 158–159
Tales of Evil 264–265
Tales of Ghost Castle 235–236
Tales of Horror 132
Tales of Suspense 143
Tales of the Mysterious Traveler 152–153
Tales of the Zombie 202
Tales to Astonish 142–143
Taloac, Gerry 216, 239
Tarantula 141
the Teller 110
Terry Thirteen 68, 70–71, 216, 226–227, 237–240
The Thing 79

The Thing from Another World 7
This Is Suspense 81
This Magazine Is Haunted 72–74
Thomas, Roy 207
Thorne, Frank 269
3-D comics 9
Tomb of Dracula 175–181, 183
Tomb of Terror 89, **90**, 91
The Tormented 130, 132
Tower of Shadows 207
Trapani, Sal 190
Trimpe, Herb 190, 205
Trinidad, Sonny 191, 200
TrueVision 9
"The Tunnel" 17
Tuska, George 203
The Twilight Zone (comic) 163–166
The Twilight Zone (TV series) 251
two-headed freaks 21, 126–127, 232
Tyler, Albert 80

"The Ugly Duckling" 89
Uncanny Tales 62–63
The Unexpected 219–222
Unknown World 78
The Unseen 108
Uslan, Michael 222

Vampire Tales 192, 199, 200
vampires 13, 18, 23, 27, 38, 57, 60–61, 76–77, 80, 88, 94, 96, 100, 101, 102, 125, 127, 134, 168, 170–171, 175–181, 186, 215–216, 229, 236, 251, 254, 256–257, 261, 262, 264, 269
The Vault of Horror 25, **26**, 27, **28**, 29–31
Venus 52–53
voodoo 13, 25, 29, 71, 78, 95, 107, 227, 257
Voodoo 102

Walpole, Horace 5
"The War That Time Forgot" 145–148, 230–231
Warner, John 191, 201
Web of Evil 122–123
Web of Mystery 98
Wein, Len 182, 193, 202, 203, 207, 212, 224, 229, 238, 239, 240
Weird Chills 121
Weird Horrors 123–124
Weird Mysteries 119, **120**, 121
Weird Mystery Tales 231–233
Weird Suspense 264
Weird Terror 109–110
Weird War Tales 228–231
Werewolf by Night 181–185, 203
"The Werewolf Hunter" 110, 112
werewolves 7–8, 12, 13, 14, 15,

16, 18, 23, 75, 81, 95, 98, 99, 124–125, 127, 136, 170, 181–185, 186, 229, 236, 241, 251, 257, 262, 264
Wessler, Carl 217, 220, 221, 257
Where Monsters Dwell 206–207
"Who Goes There?" 7
Wiacek, Bob 198
Wilde, Oscar 98
Wildman, George 251, 254, 256, 257
Williamson, Al 209
Wilson, Ron 197
Winnie the Witch 157, 248
"Wish You Were Here" 36
Witchcraft 106
witches 16, 95, 99, 132, 217, 219, 224, 225, 243, 244, 261, 264
Witches Tales 84–86
Witching Hour 217, **218**, 219
"Wolf Bait" 34–35
The Wolfman (Dell) 159–160
Wolfman, Marv 176, 178, 179, 183, 240, 246
Wood, Wally 207, 253
World of Suspense 145
Worlds Beyond, Stories of Weird Adventure 78
Worlds of Fear 74–76
Wrightson, Bernie 240–241

Yandoc, Ruben *see* Rubeny

Zeck, Mike 257
zombies 14, 29, 100–101, 202
zuvembies 202

www.ingramcontent.com/pod-product-compliance
Ingram Content Group UK Ltd.
Pitfield, Milton Keynes, MK11 3LW, UK
UKHW050540150426
5217IPUK00026B/2006